AMERICAN AVIATION

AN ILLUSTRATED HISTORY

**JOE CHRISTY
WITH CONTRIBUTIONS BY
ALEXANDER T. WELLS, Ed.D.**

TAB BOOKS Inc.
Blue Ridge Summit, PA 17214

FIRST EDITION
SECOND PRINTING

Printed in the United States of America

Reproduction or publication of the content in any manner, without express permission of the publisher, is prohibited. No liability is assumed with respect to the use of the information herein.

Library of Congress Cataloging in Publication Data

Christy, Joe.
American aviation.

Includes index.
1. Aeronautics—United States—History.   I. Wells,
Alexander T.   II. Title.
TL521.C546   1987   629.13'00973   87-6509
ISBN 0-8306-2497-X (pbk.)

TAB BOOKS Inc. offers software for
sale. For information and a catalog,
please contact TAB Software Department,
Blue Ridge Summit, PA 17294-0850.

Questions regarding the content of this book
should be addressed to:

Reader Inquiry Branch
TAB BOOKS Inc.
Blue Ridge Summit, PA 17294-0214

Contents

Foreword   v

Prelude   1

1 Those Magnificent Men and Women!   12

French Pioneers—International Air Meets—Daring Birdmen—Matty Laird—The Stinson Sisters—Glenn
Martin—Curtiss Reorganized—Keys Controls Curtiss

2 The First Air War   28

The 1st Aero Squadron—Chasing Villa in Mexico—The U.S. in WWI—The First Fighter Airplane—
U.S. Aircraft and Engine Production—Airpower Prophet—U.S. Naval Air in WWI—Combat

3 The Wings Grow Stronger   56

First Atlantic Flight—Army and Navy Racers—First World Flight

4 Naval Air and Billy Mitchell   63

Navy Aircraft Engine Development—The First Navy Dirigibles—Mitchell Court-Martialed

5 Birth of the Air Mail   78

Well, Anyway, It's a Start—The Post Office Takes Over—Jack Knight's Epic Flight

6 The Barnstorming Era   87

Charlie Meyers—WACO Is Born—Air Commerce Act—Morrow Board—Jake's Airplane Works—The
Laird Swallow—Clyde Cessna—Travel Air Formed—Walter Beech—Lloyd Stearman—Cessna Aircraft
Formed—Moellendick Bankrupt—WACO Prospers—Great Lakes Formed—Meyers Goes to Eastern

7 The First Airlines   114

The Lindbergh Boom—The Kelly Bill—Stout Metal Planes—Ford TriMotor—Fokker TriMotor—From
Nowhere to Nowhere—United Aircraft—Whirlwinds and Wasps—North American—Transcontinental
Air Transport—AVCO Formed—Stinson Aircraft—American Airways Formed—Curtiss and Wright Merge

8 Czar of the Airways   131

McNary-Watres Act—Spoils Conferences—TWA Formed—SAFEway and Delta—Reed Airline—Airway
Scrooges

9 Glass Houses   144

New Deal or Raw Deal?—The Army Flies the Mail—The "Rascals" Are Punished—The CAA Act of
1938—Pan Am Formed—The Chosen Instrument—Across the Pacific—Across the Atlantic—American
Export Lines—Postwar Overseas Routes

10   The New Deal and U.S. Airpower   164

"Neither Rain, Nor Snow, Nor Politics . . ."—Engine Development Paces the Industry—Navy Airships *Akron* and *Macon*—Transition: The Biplane Era Passes—A New Generation of Aircraft

11   WWII: The Desperate Months   186

The Philippines Lost—Coral Sea and Midway—New Guinea and the Solomons

12   The War in Europe   207

North Africa and Italy—The Italian Campaign—Assault on Fortress Europe—Overlord: The Cross-Channel Invasion

13   Victory and the Unreal Wars   230

The Aleutian Campaign—Over the Hump with the AVG and the 14th AF—The Assam Trucking Company—The CBI Fighters—The Final Thrust

14   Uneasy Peace, and Another War   248

Berlin Big Lift—Birth of the B-52—The Korean War

15   Johnson's War—And After   265

Airpower and the Flexible Response—McNamara's Brand—Faith, Hope, and Parity—Anytime, Gaddafi Baby—Carrier Power—ATF and ATA—The Balance of Power, United States Versus USSR—Midgetman—The Strategic Defense Initiative—Lasers

16   Gen-Av and Fun-Av   298

WWII Surplus—Postwar Ag-Planes—Warbirds—Air Racing—Homebuilts—The EAA—Ultralights—Piper—Beechcraft—Cessna—Business Flying—Helicopters—Minority Group—Rutan *Voyager*

17   Economic IFR   327

Jet Aircraft Engines—The 1910 Coanda Jet—The Whittle Engine—The von Ohain Engine—First U.S. Jet Engine—Boeing—Douglas—McDonnell—Lockheed—FAA Act of 1958—Deregulation—Air Controllers Strike—Slot System—Flow Control—Fare Wars—Survival of the Richest—TEFRA—Bill Lear—Gates Learjet

18   America into Space   351

The First U.S. Rockets—The Space Shuttles—The Inevitable Tragedy—Unmanned Space Vehicles—Extraterrestrials?

Appendix A: Objective Questions   365

Appendix B: Answers to Objective Questions   388

Index   391

Foreword

American Aviation: An Illustrated History was written in response to the growing need for a comprehensive aviation history textbook to be used in collegiate aviation programs. A history course is required in many flight and non-flight related programs because it is felt that students should have a perspective of the historical factors that have influenced the growth and development of the discipline.

While there are many books covering *some* phase of aviation history—aircraft, personalities, events, periods of time including wars—there are very few that cover the *entire* history—and fewer still that do it adequately. This book is the only one I have found in over 15 years of teaching an aviation history course at the post-secondary level that is designed for the college market. The book offers a well-balanced, thorough coverage of the history of aviation including significant events, personalities, and aircraft that have influenced the development of civil and military aviation. The extremely important periods covering the World Wars and the growth of commercial aviation in the United States during the 1930s is very well done.

This volume, however, is not written just as an outline of aviation history. The subject is far too fascinating to be displayed only in skeletal form. The book tells the stories that make up the drama of aviation history: the struggles between the Wrights and Glenn Curtiss; the emergence of the military airplanes with their fliers—20th century "Knights of the Air" during the Great War; barnstorming and aerial hijinks during the 1920s; the birth of the air mail and the U.S. Postal service's role in shaping development of the airline industry;

the court-martial of Billy Mitchell; the glamour and innocence of the 1930s, the era of Howard Hughes' great aerial achievements, when pioneers like Charles Lindbergh, Jimmy Doolittle, Roscoe Turner, Walter Beech, and Wiley Post flew farther and faster and higher than ever before; the air war in the Pacific, from the early defeats to the turning point at Midway and the island-hopping campaign leading to the dropping of the first atomic bomb; the war in Europe and North Africa with insight into the personalities, aircraft and events that shaped the world in the 20th century; the Berlin Airlift and the Korean War; the breaking of the sound barrier and the era of commercial jet aviation; and, finally, America's leap into outer space.

Entertaining yet extremely informative, the book represents years of research and writing by one of this country's most noted aviation historians. Complete with fascinating details and behind-the-scenes views, Joe Christy's book captures the vitality of aviation history and makes it come alive to the reader. Profusely illustrated with hundreds of rare photographs, there is no need to refer to numerous other sources for pictures.

Each chapter begins with an outline of the major sections to be covered. This is followed by learning objectives that the student should be able to accomplish upon completing the chapter. Review questions at the end of each chapter cover all of the important points. Finally, there is an appendix which includes a test bank of objective questions to further reinforce learning.

In reviewing *American Aviation: An Illustrated History,* I was guided by several criteria. The book should be interesting to read, cover the main topics that a student needs to know, flow logically from chapter to chapter, factually describe historical findings rather than hearsay, and adopt a professional orientation. Joe Christy's book has exceeded my expectations in every regard and I look forward to using it in my aviation history classes.

Alexander T. Wells, Ed.D.
Fort Lauderdale, Florida

Prelude

OBJECTIVES: At the end of the Prelude you should be able to:

- ☐ Identify the contributions to aviation made by the Montgolfier brothers and von Zeppelin.

- ☐ Describe the major accomplishments made by Cayley, Lilienthal, Pilcher and Mozhaisky.

- ☐ Explain how Professor Langley almost beat the Wright Brothers in developing a successful heavier-than-air flying machine.

- ☐ Describe the approach taken by the Wright Brothers in developing their gliders during the period from 1899 to 1902.

- ☐ Describe the successes experienced by the Wright Brothers during the period from 1902 to 1908.

- ☐ Summarize the accomplishments of Glenn Curtiss and describe the source of conflict between him and the Wright Brothers.

Man's first successful aerial vehicle was a hot air balloon launched at Annonay, France, by Joseph and Etienne Montgolfier on 5 June 1783. Having observed that smoke rises, the Montgolfier brothers decided that smoke contained a mysterious gas that was lighter than air. They constructed a 35-foot balloon ("*balon*") of linen-reinforced paper under which they built a fire fueled by damp straw and sheep's wool. Their balloon filled with the dense smoke and rose majestically into the sky.

The brothers followed their triumph with another ascent on 19 September 1783, sending aloft as passengers a duck, a sheep, and a rooster to establish that the upper atmosphere was safe to breathe. Then, the following month, French scientist Pilatre de Rozier and the Marquis d'Arlandes made a flight over Paris in a Montgolfier balloon. Man's conquest of the air had begun.

During the next 100 years, lighter-than-air vehicles—employing either heated air or hydrogen as a lifting agent—became as commonplace as their limited usefulness would allow, evolving at last into Count Ferdinand von Zeppelin's giant rigid airships, the first of which flew in Germany on 2 July 1900, more than three years before the Wright brothers took to the air in the world's first successful *heavier-than-air self-propelled* flying machine.

The invention of the airplane was preceded by a great deal more wishful thinking than scientific inquiry. A host of experimenters and dreamers

1

proposed—and even built—a number of flying machines during the nineteenth century. None was successful, although several made small contributions to the quest. Britain's Sir George Cayley and Germany's Otto Lilienthal were the most significant of the serious experimenters who preceded the Wright brothers. America's Octave Chanute, a retired structural engineer, built several multi-wing hang gliders in 1896 and 1897 that sailed up to 350 feet along the south shore of Lake Michigan. But Chanute's best machine was essentially a refinement of an earlier Lilienthal design, and Chanute's only direct contribution to manned flight was the Pratt truss system for bracing biplane wings.

Lilienthal flew his first monoplane hang glider in 1891, later switching to biplane configurations. Flying from an artificial hill near Berlin and the Stollner Hills near Rhinow, he achieved glides up to 750 feet in length before he was killed in one of his machines on 9 August 1896.

Lilienthal was a long way from achieving controlled powered flight when he died, and his calculations of lift produced by a cambered wing surface were in error, but photos of him in flight were published around the world and his work inspired many others—including the Wrights.

The extent to which Lilienthal was influenced by the work of Sir George Cayley is a matter of conjecture, but Cayley's paper *On Aerial Navigation*, published in 1810, and the successful flights of his model gliders establish that this remarkable Englishman was the first to propose the proper configuration for a fixed-wing, heavier-than-air flying machine. Cayley suggested a curved upper wing surface for increased lift, wing dihedral for lateral stability, and his models featured cruciform tails. In the early nineteenth century he was so far ahead of everyone else in this field that it may be said that nothing more of significance was added to Man's meager store of knowledge on this subject until Lilienthal began his experiments 80 years later.

Lilienthal's flights in his hang gliders actually produced almost no new scientific data; his carefully recorded figures on the lifting properties of cambered wing surfaces were found to be in error by the Wrights after they began their experiments.

But Lilienthal's influence was great, at least partly because the halftone process for reproducing photographs in newspapers came into use just in time to picture Lilienthal's accomplishments and prove to the world that man *could* sail through the air on artificial wings.

Another Englishman, Percy Pilcher, built an improved monoplane glider following Lilienthal's death, but Pilcher worked in isolation and died in the crash of his machine in 1899 without influencing the invention of the airplane. And perhaps we should mention that in Russia in 1884 (sometimes mistakenly reported as 1882), a steam-powered airplane built by Alexander Mozhaisky and piloted by I.N. Golubev was thrust into the air from a ski-jump type ramp for a few seconds, but proved incapable of supporting itself in flight.

The most controversial of the early experimenters was Professor Samuel P. Langley, a respected astronomer and secretary of the Smithsonian Institution. Langley became seriously interested in mechanical flight about 1886, and ten years later built a 25-pound steam-powered model of hickory and silk that flew three-quarters of a mile—an event witnessed by Dr. Alexander Graham Bell, who also believed that man-carrying flying machines were possible, and who reported Langley's success to President McKinley.

Langley's model achieved lateral stability in flight by means of dihedral in each of its two wings, which were positioned in tandem—an arrangement used by British experimenters Thomas Walker in 1831 and D.S. Brown in 1874, the latter having tested model gliders so configured. Langley's model also possessed cambered upper wing surfaces (first used by Sir George Cayley in 1809), although Langley's airfoil shape was very inefficient, with its deepest point much too far from the wing's leading edge.

Apparently influenced by Dr. Bell's enthusiastic account of Langley's work, President McKinley obtained an Army appropriation in the amount of $50,000 to finance construction of a full-size, man-carrying version of the "Aerodrome," as Langley called his model.

Langley hired 23-year-old Charles Manley, an

The Langley Aerodrome on its catapult in the Potomac River. It failed to fly in two attempts, suffering structural failure each time. (NASM)

engineering student at Cornell University, and designed a quarter-scale model of a full-sized Aerodrome. This flew in 1901 with a small gasoline engine.

The full-sized Aerodrome was completed in July 1903, and taken to its launch track atop a houseboat in the Potomac River. Manley had built it according to the 63-year-old Langley's instructions, and also designed and built its engine after it became clear that the Balzar engine contracted by Langley was much too heavy and produced only a fraction of the power expected. (Some historians have referred to the Aerodrome's powerplant as the "Manley-Balzar" engine, apparently in the belief that Manley merely modified Balzar's creation. Manley did expend considerable effort attempting to get more power from it, but finally gave up and designed a truly remarkable five-cylinder radial that was water-cooled and produced 52.4 hp at 950 rpm; it weighted 207.5 pounds including coolant. This engine proved its reliability in three separate ten-

hour test runs, and its weight-to-horsepower ratio was not equalled until the appearance of the Liberty engine in 1917.)

On 7 October 1903, the Aerodrome was ready for test. Manley climbed aboard, gave the signal for release of the catapult spring, swooshed down the launching rail—and fell into the Potomac. Only slightly injured, he swam to safety. A photo taken just as the machine let its launching device showed its forward wing twisted grotesquely out of shape

On 8 December 1903 Manley had the repaired Aerodrome back atop the houseboat for another try. But this time the machine's rear wing failed as it left its launching track, and Manley narrowly escaped drowning when he became entangled in the wreckage. Nine days later the Wrights flew at Kitty Hawk, and Langley abandoned his project. He died in 1906, a thoroughly honorable man, but the Aerodrome—or a reasonable facsimile thereof—would be revived eight years later and used by others to perpetrate a shameful hoax designed to

The Langley Aerodrome on its catapult in the Potomac River. It failed to fly in two attempts, suffering structural failure each time. (NASM)

discredit the Wright brothers—about which, more momentarily.

Orville and Wilbur Wright possessed a significant advantage over most of those who had preceded them in the quest of manned, mechanical flight: *They approached the question as airmen.* Except for Lilienthal, all the others had mostly proceeded with preconceived ideas as to what a flying machine should look like. They produced "eyeball" designs, and few bothered with any serious investigation of the dynamics of flight, while none gave any real thought as to how a flying machine would be controlled if it *should* succeed in getting off the ground and achieve sustained flight. Most appeared to believe that an airplane could be steered like a boat, and that wing dihedral would provide the necessary lateral stability.

The Wrights, however, were concerned with *controlled* flight from the outset, and they approached their task suspicious of every "discovery" and each bit of data that had been passed along by experimenters before them. Thus, Wilbur discovered very early that the best information available on the lifting properties of wings with various upper surface curves—painstakingly recorded by Lilienthal—was in error. The Wrights did adopt the Pratt truss system for wing bracing, but their ultimate success was exclusively theirs. They constructed a small wind tunnel that allowed them to witness the shift in the center of pressure above the wing as its angle of attack was changed, and which aided in the selection of a reasonably efficient airfoil shape for their wings. Eventually the brothers would put a similar, deliberate effort into propel-

Wilbur Wright. (National Archives)

inclusive, and accomplished more than a thousand glides from the sand hills at Kitty Hawk, North Carolina.

At the conclusion of the 1902 tests the brothers were confident that they were ready to build a powered machine, and the Wright Flyer I (Flyers II and III would follow in 1904-1905), fitted with a 12-hp gasoline engine designed by the Wrights, was ready to fly late in 1903.

Wilbur won the coin toss for the privilege of making the first flight in the new machine on 14 December, but scarcely got off the ground before overcontrolling with the forward-mounted elevator and nosed into the sand. Damaged was slight, and at 10:35 A.M. on Thursday, 17 December, Orville took his turn. He flew 120 feet in 12 seconds into a 20-22-mph wind. During the next hour and a half, three more flights were made with the brothers alternating at the controls. On the final flight Wilbur flew 852 feet wile remaining aloft for 59 seconds. Those flights, witnessed by five local people, were

Orville Wright. (National Archives)

ler research, and their marvelously reasoned solution to the problem of roll control and turning flight—wing warping—was the answer to a major aerodynamic question that others had not yet asked. The addition of a hinged rudder, interconnected to the wing-warp controls, solved the problem of adverse yaw in turning flight.

The Wrights built their first aircraft in August 1899. It was a biplane kite with a wingspan of five feet, and was flown tethered to a stake, its primary purpose being to test the wing warping system. This system warped downward the outer trailing edges of the wings on one side while simultaneously warping upward the trailing edges on the opposite side. Hinged ailerons (first used by the French experimenter Esnault-Pelterie in 1904) would soon supplant the Wrights' wing warping system, but the principle was the same.

Following tests with their kite, the Wrights built three biplane gliders, one each year 1900-1902

The 1902 Wright glider; flight control theories proven, the Wrights needed only to add a proper propulsion system—which required that they design and build their own engine and propellers. (NASM)

the first in the history of the world in which a powered heavier-than-air vehicle had taken off under its own power, achieved sustained, controlled flight, and then landed at a point as high as that from which it had taken off.

During the next two years the brothers regularly flew from Huffman Prairie, about eight miles east of their home in Dayton, Ohio. They made some 40 flights in 1905, the longest being for a distance of 34 miles. The Wrights avoided publicity awaiting patent protection and the expected sale of their invention to the U.S. and British governments. Satisfied that their Flyer III was a practical aircraft, the brothers did not fly again until the summer of 1908. Orville demonstrated a two-place Flyer at Ft. Myer (near Washington, D.C.) in September that year, the U.S. Army at last having been forced to take the Wrights seriously as reports persisted of successful flights by experimenters in France. (Accurate sketches of the Flyer III had been published in France in 1906, and although no one there understood the Wrights' system of lateral control, Henri Farman had, in 1907, remained aloft for a minute and 14 seconds and completed a wide, skidded circle. The Farman machine had no means of lateral control except for the yaw effect of its rudder.) At Ft. Myer, one of Orville's propellers failed in flight, damaged the airframe, and sent his machine crashing to the ground out of control. Lt. Thomas Selfridge, riding as a passenger, was killed, Orville seriously injured. But a month earlier, Wilbur had begun a series of demonstrations in France that captivated all Europe, and despite Orville's accident, the world had suddenly become aware that *man could fly*.

Meanwhile, Alexander Graham Bell had brought together and financed a small group of men who were interested, as was Dr. Bell, in manned

The age of manned flight begins, 17 December 1903. On his first attempt that day, Orville flew 120 feet in twelve seconds. Three more flights were made, with the brothers alternating at the controls. The fourth flight, at noon, with Wilbur piloting, lasted 59 seconds and was measured at 852 feet.

Wilbur with passenger near Auvors, France, in 1908. After witnessing one of Wilbur's many flights in France, Maj. B.F.S. Baden-Powell, Secretary of Britain's (hopeful) Aeronautical Society, said, ''That Wilbur Wright is in possession of a power which controls the fate of nations is beyond dispute.''

flight. That was the "Aerial Experiment Association," led by motorcycle racer/builder Glenn Hammond Curtiss. This group produced four flying machines based upon what could be learned about the Wright Flyers. These machines appeared between March and December 1908. The first barely flew and crashed on its second test. The next one managed to remain airborne for slightly more than a thousand feet during the best of its five attempts before crashing, while the third aircraft built by the A.E.A. members, the "June Bug," made a number of flights, the longest of which was two miles.

The June Bug was said to be Curtiss' design; it was fitted with a 30-hp water-cooled V-8 designed by Curtiss and engine builder Charles Kirkham and featured wingtip ailerons. Its best flight did not compare with the flights made there years earlier by the Wrights in their Flyer III, but the June Bug led Glenn Curtiss into the aircraft manufacturing business, and within two years Curtiss would be the Wrights' principal competitor—as well as their primary target in a series of bitter court confrontations resulting from Curtiss' alleged infringement on Wright patents.

The courts held in favor of the Wrights in every case that went to trial, but Curtiss managed to grow and prosper—primarily due to profits generated by the Curtiss exhibition teams—and held the Wrights at bay with appeals and other legal maneuvers until, at last facing a showdown in 1914, Curtiss resorted to a consciousless ploy that will forever shadow his very real contributions to aviation.

It occurred to Curtiss that if the Langley Aerodrome could be flown, then he could argue in court that the Wright patents were not based on an original invention.

Curtiss was sympathetically received by the man who had succeeded Langley as secretary of the Smithsonian, Dr. Charles D. Walcott, and Walcott not only loaned the Langley machine to Curtiss, but also sent along one Dr. Albert P. Zahm of the Smithsonian to document Curtiss's effort. It should be noted that Dr. Zahm had earlier been a Curtiss witness in court.

Glenn Curtiss (L) is pictured with Chance Vought (third from right) in 1911. Vought would also build airplanes and help found the company that is today known as United Technologies. (U.S. Navy)

Comparison of the original Langley Aerodrome and the Curtiss-modified machine of eleven years later reveals the differences. (NASM)

There were, however, other interested parties—particularly Griffith Brewer of Britain's Royal Aeronautical Society, to whom history is indebted for the true facts concerning the Curtiss caper.

Curtiss made no effort to fly the original Aerodrome. By 1914 a lot of progress had been made in airplane design. Curtiss was building flying boats by then, and had at least one able and experienced airframe designer on his staff (Douglas Thomas, designer of the famed WWI Curtiss JN-4 Jenny), and it was obvious to Curtiss that the Aerodrome was incapable of flight without significant modification.

Curtiss constructed new wings for the Aerodrome—wings of different planform, different camber, and differently braced. The Penaud-type tail (fixed surfaces with limited and very slow movement as a unit, and similar to that which Cayley had employed on his models 100 years earlier) was modified to operate with a Curtiss control system; the propellers were changed, the pilot's seat repositioned, and the machine was mounted on floats. There was still no means of lateral control except the stability provided by the dihedral angle at which the four wing panels were attached.

This hybrid could not sustain itself in flight; its longest hop was of five seconds duration. Therefore, Curtiss removed the Manley engine and its twin pusher propellers and installed a 90-hp Curtiss V-8 with a single tractor propeller in the nose of the machine. Then, on 1 October 1914, he accomplished six takeoffs that resulted in flights of 20 to 65 seconds duration. It was then up to the Smithsonian's Dr. Zahm to legitimize the hoax.

Zahm's affidavit read in part: "The machine was the same machine in construction and operation as the original structure. The frame was the same; the engine was the same; the horizontal and vertical rudder located at the rear was the same; the vertical rudder under the machine was substantially the same; the propellers were the same and the wings were identical in construction with the original machine, except, as I have heretofore stated, they were perhaps a little more roughly built and a little heavier."

Actually, Zahm wrote this affidavit before Curtiss made the engine change. It therefore did contain *one* truth when it was written. We should note that the original Aerodrome had a total weight of 830 pounds. The machine flown by Curtiss weighed 1520 pounds.

Curtiss making one of several short hops 17 December 1914 in an effort to prove that the Langley Aerodrome was capable of flight, and therefore that the Wright patents were not based on an original invention. Curtiss' ploy fooled no one. (NASM)

It is not clear who returned the Aerodrome to its original configuration, but it was placed on display in the Smithsonian Institution just as Charles Manley had built it in 1903 along with a plaque that read: "The First Man-Carrying Aeroplane in the History of the World Capable of Sustained Free Flight . . ."

That is why the Wright brothers' Flyer remained in Great Britain's Science Museum until 1948. By that time, pressure from many individuals (as well as the possibility of a Congressional investigation) brought a formal apology to the Wrights from the Smithsonian, and the Wright Flyer claimed its rightful place there on 17 December 1948, the 45th anniversary of its historic first flights. Unfortunately, Orville had died the previous January at age 77. Wilbur had been spared the hurt of the whole shameful mess, having died of typhoid fever in 1912 at age 45.

The Wrights' lawsuits against Curtiss were never settled in court. The WWI patent pool affectively placed them on "hold" until 1919, and by that time neither Orville nor Glenn Curtiss controlled the corporations that bore their names, and neither board of directors was willing to pursue the matter. Both men lived to see the merger of those companies in 1929, which formed the (then) giant Curtiss-Wright Aeronautical Corporation, but Orville had long since retired to his mansion in Dayton, and Curtiss was a Florida real estate developer. Curtiss died a year later of complications following an appendectomy.

We will encounter Curtiss-Wright in chapters to follow.

REVIEW QUESTIONS

1. What was the major contribution to the advancement of flight made by the Montgolfier brothers? What distinction is held by Pilatre de Rozier?

2. Briefly describe some of the important contributions to the science of aeronautics made by Sir George Cayley. Identify some of the significant contributions to flying made by Otto Lilienthal; by Perry Pilcher.

3. What was the reason for Professor Langley's failure to successfully launch his Aerodrome in October and December 1903? How did two obscure bicycle mechanics from Dayton, Ohio, with little formal education and no government support, succeed where some of the world's most prestigious engineers and scientists had failed? Why was the period from 1903 to 1908 such a disappointing one for the Wright brothers? Why was 1908 a turning point?
4. Explain how the Aerial Experimental Association got started. Describe some of the aircraft developed by this association. How did AEA develop a conflict with the Wright brothers?

Chapter 1

Those Magnificent Men and Women!

OBJECTIVES: At the end of this chapter you should be able to:

☐ Identify several of the early air meets and recognize some of the participants including their accomplishments.

☐ Discuss some of the daring showmen of the pre-World War I era.

☐ Describe the epic flight of Calbraith P. Rodgers.

☐ Identify several of the early women pilots.

The first commercial use of the airplane was exhibition flying. Prior to WWI there was no other way to make money with this exciting new vehicle. Engines were too unreliable; payloads too small. Man could fly, but just barely.

That was enough, however, to justify promotion of several great aerial expositions to celebrate the achievement of this age-old dream. The first was a week-long event held on the Betheny Plain near Rheims, France, in August 1909. By that time France was already beginning to lead the world in development of the airplane. Except for advances made by Glenn Curtiss (which included off-water flying), almost every innovation, every improvement to the flying machine between 1908 and 1914 originated in France. The French were ready and eager for the air age; the rest of the world had to be dragged into it.

French Pioneers

The roseate aeronautical climate in France was apparently due to several factors. Ballooning had

been born there more than a century earlier, but a more direct influence was the work of several Frenchmen who had been experimenting with flying machines since 1903, spurred by published accounts in France of the Wrights' successful gliders. These accounts included detailed drawings and photos of the Wrights' 1902 glider in flight.

Among these French aviation pioneers were Ernest Archdeacon, Robert Esnault-Pelterie, Gabriel and Henri Voisin, Leon Levavasseur, and Louis Bleriot. Englishman Henri Farman and Brazilian Alberto Santos-Dumont added their achievements to the French aviation scene.

The diminutive Santos-Dumont, heir to a coffee fortune, began with a small, cylindrical gas bag fitted with a tiny gasoline engine; in this device he flitted among the rooftops of Paris much to the delight of Parisians. He turned to heavier-than-air machines in 1906 and, after several failures, produced a 200-pound monoplane of 24 hp, the "Demoiselle," in 1909. The Demoiselle's best flight was of about 12 minutes duration. Other machines in both America and France were more advanced by then, but Santos-Dumont's contribution was significant because he was a colorful figure and his was such a class act that he provided much impetus to aircraft development in Europe at just the proper time.

International Air Meets

The 1909 Rheims Meet attracted all of the top aviators and the best aircraft designs produced up to that time. A French aviator, Maurice Tissandier, flew a copy of the latest Wright machine. The Wrights did not attend. Glenn Curtiss was there, however, with his specially designed Rheims Racer.*

Curtiss won the Gordon Bennett cup race with a speed of 47 mph, the *Prix de la Vitesse* at 46 5/8 mph, and placed second in the *Tour de Piste*. There were protests over his misrepresentation of his engine's power, but Curtiss' reputation as an airplane builder was markedly enhanced.

The success of the Rheims Meet prompted a number of similar events, the next one being an air spectacular promoted by actor Dick Ferris and held at Dominguez Field near Los Angeles in mid-January 1910. The ubiquitous Glenn Curtiss established a speed record with a passenger at 55 mph, and leaped into the air with a takeoff run of 98 feet in 6.4 seconds. But France's Louis Paulhan, flying a Farman biplane, took home top honors and most of the money for his 75-mile round trip to Santa Anita and return with an elapsed time of one hour and 58 minutes. Paulhan also established a new altitude record of 4165 feet. It was indicative of the progress being made in aircraft development. The previous altitude mark of 508 feet had been made at Rheims only five months earlier.

The next great aerial meet was at Boston Harbor during the first two weeks of September 1910. Prizes totalled $100,000, the principal one being for a race around Boston Light. This was won by England's Claude Graham-White in a Farman, barely nosing out Glenn Curtiss. Graham-White flew the 5 1/2 miles in six minutes.

The Boston Harbor Meet was the largest to date, but it was surpassed by the greatest aerial tournament prior to WWI, which was held at New York's Belmont Park, October 22-31, 1910. Described as the top society sporting event of the decade, the Belmont meet attracted not only the best pilots from both sides of the Atlantic, but what passed as the "jet set" of that era as well.

The Bennett Cup race at Belmont generated great excitement as Graham-White was hard pressed to beat out such aeronauts as America's John Moisant, flying a Bleriot; England's Hubert Latham, piloting an Antoinette; Alec Oligvie in a Wright Model C; and Walter Brookins' Baby Wright. Graham-White averaged 61 mph for the 62-mile course. Brookins crashed the Baby Wright when he turned to fly to the aid of Alfred Leblanc, who had wrecked his machine after averaging 66.2 mph in the speed dash. John Moisant won the race around the Statue of Liberty from Belmont Park, but was disqualified on a technicality and the $10,000 prize went to France's Count Jaques de Lesseps (Tenth son of the Suez Canal's builder). Ralph Johnstone claimed an important record for America when he established a new altitude mark of 9714 feet.

At Belmont the girls first appeared as pilots. Tiny Mlle. Helene Dutrieux was enthusiastically applauded by spectators for her flights, although she was not allowed to compete with the men. Other early "aviatrices," as they were called, were Americans Blanche Scott, Ruth Law, John Moisant's pretty young sister Mathilde, and a petite West Coast drama critic, Harriet Quimby. Katherine Stinson would follow in 1912, and her younger sister Marjorie in 1914.

Daring Birdmen

The success of the first great air meets, with

---

*Curtiss himself referred to this machine as the "Rheims Racer" or the "Rheims Machine." It was also called the "Golden Flyer," and there is evidence that it was the same airplane, fitted with a 50-hp engine, that some researchers have called the "Gold Bug," and which Curtiss sold to the Aeronautic Society of New York in the spring of 1909, powered with a 30-hp air-cooled V-8. It was loaned back to Curtiss in July 1909, and Curtiss appears to have built new wings for it. He registered his machine at Rheims at 30-hp, but it was found to have a new 50-hp engine.

The Henry Farman biplane of 1909 was powered with a 50-hp Gnome engine and had a speed of 37 mph. It was much in evidence at the Rheims meet.

One of the earliest aerial photos shows a spare wheel lashed to the aircraft's skid and was taken over Rheims, France, 1909.

Mlle. Helene Dutrieux flew at Belmont, L.I., but was not allowed to compete with the men.

in winged aircraft than in Beachey's and Roy Knabenshue's "rubber cows," Beachey went to Curtiss, learned to fly, and by 1911 began giving airplane exhibitions booked by Pickins. His craft was a Curtiss pusher fitted with a water-cooled V-8 engine—an engine that would evolve into the famed OX-5 of WWI.

The Curtiss airplanes of this period had at least two advantages: good engines, and pilot's controls that were more natural to use than the Wrights' control systems. (Almost every manufacturer of flying machines employed a different control system through 1911.) The Wrights used two control sticks—one moving forward and backward to activate the elevators (pitch control), and one that when moved forward put down-warp on the right wings and when pulled back put down-warp on the left wings for banking (roll control). At the top of this latter stick was a lever that controlled the rudder

their attendant publicity, correctly suggested that ready-made audiences awaited throughout the U.S. for living proof that Man could actually fly. Therefore, the Wrights, Curtiss, and Moisant organized exhibition teams and toured the country for the edification of the public and the enrichment of themselves. These teams appeared in all the large cities, while freelancers performed individually at county fairs and in smaller towns. The best of the freelancers were represented by booking agent Bill Pickins as the "Lincoln Beachey Flyers," Beachey being perhaps the most daring and soon the most popular of this nomadic fraternity.

Beachey had begun as a dirigible pilot at age 19 in 1905. He flew a sausage-shaped gas bag from which was suspended a light framework containing engine and aeronaut. But when the spectators at the Dominguez meet showed far more interest

Marjorie Stinson learned to fly at the Wright brothers' school in Dayton in 1914 and flew exhibitions in a Model B Wright pusher. (Marjorie Stinson)

Lincoln Beachey began his career as an exhibition pilot in 1905 at age 19. He flew Baldwin dirigibles with Roy Knabenshue's troupe before turning to airplanes in 1910 to become, because of his daring, the best-known of the early birdmen. Beachey died when his monoplane shed its wings during a performance at the San Francisco World's Fair, 14 March 1915. (NASM)

The Bleriot XI of 1909 had a speed of 36 mph, was powered with a 25-hp, three-cylinder Anzani engine, and was commercially available for about $2000. In such a machine, France's Louis Bleriot flew the English Channel 25 July 1909. Many Bleriots were sold and/or copied in America. Clyde Cessna built his first airplane after inspecting a Bleriot in Oklahoma City.

Calbraith Rodgers (R) made the first transcontinental flight 17 September to 10 December 1911. He crashed 19 times and arrived in California from New York with only a wing strut and rudder of his original aircraft, A Wright Model B. His sponsor was the manufacturer of "Vin Fizz," a popular soft drink. (NASM)

Crashes during the birdman era often required the services of friends armed with baseball bats to discourage souvenir hunters.

A.L. Longren of Topeka, Kansas, built this copy of a Curtiss pusher and toured the county fairs on the southern plains in 1912-1913. (Joe Durham)

for yaw control. Earlier, the Wrights had used a shoulder yoke that effected wing-warp when the pilot leaned in the direction of the desired bank.

The early Curtiss machines used a wheel atop a vertical column that raised and lowered the elevators when pulled back or pushed forward (pitch), and which controlled the rudder when turned right or left. Ailerons were activated by a shoulder yoke as in the earlier Wright machines.

Again, it was the French who eventually produced the more logical system in use today,

which incorporated foot-operated pedals for rudder control and a wheel that activated both elevators and ailerons. For many years this was referred to as the "Dep" control system, presumably because it was introduced on the Deperdussion machines in 1912. The designer of Deperdussions was Louis Becherau. Most historians have passed Becherau by, but he designed exceptionally clean mid-wing monoplanes, one of which was the first airplane to exceed 100 mph (in 1912), and raised the mark to 126.59 on 29 September 1913. Later, Becherau

Matty Laird's first airplane, built in 1913 when Laird was 17 years old, was "a loose formation of discarded material arranged in airplane form." A friend wrecked it. (E.M. Laird)

18

Katherine Stinson with her 1916 airplane, which was built for her by "Pop" Keller and Elmer Partridge. Engine was the 80-hp Gnome rotary salvaged from Lincoln Beachey's airplane. (E.M. Laird)

would design the SPAD of WWI ("SPAD" for the company that built it, *Societe Pour Aviation et Derives*).

Although the Wrights had unlocked the secrets of controlled manned flight, it remained for others to build upon those discoveries. By 1912, the pupils could teach the teachers a few things.

However, some of the most famous of the early birdmen preferred the Wright machines, perhaps at least partly because they had learned to fly with the Wright control system. Calbraith P. Rodgers was one of them.

Rodgers may or may not have been a truly competent pilot, but one thing is certain: He had more than his share of determination. He was the first to fly coast-to-coast across the United States. Sponsored by the makers of Vin Fizz, a popular grape drink of the day, and in pursuit of a $50,000 prize

Laird exhibition flight at St. Paul, Minnesota, 7 November 1916, by that time including a loop, crowded Presidential election news to a secondary position on front page of the Dispatch. (E.M. Laird)

offered by William Randolph Hearst to the first aviator to complete such a journey within 30 days, Rodgers left New York on 17 September 1911. He crashed 19 times and required 49 days for the trip, but refused to give up. He finally arrived in Pasadena on 5 November with one leg in a cast and only a rudder and a single wing strut remaining of his original Wright pusher. He had made 69 stops—many unscheduled due to weather and mechanical trouble—and actually spent 82 hours and four minutes in the air, covering 3220 miles. His average speed in the air was slightly over 39 mph.

In mid-1912 (by which time Calbraith Rodgers had died in a crash), one of America's pioneer women pilots took to the air. Katherine Stinson was not yet 17 years old when she soloed a Wright Model B at Max Lillie's flying school on Chicago's Cicero Field. She required 3 1/2 hours of dual instruction. (At $90 per hour, one tended to learn fast.) Katherine's indulgent mother, Emma, found money for a down payment on a used Model B Wright, and little Katy was soon booked for as many exhibition flights as she cared to make. Represented by Bill Pickins, she received $500 for each appearance—an impressive sum indeed in 1912 dollars. Not that she did anything spectacular by today's standards; at that time it was enough for most people to see a flying machine rise off the ground and sail overhead, and to witness such a feat performed by an unassuming young woman was indeed a memorable sight.

In 1914, sister Marjorie followed in Katherine's propwash, attending the Wright school at Dayton, Ohio. Another Model B Wright was purchased for Marjorie's use, then she too began touring the county fair circuit. Brother Eddie attended the Wright school a year later, after having spent most of 1914 living in a hangar at Cicero Field with the Laird brothers, Matty and Charles, and Buck Weaver. These four would all significantly impact American aviation in years to come.

In 1915, Lincoln Beachey was killed while performing at San Francisco's Panama Pacific Exposition. Katherine bought the wreckage of his airplane to obtain its 80-hp Gnome rotary engine

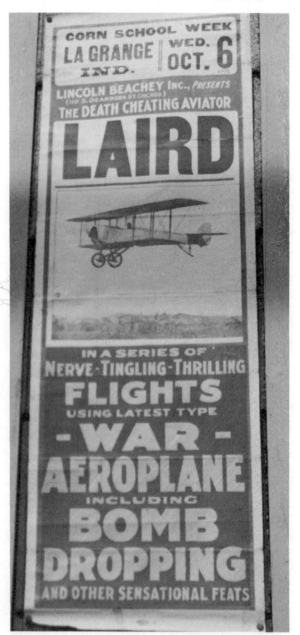

Poster announcing Laird visit to La Grange, Indiana, 6 October 1916 reveals the hype designed to attract crowds to see the "death cheating aviator." Promoter Bill Pickens had also booked Beachey, the Stinson sisters, and other top exhibition pilots of the time.

for a new biplane being built for her by Elmer Partridge and "Pop" Keller. She performed a loop in this machine, becoming the fourth American pilot

Glenn Curtiss pioneered flying boat designs beginning with his "F" Boat of 1912. (Charles W. Meyers Collection)

Flying was truly a dangerous business in the beginning. In 1910 alone, 37 pilots were killed, perhaps one in seven then flying in the U.S., although, due to the low airspeeds, most accidents were not fatal. (Charles W. Meyers Collection)

to master this maneuver, and then included a "loop-the-loop" in her subsequent appearances. (The first inside loop in history was performed by France's Adolphe Pegoud in 1913. Beachey was the first American to do it, followed by DeLloyd Thompson, Art Smith, Katherine, and, in 1916, Matty Laird. Jimmy Doolittle performed the first outside loop in 1927.) Matty Laird appears to be the first pilot to perform a loop with a passenger, that passenger being Marjorie Stinson.

Matty Laird

The mid-wing monoplane was constructed of old barrel hoops and redwood latticing. Its spruce wings, muslin-covered, were treated with hide glue and formaldehyde. It was powered with a four-cylinder engine built up from automobile and motocycle parts. It had no ailerons, no instruments, and no good reason to fly. But it did—and at the

E.M. "Matty" Laird at Chicago's Cicero Field, 1916. (Marjorie C. Stinson)

same time provided its creator with his first flying lesson.

This unlikely craft, which took to the air on 15 September 1913, was the handiwork of 17-year-old Emil Matthew "Matty" Laird, a $4.50-per-week office boy who had left school after the eighth grade to help support his family. Matty had decided to become a flier three years before, after witnessing a flight by a Wright brother's exhibition pilot, Walter Brookins, at Chicago's Grant Park.

Walter Brookins was one of several early "birdmen" (a term common at the time) hired and trained by the Wrights as exhibition pilots. Prior to WWI there was no big market for airplanes in the U.S., either civil or military, but there was money to be made—a great deal of it—simply demonstrating to the public that man could fly. The Wright's gadfly, Glenn Curtiss, also formed an exhibition team, and both were highly successful. And there was a number of freelance exhibition pilots, some flying aircraft purchased from the Wrights or Curtiss, some equipped with homebuilt copies, and a few—such as Clyde Cessna and Matty Laird—who defied the laws of gravity and reason in airplanes of their own design.

In light of what was then known about the art/science of manned flight, it seems remarkable that so many such creations actually flew. Less surprising is the fact that so many crashed. In 1910 alone 37 pilots were killed, and it was axiomatic that a crash always followed a stall. No one knew how to recover from a spin until Eddie Stinson reasoned it out and demonstrated spin recovery in 1916. The pioneers who led us out of the aeronautical wilderness were possessed of both great courage and unusual perception. The merely brave seldom survived.

Young Matty Laird's aeronautical knowledge was acquired from the building and flying of model airplanes, and many hours spent at Chicago's Cicero Field, where Wright-trained Max Lillie taught flying and which had become, by 1912, one of the most active aviation centers in America, largely due to the interest and financial help of Harold McCormick of the International Harvester Company and seed magnate Charles Dickinson.

Among the habitués of Cicero Field in addition to Laird were Buck Weaver, later a co-founder of WACO; Bill Brock, who would one day make a record flight to Tokyo; Elmer Partridge and Les Bishop, who would become pioneer air mail pilots; and "Shorty" (he was six-foot five) Schroeder, who would investigate high altitude flight for the Army, among other things. Max Lillie's students included Katherine Stinson and Chance Vought, who were destined to leave indelible marks on the pages of aviation history. Thus, the Windy City's Cicero Field—replaced in 1915 by Ashburn Field, on the site of today's Midway Airport—nurtured a significant bit of our air heritage.

Dual instruction in Lillie's Wright Model B was $90 per hour or $1.50 per minute, and one could rent the airplane for solo flight at the rate of $50 per hour, although a cash deposit of $1000 was required in case the student broke something expensive. Considering the value of the 1912 dollar, it is easy to see why so many early birdmen were forced to act as their own flight instructors.

Laird began his flight test/flight instruction program by hooking his machine to an ice scale attached to a fence post, then operating his engine at maximum rpm to determine the "pounds of thrust" thus obtained. He didn't know how much he needed, so the figure obtained was of no value to him, but the practice was common at Cicero Field and Laird felt that it served to make him appear a bit more "professional."

Matty's first surprise was the torque effect created by his propeller. After he managed to control that and taxi in a reasonably straight line, he found himself airborne, a circumstance he had not planned to confront so abruptly.

"I had thought that I would know exactly what to do," Laird said later, "But there I was, twenty feet in the air, trees rushing at me from the field boundary, and I wasn't so sure anymore. I had an overpowering urge to get back on the ground as quickly as possible."

In his haste to return to earth and give himself some time to think things out, Matty shoved forward on his control wheel, struck the ground, wiped out his landing gear, splintered his propeller, and

flipped upside down in a cloud of dust.

Matty's cuts and bruises had healed by the time his machine was repaired, and he continued—cautiously—to teach himself to fly, beginning with a long series of very short hops. At first, he would reduce power as soon as his wheels left the ground. Gradually he increased both the height and distance of each hop. By late fall he had climbed to an altitude of 200 feet and had mastered a complete 360-degree turn. After that, his progress was rapid.

During the winter of 1913-14, Matty built a small biplane and flew it evenings and weekends throughout 1914. A raise in pay at the bank where he worked allowed him to re-cover the "Baby Biplane," as he called it, with Irish linen and finish it with a new French product, cellulose-nitrate dope.

By mid-1915 it could be said that Laird had become a pilot, as skillful as most others of that day.

Edward A. Stinson, Jr. was the first to demonstrate spin recovery (1916); he was later a famed pilot and plane builder. (Marjorie Stinson)

He had rigged a small auxiliary oil tank for upper cylinder and valve lubrication of his homemade engine, and that extended the length of time it could be operated to as much as 30 minutes. Without quite realizing it, Matty had positioned himself for a career in this exciting new industry.

His first opportunity manifested itself in the form of the country's foremost booking agent for exhibition pilots, one Bill Pickins, who saw Matty fly and promptly offered to arrange professional appearances for him.

At first, Matty was booked at small county fairs and lesser events, while the more famous pilots received the most lucrative contracts. But the $350 Matty was paid to take off, circle the field a few times, and land at Sebring, Ohio, represented 4 1/2 months' pay in his regular job, so he gave notice at the bank and joined the ranks of Lincoln Beachey, Art Mix, and the Stinson sisters as a "Daring Birdman" who travelled about the country introducing the miracle of flight to the (often skeptical) citizenry.

The Stinson Sisters

During the winter of 1915-16, Katherine and Marjorie Stinson established a flying school near San Antonio, Texas, and Katherine commissioned Elmer Partridge and Pop Keller to build a new "modern" biplane for her, fitted with an 80-hp Gnome rotary engine salvaged from the wreck of the airplane in which famed exhibition pilot Lincoln Beachey had died a few months earlier. At the end of the 1916 season, Katy took this machine, along with Matty Laird's new Anzani-powered biplane, and left for a triumphal tour of Japan. Brother Eddie, having learned to fly at the Wright school, opened a flying school at Houston, Texas, while Marjorie was busy in San Antonio teaching a group of Canadians to fly who would help form the nucleus of a future Royal Canadian Air Force.

Early in 1917, Laird visited Marjorie in San Antonio and, while waiting for the exhibition season to begin, installed a new tail on a biplane Bill Brock had built for Katherine. Test-flying this machine, Matty crashed and was seriously injured.

That incident deserves more than passing com-

The Stinson sisters with Katherine's Wright Model B. Marjorie on left. Katherine was fourth U.S. pilot to master the inside loop. (E.M. Laird)

ment because it illustrates the difficulty today's serious researcher sometimes encounters in attempting to accurately record the activities of our aviation pioneers. Matty told me that this airplane entered a flat spin at an altitude of approximately 2,000 feet as he investigated control response at low airspeeds. He described in great detail his futile efforts at recovery. However, Marjorie, who was on the scene, disputed Laird's account, telling me, in no uncertain terms, that Matty simply stalled the airplane on takeoff.

Such disputes are not exactly rare. Over the years I have interviewed many great names in aviation, and while I can honestly say that every one, without exception, was courteous, modest, and really a class act, I learned quite early that some will rewrite history for you if given the chance. This forces the writer to do a lot of cross-checking. Sometimes it is not possible to firmly document the truth. All I can say in regard to the above-mentioned incident is that, cross-checking where possible, I uncovered no other questionable statements by Matty Laird in eight hours of taped conversation. When I went back to him with Marjorie's statement, he smiled and replied, "Well, that's Marjorie for you." He refused to say anything against her, and nowhere in his account did he offer anything but praise for the Stinsons.

Ralph McMillan and his homebuilt copy of a Curtiss pusher shared the billing with Laird at the Harrison County Fair, Missouri Valley, Iowa, 17 September 1915. (E.M. Laird)

It was obvious to me that Marjorie—still attractive, elegant, intense, and very sharp indeed late in life—held an extraordinary amount of personal dislike for Laird, which the years had not softened. It's one of those little footnotes to history—an intriguing if minor mystery, and all that it really means, I suppose, is that those legendary figures of our industry were, after all, only human.

Matty spent many months in the hospital as a result of his crash at San Antonio and was left with a permanent limp and an improperly knitted arm, which precluded any possibility of military service in WWI, but his most important contributions to civil aviation were yet to come.

Glenn Martin

Meanwhile, other early birds were placing a few stones in the foundation of this infant industry. Glenn Luther Martin operated a small garage in Santa Ana, California, when, in 1909, at the age

of 20, he built his first airplane. Known as the "Flying Dude" for his immaculate dress, he became one of the first motion picture pilots in 1915, appearing in the Mary Pickford film *The Girl From Yesterday*. Martin flew exhibitions, built 17 training planes

Matty Laird with his Anzani-powered exhibition airplane. Buck Weaver is at extreme left. (E.M. Laird)

25

for the U.S. Signal Corps, and moved to Cleveland in 1918 to produce bombers for the Army. Among early Martin employees were Lawrence Bell, James "Dutch" Kindelberger, and Donald W. Douglas.

When Martin moved to Cleveland from the West Coast, it was to form a new company. All of the fledgling planemakers of the birdman era, needing capital, were gobbled up by combines of investment bankers soon allied with automobile interests. The Wrights put up their U.S. and Canadian rights late in 1909 to form Wright Aeronautical Corporation with J.P. Morgan, Cornelius Vanderbilt, George Gould, and several other multimillionaires. Orville and Wilbur received $100,000 in cash, 40 percent of the stock, and a 10 percent royalty on each airplane sold (they also sold manufacturing rights in France, Germany, and England between 1908 and 1913).

Curtiss Reorganized

All this was paced by aircraft engine development at Curtiss. The first Curtiss airplane engine had been an air-cooled V-8 of 30 hp which was fitted, in turn, to the first three machines produced by Bell's Aerial Experiment Association in 1908. It was followed by improved versions of up to 60 hp, and it seems clear that Charles Kirkham, who machined and assembled these engines, was also the designer. Curtiss had no engine facility at his Hammondsport factory.

By 1912, Kirkham was building the Curtiss Model O water-cooled V-8 of 75 hp, and an improved valve-actuating system on this engine—the work of Henry Keckler and John H. McNamara—resulted in the Model OX in 1913 which, with additional detailed improvements, became the famed 90-hp OX-5 in 1916. Shortly after introduction of the Model OX, Charles Kirkham was appointed chief engineer at Curtiss; McNamara had the title of "engine superintendent."

At this point, Curtiss faced the need for significant expansion capital. He could offer a good military trainer and a good engine. Orders were coming in from Britain and Canada, while the U.S. Congress was certain to approve a pending bill that would authorize a large air training program for the Army and Navy. Therefore, Curtiss went to investment banker Clement M. Keys, who consolidated Curtiss' holdings, formed Curtiss Aeroplane and Motor Company, and marketed its stock.

Automobile mogul John North Willys emerged as the chief minority stockholder in Curtiss Aeroplane and Motor, and during WWI the Willys-Overland and Willys-Morrow plants accounted for more than 7000 of the total 12,600 OX-5 engines built, while new Curtiss factories at Buffalo and Garden City, NY, produced JN-4 and JN-6 (the latter, Hisso-powered Jennies) trainers for the Army, and JN-9 (essentially, the JN-6 on floats) trainers for the Navy. About 6750 Jennies were produced by war's end.

After the war, surplus Jennies and Canucks (the latter being the Canadian-built Jenny) became the barnstormers' primary mount, and surplus OX-5 engines could still be found in privately owned biplanes on the eve of WWII.

Keys Controls Curtiss

With the cessation of hostilities on 11 November 1918, existing wartime contracts were of course cancelled. But the government had financed construction of expanded manufacturing facilities for Curtiss and others, and Curtiss directors decided to maintain their factories, with greatly reduced payrolls, and attempt to serve whatever markets—both civilian and military—could be developed. Although there were fewer than 1000 American pilots in combat units overseas when the war ended, almost 10,000 were in training in the U.S. at hastily constructed airfields about the country, and therefore many people in the aircraft industry expected a boom in civil aviation, predicting a strong market for "flivver" planes (small and cheap single-placers), as well as larger commercial craft.

When the boom did not develop, Willys sold his stock in Curtiss Aeroplane and Motor Company to Clement Keys, who had organized the corporation back in 1916. The Willys stock, plus the shares already held by Keys, put Keys in control of the company, and wheeler-dealer Keys would dominate Curtiss—and build an aviation empire from it—when the boom did materialize in the late 1920s.

1. Where was the first international air meet held? Who were some of the participants? Where was the first meet held in the United States? Describe some of the records which were established at both meets. What was the outcome of the Bennett Cup race at Belmont Park in 1910?

2. Who were Lincoln Beachey and Calbraith Rodgers? Describe the control system developed by the French which was a considerable improvement over the ones used in the Curtiss and Wright machines.

3. Who were some of the early women pilots? What significance was the development of aircraft by Matty Laird, Clyde Cessna, and Buck Weaver?

Chapter 2

The First Air War

OBJECTIVES: At the end of this chapter you should be able to:

- [ ] Discuss the role of the U.S. First Aero Squadron.

- [ ] Recognize the importance of World War I in accelerating aircraft development.

- [ ] Describe the evolution of fighter aircraft which took place during the war years.

- [ ] Discuss some of the problems faced by U.S. aircraft manufacturers in gearing up production for the war.

- [ ] Understand the role played by Billy Mitchell in shaping the U.S. Air Service.

- [ ] Describe the role of the U.S. Naval Air Service during World War I.

- [ ] Identify some of the leading aces on both sides of the conflict and the aircraft which they flew.

At the outbreak of World War I, in August 1914, there were no military aircraft in the world. True, France, Germany, Britain and the United States military forces all possessed airplanes by that time, but none were designed for any specific military mission. The airplane had been under development in Europe for less than six years, and most of that effort had been directed toward improving performance. The Wright Model A, or Military Flyer, of 1909 cruised at slightly over 40 mph. By 1914 a speed of 130 mph had been achieved in the British single-place SE-4, but since the Army generals could envision only one possible use for airplanes—the scouting of enemy troop movements—speed was not regarded as an asset.

Actually, in the United States, artillerymen had foreseen the possibility of employing airplanes to direct artillery fire three years earlier. A 1911 newspaper report is to be found in the files of the Field Artillery Museum at Fort Sill, Oklahoma:

"Junction City, Kansas—A successful aeroplane artillery test was conducted during the War Department's aeroplane maneuvers here. Battery E, Sixth Field Artillery, Lt. Palmer commanding, was stationed on the side of a hill. An imaginary enemy was placed on the other side. Lt. Milling, Aviator, with Lt. Sands as observer, flew over the hill obtaining the enemy's position. The messages giving the information secured were dropped to the artillerymen. No wireless tests were made."

The 1st Aero Squadron

At the time of the above mentioned experiment, the U.S. Signal Corps had a total of six airplanes in service or on order. Except for pilot training at San Antonio, Texas and College Park, Maryland, this appears to be the first field test of a U.S. Army airplane. In any case, whatever flying was done by the Army through 1912 was that of true pioneers feeling their way. Then, in January 1913, Lt. Harold E. Geiger inaugurated the Signal Corps Flying School at North Island, off San Diego, California, and in December of that year War Department General Order No. 75 authorized the First Aero Squadron, although this unit was not actually formed until 15 July 1915 from students trained at North Island.

On 26 July the squadron was sent to Fort Sill, Oklahoma, for duty with the Field Artillery School. The squadron consisted of 15 officers, 85 enlisted men and eight Curtiss JN-2 aircraft, Capt. Benjamin Foulois commanding.

The Army's Capt. C. DeF. Chandler (L) and Lt. Roy Kirtland in the Wright "B" airplane were first to fire a machine gun from an aircraft, 7 June 1912. (USAF)

According to official reports, the 1st Aero Squadron "carried out various exercises" at Fort Sill, including artillery spotting and some aerial photography. One pilot, Capt. G.H. Knox, and two aircraft were lost, which led to the squadron being re-equipped with Curtiss JN-3s (extended upper wings and improved engines). Then, in November 1915, the squadron was ordered to fly its eight aircraft to Fort Sam Houston, near San Antonio. This was done without serious mishap although it was undoubtedly the longest cross-country mass flight attempted up to that time.

An uneventful winter was spent at Fort Sam Houston erecting living quarters. Then, on 13 March 1916, the 1st Aero Squadron received orders to report to Gen. John J. "Black Jack" Pershing at Columbus, New Mexico, to serve with an American punitive expedition charged with the task of capturing the Mexican rebel leader Francisco "Pancho" Villa. Early in the morning of 9 March, Villa, with 400 men, had raided the border town of Columbus, killing nine civilians and seven United States troopers. More U.S. citizens certainly would have died had not Col. H.J. Slocum charged into town with the 13th Cavalry and chased the raiders back into Mexico.

Chasing Villa In Mexico

Gen. Pershing entered Mexico with 5000 men on the 15th of March, and the 1st Aero Squadron, with 10 officers and 80 enlisted men, began operations from Columbus on the 19th. The squadron's duties consisted mainly of reconnaissance, courier, and communications assignments. Pershing was an old horse soldier and clearly felt that the airplanes were more bother than help. Considering the state of aircraft development at that time. Pershing wasn't completely wrong.

Two of the eight airplanes were lost almost at once. Lt. T.S. Bowen escaped with only a broken nose when, in a high wind, his craft "dipped and plummeted in almost a straight 50-ft fall to the ground," according to a Fourth Army press release. And a news flash reported "Flight Lieutenants Edgar S. Gorrell and Robert H. Willis, Jr. overdue and apparently down somewhere in the Chihuahua desert.'' Fears for the downed fliers' safety deepened when it was pointed out that, in the great waste over which they were flying, men on foot could wander for days without reaching help. Each carried only three days' rations and two canteens of water. An additional danger was the possibility of capture by Villa's forces.

However, both survived with little ill effect. Willis walked 32 miles to the pueblo of Casas Grandes. Later, when a crew returned to his airplane, they found that the seats and instruments had been removed and the wings slashed. Only the engine was salvagable. Gorrell was found plodding along the road three miles from another village. He had gone down with a fuel leak two days earlier. A bit of solder and a can of gasoline were all that were needed to allow him to fly his airplane back to Columbus.

Another pilot, Lt. Dargue, and his observer, Capt. Willis, crashed on the side of a mountain while on a mission to reconnoiter the roads leading into Chihuahua City. Neither was seriously injured, but their walk back to the Mexican village of San Antonio covered about 60 miles of very rough terrain.

The actual campaign into Mexico was of short duration, and the squadron had but two serviceable airplanes left when it returned to Columbus after 33 days in the field. Still, a lot of lessons had been learned in that short time. Operating their primitive craft under harsh conditions over inhospitable desert and mountains (the Sierra Madres were often higher than the absolute ceiling of the JN-3), the men of the 1st Aero Squadron proved more durable than their machines.

Pancho Villa was never captured. He and his men remained under arms in the Sierra Madres until, in 1920, the Mexican Government coaxed him into retirement with the gift of a large estate. Three years later, he was assassinated.

Meanwhile, shortly before the 1st Aero Squadron was recalled from Mexico, President Wilson had sent an ultimatum to Germany demanding the U-boat (submarine) attacks on U.S. shipping be stopped. It would be another year before America would be forced into the war in Europe, and meanwhile the 1st Aero Squadron would remain at Columbus, New Mexico. After the U.S. entered the war, the squadron would go overseas in August 1917, and, following a six-month wait for airplanes,

In November, 1910, civilian pilot Eugene Ely made the first aircraft takeoff from a ship when he flew a 50-hp Curtiss from a platform on the bow of the light cruiser *Birmingham*. (USN)

"Fly by wire" was method of launching the U.S. Navy's first airplane in 1912. The float-equipped Curtiss Triad took off from greased wires. Liason aircraft were similarly flown from Navy LSTs during WWII. (USN)

would enter combat in April 1918, flying French-built Salmson observation planes.

The U.S. In WWI

Now, the debate still continues among historians as to just how much the United States contributed to Allied victory in WWI, especially in the air. Starting with an army of 200,000 in April 1917, the United States had 2.8 million men under arms when the war ended, with 43 divisions overseas. True, they were sketchily trained and much of their armament came from France and Britain, but this was a typical American Army of "civilians in soldiers' suits," and they performed as Americans have always performed in battle. They gripped and they joked and they fought superbly.

When Americans entered the battle zones in the spring of 1918, the war had been stalemated for more than three and a half years while 10,000,000 men died in the mud. But the Bolshevik revolution took Russia out of the war and freed the Germans on the Eastern Front for a series of spring offensives in France that may well have at last defeated the exhausted British and French but for the arrival of the Americans—commanded by Gen. "Black Jack" Pershing. In fact, long before the Americans arrived in force, the mere promise of their coming gave new resolve to the tottering Allies, and the popular cry "The Yanks are coming!" was alone probably worth a couple of new divisions on the Western Front.

The Americans did, of course, make all the difference in the key battles fought during the spring and summer of 1918. They stopped a major German offensive that had broken through Allied lines east of the Aisne River and which had advanced to within 40 miles of Paris. In July, eight U.S. divisions—two of them spearheading—led the Allies to victory in the Aisne-Marne Offensive which left the Allies with the initiative. Two months later, Pershing had 27 American divisions (11 of which he used) for the St. Mihiel offensive in a successful, totally American operation. That in turn allowed the joint American-French (630,000 Americans, 138,000 French) Meuse-Argonne Drive on 26

Glenn H. Curtiss began building successful flying machines in 1908; was repeatedly sued for patent infringement by the Wrights. Curtiss pioneered flying boat designs. (Joe R. Reed collection)

September 1918 which would end the war seven weeks later on 11 November.

Those are the essential facts, unclouded by detail, but the fact that all of it was accomplished in less than seven months and at what the Allies regarded as a small sacrifice (53,403 Americans killed, 202,261 wounded), and after they had suffered four years of unbelievable carnage fighting over that same ground, led some to downgrade America's role in the Allied victory when in truth it was American troops, American food, and the U.S. Navy guaranteeing the delivery of both, that ended the bloody stalemate in Flanders and allowed the Allies to dictate the terms of peace.

Those peace terms, spelled out in the Treaty of Versailles in 1919 and primarily drafted by France, were so harsh and unrealistic that they made the appearance of Hitler all but inevitable—about which, more later.

The 1914-1918 war in the air greatly accelerated aircraft development, but the airplane did not significantly influence the outcome of that conflict, and WWI in the air was not a dress rehearsal for future air warfare. Neither side had airplanes in sufficient numbers or of sufficient performance to make airpower a decisive factor. Important con-

An early Curtiss triplane design, the Model L, crashed in test for the Army. (USAF)

The 42nd airplane purchased by the U.S. Army was this Curtiss JN-2, forerunner of the famed JN-4 "Jenny." Engine of this 1915 aircraft was the Curtiss OX-5, evolved from a series of water-cooled V-8s designed by Curtiss dating back to 1908. (Boardman C. Reed collection)

cepts in strategy and tactics emerged, but their implementation in each case was on a scale too small to establish their validity.

At the beginning of the war, airplanes on both sides were unarmed, and opposing machines often passed one another—sometimes exchanging pistol fire—on missions to scout one another's positions and troop movements. Of course, both sides recognized the desirability of denying the enemy access to their skies while remaining free to invade enemy air, and that prompted the appearance of the first fighter planes. The Germans presaged the doctrine of strategic airpower with their dirigible raids on England as early as 1915; close air support of advancing ground troops was convincingly demonstrated by Col. Billy Mitchell's fliers during the Battle of St. Mihiel.

The First Fighter Airplane

The world's first fighter plane was the Morane-Saulnier Bullet, a single-place mid-wing monoplane operated by the French early in WWI. It became a fighter when an 1885 Hotchkiss infantry machine gun was mounted on its cowling, and a wedge-

shaped steel deflector was attached to the back of each propeller blade to protect the prop from the estimated one bullet in seven that did not pass between the blades. French aviator Roland Garros is said to have shot down several German airplanes with this machine before going down behind enemy lines in April 1915.

The Germans inspected Garros' crude gun installation and soon had forward-firing, line-of-sight guns on their airplanes, although theirs utilized an interrupter gear activated by an engine-driven cam, allowing the gun to fire only between the prop blades. The British and French followed with similar systems.

The air war steadily intensified as aircraft on both sides improved. Throughout 1916, and for much of 1917, the Germans were generally better equipped. The Pfalz DIII, Albatros DIII, and Fokker DRI Triplane (the Red Baron's favorite mount) were excellent fighters for their time. Their most serious challenger was the French Spad VII, which entered combat in the fall of 1916. The British SE-5a and Sopwith Camel were in service by mid-1917 and were, perhaps, the equal of any Ger-

Curtiss R-4 of 1916 had red star on rudder, the first although unofficial attempt toward adoption of a national insignia for U.S. Army airplanes. (USAF)

man fighters with the possible exception of the Fokker DVII, which entered combat at about the same time. So the Germans were never, for any significant length of time, confronted with Allied aircraft of superior performance.

World's first fighter airplane was the French Morane-Saulnier Bullet of 1914 which mounted an 1885 Hotchkiss machine gun for line-of-sight aiming by the pilot. Wedge-shaped steel deflectors on rear of propeller blades protected the blades from the estimated one-in-seven rounds that did not pass between. (National Archives)

Had WWI continued into 1919, the Allies would certainly have controlled the air; by that time, aircraft production in the United States would have, despite much wasted effort, become a major factor, as would the 10,000 American pilots in training when the war ended. Given time, America really would have "darkened the skies over Germany" with her warplanes.

While the United States could have produced a lot of airplanes through 1919, no notable American designs would have been among them. Most would have been deHavilland DH-4 observation planes. Perhaps some would have been the American-designed Orenco D and Thomas Morse MB-3 pursuits (fighters), had the 300-hp Hispano-Suiza engines been available for them. Both of these 150-mph craft appear to be copies of the French Spad (of which the U.S. ordered 6000 on three contracts, later cancelled).

U.S. Aircraft and Engine Production

The U.S. aircraft production effort during WWI is epitomized in the story of the Liberty engine. Within days of America's entry into the war,

The British BE2 of 1914 served the Royal Flying Corps as an observation plane and light bomber early in WWI. Skids beneath nose were to prevent nose-over during landings.

a joint British-French commission arrived in the U.S. to aid manufacturers in selecting the most useful airframe and engine designs. This commission was directed to Detroit, where it was met by Jesse Vincent, the Packard Motor Car Company's vice president for engineering. As early as 1916, automobile interests had purchased the Wright patents and gained control of the Curtiss company. Therefore, aircraft and aircraft engine production would be in the hands of the car makers.

The commission recommended that U.S. factories build two-place fighter-bombers and engines of 200 to 400 horsepower. To save time, they suggested that those planes and engines be British and French designs already battle-proven. That was a realistic suggestion because, by 1917, the U.S. was years behind the combatant nations in aircraft development, and no U.S. manufacturer had any real experience in the volume production of airplanes—a product that had to be largely hand-built.

But the automobile people were in control, and whatever the problems they would solve them, *profitably.*

Vincent went to Washington and conferred

German Fokker E-1 Eindecker (monoplane) of 1915 was fitted with an 80-hp Oberursel rotary engine. Speed was 80 mph and the machine gun was synchronized by an interrupter gear to fire between the rotating propeller blades. (USAF)

The L-30, a typical German military Zeppelin, appeared in 1916 and raided London and other cities in England as well as targets on the Eastern Front. L-30 was 649 ft in length, 78 ft in diameter, 90 ft high. She could carry five tons of bombs, had ten machine guns for defense, and cruised at 60 mph. (Wingfoot LTA Society)

with the automobile executives who had been appointed by President Wilson to the key aircraft procurement posts, Edward Deeds and Howard Coffin, top men of the hastily-created Aircraft Production Board. Deeds was an associate of Charles Kettering at Delco; Coffin was a Hudson Motor Company official.

This group determined that Packard should design and build the 400-hp engine needed. It would be known as the "U.S. Standard Aircraft Engine." This engine would power the deHavilland DH-4, the airplane selected by the board for mass production. The British Bristol Fighter was a newer, superior two-place fighter-bomber, but it would not accept the V-12 engine that Vincent planned. Vincent would later say that he and E.J. Hall designed the Standard Aircraft Engine, which became known as the *Liberty,* over a single weekend following his meeting with Deeds and Coffin, but the truth was that Vincent had been working on such a design for more than a year, and had actually built two test versions.

The Liberty was no better or no worse than most aircraft engines of its day. It was billed as a triumph of engineering, but it required hundreds of modifications during its first few years of ser-

The Germans lost a number of the world's first strategic bombers to Allied fighters, although most dirigible raids were made at night when few defensive airplanes were able to fly. (Joe R. Reed collection)

A French Maurice Farman observation plane proceeding toward the Front in 1915. Engine was a 110-hp Le Rhone rotary. (USAF)

vice, and its official time-between-major-overhauls was 120 hours, although few Liberties ever ran that long without repair. (When the Army flew Liberty-powered planes around the world in 1924, engines were changed every 50 hours, but even that didn't prevent several engine failures on the four airplanes.)

The Liberty was a water-cooled engine, but it cylinders were not cast in a single block. What Vincent and Hall actually designed was a single cylinder which could be stuck into different crankcases to make engines of four, six, eight or twelve cylinders. It sounded good when stated that way, but there was nothing new about it, and the V-8 version could hardly have been taken seriously when the superior Hispano-Suiza, built under license by the Wright Corporation, had already proven itself. (Later the six-cylinder version of the Liberty—a six in-line, not a V-6—did enjoy minor success in the post-war civilian market.)

But the most interesting feature of the V-12 Liberty was its automobile-type Delco ignition system, a major component that was, of course, dear to Mr. Deed's heart. All other aircraft engines, then as today, used magnetos for a hotter spark and greater reliability.

Meanwhile, the car manufacturers and their financial backers divvied-up the market in an interesting way. Wright Aeronautical, controlled by

British F.E.2d fighter-bomber was often used to escort the vulnerable observation planes. Engine was a 250-hp Rolls-Royce. Forward gunner had a good field of fire. (USAF)

Many American pilots trained in France in the Caudron C-3, which employed wing-warping for lateral control. (USAF)

a syndicate which owned the Simplex Automobile Company (the principals being Richard Hoyt of Hayden, Stone; Thomas Chadbourne and Harvey Gibson of Manufacturers Trust, and Albert Wiggen of Chase National Bank) bought out the Glenn L. Martin Company (the third most important airplane builder behind Wright and Curtiss) and formed the Wright-Martin Company. With that kind of muscle, the Wright-Martin Company could put a hammerlock on the production of the 150 to 300-hp aircraft engine market.

Another "Wright" company was formed by wheeler-dealers Deeds, Coffin, Vincent, and Kettering. It was called Dayton-Wright (Orville Wright was listed as one of the original organizers, though he was not active in the company). Dayton-Wright was the prime contractor for the deHavilland DH-4.

At the Curtiss Aeroplane and Motor Company, John North Willys, who was something of a maverick among automobile biggies, seems to have had little or no influence with the "in" bunch comprising the Aircraft Production Board, but he didn't need it. Curtiss was well established as a purveyor of flying machines to the Signal Corps, already had

substantial orders for its JN-4 trainer by the time the Aircraft Production Board was formed, and could hardly be denied additional orders for the "Jenny," the standard Army training plane. On floats, it was the N-9 Navy trainer.

A total of 4846 DH-4s was produced: 3106 by Dayton-Wright, 1600 by Fisher Body (a GM subsidiary), and 140 by the Standard Aeroplane Company. About 1500 DH-4s were shipped overseas. However, Gen. Halsey Dunwoody, director of the Air Service's supply system, later said, "We never had a single plane that was fit for use." Those that reached the front had to be rebuilt by the A.E.F. aircraft production center at Romorantin, France.

Altogether, 13,574 Liberty engines were built before the war ended, by Packard, Ford, GM, and Marmon, but the first one did not fly over the fighting front in France until 7 August 1918.

For a reason never explained, Liberty engine production continued into 1920, by which time more than 22,000 had been built. The Army was stuck with these engines throughout the '20s, and Army observation planes designed ten years after WWI were forced to use them. The last Liberty was retired from service at Kelly Field, Texas, in 1935.

For all the money and effort invested, less than 200 American-built airplanes—Liberty-powered DH-4s—were in the battle zone and fit for service when WWI ended. The remaining 550 aircraft in American hands at the front were purchased from France and Britain. When the fighting stopped, there were 45 U.S. combat squadrons in action with a strength of 800 pilots and 500 aerial gunners and observers.

In seven months of combat, American losses were 289 planes and 48 observation balloons. U.S. pilots and gunners were credited with 781 enemy planes and 73 balloons shot down.

Eventually, in mid-1918, President Woodrow Wilson became aware of the Aircraft Production Board's blatant boondoggle and cleaned house. But the combines formed by Deeds and his cronies continued to possess their contracts, probably because there were no alternate sources at that late date. And since both public memory and political retribution are notably short-lived, both Deeds and Coffin would soon resurface in other positions of authority.

Airpower Prophet

The man who planned the highly successful U.S. Air Service tactics in WWI was Col. William "Billy" Mitchell. (We should pause to mention that the Aviation Section of the Signal Corps became the "Airplane Division" on 2 June 1917, although it was generally called the "Air Service." Separation from the Signal Corps came on 20 May 1918. On 4 June 1920 Congress approved the Army Reorganization Bill which officially recognized the "U.S. Air Service" as a "separate and coordinate branch of the Army." Then, on 2 July 1926 the Air Corps Act changed the Air Service to the "U.S. Army Air Corps," and it remained as such until 20 June 1941 when, with a new autonomy under Maj. Gen. Henry H. "Hap" Arnold, it became the "United States Army Air Forces" (USAAF). Today's independent United States Air Force (USAF) was created by the National Security Act of 1947, which became law on 18 September that year. We will try to use the appropriate term for each period discussed here.)

Mitchell had learned to fly at a civilian school and at his own expense while stationed in Washington, D.C. An excellent military record spanning 18 years service in the Signal Corps had resulted in assignment to the Signal Corps Headquarters staff and promotion to major. Mitchell had enlisted as a private in 1898 at the outbreak of the Spanish-American War, and had shown himself to be an in-

Crash of a French Farman, 1917. (Charles W. Meyers)

novative officer. Early in 1917, he convinced his superiors that he should be sent to Europe to study Allied air tactics. He was there when the U.S. declared war on Germany.

He flew as an observer with the French and went to England to talk with pilots and Royal Flying Corps brass. He was greatly impressed with Britain's Maj. Gen. Sir Hugh Trenchard, and Mitchell later wrote (Memoirs of WWI, *Liberty* magazine, 1928; Random House, 1960) that most of his philosophy on the proper use of airpower was based upon that of "Boom" Trenchard. Each clearly saw that a nation's air force should be an independent service, that a strategic air arm should be committed to the destruction of an enemy's critical industries, that tactical aircraft should be sent against the enemy's lines of supply and communication, and that close air support of an advancing ground force must include control of the air above that force.

Mitchell's immediate boss was Maj. Gen. Ma-

son Patrick, Commander of the Army Air Services and an old classmate of Pershing's at West Point. Patrick never made any public statements about Mitchell, but there is evidence that he supported Mitchell whenever possible—not only in France, but years later, when Mitchell was publicly kicking a lot of sacred military cows, to the delight of the press and to the consternation of the War and Navy Departments. Gen. Patrick was almost certainly responsible for Mitchell's appointment to the post of Chief of Air Service, First Army, with a promotion in rank to colonel, because Pershing wasn't big on placing flying officers in command positions. Most flying officers were not "regular Army," and Pershing held the professional soldier's's prejudices against reservists.

Mitchell was regular Army, and stretching friendship (with Patrick) only a little, that made him acceptable to Pershing. However, Mitchell was not a West Pointer, and that definitely left him forever

Albatros D-IIIs of Richthofen's Jagdstaffel 11, spring, 1917. A 160-hp Mercedes engine gave these fighters a speed of 120 mph. (USAF)

40

Nieuport 17 fighters of the Lafayette Escadrille at Cachy, Somme, 1916. The Lafayette was made up of American volunteers flying for France prior to America's entry into WWI. (USAF)

outside the council of the Army's General Staff. The highest permanent rank he could ever realistically expect was that of "bird" colonel. His later, temporary rank of brigadier general went with his job as the number two man in the Air Service—and it also went when he was relieved of that position.

The Army's policy of placing veteran regular Army officers in command of flying units generally worked very well. There's no substitute for experience, especially command experience. But it did produce a few unusual situations. At one flying school, when the new CO was informed that the students disliked their ancient Cuadron training planes because they employed the old wingwarping principle for lateral control rather than hinged ailerons, he ordered the planes kept indoors and out of the sun when not in use to prevent such warping. An ex-cavalry major in charge of a squadron had a hitching post installed outside the Operations office and went about the aerodrome on horseback. (There were, in fact, so many ex-cavalry officers in the Air Service that spurs were part of the Air Service regulation uniform for several years.)

The most embarrassing example, perhaps, was the case of the major in charge of the 96th Bombardment Squadron who led a six-plane formation over Germany in marginal weather and eventually landed on a German aerodrome, believing it to be an Allied field. The Germans captured the whole outfit intact. The next day they dropped a note on the 96th's base which read; "We thank you for the fine airplanes and equipment you have sent us; but what shall we do with the major?" (When later reminded of the incident, Mitchell replied, "Needless to say, we did not reply about the major, as he was better off in Germany at that time than he would have been with us.")

Mitchell's chance to demonstrate some of his theories of aerial warfare finally came on 1 September 1918 when U.S. troops under Pershing began the great St. Mihiel Drive. From his headquarters at Ligny-en-Barrios, Mitchell commanded a force of 1476 aircraft, most of them placed at his disposal by the French, British and Italians. It constituted the greatest concentration of airpower the world had seen up to that time, and would appear to indicate that the French and Italian air commanders agreed with the Trenchard/Mitchell doctrine.

The St. Mihiel salient held by the Germans was shaped like a huge horseshoe, its foremost part on the Meuse River, its ends anchored on the German Border. Mitchell sent 400 planes to each end of the horseshoe to sever enemy lines at those points and split the enemy's air defenses. Meanwhile, U.S. fighter-bombers (DH-4s, Breguets, Salmsons), along with elements of the U.S. 1st Pursuit Group, blasted in at treetop level across the horseshoe's center. While the American fliers were giving close support to the advancing infantry, the French and Italians far to the rear concentrated on the destruction of trains and trucks to immobilize all movement, effectively blocking both the possibilities of reinforcement and retreat. This was the employment of massed airpower as a tactical striking force as Mitchell envisioned it.

The operation was highly successful. The drive ended in quick victory for the American forces and the taking of thousands of prisoners who had been denied both help and an avenue of escape. Gen. Pershing was impressed; Mitchell was soon promoted to the temporary rank of Brig. Gen.

A few weeks later, Mitchell proposed to Pershing, via Patrick, that the U.S. Army form a paratroop division, but Pershing apparently did not take that suggestion seriously. Other Mitchell ideas (that the Air Service be a separate and equal department of the U.S. military, for example) *were* taken seriously—in fact, viewed with alarm. Just the hint that the upstart Air Service should someday independently take a share of the responsibility—and appropriations—for the nation's defense was enough to corrode a lot of brass. And well it might, for they were to hear a lot more from Billy Mitchell.

U.S. Naval Air In WWI

Some natural rivalry has always existed between the branches of the U.S. military, but seldom has it been more pronounced than in 1917-18 when the Army and Navy fought each other over aircraft procurement at home and the deployment of airplanes overseas. That may seem strange when

one considers that *neither* service professed much faith in the effectiveness of aerial vehicles in their respective operations, but the generals and admirals, whatever their private or public positions concerning the value of military air machines, obviously felt that, since there *were* such things, *their* branch of the service should have the authority— preferably the *exclusive* authority—to operate them. In mid-1918, long before the U.S. Navy possessed a rigid dirigible (or could fathom any use for one), the Navy managed to obtain from the Secretary of War exclusive authority to operate rigid dirigibles. Upon America's entry into the war, the Navy had rushed to sign contracts with all the major U.S. plane builders to tie up their entire production. The Army retaliated by taking charge of all sources of spruce (from which airframes were made). It was this bitter interservice squabble that hastened formation of the Aircraft Production Board.

Both services gave primary flight training to as many of its aviation enlistees as their limited facilities would permit, then shipped them overseas for advanced training (in some cases, all flight training). Therefore, many American pilots, in American uniforms, both Army and Navy, initially entered combat in French and British squadrons, because the U.S. had neither the airplanes nor the organized personnel and supporting equipment to

The British Handley Page V/1500 of 1918 was designed to carry 1000 pounds of bombs to Berlin. Wingspan was 126 feet. (USAF)

The Fokker DR-1 Driedecker (triplane) was Richthofen's favorite mount. Highly maneuverable, it was powered with the 110-hp Oberursel rotary engine and had a speed of 115 mph. (USAF)

The body of Max Immelmann in wreckage of his Fokker Eindecker. The originator of the "Immelmann Turn" fell to the guns of Lt. George McCubbin, RFC, 18 June 1916. McCubbin was flying an F.E.2b. (USAF)

More than two years of trench warfare took the lives of millions and left the war stalemated, the combatants exhausted, prior to the U.S. entry into the war in April, 1917.

establish its own air units until mid-March 1918. The Navy's first fighter ace, Lt. (jg) David S. Ingalls, scored all his air victories while flying with RAF Squadron 213.

The first aerial victory credited to a Navy air-man went to Ens. Stephan Potter on 19 March 1918, when he shot down an enemy seaplane, one of several that attacked Potter's formation of flying boats as it attempted a reconnaissance mission along Germany's north coast.

The Navy air units were chiefly concerned with coastal patrol, but began offensive operations in August 1918, when Air Squadron One, Northern Bombing Group, made a single-plane night raid on enemy submarine docks at Ostend. The first raid in force by the Navy's Northern Bombing Group was made by eight aircraft of Marine Day Squadron Nine, which dropped 17 bombs, totalling 2,218 pounds, on the German-held railroad junction at Thielt Rivy, Belgium, 14 October.

When the armistice was signed ending the hostilities of WWI, the strength of Naval aviation had grown to a force of 6716 officers and 30,693 men in Navy units, and 282 officers, 2180 men in Marine Corps units, with 2107 airplanes and 230 lighter-than-air vehicles. Of these numbers, 18,000 officers and men and 570 aircraft were overseas, serving at 20 shore stations in France, England, Ireland, Gibraltar, Italy and in the Azore Islands. The

The Curtiss H-12L flying boat used by the U.S. Navy during WWI as a patrol craft. Engines were 350-hp versions of the Army's Liberty. (USN)

DeHavilland DH-4 at Fort Sill, Oklahoma, 1918. (Joe R. Reed collection)

Navy's claims for its air units were modest: 27 enemy submarines sighted, 25 attacked, and 12 damaged. Naval aviators dropped 63 tons of bombs. The Navy's commander in chief, Adm. Mayo, refused to commend the war effort of Naval aviation, complaining that it had failed to work with his battleships.

Combat

Although the Americans made the difference in WWI, breaking the stalemate and spearheading Allied victory, we are allowed another perspective of the U.S. air contribution when we compare the number of aces (pilots officially credited with five or more enemy aircraft destroyed in aerial combat) produced by each country. Britain's RFC/RAF (the Royal Flying Corps became the Royal Air Force in mid-1918) could count 533 aces, their highest scorer being Maj. E. Mannock with 73 victories. There were 158 French aces, Capt. Rene Fonck being the greatest with 75. Of the 44 Italian aces, Maj. Francesco Baracca was tops with 34. Among the 360 German aces, Rttm. Manfred Frhr von Richthofen headed the list with 80 victories, and of the 83 American aces, Capt. Eddie Rickenbacker was the top scorer with 26 official victories.

These figures seem to suggest that U.S. Air Service pilots would have at least equalled the British record had the Americans been in combat a comparable length of time. It is a fair assumption. Gen. Trenchard himself remarked on the "aggressiveness of the Americans," and a look at the service records of a few U.S. aces underscores this factor. All were individualists, a trait not uncommon in a free society.

Take, for example, Elliot White Springs. His 12 air victories were topped by a half-dozen other U.S. pilots, but Springs typifies the attitudes, experiences, and the kind of young Americans who volunteered for the Air Service. Springs was a student at Princeton when the U.S. was forced into the war, a bright young man of small responsibility and large appetite for pleasure.

Thousands like Springs, in the best universities, were attracted to the Air Service because of newspaper accounts that had, throughout the previous year, lionized the aces and offered glowing accounts of chivalrous air duels in the skies of France. The air war was a romantic war, fought between fleet-winged machines in the crisp, unspoiled blue.

The air war was a gentlemens' war.

Springs attended aviation ground school at Princeton, and in the fall of 1917 was sent to England with 209 others for flight training. Then, in May 1918, he was posted to RFC No. 85 Squadron, which was commanded by famed Canadian ace Maj. Billy Bishop (72 victories) and equipped with SE-5a fighters. The squadron was stationed near Petite Synthe, France, and Bishop allowed his rookies a few short patrols but forbade them to fly near the front lines. That, however, was asking too much of the impatient Springs. He took off alone and flew into Germany looking for enemy aircraft.

Springs didn't find the enemy; the enemy—a flight of six Pfalzes—found him. Somehow he managed to escape and returned to his field in a badly damaged airplane. Attempting to land his crippled machine, he careened into Maj. Bishop's SE-5 and destroyed that one as well.

The next day, Bishop led six of his pilots, including Springs, on patrol in the Courtrai area where, with the advantage of altitude, they attacked a formation of 12 black Pfalz fighters. Springs, determined to vindicate himself, shot down one of the enemy as two others fell before the guns of his squadron mates. Then, returning to 85 Squadron's field, Springs, in high spirits, hot-dogged over a train for a dramatic landing—and wrecked his airplane.

Bishop determined that his eager rookie was unhurt, then sternly confronted him: "Well, Springs, pile up just two more SE-5s and you'll be a German ace. Whose side you on, anyway?"

The veteran Bishop knew, of course, that a fighter pilot's natural instincts should not be curbed, but directed. Springs would do well once a bit of responsibility was thrust upon him.

There followed a period of several weeks during which 85 Squadron escorted DH-9s of RFC 311 Squadron to bomb the U-boat pens on Germany's north coast (311 also contained Americans). Then, in June, 85 Squadron was transferred to St. Omer to help repulse what was to be the last great German offensive of the war.

While at St. Omer, Bishop was sent home to Canada to organize a Canadian air force (Canadians and other Commonwealth airmen had been fighting in the RFC), and Lt. Springs was promoted to flight commander.

Springs scored two more victories before he

The Curtiss N-9H was the Navy's version of the JN-4 Jenny trainer. (Peter M. Bowers)

French-built Nieuport 17 fighters at the U.S. Air Service training school, Issoudun, France, 1917. These aircraft were flown by all the leading Allied aces. (USAF)

himself took a burst of fire in his engine during a battle with a Hannoveraner (an armored two-seater designed for trench strafing) and went down just behind British lines. His face smashed into his gun butts as his plane flipped end-over-end and he was pulled from the wreckage in shock. Four days later, he slipped out of the hospital in his pajamas and hitched a ride back to his squadron.

Meanwhile, as planes and equipment became available, Patrick and Mitchell were reclaiming American airmen from the British and French and forming U.S. combat squadrons. The first of these, the 12th and the 94th, had begun operations in April 1918, but Springs and a number of other Americans with the RFC did not make the transition until July, when they were at last able to fight under their own flag as the 148th Aero Squadron of the U.S. Air Service.

The 148th was equipped with Sopwith Camels, fighter planes the British were replacing with the superior SE-5, as Gen. Trenchard reorganized the Royal Flying Corps and the aircraft of the Royal Navy into the independent Royal Air Force (RAF).

The Camel had its good qualities. "It could turn so fast it could bite its own tail," according to Charlie Meyers, an instructor at the U.S. Air Service training base, Issoudun, France; it had a fast rate-of-roll and was a good machine in a dogfight—if one had mastered the manipulation of its rotary engine.

The rotary radial engines, used by both sides in WWI, seem a bit incredible today. Their crankshafts were bolted solidly to the airframe, while the cylinders and propeller rotated together around the crankshaft. A rotary always ran at full throttle, and power was controlled by a button on the pilot's control stick which cut out the ignition. A great deal of blipping with the cut-out button was required on every flight, along with adjustments to a two-lever fuel/air mixture control. Castor oil was used for lubrication, and the average time-between-overhaul on the rotaries was about 20 flying hours.

On 22 August, 148th Squadron was ordered to destroy a troublesome German observation balloon, a highly dangerous assignment because the *drachens* were tethered by steel cable to winch trucks that were surrounded by antiaircraft machine guns and fearsome devices known as "flaming onions" that formed a curtain of fire around the balloons. Meanwhile, these hydrogen-filled "rubber elephants" could be hauled down very quickly—they were seldom raised above 1500 feet—and the observer, suspended in a wicker basket, often took to his parachute when attacked, fearing a hydrogen explosion. (Balloon observers were the only airmen on either side equipped with parachutes until shortly before the war's end when some German pilots received them.)

Springs was unwilling to order any of his men to make the attack, so he took the mission himself, and assigned to his flight the job of keeping enemy fighters off of him while he was vulnerable at low altitude.

Springs planned the attack carefully, and dove on the *drachen* from out of the sun. He banked steeply away as it flamed and, continuing at low altitude through the hail of lead from the balloon's defenders, sped for home.

A few days later, while flying alone, Springs dove into a formation of five Fokkers, downing two of them before his guns jammed and he was forced to dive from the fray and make a run for his home field. He was on the ground just long enough to refuel and have his guns cleared, and then took off to aid an RAF observation plane under attack by three Fokkers over Bapaume.

Attacking out of the sun, Springs shot down one of the enemy fighters over Bapaume and, in a running fight that carried well into Germany, eventually downed the other two.

We single out Springs for this report not because of an unusual combat record, but rather because his actions were *not* unusual. The traits and abilities he displayed were fairly representative of all the young Americans who participated in that war. There were many others like him, in the trenches, at sea, and in the air. They were products of their time—naive, bold, idealistic. They

were patriots, and they truly believed that they were fighting to "make the world safe for democracy."

The 148th Aero Squadron could count 66 enemy aircraft destroyed during its four months of combat. Rickenbacker's much-publicized 94th, in action three months longer, had a total of 69 air victories.

America's second-ranking ace of WWI was less typical. In fact, he was one of those rare people who defy understanding. He obviously believed in the same things that most of the rest of us claim as our standards, but he was so uncompromising in these beliefs—even when death was the only alternative to compromise—that we can only look at him with uncomprehending awe. Lt. Frank Luke, Jr scored 21 victories in a 17-day period—and nine of those days he did not fly. It is doubtful that any U.S. airman before or since has equalled that record. Luke's primary targets were as dangerous as any he could have chosen: German observation balloons. And if that is not enough to mark him as one-

The Curtiss Jenny was the standard primary training plane of the U.S. Air Service during WWI. Powered with the 90-hp OX-5 engine, it had a top speed of about 75 mph. Approximately 6750 were built by Curtiss and several war-born firms, and surplus Jennies were the barnstormers' airplanes of the 1920s. (Francis H. Dean collection)

The Liberty engine was tested in eight-cylinder configuration atop Pike's Peak. Almost all Liberties were built as V-12s. (Air Force Museum)

flight training at North Island, was sent overseas for advanced training at Issoudun, France. He then served as a ferry pilot for a time and was at last posted to combat duty with the 27th Aero Squadron late in July 1918. The 27th Aero Squadron was commanded by Maj. Harold Hartney and equipped with the French-built Spad ("Spad" from the company that produced them, *Societe Pour Aviation et Derives*).

Luke's first combat patrol came on 15 August, but no enemy aircraft were encountered. Several days later, after more "milk runs," Luke deserted his formation and dove down to destroy a German

of-a-kind, consider this: Luke is the only man in the annals of flight to be awarded the Congressional Medal of Honor for a deed done while under military arrest.

Lt. Frank Luke's story would make an absorbing book in itself, but not enough is really known about him to ensure that such a work would be accurate. Much of it would have to be speculation. We *do* know that he tended to be a loner, but on the other hand, former schoolmates characterized him as a pleasant fellow who made friends easily despite the fact that he wasn't much of a talker. A for-real John Wayne? Perhaps. As a native of Arizona, he spent much of his time as a teenager in the saddle. With a .30/30 carbine tucked in its scabbard close to his reins, he'd ride out of town trailing a pack animal and disappear for days. Some need within himself lured him into the heat-soaked desert and the silent mountains beyond. Perhaps it was a simple appreciation for raw nature—the desert is beautiful to those who truly know it—perhaps a subtler siren beckoned.

Luke learned of America's declaration of war one day in April 1917, when he rode into a small mining town after days in the trackless wasteland. He returned home and told his parents that he had to enlist because it was his duty. He was 20 years old.

Luke chose the Air Service, and after primary

Maj. Raoul Lufberry scored 17 victories as a member of the Lafayette Escadrille, He was killed soon after transferring to the U.S. Air Service. (USAF)

observation balloon. His airplane was so badly damaged in the encounter that it had to be junked. Hartney chewed him out for leaving the formation without permission, but when Billy Mitchell saw the report of the incident, he phoned Hartney and said that if Lt. Luke really wanted to "bust balloons," allow him to do so. Other pilots dreaded the assignment, and since the enemy "sausages" directed a lot of artillery fire against the U.S. positions, their destruction was always gratefully acknowledged by ground commanders.

Luke accepted the mission, although Maj. Hartney warned that only one man could be spared to accompany Luke as top cover. Lt. Joseph Fritz Wehner immediately volunteered for that duty. He and Luke had become close friends during their brief acquaintance, perhaps because Wehner, too, had been cast from a different mold. Wehner had twice been arrested and questioned by Army intelligence people, apparently because of his German background, because he had worked for the YMCA in German prison camps before the U.S. entered the war, and possibly because he spoke fluent German.

While a new Spad—fitted with special .45-caliber machine guns, one of which would be armed with incendiary ammunition—was being made ready for Luke, the squadron moved up to Rembercourt, about 12 miles behind the front lines,

to prepare for the great St. Mihiel offensive. Along with the move, the 27th Aero Squadron received a new commanding officer, Capt. Grant, as Hartney was promoted to Group Commander.

The St. Mihiel offensive began on 12 September, but Luke remained on the ground because his new machine wasn't ready. Then, on the 14th, he took Wehner with him and shot down two balloons. Wehner attacked a formation of eight Fokkers to keep them off of Luke, and the two of them made it safely back to base with no serious damage to their aircraft.

The next day, Luke got two more balloons. Wehner shot down two enemy fighters that were intent on attacking Luke, then peeled off and flamed a balloon that Frank had not seen. On the ground again, the two of them laughed uproariously over that one.

By this time, the enemy had come to know this pair of Spads very well. On the morning of the 16th, when they appeared over the lines, every German balloon in the sector was quickly hauled down.

Frank and Joe returned to Rembercourt and waited for sunset. They decided to take off just before dark, stay low, and catch the *drachens* by surprise just before they were hauled down for the night. "We'll get three of them," Luke casually informed the squadron adjutant. "The first at 7:10, the second at 7:20, and the third at 7:30." They did.

The Salmson observation plane was a superior French design operated by some U.S. units. The pilot had two forward-firing guns, and the observer two flex-mounted Lewis guns. (USAF)

A German Hanoveraner CL-II observation craft forced down intact 2 October 1918 by U.S. pilots Reed Chambers and Eddie Rickenbacker after observer was killed and pilot wounded. (Joe Durham)

However, they were a few minutes late flaming the last one because they took time out to strafe an enemy truck convoy.

They remained on the ground the next day while the many bullet holes in their airplanes were patched, then returned to action on the 18th. Near Labeuville, they found a pair of balloons and Luke attacked while Wehner circled above.

It was an enemy trap. The sky was full of Fokkers before Luke completed his first pass. The enemy fighters had apparently managed to track Wehner and Luke directly up-sun where they could not be seen. Stubbornly, Luke held his dive, and as the first balloon began to burn from a short burst from his guns, he levelled off very low and came upon the second balloon from underneath. It exploded behind him as he made a steep climbing turn in a bid for altitude. A glance behind revealed two enemy fighters dropping on his tail. Wehner was right behind them, guns aflame, but the remaining Fokkers were closing in behind Wehner.

Luke nosed down again to gain speed, reversed direction with an Immelmann turn, rolled inverted, and split-essed to bring his guns to bear on the closest of Wehner's attackers. A short burst directly into the enemy's cockpit sent that one

Crew of U.S. observation balloon prepare to launch. (Ft. Sill Field Artillery Museum)

U.S. sausage balloon explodes on ground, 1918. (Ft. Sill Field Artillery Museum)

up once again, he looked around to evaluate the situation. The remaining enemy fighters were breaking off the engagement. Wehner was nowhere in sight.

Low on fuel and countless bullet holes in his machine, Luke turned for home. On the way, he stumbled onto a German observation plane and shot it down with a short burst into the pilot's cockpit. It was his fifth victory within ten minutes, but he did not know then that he would drink no toast with Joe Wehner that evening. The Fokkers had shot down Wehner over Labeuville.

Luke's official report of that mission is very brief and closes with: "Confirmations requested, two balloons, three planes . . . Lt. Wehner is entitled to share in the victories . . ." (Wehner had eight confirmed victories when he died.)

That evening, Maj. Hartney (an ace in his own right, and aware of the close bond between Luke and Wehner) came down from headquarters and ordered Luke to take a week's leave in Paris. Luke

down. Rolling to his right, Luke got the next one as well before he was forced to level off only a few feet above the ground. It was frustrating trying to fight with so little space between him and the ground in which to maneuver. As his airspeed built

Capt. Eddie Rickenbacker (l) was America's leading ace in WWI with 26 victories. Capt. Douglas Campbell (center) scored six victories. Maj. Kenneth Marr at right. (USAF)

Lt. Frank Luke, Jr., and his Spad fighter. (USAF)

went, but was back at the end of three days, asking to be returned to duty. Hartney stalled for several days, believing that Luke needed rest, but by 26 September Luke was back in the air. Lt. Ivan Roberts volunteered to fly with him.

As they crossed the lines into enemy territory, they were joined by another Spad from a neighboring squadron. Then, in the vicinity of Consonvoye and Sivry, Luke spotted a large formation of Albatros fighters and led his three-plane element to the attack. Luke downed one of the enemy almost at once, but was forced to dive away from the fight when his guns jammed. Lt. Roberts did not return.

Luke seemed to brood over the loss of Roberts, apparently blaming himself. He took a motorcycle and left the field without permission, and when that drew a reprimand from Capt. Grant, Luke simply went to his plane and took off, also without permission.

He found a German balloon over Bantheville, but was unable to reach it before it was pulled down. He turned away as if disinterested, but then, a few minutes later, roared in on the deck and exploded the *drachen* in its nest.

He did not return to the 27th's field, but spent the night with the *Cigognes* ("Storks"), a famed French fighter squadron, flying back to his own base the next day. Capt. Grant immediately grounded him. Luke responded by taking off again, telling his mechanic that he would have his plane

serviced at a temporary forward aerodrome commanded by Capt. Vasconcelles. Grant's reaction to that was a phone call to Vasconcelles ordering Luke's arrest.

Vasconcelles apologetically relayed this order to Luke. But then, when Maj. Hartney landed there a few minutes later, Vasconcelles remained silent when Luke casually asked for—and received—Hartney's permission to attack three *drachens* hanging in the sky near Dun along the east bank of the Meuse River. Hartney was unaware of the arrest order.

Luke took off just at sunset. He stayed low and caught the first balloon crew by surprise, but left a flaming beacon in the air that quickly brought a flight of eight Fokkers that had apparently been waiting for the lone Spad and its sundown attacks.

Luke destroyed the second balloon before he was forced to turn on the Fokkers and attempt to deal with them. He shot down two of them (many believed that Luke was the best aerial marksman

Lt. Joseph F. Wehner flew top cover for Luke. (USAF)

53

Recently discovered rare photo is believed to be of Luke just as he flamed a German drachen. (Archiv Krueger)

on the Western Front), then broke away to get the third balloon which was hastily being hauled down near Milly. As the third *drachen,* exploded, Luke swung over the village of Murvaux and strafed a column of German infantry, then landed in a field beyond with a dead engine.

He jumped from his cripped plane, Colt .45 automatic in hand, and tried to escape toward the river, but enemy soldiers cut him off. From the gathering darkness, they called upon him to surrender. He replied with his Colt.

It was futile, of course, but Luke never wavered. He fell from chest wounds, with an empty pistol in his hand.

On the Allied side of the lines, Luke was listed as "missing in action" until two months after war's end. Observers at the front had seen the three balloons go down, but that was all that was known about Luke's last flight until U.S. Graves Registration Officers reached the village of Murvaux in January 1919. Their first report read:

From: Graves Registration Officer,
           Neufchateau Area No. 1.
To: Chief of Air Service, APO 717.
Subject: Grave, unknown American
           aviator.

1. Units of this service have located the grave of an unknown aviator killed on Sunday, 29 September 1918 in the village of Murvaux.

2. From inspection of the grave and interviews held with inhabitants of this town, the following information was learned in regard to this aviator and his heroism. He is reported as having light hair, young, of medium height, and of heavy stature.

3. Reported by the inhabitants that previous to being killed this man had brought down three German balloons, two German airplanes, and dropped hand bombs killing German soldiers and wounding others.

4. He was wounded himself in the shoulder and evidently had to make a forced landing. Upon landing he opened fire with his automatic pistol and fought until he was killed.

5. It is also reported that the Germans took his shoes, leggings, and money, leaving his grave unmarked.

Chester E. Staten,
Captain of Infantry,
G.R.S. Officer

Upon receipt of this report, Gen. Mitchell ordered further investigation that turned up Luke's wrist watch, which was under the sleeve of his flying suit and which the Germans had missed. An affidavit signed by the mayor and 14 inhabitants of Murvaux provided the eyewitness account upon which the Graves Registration officer's report was based. Later, this affidavit was verified by Lt. B. Mangels of Munster, Germany, who commanded German balloons numbers 35 and 64 of the 5th German Army, the last two destroyed by Luke that fateful Sunday. (*Note:* Your author is aware of previously published accounts of Luke's last flight which do not agree with this presentation. However, it appears that those versions were written without benefit of the official records, particularly, the report of Capt. Staten, and the much more detailed affidavit sworn to by the villagers of Murvaux. One such story mentions the affidavit, but then misquotes it. There is no need to tamper with the facts.

The villagers' impression that Luke dropped "hand bombs" on the enemy infantry is the kind of natural mistake one expects when the witnesses are unfamiliar with airplanes. Luke's twin .45-caliber machine guns could create a lot of havoc in the narrow, dusty street of Murvaux. The villagers also believed that Luke landed in order to get a drink of water from the river, but in all other details their account agrees with that of Lt. Mangels, the German balloon commander.)

Luke's body was removed to the American cemetery at Romagne and buried with full military honors. He was posthumously awarded the Distinguished Service cross, France's Croix-de-Guere, and the United States' highest military award, the Congressional Medal of Honor.

REVIEW QUESTIONS:

1. When was the First Aero Squadron established? Describe its makeup—aircraft and personnel. What was their first duty assignment? Why did the U.S. fall so far behind the Europeans in aircraft development?

2. What was the role of aircraft at the beginning of the war? How did this change? Identify some of the fighter aircraft used by both sides during the war.

3. Why did the U.S. aircraft manufacturers choose to build training aircraft and the British de Havilland DH-4 instead of our own fighter aircraft? What were some of the problems encountered? How did President Wilson correct the production problem?

4. How was Billy Mitchell's philosophy of air power influenced by General Hugh Trenchard? Give an example of how Mitchell implemented some of his ideas during the latter part of the war.

5. What was the role of the U.S. Naval Air Service during the war? Why did the Navy's commander in chief, Admiral Mayo, refuse to commend the war effort of Naval aviation?

6. Who were some of the leading aces on both sides of the conflict? Describe several of the combat episodes involving such American aces as Elliot White Springs and Frank Luke.

7. Why do you think that the news media romanticized the role of the fliers, dubbing them "Knights of the Air" and reporting, in great detail, their adventures in aerial combat?

Chapter 3

The Wings Grow Stronger

OBJECTIVES: At the end of this chapter you should be able to:

☐ Understand the prevailing attitude of the U.S. military in the immediate post-World War I period.

☐ Recognize the burdens placed on Germany as a result of the Treaty of Versailles which led to political and economic instability.

☐ Describe the first successful flights across the Atlantic by Lt. Commander Read, Alcock and Brown, and Major G.H. Scott.

☐ Explain why General Mitchell had his army pilots attempt a number of headline flights.

☐ Describe the first flight around the world by the U.S. Army Air Service.

U.S. military aircraft were improved during the two decades between WWI and WWII, but little credit for those advances can be given to America's leaders, either civilian or military. Military planning, at the highest levels, reverted to pre-WWI concepts. The Atlantic and Pacific Oceans were viewed as America's great natural barriers to foreign aggression, and the U.S. Navy was regarded as the primary defender of American shores—indeed, the entire Western Hemisphere. The Monroe Doctrine, which served notice to the world that the United States would tolerate no "outside" intervention into the affairs of any North, Central, or South American nation, was an unambiguous cornerstone of U.S. foreign policy.

Since every American knew that the United States was not going to start a war anywhere, there

was really no need to maintain a large, well-equipped Army. American arms were for defense only. Such a posture seemed perfectly reasonable at the time. (If man were half as civilized as he should be, it would be reasonable today.) Unfortunately, the bitter seeds that would blossom into WWII were planted at the conclusion of WWI, and America's determination to avoid future involvement in Europe's squabbles would fade when it appeared that the Nazis could well become the rulers of all Europe, including Great Britain.

It was the terms of the peace treaty signed with Germany at the close of WWI—in a railway coach at Versailles, France, 28 June 1919—that led to the Nazi takeover of Germany. Had it not been the Nazis, a similar movement almost certainly would have evolved, because the Treaty of Versailles

Military budgets of the early '20s forced the Air Service to fly the WWI DH-4s. A DH-4 training flight at Fort Sill ended against a barbed wire fence. (Mike Sweatt collection)

doomed Germany to economic servitude and the status of a second-class nation.

Germany was stripped of all her overseas territories, along with 25,000 square miles of Germany itself, and the Allies demanded that Germany pay billions in "reparations." There was no way that a bankrupt Germany could pay, in either money or goods, but the French, especially, were adamant and repeatedly sent troops into a prostrate Germany in attempts to force the Germans to pay. Many other sanctions were imposed, including the provision that Germany be allowed no military aircraft of any kind. In short, the Treaty of Versailles—which the United States refused to sign—made it impossible for Germany to regain political and economic stability. By 1923, German money was worthless and there were food riots in the streets of Berlin.

Nevertheless, the Allies did not relent, and in 1930 the final amount that Germany must pay in damages was set at 121 billion Reichmarks. Two

years later, German unemployment passed the six million mark, and the following January Adolf Hitler was elected chancellor of Germany, brought to power by eleven years of political and economic turmoil. True, the Nazis received only 33 percent of the vote in the election and Hitler, was, in effect, a compromise candidate. But all Germany, after years of deprivation and humiliation, was ready to follow a leader who could quicken its national pulse with visions of a new pride, prosperity, and Germany's return to its rightful place in the world.

During this period the American people, their representatives in Congress, and their Presidents believed that the United States could avoid future wars with other major powers, especially if no entangling commitments were made overseas. The U.S. Army shrunk to 137,000 officers and men during the '20s as military appropriations dwindled. The Air Service stood at the end of the line for its share. The Air Service/Air Corps' average yearly expenditure from authorized appropriations was 25 million dollars for the years 1921 through 1938 inclusive, while average personnel strength for those years was less than 14,000 officers and men.

For the first ten years after WWI Gen. Pershing dominated War Department policy. Although he had, during the closing weeks of the late war, been given a glimpse of the airplane's potential as a military weapon, he did not project that lesson into planning for the future defense of the nation. He removed Gen. Patrick from his post as Chief of Air Service and replaced him with Gen. Charles Menoher, an infantry commander with no background in aviation. General Billy Mitchell was appointed Menoher's deputy, and that epitomized the War Department's attitude toward the Air Service: Mitchell was able. Menoher was Army. That priority of command would continue until the eve of WWII.

The Navy, meanwhile, actually had several top officers who recognized the airplane's potential value to the fleet, among them Admirals Fiske, Fullam and Sims. Primarily due to their influence, the Navy kept its aviation program alive after the war ended and, in 1919, decided to test the efficacy of large flying boats as long-range patrol craft by attempting to fly the Atlantic. That decision may have been given a little boost by the fact that Glenn Curtiss had built a flying boat early in 1914 expressly for that purpose, although war came before the flight could be attempted. Then, the Navy contracted with Curtiss to build four large flying boats that could be flown to Europe for submarine patrol. However, only the first of those, the NC-1, was completed by war's end.

First Atlantic Flight

Rear Adm. Douglas Taylor, apparently abetted by Cmdr. John Tower (one of the Navy's first pilots) seems to have been the one who initially pushed for the Atlantic flight and who obtained permission from the Secretary of the Navy Josephus Daniels to complete the NC-2 through NC-4 sister craft for that ambitious project. The NC-2 was cannibalized to provide components for aircraft Numbers One and Four which were damaged in a hangar fire. Then, on 8 May 1919, planes NC-1, NC-3 and NC-4 left Rockaway Beach, Long Island bound for Plymouth, England, by way of Newfoundland, the Azores, Portugal, and France.

The NCs (for "Navy-Curtiss;" inevitably called the "Nancies") were large for their time. Wingspan was 126 ft, hull length was 45 ft, and each was powered with four 400-hp Liberty engines mounted in nacelles between the wings, a tractor and a pusher mounted back-to-back in the center nacelle with a tractor on each side. All-up weight was 28,000 lbs and cruising speed was 77 mph.

Delayed by engine trouble and weather, the

The Orenco D fighter was a 1918 U.S. design which had a speed of 139 mph fitted with a 300-hp Hispano engine. Curtiss built 50 for the Air Service in 1920. (USAF)

The Douglas C-1 was the standard Army transport of the '20s. It was Liberty-powered. (USAF)

three planes at last left Newfoundland on 16 May headed for the Azores, 1200 miles away.

Approximately half of the flight was made in darkness and much of the rest through recurring patches of fog. The NC-1 landed on the ocean in dense fog about 300 miles short of its destination, and the NC-3 did the same 100 miles away. The crew of the NC-1 was picked up by a passing ship, although their airplane sank in heavy seas. Cmdr. Towers taxied the damaged NC-3 on the surface, arriving in the harbor at Horta, in the Azores, 60 hours later, his airplane a wave-battered wreck.

Meanwhile, Lt/Cmdr. Albert C. Read and his five-man crew aboard the NC-4 had flown nonstop from Newfoundland to Horta in 15 hours and 18 minutes. They left Horta on the 20th, after a two-day rest, and flew on to Lisbon by way of Ponta Delgada, and ended their epic flight at Plymouth, England on 31 May. The U.S. Navy was first to fly the Atlantic—but just barely.

Two weeks later, on 14 June 1919, RAF Captain John Alcock and Lt. Arthur Whitten-Brown took off from Newfoundland in a British bomber, the twin-engined Vickers Vimy and, after 16 hours and 28 minutes (1890 miles) at an average speed of 118.5 mph, landed at Clifden, Ireland to claim

a cash price of $50,000 offered by a British newspaper publisher for the first transatlantic nonstop flight. Then, two weeks after *that*, on 2 July 1919, the British rigid airship R.34 left Scotland bound for New York.

The R.34, commanded by RAF Maj. G.H. Scott and carrying a crew of 30, landed in New York on 6 July after covering a distance of 3600 miles in 108 hours. On 9 July, Scott turned his airship around and flew back to the British Isles, thus completing the first aerial round trip across the Atlantic.

Eight years later, Charles A. Lindbergh would fly alone nonstop from New York to Paris in a single-engine monoplane, and that would be the aerial crossing of the Atlantic that would capture the fancy of the world and convince people everywhere that the airplane had become a reliable and useful machine to serve mankind.

In the meantime, several other Atlantic flights were attempted. Most ended in disaster, although the German rigid airship, Zeppelin ZR-3, was flown to America in mid-October 1924, by a German aircrew commanded by Dr. Hugo Eckener, and presented to the U.S. Navy as part payment on war damages claimed by the United States. (The U.S.

did ask for some reparations, although the amount was comparatively small and no serious effort to collect was made. The U.S. and Germany signed a separate peace treaty in 1921.)

The NC-4's successful Atlantic crossing had a predictable effect on Gen. Billy Mitchell. In the fall of 1919, he sent 60 of the Army's DH-4s across the United States in a "reliability" test. Thirty flew westward from New York as 30 others left San Francisco. Several were lost, and nothing much was proved, although it could be said that the Air Service had blazed a trail which the air mail (begun on a limited basis by Air Service planes in 1918) would later follow.

The following June (1920), four DHs, commanded by Capt. St. Clair Street, flew from New York to Nome, Alaska. They returned in October, having covered 4345 miles (much of it over unchartered wilderness) in 112 flying hours.

Army and Navy Racers

Since Air Service budgets—about five percent of the Army's total budgets—did not allow the acquisition of new airplanes in significant number, Mitchell convinced his boss, Gen. Patrick (who re-placed Menoher in 1921), that what money they had should be spent on headline-grabbing flights that would impress the public in general and the Congress in particular, especially as such activities could be justified as useful research and development. Accordingly, the Air Service (quickly followed by the Navy, of course), fostered the design and construction of a series of racing planes to compete in several popular international air races during the early twenties. The Army and Navy Curtiss racers dominated these events; although the publicity returned no discernible benefits, and the U.S. Congress remained as stingy with appropriations as ever, the races did prove the new Curtiss D-12 engine of 435 hp—a vast improvement over the wartime Liberty—and the D-12 would power Army fighter planes throughout the '20s and lead to the development of far more powerful engines of the same type.

The Curtiss D-12, a V-12 water-cooled engine, was developed by Finlay Porter from a design initiated by a long-time Curtiss engineman Charles Kirkham. It featured cast cylinder blocks (which, up to that time, had not been successful in aircraft engines of that power). The British were so im-

The four Curtiss-built NC flying boats were designed at the Naval Aircraft Factory. Powered with four Liberties (one pusher and three tractors), three of these craft attempted the first Atlantic flight in 1919. (USN)

The Navy's NC-4, commanded by Lt/Cmdr. A.C. Read, proudly taxies into the harbor at Lisbon, Portugal, 27 May 1919, after completing the first transatlantic flight from Trepassey, Newfoundland. (USN)

pressed with the D-12 that the Air Ministry purchased one and gave it to Rolls Royce, along with an appropriate government subsidy, to copy or improve. The result was the 1295 cubic-inch Kestrel of 480 hp which went into production in May, 1928. By 1937 the Kestrel XVI was rated at 750 hp as installed in the RAF's Hawker Fury fighters, and it was this engine, with its displacement raised to 1650, that became the famed Merlin of WWII.

Ironically, Curtiss, after developing the D-12 into the 600-hp Conqueror (which powered the last of America's biplane fighters) decided, in 1931, to discontinue development of liquid-cooled aircraft engines, and in America that role went by default to the (then) tiny Allison Division of General Motors. Allison was given a Navy contract at that time to build five such engines for possible use on its big rigid dirigibles. That engine, the Allison V-1710, was never installed in a dirigible (by the time it was ready for delivery, the Navy's *Akron* and *Macon* had both crashed), but it was concurrently developed during the mid-30s with the British Merlin to become a principal WWII fighter airplane powerplant. But all this takes us ahead of our story.

First World Flight

Since the Navy gained as much from the well-publicized air races of the early '20s as did the Army, Billy Mitchell came up with another idea. Although his bombers had, at least to his own satisfaction, demonstrated in 1921, and again in 1923, that the most impregnable battleship was vulnerable to air attack (about which, more later), the Air Service needed to demonstrate its potential versatility in an even more dramatic fashion. Mitchell took his idea to Gen. Patrick and Patrick officially announced it late in 1923: The U.S. Army Air Service would fly around the world!

That was indeed a bold undertaking, viewed against the background of air progress up to that time. There would be a few landing fields, no navigational aids, no radio, and no weather reports. The art of instrument flying was still far in the future, and the fliers themselves would have to perform all maintenance on their machines—a truly herculean task since it would include half a dozen complete engine changes in each of the four planes. They dared not trust the Liberty engine beyond 50 hours of flight, and it was the only engine of sufficient power available. (The new Curtiss D-12 was still in test and had been operated only for short periods in the military racers.)

A small California airframe builder, Donald Douglas, was awarded a contract to build five

The Navy's Curtiss CR-2 racer, fitted with a Curtiss D-12 engine, attained an average speed of 193.2 mph around a closed course in the 1922 Pulitzer race. (USN)

World Cruisers, four of which would attempt the journey with the fifth held in reserve. Douglas was 28 years old in 1920 when he opened for business in the rear of a barber shop with $600 in capital. But he had a degree from M.I.T.—earned in two years—and a year's experience working for Glenn Martin, during which time he designed the prototype of the Martin bombers in Army service during the '20s. Douglas had sold some torpedo planes to the Navy and, when he began design and construction of the World Cruisers, had a payroll of 112 and occupied an abandoned movie studio just off Wilshire Boulevard in eastern Santa Monica.

The World Cruisers, which were identical, had a wingspan of 50 ft, maximum weight of 8200 lbs, service ceiling of 8000 ft, and a normal cruise near 90 mph. These were hefty, two-place, open-cockpit biplanes with fittings for either floats or wheels because both would be needed in different parts of the world. Their crews were selected by Gen. Patrick from among hundreds of volunteers.

The crews and their planes were: Maj. F.L. Martin and Sgt. Alva Harvey in World Cruiser #1,

the *Seattle*; Lts. Lowell Smith and Leslie Arnold in #2, the *Chicago*; Lt. Leigh Wade and Sgt. Henry Ogden in #3, the *Boston*, and Lts. Erik Nelson and John Harding in #4, the *New Orleans*.

Equipped with floats, the four planes left Seattle shortly after sunrise on 6 April 1924 and followed the Inside Passage to Alaska through spring blizzards—one of which claimed the *Seattle* when Maj. Martin, blinded by snow, literally flew into the ground. Neither he nor Harvey were seriously injured; they walked out to civilization on their own, while the remaining three cruisers continued across the North Pacific with Lt. Lowell Smith in command.

The adventures of the three remaining crews would (and did) fill a book in itself. Weather forced them down in Russian waters off the Komandorski Islands, but as the ceiling lifted Smith led the flight into Paramushiru, navigating (as he did the entire trip) by dead reckoning. The Air Service had accomplished the first aerial crossing of the Pacific.

The cruisers flew southward over Japan's 4000 home islands to Tokyo where, for the second time,

The Army Curtiss R3C-1 was first in the 1925 Pulitzer race with an average speed of 249 mph; engine was the new Curtiss Conqueror of 600-hp, a glycol-cooled V-12. (USAF)

the crews installed new engines, and then fought heavy rains down the South China Coast to Saigon in what was then French Indochina. The *Chicago's* engine blew up over the Gulf of Tonkin, but Smith hired a native to tow the plane with a fleet of sampans to a village dock where a new Liberty deliv-

The Curtiss D-12 (V-1150) engine of 400 to 460 hp.

The *New Orleans,* flown by Lts. Erik Nelson and Jack Harding, was one of the two Douglas World Cruisers to complete the first around-the-world flight, 6 April to 28 September 1924. (Douglas Aircraft Company)

ered by a Navy destroyer, was quickly installed. The *Chicago* joined the other two planes in Saigon from where the flight turned northwestward for Bangkok, Rangoon, and Calcutta.

Switching from floats to wheels, the three cruisers left Calcutta on the first of July and made good time across India despite a newspaperman stowaway in the *Boston*'s tool compartment, sandstorms, and the oppressive heat until, a few miles short of Karachi, the *New Orleans'* engine began to disintegrate. With oil bathing the entire nose of the airplane, Lt. Nelson managed to reach Karachi.

Another engine change for the three aircraft required two days, then the fliers were off for Bagdad on 7 July. Later, they were beset by sandstorms over the Arabian Desert and threaded their way through passes in the Taurus Mountains. (The Cruiser's 8000-ft service ceiling did not permit them to climb over the mountains.) They reached Constantinople on 11 July, and five days later were in London.

By then, the six airmen were international heros. This caused a problem because crowds awaited their arrival at every stop and officials in each city along their route planned ceremonies and dinners in their honor. The fliers understood that they were representing the United States and therefore had to smile through a lot of speeches and try to remain awake through a lot of formal dinners they would have much preferred to have skipped. It all took time, and they badly needed that time to rest and to work on their airplanes.

In England, the planes received new engines and had wheels replaced by floats once again, while the U.S. Navy positioned ships in the North Atlantic along the Cruisers' course and rushed fuel to planned stops in Iceland and Greenland. No airplane had ever been to either place.

The North Atlantic, however, would exact its price. The *Boston* was forced down at sea with a dead engine. Although the Navy ship *Billingsby* rescued Wade and Ogden, their airplane sank in heavy seas.

The *Chicago* and *New Orleans* continued the flight and, after a Navy-assisted engine change in each plane on the Greenland Coast, and a link-up with Wade and Ogden in Nova Scotia on 3 September (where Gen. Patrick had sent the reserve Cruiser, christened *Boston II*), the world fliers reached Boston on 6 September, and were back at their starting point at Seattle on 28 September 1924, having been mobbed and laden with gifts at every stop across the United States.

The total distance flown was 6,345 miles, and the *Chicago* and *New Orleans* had been in the air 363 hours and seven minutes at an average speed of 72.5 mph. The fact that the journey required 177 days elapsed time primarily reflected the inadequacies of the Cruisers' engines. Each plane used nine engines averaging slightly over 40 hours on each, yet the fliers still suffered four engine failures. When it is realized that the fliers themselves performed seven of those changes, usually under primitive conditions (the Liberty engine weighed more than 700 lbs) and attended to all other servicing of their aircraft, their feat appears all the more remarkable.

There wasn't much Navy fliers could do to top the Army's world flight, which undeniably added to the United States' prestige abroad, and except for Gen. Patrick and the crews of the World Cruisers, all of whom sent warm notes of thanks

Uncovered forward fuselage reveals fuel tanks beneath seats of the Liberty-powered World Cruisers. (McDonnell Douglas Astronautics Co.)

The *Boston* goes down in the North Atlantic after rescue of her crew, Lts. Leigh Wade and Henry Ogden. (USAF)

L to R: Lt. Lowell H. Smith, Secretary of War John Weeks, M./Gen. Mason Patrick, B./Gen. William Mitchell, Lts. Erik Nelson and Leigh Wade. (USAF)

to the Navy, few others stopped to consider that the flight would not have been completed without the Navy's help, particularly over the North Atlantic.

Meanwhile, Gen. Billy Mitchell, looking to the future, had just completed an extensive tour of the Far East. On 24 October 1924, he submitted a 325-page secret report to the War Department in which he warned of a coming war with Japan:

" . . . the Japanese have specialized on their air force since 1918 . . . it now appears that the Japanese are probably the second air power in the world with between 600 and 800 airplanes . . . Japan estimates that, if war comes, America will begin the war with the methods and systems of the last war . . . She knows that war is coming someday with the United States . . . Air operations for the destruction of Pearl Harbor will be undertaken . . . the attack to be made on Ford's Island at 7:30 a.m. . . . nothing can stop it except air power . . . the Philippines will be attacked in a similar manner . . . The initial success, as things stand now, will probably be with the Japanese."

Mitchell's sadly prophetic 1924 secret report was ignored by the War Department (nowadays called the "Department of Defense"), and Mitchell became ever more public in his crusade for a strong and independent Air Force.

REVIEW QUESTIONS:

1. What was the prevailing attitude of the U.S. military in the immediate post-World War I period? Why was so little thought given to the potential of air power? Why can it be said that "the terms of the peace treaty signed with Germany . . . led to the Nazi takeover of Germany"?

2. Who was the first pilot to successfully fly across the Atlantic in a specially built Curtiss seaplane? Who were the first airmen to fly non-stop from Newfoundland to Ireland? What was the significance of the flight of the R-34?

3. What was the reason for General Mitchell to stage so many spectacular and record breaking flights during the early 1920s? What was the reaction of Congress and the public?

4. Describe the first flight around the world by pilots of the U.S. Army Air Service. Who built the aircraft for this flight? How did the War Department respond to General Mitchell's secret report regarding Japanese military air power?

Chapter 4

Naval Air and Billy Mitchell

OBJECTIVES: At the end of this chapter you should be able to:

☐ Identify some of the early proponents of Naval air power.

☐ Discuss the significance of the sinking of the German battleship *Ostfriesland* by Mitchell's bombers.

☐ Summarize the development of the Wright Whirlwind and Pratt and Whitney Wasp engines.

☐ Identify several Navy dirigibles and briefly describe their primary function.

☐ Describe the events leading up to the court-martial of Billy Mitchell.

☐ Highlight the purpose and findings of the Morrow Board.

Rear Admiral William Adger Moffett demonstrated that a man may prevail against the errors of his friends if only his enemies will help a little. Adm. Moffett greatly advanced U.S. Naval aviation during the '20s. He did so despite anti-airplane prejudices held by the old sea dogs who were his superiors, because he was aided—unintentionally, of course—by a man he detested. That man was the Army's Brigadier General William Mitchell, who consistently made the issue of U.S. Airpower front-page news and thereby kept the blood pressures of the "battleship admirals" at dangerously high levels.

William Moffett had risen to the rank of captain in the battleship Navy when in March 1921 he was appointed "Director of Naval Aviation," an office tucked into the Navy's Planning Division, and which was not expected to do much directing. The office was useful primarily as the authority responsible for whatever went *wrong* in Naval air operations, while direct control of the air units was spread among the several commands to which the units were attached.

This piecemeal administration meant that no single voice possessing real authority could speak for Naval air, and that's just the way most of the ranking officers wanted it. The Chief of Naval Operations, Admiral William S. Benson, had spoken for the saltiest of them when he declared, "The Navy doesn't need airplanes. Aviation is just a lot of noise."

There were, however, a few top Naval officers who had a different view and the courage to say so. These included Admirals Bradley Fiske, William S. Sims, and W.F. Fullam. None was radical in his thinking, and none suggested that airplanes could supplant warships in the nation's defense. They were simply agreed that the Navy needed airplanes, and recommended to the Secretary of the Navy in 1919 a development program that would establish a Naval air service "capable of accompanying and operating with the fleet in all waters of the globe."

This recommendation—actually, the last of a series forwarded by the Navy's General Board—was endorsed in its essentials by Navy Secretary Josephus Daniels. Daniels added an earlier request for funds to build a rigid dirigible, along with Admiral Sims' strong plea for an aircraft carrier, and then sought Congressional approval. That followed on 11 July 1919, with passage of the Naval Appropriations Act for fiscal 1920.

Congressional approval, while necessary, was not a guarantee. Money for Naval air was buried within the total Navy appropriation, and Naval Aviation would stand at the end of the line for its share when the Navy's Budget Bureau divvied-up the cash. Thus, the aircraft carrier that Adm. Sims had hoped for turned out to be a coal barge (the collier *Jupiter*, which was to be converted by addition of a flight deck), and the request for 108 fighter aircraft to equip America's first aircraft carrier was first cut to 75, and finally to ten.

Even that was too much to suit, Adm. Benson. In the fall of 1920, he countermanded the order to convert the *Jupiter*. But Capt. Thomas T. Craven, who was then Director of Naval Aviation, managed to get a direct order from Secretary Daniels and work on the *Jupiter* was resumed.* That cost Craven his job. Shortly after the crews returned to work on the *Jupiter*, he was replaced by Capt. Moffett.

Moffett took over Craven's desk at a propitious time. Throughout the previous year, newspapers around the country had given a lot of space to Gen.

---

*The office of Chief of Naval Operations was established 2 March 1915, and the scope of CNO's authority was challenged for years thereafter by the Navy bureau chiefs. Not until President Truman issued Executive Order 9635 on 29 September 1945 were CNO's authority and duties clearly defined.

M./Gen. Patrick (L), and Billy Mitchell. Patrick, as Chief of Air Service, was Mitchell's boss and quiet supporter from 1921 until Mitchell was forced to leave the service four years later. (USAF).

Billy Mitchell's crusade for an independent air force, and his claim, made before several Senate committees, that the airplane had rendered the Navy's surface ships obsolete. Since 1920 was an election year, the issues Mitchell raised probably received more national attention than would have otherwise been the case. His seemingly far-out pronouncements on political/military matters were custom-made to fit charges of waste, outdated policies, and maladministration at high government levels.

Then, a few days before President Harding took office in March 1921, the War Department announced that several German warships, taken as prizes under terms of the Treaty of Versailles, would be destroyed in Naval ordnance tests. Gen. Mitchell reacted predictably, and the nation's press enthusiastically took up his challenge to the Navy that the Air Service be allowed to prove that airplanes could sink battleships.

This at last prodded the Navy into covering its

Martin GMB (above) and Martin MB-2 were the bombers sent by Mitchell to prove that airplanes could sink battleships in 1921. Left to right: Donald Douglas, Eric Springer, and Lawrance Bell. (USAF)

own aviation bets. Clearly, if Mitchell's preachments should gain significant support in Congress, then it was at least possible that an independent air force, of (God forbid!) co-equal status, could emerge, and the effect of *that* on Naval appropriations was too frightening to consider. Therefore, prudence dictated that the Navy quickly establish a substantial legal equity in its own air service.

Congress obliged on 1 July 1921 with an act that created a Naval Bureau of Aeronautics (BuAer), "possessing such responsibilities and authority pertaining to Naval Air as the Secretary shall prescribe." When this office began to function on the first of September, Moffett, as its director, was elevated to the rank of rear admiral.

Meanwhile, on 21 July, an 11-plane formation of Mitchell's bombers had indeed sent the German battleship *Ostfriesland* to the bottom with two di-

rect hits and four near-misses employing 2000-pound bombs. At the time, that seemed to prove everything or nothing, depending upon one's prejudices. Ultimate proof would wait upon another day—a Sunday morning in Hawaii, to be described as a day that would "live in infamy."

It should be noted that Congresses of this period reflected little polarization of opinion over "Mitchellism." It occasioned no great debates on Capitol Hill, probably because most lawmakers saw no urgent need for major changes in the defense alignment in the absence of a definite threat: in any case, military spending was certain to remain at a minimal level for the foreseeable future. The nation was recovering from the effects of WWI, and Harding had won the Presidency with the slogan, "Back to Normalcy."

But whatever one's views on Mitchellism, it

Developed at Navy insistence, the Wright J-5 Whirlwind was America's first truly reliable and efficient air-cooled radial aircraft engine.

must be credited with aiding (however unintentionally) at a critical time the cause of that small band of visionaries within the Navy that recognized the developing need for a strong Naval air arm. With establishment of the Bureau of Aeronautics, headed by an officer of flag rank, Naval Aviation had its *Magna Carta*—albeit a poorly funded one—and a secure anchorage to attract gifted, airminded personnel.

Navy Aircraft Engine Development

Among such personnel was Lt. Cmdr. Bruce G. Leighton, Naval Aviator No. 40, a pleasant, outgoing type chosen by Moffett to head up the bureau's Aircraft Engine Section. Leighton and his engine program typified the kind of officer and the kind of action that gave BuAer its special character under Moffett. The soft-spoken Moffett believed in encouraging initiative. He told his subordinates what he wanted, but seldom how to accomplish it. That sometimes resulted in methods he himself may not have chosen, but which he always stood ready to support. He knew that loyalty begets loyalty, and future commanders must learn

to command. It was an approach that paid great returns in Leighton's case—not only for the Navy, but for the Army and civil aviation as well, because Lt./Cmdr. Leighton jawboned private industry into the development of the most successful aircraft piston engines ever built, the Wright Whirlwinds and the Pratt & Whitney Wasps.

Leighton was pointed in the right direction at the outset, because the officer previously responsible for the Navy's aircraft engines, Lt./Cmdr. S.M. Kraus in the Bureau of Steam Engineering, had determined that the air-cooled static radial engine ("static" as opposed to the rotary-type radial engines of WWI), if it could be made reliable, was best suited to the Navy's needs. It promised more horsepower for less weight, and would be easier and cheaper to maintain than the water-cooled engines then available. Therefore, Kraus had obtained some Navy money to foster development of the Lawrance Model J, a radial design of 200 hp with which Kraus hoped to power the small fighters that would be needed if and when Adm. Sims got his aircraft carrier.

The Lawrance J was the product of tiny

Lawrance Aero Engines Company, operated by Charles Lanier Lawrance, who had switched from automobile to airplane engine design after working for Allesandro Anzani in Paris prior to WWI. Returning to the U.S. in 1914, Lawrance set up shop in a New York City loft where he produced, during the next four years, some two and three-cylinder air-cooled engines. In 1919, he designed an experimental nine-cylinder static radial engine for the U.S. Army Air Service. Early in 1920, after Adm. Sims (who had commanded U.S. Naval Forces in the Atlantic during WWI) gave his support to the air advocates within the Navy and called for construction of U.S. aircraft carriers, Lawrance designed and built the Model J engine with Navy funds supplied by Lt./Cmdr. Kraus.

This prototype engine was running in test when Lt./Cmdr. Leighton was introduced to the program in March 1921. (This was actually four months before creation of BuAer, but Moffett had begun collecting his key people in anticipation of his new job.) Leighton studied the Model J and concluded that Kraus had bet on the right horse (power). Then, at the end of June 1921, Moffett backed Leighton's decision and approved purchase of 50 Lawrance J-1s, a deal apparently made possible because the Navy had some unspent monies in the fiscal 1921 budget that were about to be returned to the Treasury.

The first production J-1 passed a 50-hour test, producing its rated 200 hp, in February 1922, a month before metamorphosis of the *Jupiter* into the *USS Langley* was completed. In the meantime, Cmdr. Jerome C. Hunsaker, Moffett's chief of aircraft design at the Naval Aircraft Factory in Philadelphia, was constructing the first TS-1 fighters (43 were eventually built, 11 by Curtiss) to equip the *Langley*, so Lawrance was given a contract for an additional 200 J-1s—along with a lecture from Leighton on the need for increasing the engine's reliability factor.

By this time, however, it had become clear to Leighton that Lawrance was either unwilling or unable to find enough expansion capital to properly develop and efficiently produce engines in such quantities. In time of national emergency such a supplier would be of small value. Therefore, Leighton, knowing that both Curtiss and Packard were adamant in their stand against development of air-cooled aircraft engines, decided to pressure Wright Aeronautical Corporation into taking over the Lawrance design.

Wright Aeronautical's boss was Frederick Brant Rentschler, a sharp young man of sound family and an Ivy League education. Rentschler had served as an airplane engine inspector for the Air Service during the war and, in 1919, had formed Wright Aeronautical Corporation from the liquidated remains of the Wright-Martin Corp. Rentschler's principal products were Hispano-Suiza aircraft engines, excellent (for that time) water-cooled V-8s built under a license agreement with a French manufacturer. Both the Army Air Service and the Navy bought Wright "Hissos" in some numbers (Navy planes fitted with Hissos included the Curtiss N-9 trainer, Thomas Morse MB-3 fighter, and Vought VE-7 all-purpose aircraft); but by 1923 the Army, although stuck with thousands of war-surplus Liberties that it would have to use in its bombers and observation planes, was looking to the new Curtiss D-12 of 400 hp for its new fighters. Since there was no civil market for new airplane engines worth mentioning, that gave Leighton some muscle at Wright Aeronautical.

Leighton was just the man to use it. He told Rentschler that the Navy would buy no more Hissos or Hisso parts. Then he suggested that Wright buy out Lawrance and develop the engine the Navy wanted.

Rentschler had little trouble recognizing Dame Opportunity, especially when she stood by with a club in her hand. With his board of directors concurring, he acquired Lawrance Aero Engines for half a million dollars (and a Wright vice-presidency for Charles Lawrance). Then, Rentschler directed that his ablest engineers, George J. Mead and Andrew V.D. Willgoos, take over the J-1 engine project and crank in a large dose of reliability.

Mead and Willgoos had already learned a lot about air-cooled engine reliability—or rather, the lack of it—with their markedly-deficient Wright R-1 of 1920, a nine-cylinder radial built for the Air Ser-

The ZR-1 *Shenandoah* was completed in September 1923; it was lost two years later in a storm over Ohio. (Joe R. Reed collection)

vice. But engine men, a stubborn and secretive lot who hear things in engine exhausts that are denied to the rest of us, have always worked empirically, aided only by the metallurgist, the petroleum chemist, and a good deal of intuition. This process allowed Mead and Willgoos to announce, in September 1923, the evolution of Lawrance's J-1 into the Wright J-3. Following additional slight improvements the next year, it became the Wright J-4, the first Whirlwind. That was the penultimate step in development of an engine destined to touch off a transportation revolution and provide the basic design for all Naval aircraft engines and a majority of Air Corps engines for two critical decades. (The Air Service would become the Army Air Corps in 1926.)

Meanwhile, nervously glancing over its shoulder at Billy Mitchell, the Navy decided to install turntable airplane catapults on some of its capital ships. Originally powered by compressed air, and later by gunpowder, the first of these devices was fitted to the stern of the *USS Maryland* in May 1922. After Lt. Andrew C. McFall's Vought VE-7

floatplane was successfully flung into the air by this mechanism, such launchings slowly became routine.

Recovery of these scout planes was tricky, however, because the aircraft had to land on the sea, taxi close to the ship, and be returned to the deck by crane. This could prove interesting in a rough sea.

During the next four years, 22 ships in the fleet were equipped with catapults (12 battleships and 10 light cruisers), and most of their captains grudgingly came to appreciate the far-ranging reports of their "slingshot" aviators. The fleet had extended its vision. It could, with its take-along scout planes, establish picket lines up to 200 miles in radius about the fleet. That constituted a security blanket of no small dimensions.

Patrol of the seas to greater distances by big, multiengined flying boats evolved more slowly. That was partly due to the lack of reliable engines of sufficient power, and partly due to Admiral Moffett's great faith in large, rigid dirigibles for such duty. It was Moffett's most serious hangup.

His dirigible programs ended in disaster, and he himself died in one.

The First Navy Dirigibles

The Navy had established its right to operate U.S. military dirigibles at the end of WWI, and two such machines were included in the 1920 Navy budget. But that didn't necessarily mean that the top brass believed all that much in the usefulness of the big airships. There is a good bit of evidence that the Navy's primary concern was to prevent Gen. Mitchell from claiming such craft for the Air Service. Obviously, a lot of money could be spent for the air giants, and it would be much better to have those funds added to, rather than subtracted from, Naval appropriations. Besides, knowing Mitchell, one must expect that he would, if in possession of such craft, employ them in an attempt to unsurp at least some of the Navy's rightful areas of responsibility.

The ZR-1 *Shenandoah* was completed in September 1923, and made its first flight from Lakehurst (NJ) Naval Air Station with Capt. F.R. McCrary in command. It was a copy of a WWI German rigid dirigible. ("Rigid" airships have a structural framework, fabric-covered, within which a number of individual "ballonets" contain a lifting gas. The "non-rigids" such as modern blimps have a single fabric envelope without internal framework.)

The ZR-2, purchased from Britain and called the "R-38" by the British, had been completed two years earlier, but during a trial flight broke in half and fell into the Humber River at Hull, England, carrying 28 Britons and 16 Americans to their deaths.

The Navy's ZR-3 *Los Angeles* was ordered from the Zeppelin works at Friedrichshafen, Germany in June 1922, after the Allied Reparations Commission levied a $33 billion "war damage" claim against Germany. As partial payment on this assessment, Germany built the ZR-3 for the U.S., along with similar craft for France and Italy. The *Los Angeles* was delivered in mid-October 1924, and served with the fleet for eight years until, during a fit of economizing, it was scrapped. It was the only dirigible to be successfully operated by the Navy.

Perhaps contributing to the *Los Angeles'* relatively long service was the fact that it was designed and built by those most experienced with such craft (Count von Zeppelin built his first dirigible before the Wright brothers flew), and because of the caution attending operation of the *Los Angeles* after the *Shenandoah* was lost. Caught in a line squall over Byesville, Ohio during the early morning hours of 3 September 1925, the *Shenandoah* was torn apart and its wreckage scattered. There were 29 survivors, but 14 were killed, including Lt./Cmdr. Zachary Lansdowne, the airship's commander.

This disaster stalled the Navy's airship programs for a time. It would be another three years before Adm. Moffett could get money for more—and bigger—dirigibles. But the *Shenandoah* tragedy served the Navy in an unexpected way: it provided the vehicle that carried Billy Mitchell to oblivion.

Mitchell Court-Martialed

After the sinking of the *Ostfriesland* in 1921, Mitchell was quietly supported in his abrasive crusade for a strong independent air force by his new boss, Maj./Gen. Mason Patrick, who replaced the more conservative Gen. Menoher as Chief of Air Service late that year.

Patrick also agreed with Mitchell on how best to get the most from tiny Air Service appropriations. Lacking funds to buy new airplanes in meaningful numbers, Gen. Patrick spent as much as possible on research and development. At some future date, the need to defend America in the air must become evident; when that time came superior planes must be ready. Therefore, Patrick okayed Air Service participation in national and international air racing, and daring long-distance flights as a means of developing high-horsepower aircraft engines and advanced airframe designs.

Such activity gathered favorable news coverage for the Air Service. This was important, because from the time that Mitchell began to kick up a fuss over the proper role and status of U.S. airpower, there was a federal investigation of some kind—20 in all, between 1919 and 1925—looking into the "aviation question." The most thorough

The ZR-3 *Los Angeles* was German-built and entered Navy service in 1924; retired in the early '30s. Improper handling resulted in this nosestand while anchored to mast in 1927. (USN)

of these was that of the Lampert-Perkins Committee in the House of Representatives (68th Congress) which, in 1924, made recommendations largely favorable to the Mitchell-Patrick position. But the Lampert-Perkins Committee report was soon submerged in another controversy when the Army's General Staff decided that Mitchell should not be reappointed as Assistant Chief of the Air Service. Indeed, as his tour of duty ended he was "allowed" to revert to his permanent rank of colonel and transferred to Fort Sam Houston, Texas.

Mitchell probably expected as much. The Army General Staffs of that era were made up of old horse soldiers, dominated by Gen. John J. "Blackjack" Pershing, and to a man all were schooled in strategy and tactics that had not changed since the Civil War. Mitchell had become as bothersome to them as he was to the Navy.

Many newspapers cried "Shame!" and the public generally agreed that Mitchell was being punished for daring to disagree with his superiors. Columnist Mark Sullivan may have summed it up best when he observed: "The American people admire a man who has the courage to sass his bosses." There is small evidence that the people were actually much concerned with the issues raised by Mitchell. His public support was simply rooted in that basic human trait which compels us to cheer for the underdog.

Whether or not Mitchell understood that, he did know that the public constituted his only court of appeal. He recognized that his career was finished; the most he could do was to inform the people of the facts and let history be his judge. He therefore continued to make strong statements to the press, alleging gross mismanagement of America's military establishments, and he ignored orders to obtain prior approval from his superiors for these public utterances.

The inevitable showdown came two days after the *Shenandoah* went down (and while a Navy flying boat was missing over the Pacific), when Mitchell handed reporters a lengthy prepared statement in which he charged that these losses were due to the "incompetency, criminal negligence, and almost treasonable administration of the national defense by the War and Navy Departments."

Mitchell went on to accuse the Army and Navy of forcing officers to falsely testify before various Congressional committees, condemned the War Department for retaining the Air Service's obsolete "flying coffins", and concluded by saying: "I can no longer stand by and see these disgusting performances by the Navy and War Departments, at the expense of the lives of our people, and the delusion of the American public."

That, of course, resulted in headlines of arresting proportions, and before the stunned War and Navy Departments could regroup for a common defense, Mitchell followed up with a demand that the President appoint a panel of representative Americans to investigate these departments.

President Calvin Coolidge, a humorless, unimaginative man thrust into the White House by President Harding's sudden death in mid-1923, first directed that Mitchell be court-martialed under the 96th Article of War. Then Coolidge appointed a nine-member President's Aircraft Board "to make a study of the best means of developing and applying aircraft in national defense."

No one ever accused this board of being representative of the American people. It was headed by Coolidge's school chum Dwight Morrow, a partner in the J.P. Morgan banking firm, and contained Senator Hiram Bingham, already on record as opposed to Mitchellism; Maj. Gen. (ret) James Harbord, who had sought Mitchell's resignation earlier; and Howard Coffin who was, it will be recalled, chairman of the bungling Aircraft Production Board of WWI.

This hip-pocket assembly, popularly called the "Morrow Board," sat for about three weeks, and Coolidge timed release of its report to immediately precede the verdict in the Mitchell trial. This report summed up its rejection of Mitchell's proposals with the statement: "The next war may well start in the air, but in all probability it will wind up, as the last one did, in the mud." Then it dangled an aerial carrot, recommending acquisition of new and modern airplanes for Navy and Air Service.

As for the verdict in the Mitchell trial, there was never any doubt about that once the court ruled, shortly after the proceedings began on 28 October 1925, that *truth was not a defense*. Whether or not Mitchell's statements were true had no bearing on the case, the six generals sitting in judgment decided. Mitchell was *not* charged with lying, but with "conduct prejudicial to good order and military discipline." It was a catch-all canon applicable to everything from kicking a horse to making an improper advance to another officer's wife. And although Mitchell pleaded not guilty to each of eight counts, he knew that the whole procedure was mere formality. The proceedings were in the best Judge Roy Bean tradition: Give'em a fair trial and then hang 'em.

Mitchell was eloquent, and managed to turn the whole affair into an indictment of his accusers—at least, for the record. Then he directed his legal counsel to withdraw from the case and make no closing argument.

The court's guilty verdict was announced on 17 December 1925. The only dissenting vote was cast by Gen. Douglas MacArthur. The court decreed that Col. Mitchell be suspended from rank, pay, and allowances for five years. Mitchell responded by resigning from the Army.

But nothing is so hard to destroy as the truth, and the principles that Mitchell championed were firmly held by others in both the Army and the Navy. The time would come when their counsel would be sorely needed.

Billy Mitchell, however, would not live to see that day. He would die five years before the Japanese attacked Pearl Harbor—exactly as he predicted they would, early on a Sunday morning.

REVIEW QUESTIONS

1. Describe the predominant attitude in the early 1920s by the "battleship admirals" and "horse soldier generals" towards aviation. Who were some of the leading military men who opposed this attitude? How was the Naval Bureau of Aeronautics created?

2. What was the purpose of the sinking of the *Ostfriesland?* Did the event achieve its purpose? Why?

3. Why was the development of the Wright Whirlwind and Pratt and Whitney Wasp engines such a breakthrough in engine design? Who was Charles L. Lawrance? Frederick B. Rentschler?

4. Identify some of the Navy's early dirigibles. How were they used? What was their fate?

5. Why was Billy Mitchell court-martialed? Why did General Mason Patrick allow army pilots in air racing and daring long-distance flights?

6. Did the public support General Mitchell's charges? Do you think Mitchell was surprised at the outcome of the trial? What is meant by the statement "truth was not a defense"? What was the purpose of the Morrow Board?

Chapter 5

Birth of the Air Mail

OBJECTIVES: At the end of this chapter you should be able to:

☐ Describe the first attempt at air mail service in the United States.

☐ Discuss some of the problems encountered by the Post Office Department in inaugurating air mail service.

☐ Identify the type of aircraft flown on the early air mail routes.

☐ Discuss the significance of Jack Knight's epic flight.

The nation's airline system grew from the airmail routes of the early 1920s. A relative handful of civilian pilots, employed by the U.S. Post Office Department, flying WWI surplus biplanes, pioneered the transcontinental airways. They flew their schedules with remarkable constancy, without radio aids, with few instruments and sketchy weather reports. Their contribution to civil aviation in general and a future airline industry in particular was out of proportion to their number.

Well, Anyway, It's a Start

The morning of 15 May 1918 dawned bright and crisp in the nation's capitol. It was a proper morning for the historic event jointly planned by the Post Office Department and the U.S. Air Service, the inauguration of the world's first scheduled aerial mail service. But despite nature's invigorating promise, it was a morning that Lt. George Leroy Boyle should have, as the saying goes, "stood in bed." As things turned out for Boyle that day, his contribution to the momentous event was an embarrassing one.

Actually, it wasn't Boyle's fault. He should not have been given the honor of flying that first load of mail. He was a new pilot; he had never flown beyond sight of his training airfield.

A regularly scheduled aerial mail system in the United States had been the dream of U.S. Senator Sam Sheppard of Texas since 1910, and he had argued for it—first in the House of Representatives later in the Senate—until, with the support of Postmaster General Albert Burleson, Sheppard managed to obtain Congressional approval for an experimental route between New York city and Washington, D.C. in 1916. The necessary funding was included in the steamboat mail appropriation for fiscal 1918. Therefore, President Woodrow Wilson, who viewed such a service as good training for Army pilots as well as possibly being of some value to businessmen after the war, directed Secretary of War Baker to provide planes and pilots to fly the route, with a stop in Philadelphia, each way every day except Sunday. The Post Office Department would administer the program.

The President and Mrs. Wilson, along with a num-

Maj. Reuben Fleet briefs Lt. George Boyle as Boyle prepares to take off with the nation's first load of scheduled air mail on 15 May 1918.

ber of other dignitaries including Assistant Secretary of the Navy Franklin D. Roosevelt, were gathered at the polo field on the banks of the Potomac by 10:30 A.M. on that pleasant spring morning to give the aerial mail an appropriate sendoff. The airplane, a Hisso-powered Jenny, had arrived an hour earlier, flown in from Philadelphia by Maj. Reuben Fleet, who had been placed in charge of the Air Service's part in the joint effort. (Reuben H. Fleet was a National Guard officer who learned to fly at the Army's school on North Island, San Diego, in 1917. He came from a pioneering lumber family in the State of Washington. His Army rank and position in Washington, D.C. reflected both family political influence and Fleet's early enlistment. In 1923, Fleet would form Consolidated Aircraft Corporation from the remains of Dayton-Wright and tiny Gallaudet Aircraft Corporation, and Consolidated would merge Vultee Aircraft in 1943 to form Convair. We will take note of the Consolidated flying boats and Convair airliners in subsequent chapters. Mostly, Consolidated/Convair produced military aircraft.)

Maj. Fleet produced a map that depicted the railroad tracks in the area and huddled with Lt. Boyle to point out the location of prominent checkpoints along Boyle's route to Philadelphia.

Boyle climbed into the cockpit, the shutters of press cameras clicked, and Sgt. E.F. Waters grasped the Jenny's eight-foot propeller. "Switch off!" he called.

"Switch off," Boyle responded.

Waters pulled the prop through a few turns to prime the engine, then yelled, "Contact!"

"Contact!" Boyle echoed, flipping the ignition switch.

Waters swung the prop. The engine fired on one or two cylinders, blue smoke belched from the exhaust, and the prop stopped stiffly.

Two more attempts were made to start the engine. The "sparking plugs" were checked; then someone peered into the fuel tank and discovered the problem.

At last properly fueled, Lt. Boyle took off with 140 pounds of mail bound for Philadelphia. He circled the field, gaining altitude, and flew away—in the wrong direction.

The first scheduled air mail out of the nation's capitol was quietly put aboard a train at Waldorf, Maryland, approximately 24 miles from its point of origin when Lt. Boyle landed in a plowed field, hopelessly lost.

The other pilots completed their flights successfully. Lt. Torrey Webb took off from the infield at Belmont Park, Long Island, at 11:30 A.M. and arrived at Philadelphia's Bustleton Field at 12:40 P.M., where Lt. James C. Edgerton was waiting to take the 150 pounds of New York mail on to Washington. Edgerton touched down at the polo grounds at 2:30 P.M. Meanwhile, Lt. H. Paul Culver, after a long and fruitless wait for the northbound mail, left Philadelphia for New York carrying about 200 letters.

But it was a beginning, and in the days that followed, the Army pilots (without Boyle) managed to maintain the service with commendable constantcy under the direction of Capt. Benjamin B. Lipsner. Lipsner was not a pilot, but he was a hard worker and able administrator.

During the first year of operation, 1208 air mail flights were completed. There were 90 forced landings—53 due to weather and 37 chargable to engine failure. In anticipation of increased mail loads, a couple of Curtiss R-4Ls were placed in service on the New York-Philadelphia segment during the first month of operations. The R-4L was larger than the Jenny, and powered with the 400-hp

The Army flew the mail in Jennies fitted with 150-hp Hispano-Suiza water-cooled V-8 engines; these craft were designated JN-6H. (George Pollard)

Liberty engine. The Jennies were JN-6H versions, fitted with the 150-hp Hispano-Suiza produced by Wright-Martin and known as the Wright Model A engine.

The Post Office Takes Over

The Army pilots had the service well established by the middle of July 1918 and the Post Office Department was ready to operate the system. At that time, the price of an air mail stamp was reduced from 24¢ to 16¢; Capt. Lipsner was separated from the Army to become the first superintendent of the air mail, six new airplanes were ordered, and half a dozen civilian pilots were recruited. The first civilian air mail pilots were Max Miller, Ed Gardner, Maurice Newton, Ed Langley, and Robert Shank, plus a reserve pilot by the name of Boldenweck. Newton came from the Sperry Gyroscope company; the others had been instructors for the Air Service.

The new airplanes, built by the Standard Aircraft Company of Elizabeth, NJ (a small company owned by Mitsui in Japan) were designated Standard JR-1Bs and, equipped with 150-hp Hisso engines, were superior to the Jennies in that they were a little faster and had significantly longer ranges.

On 12 August 1918 the civilian pilots began flying the mail between New York and Washington, D.C., employing the same shuttle system used by their predecessors and with equal reliability. At the end of a year, including the period flown by the Army pilots, the service had generated postal revenues totalling $162,000. Total cost of the operation was given by Superintendent Lipsner as $143,000 for an average of $64.80 per hour of flying time. Up to 300 pounds of mail could be carried in the Standards when flown with half of their normal 60-gallon fuel supply.

The Post Office Department would continue to operate an ever-expanding system until, in 1925, the Congress decided that the pioneering had been done and that the time had come to turn the air mail over to private contractors. The Congress was substantially influenced by the railroad lobby. As the air mail sacks had steadily grown fatter, the railroads had increasingly complained that it wasn't fair for them to compete with the government in transporting the mails.

On 2 February 1925 Congress passed HR 7064, the Air Mail Act, sponsored by Representative Clyde Kelly of Pennsylvania, known as "the voice of the railway mail clerks." And the railroaders undoubtedly felt comfortable with the Kelly Bill. Except for the air mail's first year of service, it had never made a profit. As the routes grew to span the nation coast-to-coast, costs had outstripped revenues by a margin of three-to-one. If the Post Office Department was so far from making money on the air mail, how could private operators expect to make it pay?

The Post Office Department had not expected profits. From 18 July 1919 until 1 July 1924 the special air mail rate was abandoned and the planes loaded with as much first class mail as they could carry. The important thing was to establish the system.

In May 1919, the Chicago-Cleveland segment began operation, and six weeks later scheduled air mail service between Cleveland and New York over the Alleghenies was inaugurated. By the time the air mail was two years old it had reached Omaha, and on 8 September 1920 the Post Office offered regular transcontinental service between San Francisco and New York. The trouble was, it wasn't air mail all the way. The planes flew only during daylight hours, and the mail was transferred to trains overnight. Not much time was saved, but airfields

Mail is put aboard the DH-4B of mail pilot E. Hamilton Lee. Lee would eventually retire from United Air Lines in 1949. (NASM)

The wartime DH-4s were completely rebuilt for service with the Post Office Department's air mail routes. Fuselages were plywood-covered. (American Air Lines)

were built coast-to-coast, and the pilots gained experience (especially in dealing with the weather), while the longer and more difficult routes provided useful lessons in the operation and maintenance of their airplanes.

There were 98 airmail planes in service by the end of 1921, about half of them war surplus de-Havilland DH-4s. As time passed, the DH-4 became the standard airmail machine. These craft were obtained at no cost from the Army and rebuilt by the Post Office mechanics for about $2000 each. The Liberty engines, also free from large government stocks, required a number of modifications to pistons, gears, and oil systems and were made reasonably dependable. The resulting aircraft were not exactly ideal for the job, but were relatively cheap, and since there was at the time little incentive for the few airplane companies to develop new commercial airplanes, the Post Office Department had small choice.

Advances in a number of technological disciplines had to come together to produce significantly better airplanes. Better engines depended on the work of metallurgists and petroleum chemists as well as engine designers. More efficient airframes awaited development of improved airfoils and more suitable materials, allowing designs that would provide structures of greater strength-to-weight ratios, along with minimum maintenance and maximum durability.

All of that cost money and could be justified only by the promise of a reasonably profitable market. But during the early '20s, there existed almost no market for new civil aircraft, and the military budgets were reduced to levels that allowed no funds for the acquisition of new airplanes in meaningful numbers.

Nevertheless, during this time, the country was blessed with a series of postmasters general (and a generally favorable Congress) that supported

America's air mail effort and, by 1926, when the Post Office Department began letting contracts to private operators to fly the mail, the airway was lighted coast-to-coast for 24-hour operation, and 17 weather reporting stations, linked by radio, were positioned along the route.

A total of 289 flashing beacons marked the airway, including those at emergency fields and in between. There were no radio aids to navigation, but on clear nights a pilot could always see several beacons ahead on his course. The lighted emergency fields averaged about 30 miles apart.

That was as safe as the Post Office Department could make it. Instrument flying as we know it today was still years in the future. A few veteran mail pilots learned to maintain control under instrument conditions for short periods of time once the gyro-activated turn needle became available to them in 1924. Keeping the turn needle centered, or average-center in rough air, kept the wings level, while the altimeter's tendencies indicated a climbing or descending attitude. If a pilot lost control or found himself in or above clouds with fuel near exhaustion, he deliberately stalled the airplane and applied full rudder to enter a spin. A spin was a known condition, and a safe way to lose altitude without gaining excessive airspeed. Then the pilot's only concern was that he would break into clear air beneath the clouds with sufficient altitude remaining to recover from the spin.

The pilots did have an alternative to such a procedure. Seat-type parachutes were issued in 1919, although most were slow to wear them.

Mail pilots received a maximum base pay of $3600 per year, plus 5¢ to 7¢ per mile flown. Normally, each pilot flew five to six hours per day, two to three days per week.

But Homer Berry, one of the pilots flying between Cheyenne and Rock Springs, Wyoming, supplemented his income by operating his personal airline, carrying passengers between Laramie and Rawlins for $50 each. However, Berry's free enterprise venture cost him his job when one of his customers attempted to make a reservation at the Post Office in Cheyenne.

Resourcefulness was the mark of the early mail

Jack Knight in the cockpit of his DH-4. Knight would retire from United Air Lines in 1937 as a DC-3 captain. (United Air Lines)

pilot. When Frank Yeager encountered dense fog flying his run from Omaha to Cheyenne, he landed on the prairie and taxied more than thirty miles to his destination. He turned around at each fence, circled back for a run to gain flying speed, hopped to the other side, and continued on his way.

Today, every non-instrument pilot knows that "pushing the weather" is an invitation to disaster (although some do it, accounting for almost 40 percent of all fatal accidents in civil aviation), but the pioneering mail pilots had small choice. There was no other way to establish the air mail service. If humanly possible, the mail had to go through. And it did so at high cost. Once coast-to-coast service was established, an average of 40 pilots was employed by the Post Office Department. During the time the Post Office operated the system, 43 pilots were killed and 23 seriously injured.

Why did they do it? Dean C. Smith, a seven-year veteran of the service, put it this way:

"I knew that I could fly and fly well . . . I cer-

Charles Lindbergh flew DH-4s over the St. Louis-Chicago mail route before making his historic flight to Paris in 1927. (Joe R. Reed Collection)

tainly had no wish to get killed, but I was not afraid of it. I would have been frightened if I had thought I would get maimed or crippled for life . . . then, too, sometimes I was called a hero, and I liked that . . . But what I could never tell of was the beauty and exultation of flying itself. . ."*

Jack Knight's Epic Flight

There was also pride. That was demonstrated one winter night before the airway was lighted. Senator Warren Harding, who had taken the position that the air mail was a waste of money, was elected President in November 1920 and would be inaugurated the following March. Foreseeing the likelihood that Harding would shoot down the service once in office, Postmaster General Burleson and his Assistant Postmaster General Otto Praeger (actually, the active boss of the air mail system), decided that if the mail could be flown all the way across the United States, without transferring it to trains during the hours of darkness,such a demonstration should have a dramatic effect on the public and influence the faint of heart in the Congress.

Therefore, at 6 A.M. on Washington's Birthday, 1921, two mail planes took off from Hazelhurst Field, L.I., New York, headed west, and two left

Marina Field, San Francisco, at 4 A.M. (Pacific Time) flying east. Pairs of relay planes awaited at all the regularly scheduled stops in between.

Flying eastward, pilot W.F. Lewis crashed to his death shortly after takeoff from Elko, Nevada, but J.L. Eaton continued eastbound, arriving in Salt Lake City shortly before noon. Jim Murray then took Eaton's load on to Cheyenne, touching down there just before dark. Frank Yeager, waiting in Cheyenne with his Liberty engine warmed, was airborne within five minutes, his big deHavilland biplane established on course for North Platte, Nebraska in gathering darkness. It was clear and cold over the high plains and Yeager was able to follow the "iron beam" (Union Pacific railroad tracks) into North Platte, landing in the snow at 7:50 P.M. where James H. "Jack" Knight was waiting to take the eastbound mail into Omaha.

Meanwhile, the westbound flights had got only as far as Chicago, where they were grounded by a blinding snowstorm. Even as Knight prepared to leave North Platte, the westbound air mail was being put aboard a train in Chicago. Knight did not know it, but there would also be no airplane waiting in Omaha to take his mail sacks eastward. That pilot, too, was sitting out the storm in Chicago.

---

*By the Seat of My Pants, Dean C. Smith, Little, Brown and Company, 1961.

A last-minute check of Knight's DH-4 revealed a badly cracked tailskid, and repairs delayed his departure until 10:44 P.M., but the winter night remained reasonably clear over Nebraska, and people in the towns of Lexington, Kearney, and Central City lit huge bonfires as they heard the sound of Knight's approaching engine. Jack Knight was grateful. He didn't really need the fires because he had sufficient visibility to see the railroad tracks and other prominent checkpoints, but the peoples' cold vigil below reached out to him from the darkness and he was touched by their concern and support.

Knight reached Omaha at 1:10 A.M. in the early morning of the 23rd and, as he warmed himself by the big pot-bellied stove in the operations office,was told of the huge winter storm over the Midwest that had apparently doomed the air mail service's trailblazing effort. The backside of the storm was somewhere between Omaha and Chicago. Knight had never flown the route east of Omaha.

He filled his coffee cup and backed up to the stove again. Perhaps he thought about the bonfires. He stuffed folded newspapers across his chest inside his fur-lined flying suit, filled his coffee thermos, and announced to the surprised station manager that he would take the mail to Chicago.

Knight left Omaha at 2 A.M. He intended to land at Des Moines for fuel. Gradually a thin haze turned into broken clouds and he dropped low, following the Rock Island tracks into Des Moines. The city was asleep and the airfield appeared deserted. Knight buzzed the field and, unable to gauge the depth of the snow cover, decided to try for Iowa City, 120 miles to the east. Whatever the conditions, it would be necessary to land there for fuel. Steadily the clouds thickened, and halfway to Iowa City his prop began whipping a blizzard of snowflakes about the cockpit. He flew as low as he dared and was allowed intermittent glimpses of the ground. He guessed the crosswind at about 25 mph. It was a good guess. He was forced to climb a few hundred feet as Iowa City loomed out of the swirling snow. He was unable to locate the darkened airfield, but a night watchman heard him circling, rushed to the center of the field, and lit a flare.

The two then refueled the airplane, then Knight sat in the office close to the stove. It was 200 miles to Chicago.

Knight took off into the darkness at 6:30 A.M. The snow had stopped falling, but the sky was murky, with large areas covered by ground fog over the Mississippi Valley. He held to his course and concentrated on keeping his wings level. He was cold, and very tired. Slowly, the sky grew lighter and the sun appeared. The ground below remained shrouded in mist, but smoke spreading from the Windy City's industries marked his destination and the big wheels of Knight's DH-4 were rolling in the snow covering Checkerboard Field at 8:40 A.M.

The mail had come by air all the way from San Francisco, and Jack Knight had flown 830 miles through the winter night to make it possible.

Pilot J.D. Webster departed Chicago for Cleveland at 9 A.M. and Ernest Allison took the mail from there to New York, arriving at 4:30 P.M. to complete the bold demonstration. Seven pilots had spanned the 2660 air miles between San Francisco and New York in 33 hours and 20 minutes with the United States mail (slightly less than 26 hours flying time). The fastest transcontinental trains required 108 hours for the same journey.

The feat was headlined in newspapers throughout the country, and President-elect Harding, who knew a good bandwagon when he saw one, praised the air mail service and later supported the Post Office Department's request for money to light the airway. It was one of those times in history—and there are many more of them than one might think—that the determined act of one individual made all the difference.

The airway was lighted from coast-to-coast by 1 July 1924 and, following a 30-day test, the air mail began scheduled day and night operation. The transcontinental route was divided into three zones—New York-Chicago, Chicago-Rock Springs, and Rock Springs-San Francisco—and postage was fixed at 8¢ per ounce for transit of each zone.

It was a beginning. The Post Office pilots, in their war-surplus machines, had pointed the way.

1. The first air mail route was established between which cities? Describe Lt. Boyles's ill-fated flight. How long did the Post Office Department continue to fly the mail?

2. What was the reaction of the railroad lobby to the Kelly Act? Discuss some of the advances in aviation that took place during the early 1920s which aided in the development of air mail service. What were some of the problems encountered by the Post Office pilots flying at night or under poor weather conditions?

3. What was the purpose of the Post Office Department staging a cross-country flight in February 1921? What was the significance of Jack Knight's flight? When was the airway system lighted from coast to coast?

Chapter 6

The Barnstorming Era

OBJECTIVES: At the end of this chapter you should be able to:

☐ Identify some of the barnstormers of the early 1920s and recognize their contribution to the growth and development of aviation.

☐ Describe the purpose and significance of the Air Commerce Act of 1926.

☐ Explain why Jake Moellendick is recognized as the father of Wichita's aviation industry.

☐ Describe how Clyde Cessna, Walter Beech, and Lloyd Stearman formed Travel Air Manufacturing Company and their own individual companies.

Production of the first private and commercial airplanes in the U.S. began in 1919. Few were sold because there were few practical uses for those open-cockpit machines powered by unreliable and inefficient engines. The barnstormers and air mail pilots were almost the only visible evidence of civil aviation into the mid-1920s, but the essential ingredients for a boom were coming together.

Charlie Meyers

Charles W. Meyers was not a tall man. He was, in fact, rather short. One comes to realize this only in retrospect, because you would never notice it in his presence. There was something about Charlie—an indefinable *something* that caused the world to stand aside while he passed. He was a man of courage and talent; he was a man of the sky.

Charlie grew up on Long Island and made his first flights in 1913, at age 17, in gliders of his own

design. Prior to WWI, he found a job with Aeromarine Plane & Motor Corporation in Keyport, NJ, one of about a dozen very small plane builders (including Sloan, Standard, LWF, Burgess-Dunn, etc.) that were at the time hoping to share the miniscule airplane market dominated by the Wrights, Curtiss, and Martin.

Meyers learned aircraft construction at Aeromarine, and by mid-1916 had managed to obtain about 12 hours' flying time with company test pilot Allen Adams as his instructor. Thus equipped, Charlie offered his services to the U.S. Army Signal Corps' 40-plane air arm. Rejected, he went to Canada, where his limited flying experience was more appreciated. Britain and her dominions had been at war in Europe for nearly two years. After an hour and 45 minutes additional air time with a Canadian officer, Charlie was commissioned in the Royal Flying Corps and made an instructor. Later

Briefly airborne in a glider of his own design, 17-year-old Charles Meyers begins a lifetime as a pilot in 1913. (Charles W. Meyers Collection)

he was sent to England, where he spent the remainder of the war training British and American pilots in Avro 504s.

Back in the United States after the war, Charlie bought a surplus Canuck (Canadian Jenny), joined forces with E.P. Lott and George "Buck" Weaver, who were similarly equipped, and went barnstorming. Weaver, it should be noted, had worked as an assistant to Matty Laird on the county fair circuit before the war, and had become an Air Service instructor at Rich Field, Waco, Texas, during the war. Also at Rich Field was Master Signal Electrician (sergeant-mechanic) Walter Beech.

Meyers, Lott, and Weaver were joined in midsummer by Elwood "Sam" Junkin and Clayton Bruckner, and their five-plane aerial circus fared very well, selling three-minute rides from Midwestern pastures for $20.

WACO Is Born

The group decided to spend the winter in Lorain, Ohio and, having convinced themselves (as had others, including Matty Laird and the Lockheed brothers) that a profitable market awaited the appearance of a small and inexpensive personal airplane, pooled their resources to design and build

Meyers was unhurt in the crash of his glider, but hammed it up for his father's camera. (Charles W. Meyers Collection)

88

Meyers, on wing, and Clayton Bruckner load Jenny with newspapers, which they delivered to Ohio farm families by air in 1919. It was a way to make a dollar with a war surplus airplane. (Charles W. Meyers Collection)

a tiny single-place parasol monoplane fitted with a two-cylinder Lawrance engine. They called it a "WACO," since Buck Weaver was the prime mover behind the project and they worked under the name of Weaver Aircraft Company, and because Buck had fond memories of his service at the Army training field near Waco, Texas. (While Texans pronounce it "Way-ko," the personnel at Rich Field called it "Wah-ko," and all WACO airplanes were so called.)

Buck narrowly escaped serious injury in the crash of the first WACO after its engine failed on a test flight, and he left the company soon afterwards, but Bruckner and Junkin were determined to build airplanes and eventually produced the successful WACO 9 in 1925. WACO's success during

First WACO was this anemic single-place monoplane fitted with a 26-hp Lawrance air-cooled two-cylinder engine. This 1919 craft was destroyed in test. (Charles W. Meyers Collection)

Buck Weaver hopping passengers in 1920 in his Canuck (Canadian Jenny). The barnstormers could charge $20 for a three-minute ride during the early '20s. By 1925, competition lowered the price to $2 or $3 per passenger. (Charles W. Meyers Collection)

In the Carolinas in 1921; Meyers (center) converted a war surplus Thomas Morse Scout to two-place and substituted an OX-5 engine for the plane's original rotary. At right is fellow barnstormer Harry Herman. (Charles W. Meyers Collection)

the late '20s would be largely owed to Charlie Meyers, but no one at Weaver Aircraft Company suspected it then, and Charlie left the group early in 1920 to barnstorm in the Carolinas.

Meyers was typical of the gipsy barnstormers of the early '20s, and among them were many whose names are familiar today: Walter Beech, Clyde Pangborn, Wiley Post, Charles Lindbergh, Roscoe Turner, and Clyde Cessna, to name a few. They took chances because it was necessary, but few were irresponsible daredevils; a busted airplane earned no money. They operated from the nation's cow pastures because there were no civilian airports except for the sod fields used by the air mail pilots. If they spliced a broken wing spar with a piece of yellow pine from an orange crate, that was an economic necessity. If they replaced a worn rocker arm brushing in an OX-5 engine with the

steel barrel from an Eversharp pocket pen, that was because it fit and it worked. In any case, there were no aviation regulations, no pilot licenses required, and no airworthiness certificates needed for their machines. The sky was free, and anyone with a few hundred dollars to pay for a surplus Jenny or Standard could do whatever he pleased—or was able to do—with it. Barnstorming was a matter of survival of the fittest, and the only way most could both fly and eat with some regularity. No one ever got rich at it. Indeed, it was commonly said within this hardy clan that "The greatest danger in flying is starving to death."

Nor was all of it pure fun. As barnstormer Earl C. Reed put it, "There were more pleasurable things than overhauling an engine somewhere on the plains when the temperature stood at 105 degrees. No one ever looked forward to hand-

The "TLR Flying Circus" consisted of a surplus Standard, pictured, and a Jenny. Owner Reed in center; pilot is Beeler Blevins, with paying passengers in front cockpit. (Earl C. Reed)

propping a Hisso engine after a cold night in the open, or washing the cow dung from the underside of the wings, or sitting miserably under a wing during a thunderstorm, your raincoat draped over the wooden propeller to keep it from soaking up moisture which could cost rpms. But we were fliers, and that whole vast sky out there belonged to us alone, and that was enough."

But the times were changing. By 1925 the ever-increasing number of barnstormers was finding customers ever more scarce and the price of a ride around the patch had dropped to $2 or $3 per passenger. A few innovative entrepreneurs would continue to barnstorm right up to the eve of World War II, offering night flights in Ford and Stinson Tri-motor airliners, along with spectacular airshows. At $1 per head, even with a full load of 15 passengers, that was hardly an airlift to affluence.

Air Commerce Act

So the barnstormer faded from the scene because he could no longer survive economically. But he would have gone anyway. The Kelly Bill promised profits to civilian air mail contractors, and if there was money to be made in aviation, the investment bankers were interested, and bankers like things tidy and well-regulated. The U.S. Congress obliged with the Air Commerce Act of 1926, which provided for the first aviation regulations, and required federal licenses for all civil pilots and aircraft.

Morrow Board

The Air Commerce Act of 1926 also drew upon recommendations of the Morrow Board, a commission appointed by President Calvin Collidge in response to sensational public charges by the Air Service's Gen. Billy Mitchell accusing the Army and Navy of gross incompetence and near treason in their refusal to recognize the importance of air-power to the nation's defense. The Morrow Board (officially, the President's Aircraft Board) was chaired by the President's old college chum, Dwight Morrow, a partner in the J.P. Morgan banking firm; among its eight members was Howard E. Coffin of the discredited WWI Aircraft Production Board.

Reed's Standard is damaged in a cow pasture landing incident, a not uncommon sight. Military insignia was painted-out with green barn paint. (Earl C. Reed)

It seems incredible today, in view of the testimony given before this assembly during its three weeks of hearings, that Dwight Morrow and his cohorts could have decided that Mitchell was wrong. But they dutifully rejected "Mitchellism" (which called for a strong, independent air force, and accurately predicted a surprise attack on Pearl Harbor by the Japanese, among other things) and, having accomplished their primary purpose—the denigration of Mitchell—Morrow, Coffin, and friends offered some suggestions for the federal regulation of civil aviation.

The Morrow Board's recommendations for civil aviation were modified by Secretary of Commerce Herbert Hoover, with some input from the NACA (forerunner of NASA) and Senator James W. Wadsworth of New York, an advocate of federal air regulations for several years. The result was the Air Commerce Act (also known as the Bingham-Parker-Merritt Bill, for its sponsors), which has often been characterized as U.S. civil aviation's Magna Carta. It was hardly that. True, sensible regulation was due and desirable. However, it was but one leg of the required triad. Of equal importance were more efficient airplanes and an infusion of risk capital. If civil aviation had a Magna Carta, it was the Kelly Bill, which offered a dependable source of revenue to private operators. That, in turn, attracted investors. More efficient airplanes were certain to follow.

More efficient commercial airplanes evolved slowly during the early '20s because of the very

The civilian fliers of the post-WWI years were forever seeking ways to make a dollar with an airplane. Vic Carlstrom (R) established inter-city records in 1919 with a Curtiss Model R powered with a Curtiss VX engine of 180 hp. Curtiss' chief motor engineer, Charles Kirkham, is second from left; early exhibition pilot Art Smith, center and with back to camera at left is Matty Laird, then using a crutch as a result of a crash in Katherine Stinson's Brock-built machine two years before. Photo taken at Chicago's old Ashburn Field. (E.M. Laird)

limited and ill-defined market, and the fact that designers had little choice in the selection of a proper engine. Nevertheless, some progress was made because of those who saw the future potential of commercial aviation.

In Chicago, Matty Laird envisioned that potential and presumptuously painted a sign on his Ashburn Field hangar that read "E.M. Laird Company" after agreeing to build an airplane for barnstormer Billy Burke early in 1919. But the immediate market, Matty believed, was for an inexpensive personal or sport plane, a market generated by the thousands of pilots so recently trained by the military.

Matty was wrong, of course. That same euphoric expectation was shared by others then, and again 25 years later after WWII, and materialized neither time.

Matty sold but the one Laird Model S—a two-place biplane powered with an 80-hp rotary engine—and although Burke was pleased with the craft, no other customers appeared. Matty then began planning a larger, three-place "Commercial" biplane, and had three-view sketches of it on hand when Burke returned late that fall.

Jake's Airplane Works

Now, Burke was a successful Buick-Franklin automobile dealer down in Okmulgee, Oklahoma, but his passion was airplanes. He had instructed at Rich Field during the war, and when offered the chance to manage a newly organized and apparently well-financed flying service in Wichita, Kansas, Burke took it and soon was off to Chicago to look for airplanes that were more efficient than the pair of tired Canucks possessed by the Wichita Aircraft Company.

The three ex-Army pilots who had organized

Meyers' barnstorming airplane of 1923 was a craft of his own design and construction. Built in a barn, it was powered with a surplus OX-5 engine of 90 hp. (Charles W. Meyers Collection)

The barnstorming era produced another phenomenon, the "wing walker," who performed gymnastics on the outside of airplanes in flight as a means of attracting crowds from which paying passengers could be solicited. (Joe R. Reed)

W.A. "Billy" Burke, one of the three original founders of Wichita's first airplane factory. Billy is shown while an instructor at Rich Field, Waco, Texas, during WWI. Also at Rich Field were Buck Weaver and Walter Beech. (E.M. Laird)

the Wichita Aircraft Company as a barnstorming and air taxi service had the financial backing of several Wichita businessmen, including hotelman George Siedhoff, contractor J.H. Turner, and Jacob Melvin Moellendick. Jake Moellendick must be recognized as the father of Wichita's aviation industry—although, as things turned out, he was a lousy parent.

Jake had earlier followed the oil-drilling rigs from Okmulgee's well sites to the booming Wichita discovery, arriving with little more than the shirt on his back. But Jake was a true high-roller. As far as he was concerned, if a man couldn't be rich he may as well be broke. He was a driller, and a good one (the top job on a drilling rig), but working for wages, however high, just wasn't Jake's idea of living. Therefore, he often offered his services in exchange for a "piece of the hole," and the nature of oil wildcatting being what it is, his offer was

sometimes accepted. Sure enough, one day Jake's bit twisted into pay dirt, and his bank account suddenly began growing faster than Jake could deplete it—which is saying a lot, because he had a large appetite for personal pleasure. Jake Moellendick was soon an important man around Wichita. He was also loud, abrasive, and usually drunk.

So Moellendick was a natural target for the partners in the Wichita Aircraft Company when they went looking for additional capital. Theirs was the kind of long-shot proposition that was made to order for Jake. He not only bought in, but became the majority stockholder.

Aware that this made him the boss, Jake immediately started bossing. He didn't know anything about airplanes, but he knew a man who did—his old friend Billy Burke down in Okmulgee. Jake sent for Burke, and that is what led to Burke's appearance at Matty Laird's "airplane factory" late in 1919.

Burke was so impressed with the sketches of the proposed Laird Commercial that he thrust aside all thought of the Wichita Aircraft Company and immediately suggested that they move the Laird operation to Wichita, where the economic climate was much better, and manufacture the Commercial in quantity. Inevitably, perhaps, that led back to Jake Moellendick and formation of the E.M. Laird Company of Wichita, which was a three-way partnership with Laird contributing his equipment and know-how, and Burke and Jake each putting up $15,000 in cash.

The first product of Wichita's first airplane manufacturing plant was test-flown in mid-April 1920, by which time the Laird company had absorbed Jake's original air taxi operation and acquired its airfield at 29th and Hillside. Among the spectators as Matty completed the test flight was hotelman Bill Lassen, who remarked that the plane flew "just like a swallow," whereupon Moellendick announced that Lassen had just named it.

The Laird Swallow

The Laird Swallow was an immediate success by the standards of that time. The first company advertisement, appearing in the June 1920 issue of

The first Laird Swallow under construction in Wichita. Built of wood and fabric, the early Swallows were, essentially, Jenny replacements that carried two in the front cockpits, and were advertised as the country's first commercial airplanes. (E.M. Laird)

Aviation, described it as the "First commercial airplane; capable of carrying a pilot and two passengers with fuel enough for 225 miles at full speed." This announcement was greeted by orders for 11 airplanes, and freewheeling Jake Moellendick opened the company throttle, calling for production of 20 Swallows for the rest of the year.

That also called for additional employees, among whom was Lloyd Carlton Stearman, a 20-year-old architectural student who had learned to fly in the Navy during WWI. A few months later, Walter Beech and Buck Weaver were hired as pilot-salesmen as Jake pumped more cash into the company, began construction of a new factory building,

and asked Matty to design a twin-engine transport plane. Jake had visions of starting his own airline.

Buck Weaver test-flew the twin-engine Laird in July 1921. However, the big seven-place biplane was underpowered (with a pair of OX-5s) and spent most of its time in the hangar until Laird reworked it around a single 300-hp Packard engine, after which Beech wrecked it following engine failure.

That loss, coupled with the crashes of two Swallow demonstrators, the cost of the new building, and the general business recession of 1921, required more transfusions of cash from Jake, while Jake seemed to become more difficult to get along with in direct proportion to his investment in the

Brand new Laird Swallows on the field at Wichita, 1921. (E.M. Laird)

Standing before the twin-engine Laird Transport in 1921 are employees of Jake's airplane works. Buck Weaver is second from left; Jessie Chacon, later with Travel Air and Beech, second from right; Jake Moellendick in straw hat third from right; Charles Laird fourth from right; Lloyd Stearman in cap, center.

company. Both Burke and Weaver left the company early in 1922 after fights with Jake, and Laird quit in September 1923. Forty-three Swallows had been built.

Jake reorganized the company, changing its name to Swallow Airplane Manufacturing Company. Walter Beech became the chief pilot, and Lloyd Stearman moved up to the position of chief design engineer.

But scarcely had Jake got things moving again before his two top hands raised another issue: Stearman and Beech were convinced that the Swallow's wood-framed fuselage should be redesigned and constructed of tubular steel. Jake refused to listen, and the argument ended when Beech and Stearman resigned on the spot. Jake continued with Matty's brother, Charles Laird, as chief of design, and with Red Jackson as chief pilot.

Laird returned to Chicago and Ashburn Field, where he soon introduced the Laird Commercial,

the first of a long line of quality-built single-bay biplanes with steel tube fuselage frames—including some famous racers—that would be advertised throughout the '20s and early '30s as the "Thoroughbreds of the Airways." Laird would never again accept a partner.

Swallow, meanwhile, had a head start in the civilian airplane market. Its products, well crafted, had established a good reputation for the company, and with almost no competition (the Curtiss Oriole was priced higher and was a poor performer), was in position to dominate its market for the foreseeable future if properly managed. Lloyd Stearman, during his brief tenure as chief engineer, had redesigned the original Laird Swallow, eliminating one set of wing struts on each side to make a trimmer, more efficient single-bay biplane, a configuration that would be the standard for all two and three-place biplanes to follow, and Charles Laird modified that airframe to allow installation of Hisso

Businessmen-pilots of the '20s used their airplanes more for advertising than for business travel. Walter Beech sold this Laird Swallow to a Wichita businessman in 1922. (E.M. Laird)

Clyde Cessna's 1912 "Silver Wings" was a homebuilt copy of the French Bleriot. Clyde favored monoplanes from the beginning. (Cessna Aircraft Company)

engines up to 180 hp.

Beech and Stearman quit Swallow in October 1924, and it is just possible that there was more behind it than Jake's refusal to switch to metal framing in the Swallow fuselage. Stearman had drawings of a new biplane that looked very good to Walter, and perhaps Walter may be pardoned if he decided that what Stearman could do for Jake might just as well be done for Beech. In any case, Beech looked up barnstormer Clyde Cessna, whose maturity and judgment Walter respected, and proposed that the two of them open their own airplane manufacturing plant to build Stearman's new design.

Clyde Cessna

Clyde Vernon Cessna had a solid background in aviation. He had been a 31-year-old farm implement mechanic in Enid, Oklahoma, when, in 1910, a trio of early birdmen staged an exhibition in Oklahoma City. Clyde attended and was smitten. He made sketches of the Bleriot monoplane flown by one of the "aeronauts" and, back in Enid, ordered a bare fuselage from the Queens Aeroplane Company of Bronx Park, NY (which was licensed to

make Bleriots in the U.S.). He designed and built his own wings, depending on the sketches he'd made in Oklahoma City. The tail section and control systems were added from memory, and he converted a 4-cylinder 60-hp Elbridge marine engine to power his creation. The craft was ready for its first flight in May 1911.

Like so many early birds, Clyde had to teach himself to fly and test his airplane simultaneously. Both projects suffered. But on his 13th attempt, Cessna got off the ground and back down again without doing serious violence to either his machine or himself. He thereupon quit his job and took off on an exhibition tour.

An accident early in his flying career wrecked the plane and put Clyde in the hospital for a few weeks. By then, however, he had flown a couple of successful exhibitions—the first, at Cherokee, Oklahoma, earned him $300—and he had other county fair dates contracted.

During the winter of 1911-12, Cessna took his wife and two children, Eldon and Wanda, to the Cessna family homestead near Rago, Kansas, and built a new plane powered with an Anzani engine. This craft, the "Silver Wings," prophetically em-

Cessna with his 1914 airplane at Burdette, Kansas. (Cessna Aircraft Company)

ployed the leaf of a buggy spring in its landing gear.

For the next four years Cessna worked the county fairs in season and built a new and improved airplane each winter. Late in 1916, he built three airplanes in the plant of the Jones Motor Car Company at Wichita when the makers of the Jones Light Six offered free use of their facilities in exchange for the advertising value of this activity. One of these craft, the "Comet," had an enclosed cockpit and was capable of almost 100 mph. Clyde found buyers for the other two.

Cessna was not accepted for military service in WWI (he was 37 years old), so he spent the war years on his farm at Rago growing wheat. He returned to barnstorming in 1919, and in the late summer of 1923 purchased a new Swallow from Walter Beech. Clyde had made money barnstorm-

ing, and was the kind of man who saved much of it.

Clyde wasn't especially enthused over the prospect of producing Stearman's biplane; he had favored monoplanes from the beginning, and had recently come to believe that monoplanes with cantilever wings—that is, wings without external bracing, such as Bill Stout was building for Henry Ford—would be the most efficient. But the monoplanes would surely follow if the proposed company was successful.

Travel Air Formed

Cessna put up $6200, Beech got together $5700, and Stearman's minority share was represented by $200 and his drawings of the new airplane. Other investors included Daniel C. Sayre, Walter Innes, Jr., and other Wichita businessmen.

The company was incorporated 5 February 1925 as the Travel Air Manufacturing Company with Cessna as president and Beech vice-president.

Walter Beech

Both Beech and Cessna were reared on farms—Walter being a native of Tennessee—and both were into automobile mechanics before WWI, but there the similarity ended. When they joined together to form Travel Air late in 1924, Clyde was 45 years old and Walter 33. Clyde was a quiet, deliberate type, a solid family man with grown children. Walter was an outgoing, ambitious man, an excellent salesman, and a bachelor who is said to have had a fine appreciation for a "well-turned ankle," to put it in the idiom of that time.

When and how Walter learned to fly is very difficult to determine. The official line at Beech Aircraft Corporation has long been that Walter rebuilt a Curtiss pusher in Milwaukee in 1914, taught himself to fly it, and was a flight instructor at Rich Field during WWI. Walter worked for a truck manufacturer prior to the war and was sent to Europe to represent that firm. He held the rank of sergeant (master signal electrician) at Rich Field, and several

who knew him there have confirmed that he was in charge of the engine overhaul shops. However, when Walter showed up in Arkansas City, Kansas, in 1919 at the Williams-Hill Flying Service, he was hired as a pilot (Pete Hill had known Walter at Rich Field). Apparently, Walter learned to fly while serving in the Army as a mechanic, a not uncommon practice at the time. In any case, Walter barnstormed for Pete Hill and Errett Williams until Moellendick hired him early in 1921.

Lloyd Stearman

Lloyd Stearman was 26 years old when he joined with Walter and Clyde to form Travel Air. Lloyd, from Harper, Kansas, was an intellectual who played the violin and relaxed with classical music, and who had learned to fly in the Navy at San Diego in 1918. He was working as an architect for the S.S. Voigt firm in Wichita when his continuing interest in aviation took him to the Swallow company—at reduced pay—in the summer of 1920.

Travel Air produced 19 of their OX-5 Model 2000 biplanes during 1925 and production more than doubled to 43 units the following year, aided by Beech's showing in the Ford Reliability Tour

The first Travel Air, fitted with fully-cowled OX-5 engine. A total of 19 was sold in 1925. (Beech Aircraft Corporation)

Walter Beech and Travel Air powered with a Curtiss C-6 engine of 160 hp. Walter flew this airplane to first place in the 1928 Ford Reliability Tour. (Beech Aircraft Corporation)

both years. By the end of 1926 Travel Air had moved onto Wichita's new municipal airport on East Central Avenue, and both Stearman and Cessna had left the company to build airplanes on their own.

Stearman left in September 1926 and, with backing from West Coast Travel Air dealer Fred Hoyt, produced the Stearman C-1 and C-2 in Venice, California. Several of the latter craft went to Walter Varney, one of the first contract air mail operators. Then Lloyd was lured back to Wichita in November 1927, when several local businessmen, led by Walter Innes, raised $60,000 to put the Stearman Aircraft Company solidly to business, where it would remain until absorbed by the Boeing Division of United Aircraft Corporation two years later. Stearman and Varney would join with others in 1932 to purchase and revitalize the bankrupt Lockheed company in Burbank, California.

Cessna left Travel Air in April 1927 to organize his own company. Although Travel Air was producing a cabin monoplane by that time, the Model 5000, the 5000 was not the kind of monoplane that Clyde wanted. In any event, it was inevitable that he would leave. Cessna, Stearman, and Beech could

Olive Ann Mellor (R) was Travel Air office manager and girl Friday; she sold tickets while Walter hopped passengers on Travel Air paydays. She and Walter were married in 1930. (Beech Aircraft Corporation)

not long remain under a single roof. They differed greatly in character, and the traits they had in common sharply conflicted. Each had strong convictions and the courage to pursue them. Travel Air suffered from an overabundance of talent possessed by men who were poor compromisers.

Earlier, late in 1926, Clyde had built—in his spare time and at his own expense—a trim cabin monoplane fitted with a 120-hp Anzani engine. But in order to offer it to an air mail contractor, Walter decreed that Clyde's design be substantially modified with a new, deeper fuselage, Travel Air tail, and powered with the new 225-hp Wright Whirlwind engine. The resulting airplane was successfully marketed as the Model 5000, but it was no longer Clyde's airplane.

Cessna Aircraft Formed

Clyde organized the Cessna Aircraft Corporation, moved into a modest plant at 200 East Douglas in Wichita, and began work on his Model A cabin monoplane, a design that was to be the basis for Cessna airplanes for the next 25 years.

The Model A Cessna, originally called "Type 3-120," was powered with a 120-hp Anzani engine, was four-place, had a top speed of 120 mph, and sold for $3575. The French-designed Anzani engines were generally considered cantankerous beasts with excessive vibration, but Clyde had flown them extensively and had worked out modifications that made the Anzani-Cessnas reasonably reliable.

Nevertheless, aware of the Anzani's reputation, Clyde also offered his new ship with a choice of engines. The Warner-powered Cessna AW, and the Whirlwind-Cessna certificated in 1928 as the Model BW, became the most popular. The BW, with 225 hp, had a top speed of 150 mph, landed at 45, and its initial climb rate was 1400 fpm. It was widely flown as a racer in the air meets that were popular during those years.

In August 1927 the company name was changed to "Cessna-Roos Aircraft Corporation" when Victor Roos came in as a stockholder. Roos had been associated with Guiseppe Bellanca in the short-lived Bellanca-Roos company of Omaha (which made Anzani-powered monoplanes very

The 1927 Cessna Model A was Clyde's first project after leaving Travel Air and forming his own company. (Cessna Aircraft Company)

The 1929 four-place Cessna DC-6A was powered with a Wright Whirlwind J6-9 engine of 300 hp, and maximum speed exceeded 160 mph. Price at factory was $11,000. (Cessna Aircraft Company)

similar to the Cessna Model A). But Roos' tenure with Cessna was also brief, for he sold out to Clyde before the end of the year and took a job as general manager at Swallow.

Swallow badly needed some managing. Moellendick's latest caper had bankrupted the company and Jake was in a sanitarium for treatment of alcoholism.

Moellendick Bankrupt

The first six months of 1927 had been profitable ones at Jake's airplane works. Then, in June, Capt. William Erwin, a WWI ace and barnstormer, appeared in Wichita and asked Moellendick for an airplane capable of flying nonstop to Hawaii. Erwin said that he had some backing from a Dallas newspaper, and if Jake would sell him an airplane on credit, Erwin was confident that he could win the $25,000 offered by Hawaiian pineapple king James Dole to the first civilian pilot to reach Hawaii after August 12th. There was also a $10,000 second prize.

It was the kind of proposition that Jake could not resist. Charles Lindbergh had flown to Paris just two weeks before, and the world was enchanted with the evidence that men could span the oceans in a matter of hours. People of far lands who could not name the president of the United States knew

Typical biplanes of the middle '20s were, right to left: Standard (WWI surplus); Alexander Eaglerock, commonly called the "Eaglebrick," built in Denver, designed by Al Mooney; New Swallow, and WACO 10. All above are powered with OX-5 engines except the Standard, which was usually refitted with a Hispano-Suiza engine of 150 or 180 hp. (Earl C. Reed)

all about Lindbergh, the "Lone Eagle," and his Ryan monoplane, the *Spirit of St. Louis.*

Jake blew the whistle on the Swallow production line. Ignoring the protests of Swallow dealers and minor stockholders, Moellendick ordered all hands to work on a new long range monoplane for Erwin.

The plane was completed early in August; Bill Erwin christened it in the *Dallas Spirit,* then ferried it to Oakland to prepare to earn the money to pay for it. It had already cost Jake plenty—both directly and in lost sales of the Swallow production aircraft.

By that time, two airplanes—a Fokker Trimotor piloted by Army fliers Les Maitland and Al Hegenberger, and the prototype Travel Air 5000 crewed by Ernie Smith and Emory Bronte—had made the flight to Hawaii and, although too early to collect the Dole prize, had dimmed the glory for the nine entrants that were ready for takeoff on 16 August.

Of the nine, only two made it to Hawaii. Art Goebel and Navy Lt. Bill Davis in a Travel Air 5000 got there first. Martin Jensen and his navigator, Paul Schluter, in a monoplane built by Vance Breese, arrived two hours later. (When Jensen landed, his wife, Marguerite, a nervous wreck from her anxious, 26-hour vigil, marched to his plane and, hands on hips, demanded, *"Martin Jensen, where the hell have you been?"*) One plane was disqualified and not allowed to take off. Two cracked up during takeoff runs. Two turned back during the first hour. And two disappeared over the silent Pacific.

Five people died in the two machines that disappeared: Jack Frost and Gordon Scott, flying the first Lockheed Vega to be built, and Augy Pedlar flying a Buhl Airsedan carrying Cy Knope and a pretty 22-year-old sixth grade school teacher, Miss Mildred Doran.

The big silver and green Swallow monoplane, *Dallas Spirit,* was one of the two that turned back. Six feet of fabric had stripped from its fuselage aft of the navigator's station. But Erwin patched the Swallow, and the next day calmly announced that he and his navigator, Alvin Eichwaldt, were taking off for Hong Kong by way of Hawaii and Manila, and would search for the downed planes enroute. That seemed so preposterous that few believed Erwin. However, there were prizes offered for the first flights to Manila and to Hong Kong, however improbable such feats might have been at the time.

Apparently, Erwin and Eichwaldt were serious.

Winners of the 1927 "Pineapple Derby" were Art Goebel and Lt. Bill Davis flying this Travel Air 5000. (Beech Aircraft Corporation)

They flew a straight and unwavering course for Hawaii, tapping out frequent Morse Code messages to inform the world of their progress. Then, seven hours out and in darkness, Eichwaldt sent the following:

"9:02 P.M. This is the *Dallas Spirit*. We went into a tailspin—SOS—belay that. We came out of it, but were sure scared. It was a close call. The lights on the instrument panel went out and it was so dark that Bill couldn't see the—we are in a spin—SOS . . ."

Nothing further was ever heard from the *Dallas Spirit*.

That broke the Swallow company, and Jake had no money with which to rescue it. His oil-drilling partnership with Charles Landers had sunk a series of dry holes to drain his cash reserves and

he had exhausted his credit. A short time later the Swallow company was forced into receivership and Jake, beset by the Erwin-Eichwaldt tragedy and financial ruin, was taken to a sanitarium.

Months later, Moellendick went back to the oil fields and started over. But times—and Jake's luck—had changed. He returned to Wichita in 1929 and, as the *Wichita Eagle* put it, "joined the Sullivan Aircraft Corporation." Sullivan built but one airplane before closing its doors, a fate suffered by a dozen or so other would-be plane makers in Wichita during the late '20s.

Jake died 23 March 1940. He was penniless. Anonymous aviation people paid for his burial in Wichita Park Cemetary, just across the street from the old Swallow Field.

Today not many people in Wichita can tell you

Real life "Jonathan Livingston Seagull," Johnny Livingston (L), takes delivery of a WACO 10 from Clayton Bruckner.

Berry Brothers aircraft paints flew a WACO 10. Photo is dated 16 September 1929. (George Pollard)

who Jake Moellendick was, not even among the thousands employed at Beech, Cessna, Boeing, Learjet, and their suppliers. And although it is unlikely that any of them would be there had it not been for Jake, he has no monuments in Wichita, no streets or schools named for him. Sure, he was ornery and overbearing and maybe some other things, but he had guts, and faith, a vision of the future, and he left behind something of value. What else should we ask of a man?

The Swallow Airplane Company, following Jake's departure, was efficiently operated by Vic Roos, W.M. Moore, and C.A. Noll under a "purchase partnership" agreement, and was soon solvent again. They added a two-place sport-trainer to the production lines and had reason for some optimism until overtaken by such competitors as Travel Air, WACO, and Eaglerock. The last Swallow biplane was the Sport HC model of 1931, which was fitted with a 70-hp Continental radial engine. It found few buyers until Swallow, along with many other aircraft manufacturers, succumbed to the Great Depression.

WACO Prospers

WACO was one that survived the depression. After Buck Weaver's departure, Sam Junkin and Clayton Bruckner ended up in Troy, Ohio, in 1923, after brief tries in Alliance and Medina. They called their airplanes "WACOs," but worked under the name Advance Aircraft Company (Advance would at last become WACO Aircraft Company in June 1929).

The first WACO built at Troy was the Model 6, similar in configuration to the early Laird Swallow, although lacking the Swallow's modest success. A Model 7 followed, essentially a cleaned-up 6, then the Model 8, which was a four-place cabin biplane powered with a 6-cylinder Hall-Scott engine. Advance produced fewer than 10 airplanes through the Model 8.

Advance Aircraft's lean days came to an end with the appearance of the Model 9. Thirty of this model were sold during its first four months of production late in 1924 and early in 1925, and 275 were built by the time the improved WACO 10 was introduced in April 1927.

Aerobatic pilot "Fearless Freddie" Lund rolls a Whirlwind-powered WACO Taperwing in the early morning sun over Ohio.

The WACO 10 was designed and tested by Charles W. Meyers. Meyers, you will recall, had worked with Bruckner and Junkin during the winter of 1919-20. In the intervening years he had barnstormed and built a couple of airplanes of his own, one being the Meyers Midget, a tiny biplane that attracted national attention at the 1926 National Air Races, and which Charlie hoped to market in kit form. That plan was abandoned when he crashed it in a Philadelphia railroad yard in the fall of 1926. And that was when he went to Troy, Ohio, in response to a telegram from Clayton Bruckner.

"After the crash of my Midget, I went to WACO," Charlie recalled. "Designer Sam Junkin

had just died, and when I arrived there Clayt Bruckner didn't know what he was going to do. He could make anything, and he knew shop procedure, but without Sam he was thinking of folding up. But he had enough material on hand for some twenty-odd Nines, so I suggested we put them together. In the meantime, I got busy thinking and designed a follow-up airplane . . . the WACO 10. We got up to a five-a-day production on those, and even so were sending people to Travel Air because we couldn't supply them."

WACO sold 435 of the 1000 new civil aircraft built in the U.S. in 1927, and late that year the WACO 10 airframe was given a J-5 Whirlwind en-

John Wood, winner of the 1928 Ford Reliability Tour, with his WACO Taperwing and new Chrysler roadster.

gine as an option, which made it the WACO Sport ASO model. Then, when Charlie Meyers designed a set of tapered wings for this airplane, using a slightly modified version of Max Munk's new M-6 airfoil, the resulting WACO Taperwing ensured that Walter Beech's increasingly-popular Travel Airs would have all the competition they needed.

Great Lakes Formed

By the late fall of 1928, the Advance Airplane Company was indeed prospering, as was the entire aircraft industry in the U.S. Many new plane builders had come into existence during the preceding two years to ride the boom, and WACO's sales manager, Charles Van Sicklen, had discovered an opportunity to get into airplane manufacturing with a minimum of risk. He had learned that Glenn Mar-

tin wanted to move from Cleveland to Baltimore, and would leave behind a contract with the Navy for some torpedo bombers then in production at the Cleveland plant. Van Sicklen found financing and formed the Great Lakes Aircraft Corporation, taking Charlie Meyers with him.

In Cleveland, Meyers teamed up with young Cliff Leisy in the old Martin factory to design a two-place sport-trainer that would make use of the 4-cylinder air-cooled Cirrus engine of 90 hp. The Cirrus was the American version of the British de-Havilland Gipsy engine, and was built under license in the U.S. by the American Cirrus Motor Company; its use was dictated by the fact that Cirrus Motor Company money was invested in the original Great Lakes Corporation.

The Great Lakes Sport-Trainer, Model 2T-1,

Meyers Midget, with M-6 airfoils, flew 106 mph in closed-course race with 32 unreliable horsepower.

initially appeared with straight wings and was found to be tail-heavy in flight, so Meyers and Leisy solved that the quickest and cheapest way possible: They gave the little biplane nine degrees of sweep-back in its top wing panels, and the happy result of that was a distinctive craft with excellent performance that was popular then, as well as a generation later, when it was revived and put back into production with a modern engine. The original Great Lakes company, however, disappeared forever into the maw of the Great Depression after some 500 Sport-Trainers were built with Cirrus and Menasco engine installations.

Charlie Meyers left Great Lakes in 1931, about a year before its demise, to fly the Goodrich Rubber Company's Lockheed Vega, *Miss Silvertown*, testing the new wing deicer boots. Charlie eventually "Busted hell out of *Miss Silvertown*" (his phrasing) following engine failure with a load of ice. (The early P&W Wasp engines had inadequate carburetor heat available. If one picked up carb ice, the standard procedure was to lean out the fuel/air mixture until the engine backfired, then, according to

Charlie. "That either got rid of the ice or blew the damn carburetor off.")

Meyers Goes to Eastern

After months of seeking out bad weather for

Charles Meyers, codesigner of the Great Lakes 2T-1 Sport Trainer, was also company test pilot, and raced modified versions of the Great Lakes. (Charles W. Meyers Collection)

The Great Lakes biplane was a favorite of aerobatic pilots into the '60s. This one was flown by three-time national champion, the late Harold Krier. (Krier Brothers Collection)

A popular sportplane of the late '20s was the Model 113 Monocoupe, a two-place craft with a 65-hp air-cooled Velie engine, which sold for $2865 in 1929. Stinson Detroiter in the foreground. Both aircraft were returned to flying condition in the mid-'60s.

Ryan B-5 of 1929 was produced by the Ryan Aircraft Corp., St. Louis, which company purchased the Mahoney-Ryan company of San Diego which had built Lindbergh's Spirit of St. Louis. The Ryan Broughams were all advertised as "sister ships" to Lindbergh's famous airplane. (Cassagneres Collection)

Another, and highly successful, St. Louis-built airplane was the Curtiss-Robertson Robin. The prototype, and many production Robins, were powered with OX-5 engines or an OX-5 modification known as the "Tank." Others were fitted with the Curtiss Challenger radial. The Robin was three-place.

Captain Meyers shortly before his retirement from Eastern in 1956. Meyers maintained his pilot's certificate for another dozen years, flying a Cessna Skyhawk for pleasure. (Eastern Air Lines).

the deicer tests, Charlie was hired by Eastern Air Transport to fly the mail in one of their Pitcairn biplanes. He remained with them after they became Eastern Air Lines, and flew everything from Curtiss Kingbirds to Douglas airliners. He retired from Eastern in 1956 as a senior captain flying DC-7s.

Charlie maintained his pilot's certificate and flew his Cessna Skyhawk for another dozen years, during which time he taught a grandson to fly. He died of natural causes in 1972, leaving behind a part of our air heritage, along with his wife Jessie, whom he married during barnstorming days, and two daughters, both married to airline captains.

REVIEW QUESTIONS:

1. Identify some of the barnstormers of the early 1920s. What did they do? Why can it be said that they contributed to the growth and development of aviation? Why did the Air Commerce Act of 1926 mark the beginning of the end of the barnstorming era?

2. What were some of the Morrow Board's recommendations for civil aviation? Who was Jake Moellendick? Why is he considered the father of Wichita's aviation industry? How was the Swallow Airplane Manufacturing Company formed? What happened to Matty Laird?

3. How did Clyde Cessna get started in aviation? What characteristic of the original Bleriot Monoplane did Cessna adhere to in all of his aircraft? How was Travel Air Manufacturing Company formed? Why did the company break up?

Chapter 7

The First Airlines

OBJECTIVES: At the end of this chapter you should be able to:

☐ Explain the significance of Charles Lindbergh's epic flight to the growth of aviation.

☐ Discuss the importance of the Kelly Bill to the development of airlines in the U.S.

☐ Identify the successful bidders on the first Contract Air Mail (CAM) routes.

☐ Understand how the Ford Motor Company got started in aviation and developed the famous TriMotor.

☐ Describe the formation of the following three aviation empires which monopolized the industry: United Aircraft and Transport Corporation, North American Aviation, and Aviation Corporation (AVCO).

The late 1920s witnessed the formation of important aviation empires. The airplane's great potential as a commercial vehicle was at the threshold of realization, and significant risk capital appeared as investors poured money into a small and fragmented industry unaccustomed to such munificence. It was a turbulent, exciting time. It was a time for wheeler-dealers.

The Lindbergh Boom

Charles Augustus Lindbergh was not solely responsible for the boom in private and commercial flying that followed his solo flight from New York to Paris in May 1927. Civil aviation was ready to dramatically expand in America by 1927, and the boom was simmering on a back burner when Lindbergh lifted the lid.

The trend was discernible as early as 1925, when more than 300 new civilian planes found buyers, compared to a total of 60 the year before. In 1926, new plane deliveries topped 650, aided by orders from private contractors to the air mail service. So the airplane's potential as a commercial vehicle was at the threshold of realization when Lindbergh made his historic flight and turned the world's eyes skyward.

This is not to denigrate Lindbergh. He planned and executed his trailblazing flight with skill and courage, and afterwards he could have accepted any of dozens of motion picture or other offers that would have made him very rich indeed, but he re-

Lindbergh's specially-built Ryan monoplane was powered by a 220-hp Wright Whirlwind J-5C. Lindbergh paid Ryan $10,580 for the *Spirit of St. Louis.* (Teledyne Ryan)

fused to exploit his fame. This hero was for real.

It has been said that Lindbergh "sold" 10,000 airplanes overnight, and whether or not that is true, heavy money did flow into aviation enterprises in the wake of his exploit, and some of it, at least, did some lasting good because another man, one Walter Folger Brown, was determined that the United States should have the finest domestic airline system in the world.

Brown was in position to make it happen. He was President Herbert Hoover's postmaster general, and as such he administered the provisions of the 1925 Kelly Bill. When Brown saw that the Kelly Bill did not give him all the muscle he needed, he wrote a new law that did. It would be known as the McNary-Watres Act of 1930.

The Kelly Bill

The Kelly Bill (HR 7064) provided for payment to operators of up to four-fifths of the postal revenues carried, but that proved cumbersome and the bill was amended on 3 June 1926 to allow payment of up to $3 per pound for the first 1,000 miles, and 30¢ per pound for each additional 100 miles. As a measure against irresponsible bidding or the undercutting of established operators, a 1928 amendment established a 5¢ per ounce minimum for operators that had satisfactorily flown the mail for two years, and allowed them to exchange their contracts for 10-year route certificates.

The Post Office Department lost money under these provisions; in 1929, for example, actual payments to operators totalled $11,618,000, while air mail revenues came to $5,273,000.

The Post Office expected that. From its own experiences in flying the mail it knew that the only profitable routes had been those established at the beginning—short routes of 200 miles and with 24¢ stamps. But it also understood that the air mail would be truly useful only when it reached all parts of the nation, and with postage rates in keeping with the general economy. In 1929, air mail postage was 5¢ per ounce and that appeared realistic for the times.

Meanwhile, the Post Office hoped—expected—that the operators would add passenger service to supplement their mail pay and, as passenger revenues increased and larger, more efficient aircraft were put in service, mail pay could be negotiated downward. The Post Office Department, in the person of Postmaster General Harry S. New in the Coolidge Administration, made all that clear to the first contract operators.

There was, of course, a great deal of opposition to a subsidy for the air mail carriers—notwithstanding the fact that the railroads had been built with generous land subsidies from the federal government, and the steamship lines continued to receive subsidies with no end in sight. Those who favored the Post Office's subsidy to the air operators insisted that some form of government help was essential to the development of a domestic airline system because private capital would never be available in sufficient amounts and could not justify the large short-term losses with the promise of profit perhaps years in the future. But the subsidies would disappear, they insisted, as air travelers brought new profits to the operators.

The problem was that most of the contract air mail operators were not anxious to carry passengers—not as long as they could get up to $3 per pound for carrying mail in open cockpit biplanes.

However, the Kelly Bill did give the postmaster general considerable control over the operators. He could, for example, award routes only to those bidders that *he* regarded as responsible, and when bids were opened for the first eight routes on 7 October 1925, Postmaster General New awarded but five contracts because he was not satisfied with the equipment, financial status, or operating experience of the remaining bidders.

The five successful bidders were Colonial Air Lines, Contract Air Mail Route 1 (CAM-1), New York-Boston; Robertson Aircraft Corporation, CAM-2, St. Louis-Chicago; National Air Transport, CAM-3, Chicago-Dallas/Ft. Worth; Western Air Express, CAM-4, Los Angeles-Salt Lake City; and Varney Speed Lines, CAM-5, Elko, Nevada-Pasco, Washington. Two weeks later, Henry Ford's Ford Air Transport was awarded CAM-6 and CAM-7 for the Detroit-Cleveland and Detroit-Chicago routes. Then CAM-8, Seattle-Los Angeles, went to Pacific Air Transport, and CAM-9, the Chicago-Twin Cities route, was awarded to Charles Dickinson, millionaire Chicago seed merchant.

The first contract air mail routes were flown in open-cockpit biplanes. Here, a Curtiss Carrier Pigeon of National Air Transport lands at Kansas City. Barnstormer Ben Gregory's Standard is in foreground; a New Swallow in background. (Earl C. Reed)

Laird Speedwing (L) and Laird Commercial flew CAM-9 in the beginning. Northwest Orient Air Lines would grow from this route. (E.M. Laird)

CAM-1. Colonial started in 1923 as the Bee Line, an air taxi service apparently meant to occupy the free time of a group of ivy league types of good family and old money. Its stockholders included William Rockefeller, Cornelius Vanderbilt Whitney, Sherman Fairchild, Juan Trippe, and Harris Wittemore of Connecticut and Bond and Share. After winning CAM-1, it became Colonial Air Transport.

CAM-2. The Robertson brothers, Frank and Bill, were WWI pilots who were able to obtain financing from St. Louis businessmen. One of their pilots was Charles Lindbergh.

CAM-3. National Air Transport had been organized immediately after passage of the Kelly Bill by Clement Keys of Curtiss Aeroplane and Motor Company, William Rockefeller, Charles Kettering of GM, and the ubitquitous Howard E. Coffin.

CAM-4. Western Air Express was put together in July of 1925 by former automobile racing driver Harris "Pop" Hanshue, and was backed by Harry Chandler, publisher of the Los Angeles *Times,* and other West Coast investors.

CAM-5. Varney Air Lines (at one time called Varney Speed Lines), was put together by Walter Varney, who had been in aviation since 1916, and his airline grew from a flying school and air taxi service in San Mateo, California. Varney would be in and out of the airline business (selling out at a profit each time), including one operation in Mexico.

CAM-8. Pacific Air Transport belonged to Vern C. Gorst, another old timer who had been a pilot since 1912, and who operated a West Coast bus line.

CAM-9. Charles Dickinson's operation of CAM-9 pointed up the need for prior experience in maintaining scheduled air mail service. Although he was a rich man, Dickinson identified with aviation's little guys, and he bid on CAM-9 only to keep National Air Transport (NAT) from getting it—as Dickinson put it, ". . . to keep Wall Streeters from reaping the profits from an industry nurtured to the point of gain by the risks and sacrifices of men the system was bypassing." Dickinson made sure of the contract by offering to carry the mail between Min-

Northwest Airways' first airliners were Hamilton Metalplanes, built in Milwaukee by Tom Hamilton (also responsible for Hamilton Steel Propellers), and designed by Jim McDonnell, who would later form McDonnell Aircraft—today, McDonnell-Douglas. Charles "Speed" Holman was chief pilot at Northwest.

neapolis and Chicago for 48 percent of the postal revenues, a very low figure at a time when 80 percent was the maximum.

Dickinson's CAM-9 began operation 7 June 1926 equipped with three new Laird biplanes, plus a cabin biplane built by Elmer Partridge and an open-cockpit craft constructed by H.J. "Pop" Keller. In addition to Partridge, Dickinson's pilots

included Matty Laird (temporarily), Billy Brock, and Charles "Speed" Holman. Partridge and Laird were the only two men to fly the mail in airplanes they had designed and built themselves.

CAM-9 was 400 miles in length, possessed no airway beacons, and had been abandoned by the Post Office Department six years earlier because of a series of crashes induced by bad weather. The

Maiden Dearborn was one of a pair of Liberty-powered Stout 2-ATs operated by the Ford Motor Company in scheduled service between Detroit-Chicago and Detroit-Cleveland transporting automobile parts prior to flying the mail. (Ford Motor Company)

weather hadn't changed since 1920. Partridge smashed to his death on his initial flight. Laird and Keller, flying OX-5 airplanes, were forced down by weather. Only the two Whirlwind Lairds made the trip successfully. In following weeks, the pair of Lairds kept CAM-9 alive and on a reasonable schedule, but Dickinson was losing money on every trip, and began looking for an honorable way out of the air mail business.

He went to Bill Stout, whom he had known as a member of the Aero Club of Illinois back in 1910. Stout (who would later take over Henry Ford's airlines), required little sales talk. He quickly rounded up H.H. Emmons (a lawyer and a member of the WWI Deeds-Coffin Aircraft Production Board) and banker Frank Blair of Detroit, brought in Col. L.H. Brittin, and incorporated under the name Northwest Airways. Northwest successfully rebid CAM-9, and one of its first pilots, in addition to Speed Holman, was David L. Behncke, who would later found the influential Air Line Pilots Association. Northwest Airways, of course, would one day be known as Northwest Orient Air Lines.

CAM-6 and CAM-7. Henry Ford's CAM-6 and CAM-7 began flying the mail on 15 February 1926, the first private operator to do so, because Ford 2-AT Transports had been flying over these routes, carrying automobile parts and Ford Motor Company personnel on schedule, since the previous April.

Henry Ford had become interested in aviation at least as far back as 1914, when he sent one of his best attorneys to help Glenn Curtiss in Curtiss' court battles with the Wrights. And that interest had been rekindled late in 1923 as the result of an improbable letter written by an improbable man, William Bushnell Stout.

Stout Metal Planes

Bill "Jackknife" Stout, a mechanical engineer, interested in aircraft design since leaving school (there were no university degrees offered in aeronautical engineering until 1922), was a flier and an extrovert. He had founded and edited *Aerial Age,* one of the earliest U.S. aviation magazines, worked for Jesse Vincent at Packard, and, in WWI, was in charge of invention studies at the Army's McCook Field. Stout's letter, sent to a hundred of the nation's top industrialists, informed each that he needed capital to build a new kind of airplane

Bill Stout's first airplane was his 1919 Batwing, planned as a prototype of a Navy torpedo bomber. (Earl C. Reed)

The Stout Air Sedan, which impressed the Fords, reflected Batwing's influence. (Ford Motor Company)

and suggested that each send Stout $1,000. The letter ended with the unsettling statement that no contributor should expect to see his money again.

Apparently, Bill Stout had a good reputation: 25 people sent checks, among them Edsel and Henry Ford.

The plane Stout wanted to build was a three-place monoplane fitted with an OX-5 engine; it was

The German Junkers J-1 of 1917 was an all-metal aircraft with full cantilever wings, one of a number of Prof. Junkers' "Tin Donkeys." Stout introduced the Junkers concept to America. (Joe Durham)

Stout Air Pullman was the prototype of the 2-AT model. Pilots did not like the enclosed cockpit, so the 2-ATs that followed, as the first TriMotors, left pilots in the open.

evolved from his earlier "Bat Wing" and incorporated two advanced features: all-metal construction and a wing braced from within. Both principles were unusual in the U.S., although the German Junkers company had built such craft as early as 1915, and Eddie Stinson was flying a Junkers in the U.S. at that time.

Bill called his airplane the Stout Air Sedan. Only one was built, and it barely flew, but the Fords were convinced of the soundness of Stout's approach to airplane design. Within a few months the Ford Motor Company provided a factory building, an airfield, and put the Stout Metal Plane Company in business.

During 1924 Stout produced two machines, the Model 2-AT ("AT" for Air Transport"). These were eight-passenger versions of the Air Sedan, but powered with 400-hp Liberty engines and with redesigned wings, the latter being the work of George Prudden, Stout's chief engineer (later noted for his design work at Lockheed after a brief fling at marketing a small trimotor under his own name in 1928).

Stout's pair of 2-ATs were tested and ready for service by the time Congress passed the Kelly Bill and, with two more added to the Ford fleet (11 were eventually built, seven sold to other lines, and all

had perfect safety records), began scheduled operation. Meanwhile, in July 1925, the Ford Motor Company had bought out the Stout Metal Plane Company.

Ford's entry into aviation at that time gave the industry important psychological as well as practical benefits. He was respected for his business acumen, and his participation encouraged other sources of money. On the tangible side, Ford built the first concrete runways in the U.S., the first control tower, pioneered in air-to-ground radio communications, and spent large sums advertising air travel in leading magazines.

Ford TriMotor

Early in 1926, at Ford's direction, Stout and his engineers produced the first Ford Trimotor Model 3-AT. Large (for that time) multi-engine airplanes had become more practical with the introduction of the Wright Whirlwind engine. The 3-AT, however, was less than a rousing success and was providently destroyed in a hangar fire. Then Stout's crew went to the other extreme and produced a winner, the prototype of the classic "Tin Goose." The Goose flew on 11 June 1926 with Shorty Schroeder at the controls, and it would become a major tool in the development of the emerging airlines.

Boeing and Fokker also contributed early multi-engine planes in significant numbers. In fact, the Ford Trimotor was undoubtedly inspired by the first Fokker Trimotor, which appeared a year earlier and which the Fords had bought for Cmdr. Richard Byrd's attempt to fly over the North Pole.

Fokker TriMotor

Anthony Fokker was a Dutchman who built his first flyable airplane in 1910 and later designed some very good fighter airplanes for Germany during WWI after the British and French refused his services. Following the lead of Professor Junkers, Fokker adopted cantilever wings (no external bracing) and metal-framed fuselages, and, with a factory in Amsterdam after the war, opened an office in New York with Robert B.C. Noorduyn in charge. (Noorduyn would later open his own aircraft factory in Montreal.) By the time the Ford Trimotor appeared, Fokker was building airplanes as the Atlantic Aircraft Corporation in Teterboro, New Jersey.

From Nowhere to Nowhere

As expected, almost none of the new operators showed a profit in the beginning. Average income was approximately 43¢ per mile, while operating costs began at about 50¢ per mile and went as high as 80¢ per mile. Few were discouraged, however, because they were sure that the government would never allow the service to die. The operators were confident that if they showed good faith and operated as dependably as possible, reasonable adjustments in mail payments would be made after a decent interval. And such adjustments were made by way of amendments to the Kelly Bill, notably in 1926 and again in 1928 as previously mentioned. By the end of 1928, when air mail postage was reduced to 5¢ per ounce, most operators were making money, averaging 90¢ per plane mile. A year later, this was up to $1.10 per mile. The 5¢ air mail stamp increased loads by 95 percent, and since the air carriers were then being paid by the pound to fly the mail, that meant that their incomes almost doubled while their costs increased very little.

The Post Office Department—with the Republican Congress concurring—wanted it that way. Air mail revenues were far below the cost of the service, but many new routes were added during this period, and some operators were buying equipment that accommodated a few passengers because most understood that a change in Washington could modify or even reverse the government's policy of

First Ford TriMotor was the 3-AT. Performance matched its looks. (Ford Motor Company)

Ford 4-At TriMotor was flown by Shorty Schroeder at the Philadelphia Air Races in September, 1926. The 4-AT carried eight passengers; was powered with Wright J-4 Whirlwinds. (Ford Motor Company)

subsidizing the air mail carriers—and, in any case, it could not be expected to last forever. Most understood that they were expected to develop enough passenger and air freight business to allow reductions in mail pay to levels below that of air mail revenues.

While there was some indication that this would happen at some future date, the lines were evolv-ing slowly, largely because the routes were too fragmented to attract such business. Too many CAM routes were flown "from nowhere to nowhere," and those that flew "somewhere" had no connecting flights to serve potential air passengers. For example, Boeing Air Transport flew Boeing Model 40A biplanes between San Francisco and Chicago that had cabin space for two hardy passengers, but

Fokker F-10 of Western Air Express was a 12-passenger airliner fitted with three Pratt & Whitney Wasps of 420 hp each. (TWA)

NAT, which took the mail on to New York from Chicago, had no provision for passengers.

NAT's Curtiss Carrier Pigeons were hefty biplanes designed for the large mail loads of CAM-3 and the New York-Chicago route that NAT was awarded in September 1927. They were Curtiss-built because C.M. Keys at Curtiss was a principal organizer of NAT. Boeing Air Transport (BAT) flew Boeing airplanes for the same reason, and this would be the case as other major operators appeared, with American Airways flying Stinsons since both had a common corporate parent. Thus, the trend to what may be called "semi-cartels" was apparent by the time the Hoover Administration took charge of the White House on 4 March 1929.

United Aircraft

By then, the aviation empires of the several financial power blocs were identifiable. The first to emerge was United Aircraft and Transport Corporation. It was put together after William E. Boeing of the Boeing Airplane Company in Seattle was awarded CAM-18, the transcontinental route between Chicago and San Francisco, following the second round of air mail bids in January 1927. Boe-

ing had waited because the transcontinental line was not offered to private contractors until that time, and he was not interested in anything less.

Bill Boeing came from a pioneer lumber family in the Pacific Northwest, and his Boeing Airplane Company could trace its beginning back to the Pacific Aero Products Company, formed by Boeing and Conrad Westervelt in 1915 to build what were, essentially, improved copies of the Martin training plane. Boeing sold 50 of those craft to the Navy early in WWI, and had concentrated on military orders ever since.

Whirlwinds and Wasps

United Aircraft was the creature of Bill Boeing and Frederick Rentschler, with Chance Vought included as a sort of junior partner. You will recall that Rentschler formed Wright Aeronautical from the remains of the WWI Wright-Martin company to manufacture Hispano-Suiza engines. In 1922 the Navy convinced Rentschler that Wright Aeronautical should buy out tiny Lawrance Aero Engine Company and develop Charles L. Lawrance's promising 200-hp air-cooled radial engine. It had not been a difficult decision for Rentschler because

The Wright Whirlwind J-6 series of 225 hp. (Hudek Collection)

The R-1340 Pratt & Whitney Wasp of 400 hp. In later years, this engine was rated at 600 hp. (United Technologies)

the Navy—his best customer—said it would buy no more Hissos, and that it expected to standardize on air-cooled radials for its shipboard airplanes.

Rentschler's enginemen, George Mead and Andy Willgoos, had brought the Lawrance J-1 engine to a high state of reliability as the J-4 Whirlwind by 1924, and Rentschler recognized the opportunity of a lifetime. Aware that Sam Heron and Ed. T. Jones at the Army's McCook Field engine research facility had developed a superior air-cooled cylinder and valve system, he resigned from Wright Aeronautical and took Mead and Willgoos with him. Rentschler quickly found financing (from Niles-Bement-Pond, which owned the idle Pratt & Whitney Tool Company factory in Hartford, Connecticut; a principal stockholder and officer in Niles-Bement-Pond was the unsinkable E.A. Deeds), and thus was formed the Pratt & Whitney Aircraft Company. And employing the Heron-Jones air-cooled cylinder, Mead and Willgoos quickly produced the first P&W Wasp engine, the R-1340, initially rated at 400 hp.

The Wasps and Hornets that followed in quick succession were fabulously successful, being purchased in great numbers by the Navy, Army, and civil aviation alike, and when Boeing joined forces with Rentschler to form United Aircraft and Transport Corporation in October 1928, they were looking far down the pike at civil aviation's great potential, determined to profit as much as possible from it.

Beginning with the purchase of Chance Vought's company and Pratt & Whitney, they also acquired—within a year, and mostly by way of stock swaps—Hamilton Propellers, Standard Steel Propeller, Stearman, Northrop, and Sikorsky. They brought Boeing Air Transport into the fold as United Air Lines, and then went after the New York-Chicago air mail route in order to possess the entire transcontinental route coast-to-coast.

North American

The bug in United's cup of tea was, of course, National Air Transport, which had the air mail contract for the New York-Chicago route: NAT had the same visions of aeronautical sugarplums dancing in its corporate head as did United. NAT was controlled by the Curtiss-C.M. Keys group and Keys was also dreaming of an aviation empire.

The battle was an expensive one for United, because it drove NAT stock from $15 per share to $30, and while United was buying up NAT common, Keys formed North American Aviation, a holding company backed by Bankamerica-Blair, and proposed an exchange of stock between NAT and North American. That would have given Keys a preponderance of the votes in NAT, which he did not have as things stood. But Boeing and Rentschler obtained a temporary court injunction to delay Keys' ploy, and by the time a hearing was scheduled on the matter, United had enough NAT stock and proxies to take NAT into the United family.

Meanwhile, Boeing and Rentschler had bought out Walter Varney, whose air mail route had been expanded to fly between Seattle and Salt Lake City, and shortly afterwards would purchase Vern Gorst's Pacific Air Transport, which flew between Seattle and Los Angeles, as well as Bill Stout's non-mail line, which had succeeded Ford's Detroit-Cleveland route. As the emerging airlines faced the era of expansion, United was already fat and sassy.

Clement Key's North American Aviation grew apace, although it eventually took a different turn.

Clement M. Keys (R), aviation empire builder. (Francis H. Dean)

Formed solely as a holding company, North American was soon backed by General Motors (which gained full control in 1933) and Hayden, Stone & Company, along with Bankamerica-Blair; it had Curtiss Aeroplane and Motor Company as its cornerstone. Other important properties soon acquired included Eastern Air Transport (New York-Atlanta at that time), Sperry Gyroscope, the Ford Instrument Company, Keystone Aircraft (bombers), Moth aircraft, Curtiss-Caproni, and New York Air Terminals, Inc. Robertson Aircraft, in St. Louis, and Walter Beech's Travel Air company would be added in mid-1929, but first, North American's airline was born as Transcontinental Air Transport (TAT).

Transcontinental Air Transport

TAT was unique in that it was a combination air and rail passenger service. Leaving New York at night via Pennsylvania Railroad pullmans, the passengers were transferred to Ford Trimotors that next morning at Columbus, Ohio. They flew to Waynoka, Oklahoma, then boarded a Santa Fe pullman for Clovis, New Mexico, where another Ford airliner waited to take them on to Los Angeles. The trip was comfortable and safe, but it was also expensive (16¢ per mile), and not much faster than a transcontinental train. TAT lost $2,750,000 during its 18 months of operation, but would be rescued by a forced merger with Western Air Express to become TWA—about which, more momentarily.

AVCO Formed

The third large aviation combine to appear at this time gathered its holdings together as the Aviation Corporation (AVCO). AVCO was incorporated in March 1929 with a working capital of $35 million, and its directors included Sherman Fairchild; three investment bankers; D.K.E. Bruce (son-in-law of Andrew Mellon); Robert Dollar, steamship magnate; Harry S. New, former postmaster general; and Gen. Mason Patrick, former chief of the U.S. Air Service. While $35 million may not sound too impressive these days, we should keep in mind that these were 1929 dollars—equal, perhaps, to ten times that amount today.

AVCO began by acquiring Embry-Riddle's operation over CAM-24, Chicago-Cincinnati. T.H. Embry and Paul Riddle had previously run a flying service in Cincinnati and were dealers for the new Fairchild monoplane built in Hagerstown, Maryland. Sherman Fairchild had entered the airplane manufacturing business because there was no airplane on the market that provided a suitable platform for the excellent aerial cameras he had perfected. Fairchild promoted AVCO with the help of the above-named fellow incorporators, and within a short time this new holding company controlled a number of companies, including its own subsidiary holding company, Colonial Airways Corporation, originally organized as Colonial Air Transport, which held CAM-1. AVCO then looked toward the South, where it found Southern Air Transport (SAT) with several of the essential mail contracts.

SAT could trace its roots back to Temple Bowen, a tough old bus operator whose Texas Air Transport flew the mail between Dallas/Ft. Worth and Galveston and San Antonio. Bowen sold out to A.P. Barrett's Southern Air Transport in 1928, and Barrett, a Tennessean who had gone to Texas with nothing and parlayed a charming manner and a politician's instincts into a natural gas supplier serving five states, then purchased Gulf Coast Airways, which flew between Atlanta and Houston by way

of New Orleans. It was at that point that AVCO negotiated an exchange of stock with SAT that gave AVCO controlling interest in these important southern routes—and Barrett a vice presidency in AVCO.

AVCO purchased other small operators, such as Interestate Air Lines (Chicago-Atlanta, CAM-30), and successfully bid on an air mail route in Alaska. Then it went after Universal Aviation Corporation.

Universal was backed by a group of St. Louis, Chicago, and Minneapolis bankers and, like the other aviation combines, was started during the halcyon days of the Lindbergh Boom when almost any aviation stock could find eager investors (the stock of Seaboard Air Lines experienced a sudden increase in value following the Lindbergh flight to Paris until it was discovered by investors to be an East Coast railroad).

Universal was built from Robertson Aircraft Corporation, which flew the mail between St. Louis and Chicago, a well-managed company that was well known because of Lindbergh's employment there prior to his epochal flight to Paris.

Universal successfully negotiated with the Post Office Department for the Cleveland-Louisville route, CAM-16, acquired some small flying services, and bought Tom E. Braniff's Braniff Air

Fokker F-32 had four P&W Hornets of 575 hp each, two tractors and two pushers. The F-32 had a span of 99 feet and seated 32 passengers. Ten were built for Western Air Express and Universal Air Lines. (Hudek Collection)

Stinson SM-1 Detroiter flown by Ruth Elder and George Haldeman attempted Atlantic flight five months after the Lindbergh flight to Paris. Elder and Haldeman were plucked from the ocean near the Azores by a passing ship. (Hudek Collection)

Lines, a passenger service at near bus fares flying between Kansas City and Dallas/Ft. Worth. (In 1930, Braniff and his elder brother would start another airline).

Late in 1929, Universal directors voted to accept an exchange of stock with AVCO that left AVCO with a 95 percent controlling interest in the Universal properties.

Meanwhile, AVCO was buying into every other aviation firm it could find, including E.L. Cord's Lycoming Motors and Stinson Aircraft Corporation.

Stinson 6000-B was a nine-place airliner flown by American Airways. Engines were 215-hp Lycomings. These craft were in service 1932-1936 inclusive. (American Air Lines)

Stinson Aircraft

Eddie Stinson built the first of his famous Detroiters in a Congress Street loft in Detroit and tested it on 25 January 1926 at Selfridge Field. It was a four-place cabin biplane with wheel brakes and electric starter. Eddie's financial backers, a group of Detroit industrialists, were impressed with the machine. An empty factory was obtained in nearby Northville, Michigan, and the Stinson Aircraft Corporation organized. The first production model of the Stinson biplane Detroiter, completed in August 1926, was sold to Reed Chambers' Florida Airways, CAM-10. The first Stinson monoplane appeared ten months later. By that time Eddie was wearing spats, smoking 25¢ cigars, and had 200 workers on his payroll.

American Airways Formed

At that time, AVCO organized American Airways and brought all of its subsidiary holding companies into American. Eventually, all the subsidiaries were dropped and AVCO ended up as the sole stockholder of American Airways (which would be renamed American Air Lines in 1934). That simplified the corporate structure considerably, but the airline itself was still a collection of disjointed routes, and it would fall to the new postmaster general, Walter F. Brown, acting under the powers given to him by the next amendment to the Kelly Bill, the McNary-Watres Act of 1930, to fill in the blanks, which would allow American Airways to become a major airline system.

All of the new aviation combines—indeed, the entire aircraft industry—anticipated continued prosperity as the Republicans maintained control in Washington with the 1928 elections, and although there were disquieting signals from Wall Street early in 1929, few paid heed. Significant money continued to be available to aviation enterprises, and the combines continued to expand.

Curtiss and Wright Merge

In August 1929, C.M. Keys engineered the merger of Curtiss Aeroplane and Motor with Wright Aeronautical Corporation to form Curtiss-Wright Aeronautical Corporation, a $200 million corporate marriage that brought 29 aviation stepchildren under the same roof, including Travel Air, acquired within days of the Curtiss and Wright vows. Curtiss-Wright, of course, was related by corporate marriage to North American Aviation.

Later, in July 1930, North American founded China Airways Federal Corporation to buy 45 percent of Chiang Kai-sheck's China National Aviation Corporation (CNAC). Pan Am would end up with that stock after the Democrats at last returned to the White House in 1933, but that is getting ahead of our story. (If you have concluded that Keys, Boeing, and Rentschler were wheeler-dealers, just wait until we examine the maneuverings of Juan Trippe as he built Pan Am.)

First, however, comes Walter Folger Brown, who was either a dictator who served the money interests in civil aviation or a dedicated public servant. That is a determination you will have to make for yourself.

REVIEW QUESTIONS:

1. Why can it be said that Lindbergh's flight was a catalytic event? Describe some of the provisions of the Kelly Bill. Why weren't the carriers anxious to carry passengers?

2. Identify some of the early CAM routes and the successful bidders. How did the Ford Motor Company become involved in aviation? Describe the formation of United Aircraft and Transport Corporation by Boeing and Rentschler. Who was Clement Keys? Name some of the companies under the North American holding company. Who were some of the founding directors of AVCO? Name some of the

companies which were acquired and came under its holding company umbrella.

3. How did the Stinson Aircraft Corporation get started? How was American Airways formed? Who engineered the merger of Curtiss Aeroplane and Motor with Wright Aeronautical Corporation?

Chapter 8

Czar of the Airways

OBJECTIVES: At the end of this chapter you should be able to:

☐ Discuss the importance of the McNary-Watres Act in shaping the early airline route structure.

☐ Summarize the purpose and results of the "Spoils Conferences."

☐ Describe how TWA and Delta were formed.

☐ Describe the fate of many smaller carriers such as Reed Airline and Century Air Lines.

☐ Explain how the competition between Ludington Line and Eastern Air Transport led to the air mail scandals of 1934.

America's domestic airline system was pieced together during a critical five-year period, 1928-1932 inclusive. Surrounded by controversy and charges of political favoritism, the routes were parceled out behind closed doors, nurtured by government subsidy, and directed by the postmaster general. No single person, before or since, has held such power over the nation's airways. The question is, did Walter Folger Brown wear a white hat or a black one?

McNary-Watres Act

Walter F. Brown was a Toledo attorney who had toiled faithfully in the Republican orchards for more than two decades when President-elect Herbert Hoover rewarded him with the portfolio of the U.S. Post Office Department. After taking office in March 1929, Postmaster General Brown spent months studying the air mail system and the state of commercial aviation in America. Then, in February 1930, he appeared before the House Committee on Post Office and Post Roads to urge passage of HR 11704, an amendment to the Kelly Bill popularly known as the McNary-Watres Act after its sponsors, Senator Charles McNary of Oregon, and Representative Laurence Watres of Pennsylvania. Actually, Brown himself was the author of this significant bit of legislation, with some input from William P. McCracken, a former assistant secretary of commerce who had initially administered the Air Commerce Act of 1926, and who was, by 1929, a lobbyist for airline interests.

Congress approved the McNary-Watres Act 29 April 1930, and the important provisions in the new law were: 1) Operators were to be paid for flying the mail according to space available for mail in their airplanes, which could be as much as $1.25 per mile for a Ford or Fokker Trimotor; 2) The

Walter Folger Brown, President Hoover's postmaster general, fostered legislation that gave him the power to build America's domestic airline system. He used that power ruthlessly. (U.S. Postal Service)

velopment of safer and more efficient machines, and as passenger revenues increased, mail payments could be decreased; eventually, the airlines would be self-supporting and would carry the mail at rates that would be below that of the postage represented.

Brown and the Congress were obviously right, because the contracts let in 1929 averaged $1.10 per mile; by 1933 the average was down to 54¢ per mile over a vastly expanded system. Then, on the brink of self-sufficiency, the whole structure would be pulled down by the Roosevelt Administration, as we shall see momentarily.

It is possible that the Republican lawmakers did not fully realize the extent of the power they were giving to the postmaster general with the McNary-Watres Act. The authority to extend or consolidate routes could be (and was!) broadly interpreted, as was the inclusion of "responsible" in the "lowest responsible bidder" provision. The requirement that a bidder have six months experience over a route of at least 250 miles effectively eliminated most small, poorly financed operators. Taken together, what these provisions really meant was that only the fat cats need apply. Postmaster General Brown meant to erect a great airline system, possessing the best available equipment and the most effective management. There wasn't much room in his plan for the little independents with limited resources. Brown had the muscle and he intended to use it.

Spoils Conferences

That became apparent just two weeks after passage of the McNary-Watres Act, when Brown called a series of meetings in Washington to divvy up the new air mail contracts (these meetings would later be called the "spoils conferences" by the Democrats). Brown made it clear to the invited operators (those regarded as "uncooperative" were not invited) that he intended to have three transcontinental routes and that each must be under a single management. United had the northern route and Brown was quite satisfied with it. The middle route would be established by the merger of TAT and Western Air Express, and American Airways

postmaster general could extend or consolidate routes "when in his judgment the public interest will be promoted thereby;" 3) Routes would be awarded to the lowest responsible bidder who had owned an airline operated on a daily schedule of at least 250 miles over a period of six months.

These provisions gave Brown almost absolute control over the airlines, and practically guaranteed profits to those who cooperated. The act offered the air mail contractors outright subsidies, and in that respect the primary intent of Congress and the Post Office Department seemed clear: Give the operators substantial incentive to acquire large multi-engine airplanes and develop passenger revenues. That, in turn, would promote the de-

In 1926, Harris "Pop" Hanshue's Western Air Express flew its profitable Los Angeles-Salt Lake City air mail route with half a dozen Liberty-powered Douglas M-2s. (TWA)

Pacific Air Transport, later absorbed by United, began flying the mail between Los Angeles and Seattle in September 1926, equipped with six Ryan M-1s. PAT's pilots included Lee Schoenhair, who later flew for Goodrich and would contract with Matty Laird for the famous Laird "Solution" racing plane, and Ralph Virden, who was fated to die while test-flying the Lockheed P-38. (Cassagneres Collection)

would have the southern route, because Brown would extend or consolidate where necessary to take American all the way to the West Coast without the threat of "outside" bidding. Just in case some troublesome bidder should crop up, Brown had a remedy for that, too. When the contracts were duly advertised for bidding, he inserted the provision that qualified bidders must have flown at night for six months over a route of not less than 250 miles. Since only the big carriers could meet that qualification, it was met with anguished cries of protest. Brown calmly pointed to the original air mail act, the Kelly Bill, which clearly stated that the postmaster general was empowered to "make such rules, regulations, and orders" as were necessary for the carrying out of provisions of that law.

The independents on the outside looking in were understandably angry. Brown's approach was unfair and counter to the basic tenets of free enterprise. But the major operators soon came to resent Brown almost as much as did the little guys who were squeezed out. The postmaster general

favored them because they had the means to build the system he envisioned. True, he saw to it that they made money, but along with the federal largess came total federal control, and Ringmaster Brown's fat cats obediently lined up on their designated perches as he cracked his mail-pay whip.

Two contributing factors that worked in Brown's behalf was the airlines' deep distrust for one another, and the fact that the nation was sinking into the Great Depression following the stock market crash in October 1929. But the central fact that none could ignore was that no airline could survive with the airplanes then available with passenger fares alone. The difference between profit and loss was an air mail contract. Therefore, the airline operators did things Brown's way or not at all.

TWA Formed

An early example of that was the forced merger of Western Air Express (WAE) and TAT. Pop Hanshue's WAE was one of the few lines that had

John K. "Jack" Northrop pioneered all-metal stressed-skin construction after leaving Lockheed (where he designed the wooden Lockheeds, beginning with the Vega), and his Northrop Alpha was purchased by Transcontinental and Western Air (TWA) and National Air Transport (NAT) in 1930. Forward cabin was configured for three to six passengers on most Alphas. (Don Dwiggins)

made money from the start. Flying CAM-4 between Los Angeles and Salt Lake City, WAE connected with United, and since so many people in the Los Angeles area had ties in the east, Hansue's mail loads were large. WAE netted about $1 million per year on this route. Then, in 1929, WAE inaugurated a passenger service, *sans* mail pay, between Los Angeles and Kansas City. Although the passenger line lost money, Hanshue kept it in operation because he believed that it would be the logical west half of the transcontinental middle route that was certain to come, and because he knew that the more direct route to the East Coast from Los Angeles would drain business from CAM-4.

TAT went all the way across the country from New York to Los Angeles, as previously mentioned, flying in daylight and transferring its passengers to trains at night. It was a big money loser, and Hanshue wanted no part of it. Brown liked TAT because it was well-financed and had good equipment and experienced management, it had an aura of permanency and responsibility about it, and it had a pioneering equity in the route every bit as valid as WAE's. Besides, Brown was unwilling to split a coast-to-coast route between two different managements. The fact that, under Brown's own rule, TAT was not a qualified bidder due to its lack of night flying experience was not a problem, the postmaster general pointed out, because, if the two lines merged, WAE would bring the necessary night flight experience to the new company.

Hanshue and his directors fought the merger, but in the end they had to capitulate. On 13 February 1931 Western Air Express and Transcontinental Air Transport exchanged stock on an equal basis and became Transcontinental & Western Air—TWA.

Hanshue was bitter, especially after TWA lost $1 million during its first year of operation. He blocked the purchase of Curtiss Condor airliners, which former TAT people favored due to their affiliation with Curtiss via North American. But TWA bought Fokker Trimotors instead, also due to TAT's affiliation with North American, because General Motors owned the American Fokker Company and was a major stockholder in North American.

SAFEway and Delta

The only bidder on the transcontinental south-

Oilman Erle Halliburton owned Southwest Air Fast Express (SAFEway), which operated Ford TriMotors in Missouri, Arkansas, Oklahoma, and Texas; was absorbed, after a flight, by American Air Lines, with Postmaster General Brown forcing the merger. (Burrell Tibbs)

ern route was AVCO's American Airways, although American did not get the route without challenge. Two men who thought they should have it were Erle Halliburton, an Oklahoman who operated Southwest Air Fast Express (SAFEway), and C.E. Woolman of Delta Air Service.

Halliburton made his money in oil (Halliburton Oil Well Cementing Process), and his passenger airline, which flew Ford Trimotors out of Tulsa into Texas, Kansas, and Missouri, was very close to the break-even point despite fares that were near those of the bus lines.

Woolman's Delta Air Service began as a cropdusting business in Louisiana in the early '20s, and his airline, started in 1925, flew between Birmingham and Dallas across the deep South.

Both Delta and SAFEway were excluded from the bidding by Brown's night flying requirement. Woolman sold out to American Airways just as Brown intended, but Halliburton chose to fight and was preparing to go to court when American bought him out for $1,400,000. SAFEway's hard assets totalled less than $800,000. Thereafter, Halliburton continued in his very successful oilfield business, although Woolman would return with another Delta airline after President Franklin Roosevelt's "New Deal" forced the airlines into a 180-degree turn in 1934.

By the spring of 1931, one could travel by air between all major American cities, as well as a great many lesser ones. United, TWA, and American offered daily schedules coast-to-coast. Eastern (affiliated with TWA through their North American parent) flew up and down the East Coast; United served the West Coast over the old Pacific Air Transport route, and also branched south at Chicago to fly into Texas. Northwest, meanwhile, was receiving route extensions from the postmaster general to take it across the northern states toward Seattle as fast as it could digest them. Although the independents should have gotten the word by then, they nevertheless continued to proliferate, most seeking to establish pioneer equities over routes between smaller towns, hoping for a mail contract. Most were sincere if unrealistic, proceeding on faith and belief in fair play, honest effort, and the free enterprise system. Sad to say, most of them fared poorly. Others, who were less constrained by such traditional values and dared buck the system, managed to make something out of nothing.

Reed Airline

An example of the former, and typical of dozens of other small independents, was Joe Roy Reed. Reed was an honorable man who seemed perpetually in good humor. He had learned to fly during WWI at Ft. Sill's Henry Post Army Airfield, barnstormed in the early '20s, and returned to active duty with the Air Corps Reserve in the late '20s, flying Douglas O-2Hs with the 320th Observation Squadron at Post Field. Reed, like many of his contemporaries, foresaw the ultimate role of the airplane as a commercial vehicle and, at some point while serving as an Army aviator, acquired his airline dream. In 1929, he left the Air Corps to pursue his dream.

Reed had already selected his route. His southern terminus would be Wichita Falls, a rich north-Texas city of 50,000; he operated from there to Lawton, Oklahoma, 40 miles northward, which could only boast of some 20,000 people (but was adjacent to Fort Sill and potential military business), then 85 miles to Oklahoma City, where he would connect with United's Chicago-Ft. Worth run and, finally, 95 miles to Ponca City, his northern terminus.

The only weak point in Reed's planned route was the lack of facilities at Lawton. Lawton had no airport, and apparently no suspicion that it needed one. Therefore, Reed began a campaign to convince those worthy citizens that they should move to share the blessings of the air age. He spoke before school assemblies, women's clubs, the chamber of commerce and, eventually, the city council. It took almost a year, but he aroused sufficient interest to provoke a bond issue, approved by the voters in the amount of $35,000, for the construction of a municipal airport.

Reed took a lease on the new Lawton airport and, with savings in hand—plus a frightening note at the bank—bought a Spartan C-3 biplane for charter and instruction and began searching for a

Typical of America's small-town airports of the early '30s was the sod field at Lawton, Oklahoma, home base for Reed Airlines. Author Joe Christy's first flying lessons were received in the Spartan C-3 at right. Ryan Brougham at left.

secondhand airliner that possessed a price tag to match his limited working capital. His first ad in the local paper read: "Learn to Fly! Pilots make big money! Complete flying course $250! Rides $2!"

The new airport was dedicated on Labor Day 1930, and Reed worked through the fall getting his base of operations set up and more or less self-supporting. He was forced to cut the price of his "complete flying course" to $175, but at the beginning of 1931 he had eight students, some charter business, and had hired a mechanic from the local Pontiac garage who apparently encountered no problems in transferring his bolt-busting talents from automobiles to airplanes.

In the meantime, Reed had located his airliner, a six-place Travel Air 6000B monoplane owned by the Wadlow Brothers Flying Service in Wichita, Kansas. It had sold new for $13,500. The Wadlows, feeling the pinch of the depression, were willing to sell it for $7,500, the amount they had paid Central Air Lines for it a few months earlier. (That was one of at least three "Centrals." It was established in 1928 and flew between Wichita and Tulsa for a time. Another, established in 1930, flew a Detroit-Washington route and merged with Pennsylvania

Airlines in 1936 to form Pennsylvania Central Air Lines; it was renamed Capital Air Lines in April 1948, and absorbed by United 1 June 1961. The third began service in November 1949, flying between Dallas/Ft. Worth and Wichita, and was merged with Frontier Air Lines 1 October 1967.)

Central had christened the Travel Air *Romancer* because, in late February 1929, Charles Lindbergh had borrowed it for a flight to Mexico City and a visit with his fiancée, Anne Morrow, whose father was ambassador to Mexico (the same Dwight Morrow whose 1925 Morrow Board repudiated Billy Mitchell's position on U.S. airpower). There, the Travel Air lost a wheel on takeoff with Miss Morrow aboard. The famed flier stacked cushions around her and landed in the thin air of Valbuena Airport, flipping upside down, though leaving Anne uninjured. This incident, coming just a few days after public disclosure of the Lindbergh-Morrow engagement—surely the most extensively reported romance of the roaring '20s—bathed the orange-and-green Travel Air in publicity and pixie dust, making it a symbol of the ideal romance, with adventure in the clouds thrown in for good measure, that an adoring public could vicariously share with

The six-passenger Travel Air 6000B *Romancer* and airline owner and chief pilot Joe R. Reed (R) with speed flyer Frank Hawks.

the Lone Eagle and his mate.

Therefore, when Lindbergh offered to buy the slightly damaged Travel Air from Central, those officials would not hear of it. The airplane was easily fixed good as new—in fact, somewhat *better* than new, as any public relations man would testify.

The immediate result was some 50-odd airborne marriages in the *Romancer* that, added to its regular airline runs between Wichita and Tulsa, must have given it a utilization rate that would warm the heart of any airline president. But Central fell upon evil times with the deepening depression, and the enchanted Travel Air felt a new hand on her control wheel—the hand of a man who appreciated her for herself rather than for her past associations.

"She was a sweetheart to fly," Reed later recalled. "She had an indicated cruise of 95 mph, which was respectable enough then, and a short-field landing and takeoff performance that would be respectable now. She was licensed for a pilot and five passengers, along with 30 pounds of baggage for each, but if six or seven fares showed up, it didn't strain her any to add a couple of kitchen chairs in the aisle in order to accommodate everyone."

In 1931 there was no legal barrier to the formation of an airline. All it took was a little money and a lot of faith. And in the middle of the Great Depression there was little question concerning the fares to be charged—it was merely a matter of competing with the bus lines. Reed's first published rate table listed ticket prices very near those of the bus lines.

When asked about federal regulation, Reed chuckled. "That was before the time of the FAA, or even the CAA, although the Department of Commerce had been issuing pilot's licenses since 1926.

I recall that they did make a rule requiring airline pilots to pass an instrument flying test, which I did, but nothing was ever said to me about having a blind panel in the airliner, which I did not have."

Reed Airline began operations 1 September 1931 and the *Romancer* averaged four passengers per flight during the first month. That was not solely due to low fares, but at least in part to Reed's tireless huckstering—and perhaps because he would cheerfully bend a schedule to make a paying customer happy. For example, a lady with two preteen children wanted to go to grandmother's farm for a visit. Grandma lived 25 miles west of Oklahoma City so the Lawton-Oklahoma City flight that morning deviated from its normal route. Reed obligingly put the *Romancer* down in grandma's south forty, then, with a wide grin to his other paying customers, took off and continued to the capitol city. (That incident is recorded from firsthand knowledge; I was one of the kids.)

Early in 1932, Reed added another Travel Air 6000, hired young Joel Pitts for $65 per month plus expenses to fly it, and began pressing the Post Office Department for an air mail contract.

At the end of his first year, having met 94 percent of his schedules, Reed noted a small but steady increase in boardings and optimistically purchased a third airliner, a sesquiwing Buhl Air Sedan

Travel Air 6000s under construction at Walter Beech's Travel Air plant in Wichita. Travel Air biplanes in background. (Beech Aircraft Corporation)

In addition to two Travel Air 6000s, Reed Airlines also operated a 300-hp sesquiwing Buhl Air Sedan. The Buhl was built in Marysville, Michigan. The company's chief pilot, Lou Meister is at right. (Charles W. Meyers Collection)

(sesquiwings were of biplane configuration, but the lower wings were far smaller than the upper ones) and hired another pilot. Throughout 1932 and 1933, during which time the depression imposed its hungriest days on the southern Plains, Reed Airline met its schedules and almost broke even financially, while Reed made several pilgrimages to Washington pushing for the air mail contract that would, in the end, determine the fate of his bold venture.

In retrospect, it is easy to see that Reed Airline never had a chance. But Reed held on by slashing his rates 20 percent, reduced the price of his solo flying course at his home field to $120, and returned to Washington in March 1934 to make a final attempt at securing a mail contract. He was denied.

Reed Airline met its last schedule on 1 April 1934. Reed sold his airplanes to the Charles A. Babb aircraft brokerage firm in Glendale, Califor-

nia, and the *Romancer* went to Central America where it faded into oblivion.

Joe Reed traveled a lot late in life (he died in 1982), but the young captains of Metro Air Lines' Convairs never knew why the white-haired gentleman with the wide smile always waved at them as he boarded the airplane at Lawton.

Airway Scrooges

E.L. Cord was a different kind of man. And while it is not easy today to characterize him (even *Time* magazines of the '20s and '30s, a usually productive source for research into that lusty era, ignored Cord), it is safe to conclude that Cord was more than a match for the likes of C.M. Keys or even Walter F. Brown.

Cord had risen from car salesman to head of the Auburn Automobile company (which should tell us something) when he detected opportunity in the

Stinson 6000B of E.L. Cord's Century Air Lines. Cord cut fares and suffered a pilot's strike in an unsuccessful bid to obtain an air mail contract, but he ended up in control of American Air Lines. (Edward Peck)

airline business and, in 1931, started two small passenger lines, Century Air Lines and Century Pacific Lines, each of which paralleled high-density routes flown by American Airways out of Chicago and San Diego.

It is not clear whether Cord, without mail contracts, expected to successfully compete with the big AVCO line, or whether he planned from the beginning to make such a nuisance of himself that American would be forced to buy out his Century lines at an inflated price. The latter seems more likely, because Cord not only undercut American's rates but offered to fly the mail over American's routes for approximately half the amount that American got for it. Cord maintained that American—and most other airlines—were poorly managed and, with proper cost controls, could profitably operate with far less money from the Post Office Department. As if to underscore his position, Cord forced a strike by his own pilots late in 1931 when he decided that the $7200 per year average pay for captains—fostered by Tex Behncke's infant Airline Pilot's Association (AFL-sponsored)—was ridiculous at a time when plenty of qualified pilots were looking for jobs.

It wasn't Cord's low rates or his fight with the union that set the industry on edge, but his claim that the airlines were being grossly overpaid for fly-

ing the mail tended to give the operators a nervous twitch—especially American, because it was receiving 70 percent of its revenues from mail contracts,

Interior of the Stinson 6000 TriMotor airliner. (Joseph P. Juptner)

141

or about one-third of all air mail appropriations for transporting approximately 10 percent of the mail.

The same charges had been made before by other independents, but Cord was a credible threat because, whether or not he was bluffing, he apparently had the resources to back up his low bid and, although the operators were assured by the postmaster general that Cord had no chance at a mail contract, that could change with a new administration in Washington. So American decided the best way to silence Cord was to buy his airlines and make him an AVCO stockholder.

Cord's price was 140,000 shares of American Airways, and that was enough to make him a director of AVCO. Shortly afterwards, when other AVCO directors sought to buy into the Curtiss-Keys combine—which is to say, North American Aviation—Cord saw that such a deal would weaken his position at AVCO, successfully fought the transaction, and emerged in control of AVCO, holding 19 percent of American Airways stock.

Cord would remain a strong and unsettling influence in the industry until after the "air mail scandals" of 1934; then, apparently to avoid answering some embarrassing questions posed by the Securi-ties and Exchange Commission, he fled to England.

Another independent, very much like Cord's Century lines, was Ludington Line, which flew between New York and Washington from September 1930 until February 1933, when it was forced to sell out to Eastern Air Transport. The Ludington brothers got their investment back, and that was all. But Ludington Lines was destined to greatly—if indirectly—influence the future of the entire industry.

Ludington actually showed a small profit flying passengers. Largely financed by the socially prominent Charles and Nicholas Ludington of Philadelphia, and sharply managed by Gene Vidal (formerly with TAT and another Ivy League), Ludington Lines instituted "Every Hour on the Hour" service over a short, high-density route, offering rates close to those of the railroads. Every economy was utilized: The equipment was Stinson Trimotors that, at $18,000 each, cost about half as much as Ford Trimotors. Ludington Captains flew alone, handled baggage, taxied on one engine, and cruised on automobile gasoline in flight.

Ludington operating costs were therefore approximately 35¢ per mile, an amount usually

Ludington Lines employed low-cost ($18,000) Stinson Model 6000 TriMotors, and effected every possible economy of operation to fly "every hour, on the hour" between New York and Washington, but the Lundingtons were forced to sell to Eastern when denied a mail contract by Postmaster General Brown. (Gerald Balzer)

equalled or exceeded by passengers' fares alone; whatever Ludington could get for flying the mail would have been pure profit.

But Eastern Air Transport was awarded the mail contract between New York and the nation's capitol at 89¢ per mile, and when a Ludington official bitterly complained to a Washington newspaper reporter about Eastern's contract, awarded despite Ludington's bid of 25¢ per mile, that enterprising young reporter, one Fulton Lewis, Jr., sensed a good story and began digging into Post Office Department records.

The deeper Lewis dug, the more excited he became. He found abundant evidence that Ludington's treatment at the hands of the postmaster general was typical of that accorded to the small independents. Lewis learned of the meetings between Brown and the selected airline executives when the important routes were planned soon after passage of the McNary-Watres Act, and he discovered how thousands of miles of the air mail routes had been parceled out to the big combines by way of the "route extension and consolidation" clause, immune from any threat by outside bidders.

It has been suggested that since reporter Lewis was the son-in-law of Postmaster General Brown's chief political rival, Lewis' motives in pursuing the air mail story were less than pure. That is unfair to Lewis and irrelevant to this account. True, he developed but one side of the story—a common fault in news reporting, then and now—but the media's never-ending search for misconduct in government is a valuable service to the nation, whatever prompts it.

Oddly, Lewis' boss, publisher William Randolph Hearst, refused to allow publication of Lewis' scoop, and whatever Hearst's motive, his repression of a story so pertinent to the public interest would seem to be at least as immoral as Postmaster General Brown's alleged misdeeds.

Although Lewis was denied the satisfaction of breaking the story of the "air mail scandals," his material was the basis for the inquisition visited upon the industry after the Democrats returned to office in 1933.

REVIEW QUESTIONS:

1. What was the purpose of the McNary-Watres Act of 1930? List some of its important provisions. Why did Postmaster Brown call a series of meetings with airline executives shortly after passage of the act? Why did it become known as the "Spoils Conferences"?

2. How was TWA formed? Why did Harris Hanshue fight the merger? Why were SAFEway and Delta excluded from bidding on the transcontinental southern route?

3. Describe the plight of such airlines as Reed and Century. How did the bidding for the New York to Washington, DC air mail route between Ludington Line and Eastern Air Transport lead to the air mail scandals of 1934.

Chapter 9

Glass Houses

OBJECTIVES: At the end of this chapter you should be able to:

☐ Describe the purpose and political implications of the Black Committee.

☐ Summarize Walter F. Brown's testimony and response to the Ludington-Eastern Air Transport affair.

☐ Explain why the Army was ordered to fly the mail and their experience from February to May 1934.

☐ Define the purpose of the Air Mail Act of 1934 (Black-McKellar Bill) and the Civil Aeronautics Authority Act of 1938.

☐ Describe how Pan Am was formed and how Juan Tripp was able to obtain the Key West to Havana route.

☐ Discuss some of the problems faced by Pan Am in developing service into Central and South America.

☐ Describe the postwar competitive environment for international routes.

The day of reckoning for W.F. Brown and his favored airline operators was poorly managed by their prosecutors. Nevertheless, the domestic airlines were severely punished.

Meanwhile, a U.S. overseas airline, enjoying an even greater degree of federal favoritism, along with generous subsidies, continued to grow. Justice, if that is what it was, could wait.

New Deal or Raw Deal?

The Special Committee on Investigation of the Air Mail and Ocean Mail Contracts, popularly called the "Black Committee" after its chairman and chief inquisitor, Senator Hugo L. Black, was authorized by the Senate a month before President-elect Franklin D. Roosevelt took power with his "New Deal" in March 1933.

Senator Black was an Alabama Democrat with a mail-order law degree. At age 47 he was unprepossessing in appearance, with sandy, thinning hair, a folksy manner, and a dry wit. He was an economic liberal and a social conservative, an ambivalence endemic to southern politics. He was a small man with a large ambition, and he would be appointed to the Supreme Court by FDR in 1937, but when his committee began its hearings in 1933, Black was little known outside Alabama. The air mail scandals—real or manufactured—would make him a national figure.

The Black Committee was made up of two Republicans and three Democrats. The former were White of Maine and Austin of Vermont. The Democrats, in addition to Black, were King of Utah and Pat McCarran of Nevada (later, McCarran's conduct in the Senate as a tireless crusader for Pan Am's monopoly on overseas routes would leave *his* ethics subject to question). However, when this worthy body began taking testimony later in September 1933, in Room 312 of the Old Senate Office Building, it was immediately apparent that Hugo Black was to be the star of the show.

There were, of course, plenty of disgruntled independents in—or formerly in—the airline industry to ensure that the Black Committee became acquainted with the material gathered by reporter Fulton Lewis, Jr.

The Black Committee pecked at the ocean mail mess (it was an old story and strictly ho-hum stuff to news reporters) in a desultory manner, marking time while the goings-on in the room next door grabbed the headlines. Black was an accomplished politician and had no intention of allowing other newsworthy events to detract from his performance. Next door, the Senate Banking and Currency Committee was, in effect, putting America's private banking institutions on trial for whatever blame could be charged to them for the 1929 market crash and the ensuing worldwide depression. Since the witnesses called to testify before that committee included such famous names as J.P. Morgan and the partners in Morgan's investment/banking empire (among Morgan's partners was Dwight Morrow, Charles Lindbergh's father-in-law), all of the news reporters were next door.

But the Senate's banking probe eventually died of malnutrition and, in October, Black was ready to raise the curtain on his exposé of the former postmaster general and his airline cronies.

Now, in justice to Black (no pun intended), we should concede that the Democrats had been out

of office for 12 long years, and were understandably anxious to discredit the policies and programs of the Republicans. Black smelled thievery and conspiracy in the air mail program and, in the long tradition of old-fashioned, gallus-snappin' politics, he saw the opportunity to right some grievous wrongs, save some taxpayers' money, and make a great deal of political hay in the process.

Therefore, even today it's not easy to decide whether or not the New Dealers acted in good faith, or at what point the good faith degraded into simple demagoguery—or a stubborn determination to save face at whatever cost.

True, there was undoubtedly plenty of thievery and political favoritism to be uncovered in the previous Republican administrations had the Democrats looked for it in the right places, but they seem to have seized upon the air mail question prematurely, and made it into a media event, before it became evident that there was another side to the story. The testimony before the Black Committee did indeed confirm the facts gathered by reporter Lewis. However, it soon became clear that the airline operators—big and small alike—had simply followed the rules set down by Walter. F. Brown.

As for Brown himself, he denied nothing. His testimony made it equally clear that he was determined to give the American People the greatest air carrier network in the world, and that could not be done by awarding air mail contracts to small independents who merely wanted to fly the mail over hundreds of short routes and, for the most part, were not interested in developing passenger services. Such a policy would indeed be a waste of the taxpayers' money. As for Ludington, it was merely skimming cream from a short, high-density route. If Ludington had to provide service comparable to that of EAT over great distances, its costs would match EAT's 70¢ per mile. EAT was simply the more responsible bidder, and was making a significant contribution to the overall airway network. It required money—lots of money—to build the stable systems that covered the nation, and therefore Brown dealt with the companies that had plenty of capital, although he had often been less than gen-

The Curtiss T-32 Condor, fitted with a pair of Wright Cyclones, seated 12-15 passengers, and served both American and Eastern from mid-1933 through 1936. Brown favored the well-financed lines that were willing to promote passenger service. (American Air Lines)

tle with them. He forced the major lines to accept route extensions when he considered those extensions to be in the public interest.

Yes, he got rid of independents who appeared to intend to speculate with a mail contract. He had been ruthless and his enemies were legion. And he was completely unrepentant. As one aviation reporter put it, "About all that can be said in Brown's favor is that he has given the United States a domestic airways system second to none; and there is not a shred of evidence that Brown himself has made anything from it except a lot of enemies."

So the Black Committee established that Brown had been a dictator. No formal charges were brought against him because he had apparently acted within the law. However, President Roosevelt, acting on the advice of Attorney General Homer Cummings, announced on 9 February 1934 that all air mail contracts would be cancelled on the 19th. He told reporters that the airways system had been mapped out in a series of "spoils conferences"

attended by Walter F. Brown and a handful of his favored airline operators, that small operators were denied the chance to bid on air mail routes, and that some airlines had been grossly overpaid for carrying the mail.

The Army Flies the Mail

Then Roosevelt called in Gen. Benjamin Foulois, chief of the impoverished Army Air Corps, and asked if the Army could fly the mail. Foulois, of course, had no choice but to reply in the affirmative, but he knew full well that the Air Corps had neither the airplanes nor trained pilots to take over scheduled all-weather flying.

The Air Corps began flying the mail on 19 February. Although Roosevelt's postmaster general, James Farley, agreed that only 9000 miles of the 27,000-mile system would be served and no passengers carried, the Army faced an impossible task. With only 10 days' preparation, airplanes with few instruments (some even lacked compasses), and non-instrument pilots, the attempt was made during the worst weather of the year. At the end of a week, five pilots were dead and six critically injured. And that was just the beginning.

By the second week in March, the mounting toll of accidents appalled the nation and President Roosevelt began looking for a way out. On 10 March he announced that the air mail would be returned to the airlines as soon as possible.

A total of 12 Army fliers died before the mail could be handed back to the airlines, and had the air carriers actually been guilty of collusion, that was the time to get together for their mutual good. But they were so anxious to get back their mail pay, and so great was their distrust of one another, all submitted very low bids for their former routes, confident that fair adjustments could be negotiated later.

Jim Farley piously pointed to these bids as proof that the airlines had been overpaid, as the new administration had said all along.

But no one was listening to Farley at that point. The press and the public's reaction to the deaths of the Army fliers, as the result of what many believed to be a political witch hunt, overshadowed any culpability that may have otherwise been borne by Brown and the airlines.

The New Dealers obviously felt that they should not be the subject of such calumny since their intentions were pure. More than ever, they had to insist that the airlines were guilty as charged, and then fix an appropriate punishment.

The "Rascals" Are Punished

The extent to which the New Dealers were merely trying to save face with their continuing vendetta against the airlines, or whatever the measure of their belief that Brown and the major operators had conspired to loot the U.S. Treasury, is impossible to determine. It appears that Senator Black never wavered in his hard-nosed position, and was willing to destroy the whole airline system that had been built during the Coolidge and Hoover Administrations. But President Roosevelt, while agreeing that the airline rascals should be made to suffer, was unwilling to see the system completely

The Curtiss O-39 observation plane was typical of the several types pressed into service to fly the mail when FDR cancelled all air mail contracts in 1934. Lt. Otto Wienecke died in an O-39 approaching Cleveland in a snowstorm. (Francis H. Dean)

dismantled. Therefore, Postmaster General Farley's job was to get the system back in operation with a New Deal label on it, and with substantial penalties to the semi-cartels that owned the big airlines.

Farley managed that by decreeing that no airline which had been represented at the 1933 spoils conferences would be given a mail contract, and that the major air mail routes would be awarded only to bidders possessing multi-engine aircraft. That is why American Airways suddenly became "American Air Lines;" Northwest made a similar change; EAT became "Eastern Air Lines," while TWA, a bit bolder, simply added "Inc." to its name, and United Air Lines remained unchanged because its original mail contract had been obtained in the name of Boeing Air Transport. The multi-engine provision kept most of the independents from bidding on the major routes (shades of W.F. Brown!).

Some of the more responsible independents were admitted to the fold. Tom Braniff was back,

Cowboy humorist Will Rogers, who poked fun at Democrats and Republicans alike, was a firm supporter of the airlines and criticized the New Dealers' handling of the "Air Mail Scandals." The Ford TriMotor in background belonged to Maddux Air Lines, a West Coast operation that merged with TAT before the shotgun wedding of TAT and WAE, which produced TWA.

The nation's press blamed President Roosevelt and his postmaster general, James Farley, for the deaths of the Army fliers. This example appeared in *Aero Digest* magazine. (*Aero Digest*)

and was awarded United's route from Chicago to Texas; C.E. Woolman squeezed through Farley's door to put Delta back in business in the South.

Meanwhile, new regulations were drawn to punish the industry. These were contained in a bill written by Senator Black and the chairman of the Senate Post Office Committee, Democrat Kenneth McKellar of Tennessee. The Black-McKellar Bill (Air Mail Act of 1934), with the President's endorsement, sailed through Congress 12 June 1934, a month after the mail had been returned to the airlines. This legislation repealed all antecedent laws and left the air carriers subject to control by three federal bodies. Air mail contracts, routes, and schedules would be determined by the Post Office Department; the fixing of rates and air mail payments fell to the Interstate Commerce Commission, while the Bureau of Air Commerce would continue regulation of the airways and the licensing of pilots and aircraft.

The new law extended the temporary—and financially unsound—contracts signed when the mail was returned to the airlines following the cancellations, and limited the system to its existing routes. All airlines were required to separate themselves from manufacturing affiliates, and all routes were to be rebid each year.

All of the major airlines operated at a loss. United's first quarter deficit was $852,000, a crippling sum in 1934 dollars. TWA and Eastern, then owned by North American Aviation, lost $405,000 between them during the same period. American was able to cut its losses by reducing schedules. But all could look to the future with little hope. Long-range planning was impossible as long as the routes went up for grabs each year, while separation from manufacturing affiliates meant not only large auditing and legal fees, but reduced capitalization at a time when airline stocks were down to a fraction of their pre-cancellation values (United Air Lines stock dropped from 35 to 14; North American, listed at 8 just prior to the cancellation, dropped

to 2 5/8, while AVCO plunged from 10 to 4 during the same period). It was a bad time for the air carriers to be cut off from their solvent parent combines.

There were a few glimmers of hope during the next four years. New airliners appeared—the Douglas DC-2 and DC-3—that were so efficient they promised profits on passenger traffic alone. Another was found in the small print of the Black-McKellar Bill—a clause that empowered the President to appoint a Federal Aviation Commission to recommend future legislation. It was this latter hope, transformed into reality, that produced the Civil Aeronautics Act of 1938, which at last brought sanity and stability to civil aviation in the United States.

In 1935, the 23 scheduled airlines that made up the domestic system owned 459 airliners with a total value of $12.5 million. They employed 652 of the 736 pilots holding an Air Transport Rating. Department of Commerce records also reveal that the airlines employed 335 copilots and 212 "hostesses and stewards," which roughly suggests how many of the 459 airliners were multi-engined. This source lists 679,000 passengers carried in 1935, at an average rate of 5.7¢ per mile. Total air

A low cost ($37,500) airliner for the short-haul air carrier of the mid-'30s was the Stinson Model A, powered with three Lycoming R-680 engines of 260 hp each. The Model A carried eight passengers and a crew of one. American and Delta flew Model As, as did Central.

carrier employment was 8,333.

This tiny industry, less than 10 years in existence, beset by political shenanigans and economic impossibilities, nevertheless would prevail. It would manage to do so for another three years before Senator Pat McCarran, allied with Representative Clarence Lea, gained presidential approval of what was to become known as the Civil Aeronautics Act of 1938—legislation that was pronounced "fair and sound" by the Airline Pilots' Association, and which at last loosened the industry's crippling bonds.

THE CAA ACT OF 1938

The new law, which established the Civil Aeronautics Authority (CAA), authorized the President to pick its administrator with the approval of the Senate. The remaining members would also be presidential appointees, but during their six-year terms could not be dismissed except for cause.

In practice, this worked well, and made for a reasonably autonomous authority because the Supreme Court had previously held that federal regulatory bodies were beyond the overt control of the President.

This board had plenty of power. It formulated policy and determined rates. Its decisions were law with regard to civil aviation. Left to the postmaster general was his time-honored right to enforce rules and regulations for transporting mail and determining schedules for mail transporters, but the amounts paid to the airlines for carrying the mail were set by the CAA.

The CAA took over the aviation property and personnel of the Post Office Department, the Interstate Commerce Commission, and the Bureau of Air Commerce on 22 August 1938, and established an Air Carrier Economic Regulation Division to control the airlines. This division immediately moved to protect the established air carriers by decreeing that only those lines to which it issued "Certificates of Convenience and Necessity" would be allowed to operate scheduled air services, a rule that would remain in effect until the industry was

Following two record-breaking round-the-world flights in 1931 and 1933, former barnstormer Wiley Post went on to explore the problems of high-altitude flight and the design/test of pressure suits. (Rand Corporation)

Pan Am's first airliners were three Fokker TriMotors, two F-7s (above) and a C-2. As with the early Fords, pilots remained in open cockpits in the F-7s. Engines were Wright J-5s. Scheduled passenger service between Key West and Havana began in January 1928. (Pan Am)

deregulated 40 years later. Operators could not open new routes or abandon existing ones without CAA approval, and it abolished the contract air mail system in favor of negotiated rates. It was a remarkably good law, and it served the best interests of the airlines, general aviation, and the public.

In 1940, Roosevelt forced reorganization of the CAA and created the Civil Aeronautics Board (CAB) to regulate the airlines and investigate air accidents. The CAB was essentially independent, but the CAA was returned to the Department of Commerce. No one liked it that way except the President, who never explained why he demanded such action from the Congress (the Congresses of the Roosevelt era normally acted as FDR wished); however in practice, the regulation of civil aviation seemed little affected by the change, and the CAB would survive for more than 40 years under seven subsequent Presidents.

Concurrent with development of the U.S. domestic airline system was the extension of American wings to foreign shores, and one airline was destined—indeed, *chosen*—to fly the oceans: Pan American Airways.

Pan Am Formed

Juan Terry Trippe built Pan Am with in-

fluence, money, ruthlessness, and ability. He regarded competition as wasteful, and "robber baron" was just one of the more printable sobriquets that were used by his contemporaries to describe him.

Trippe was 28 years old when he started Pan Am in 1927. He had the proper requisites for empire-building. Born to wealth, educated in the best schools, and possessing as friends other young men of influential families, Trippe was assured of a hearing before those holding both financial and political power. He made the most of it.

Trippe had learned to fly in the Navy during WWI, and gained some experience between 1923 and 1925 operating, with a surplus Navy airplane, "Long Island Airways," a charter service. That part-time venture expired quickly and Trippe joined Colonial Airways as a minor executive. He left Colonial when it began scheduled service in 1926 as CAM-1, worked briefly for the banking firm of Lee Higginson & Company, and tried to decide whether or not he should accept the security (and, presumably, the boredom) of a position in his family's business, Trippe & Company, Brokers and Investment Bankers.

With aviation in his blood and avarice in his heart, the decision was not a difficult one. Juan Trippe inhaled deeply of the roseate atmosphere that bathed all things aeronautic following Lindbergh's flight to Paris and saw opportunity. It was an opportunity reserved for those who could think big, and one must credit Juan with that: He could think big.

He established that when he out maneuvered two other airlines to obtain a mail contract for a route between Key West, Florida, and Havana, Cuba. That 90-mile stretch held little value in itself, but as one of only two gateways to the Caribbean and Latin America, its potential was tremendous.

Trippe's company, entirely on paper when he submitted his bid to Postmaster General New, was the Aviation Corporation of the Americas (not to be confused with AVCO), and his rivals were Florida Airways and Pan American, Inc.

Florida Airways, organized by John Harding and war aces Eddie Rickenbacker and Reed Chambers, wanted to extend its Atlanta-Jacksonville run, CAM-10, through Miami and thence to Havana.

Pan American, Incorporated, was originally formed by Air Corps Major H.H. "Hap" Arnold (later, general, and chief of the U.S. Army Air Forces), and John K. Montgomery, a former Navy pilot, after Arnold became alarmed at the expansion plans of the German airline, SCADTA, based in Columbia, which proposed service to Panama. Arnold decided to remain in the Air Corps for patriotic reasons after the Billy Mitchell court martial, and Montgomery was joined by G. Grant Mason. Their major backer was Lewis Pierson of the Irving Trust Company.

Pan American, Inc., seemed in a favored position to gain a mail contract for the Florida-Havana route because Mason had obtained exclusive landing rights in Cuba from Dictator Gerado Machado. However, it appears that Trippe may have had his own private spoils conference with the postmaster general, because he went to Cuba and somehow convinced Machado that the dictator should tear up his agreement with Pan American, Inc., and replace it with one granting Trippe's company exclusive landing rights in Cuba.

Thus armed, Trippe won the air mail contract at the maximum rate allowed under the law. He purchased, at bargain prices, both Pan American, Inc., and Florida Airways, renamed his company Pan American Airways, and began scheduled operations 28 October 1927 when Capt. Hugh Wells

Sikorsky S-38 amphibians carried eight passengers (as did the Fokkers); entered service with Pam Am late in 1928. Engines were 420-hp Wasps. (Pan Am)

The 13-passenger Ford 5-AT-B began flying Pan Am's Mexico and Central American routes in March, 1929. Pan Am paid $55,000 each for these Wasp-powered craft. (Pan Am)

took off from Key West with a handful of mail in the Fokker TriMotor NC-53. Passenger service to Havana began the following January.

The Chosen Instrument

From this 90-mile base route, Trippe reached out to the Dominican Republic and, in July 1928, gobbled up West Indian Aerial Express, which had been in operation just seven months, flying between Haiti and Puerto Rico. WIAE investors retrieved some of their money because the postmaster general insisted upon it. The Post Office Department and the State Department agreed with Trippe very early that Pan Am should be the United States' "chosen instrument" to carry the American flag on overseas air routes. Perhaps conscience-stricken, the postmaster general demanded that Pan Am at least purchase the equipment of the operators destroyed along the way.

In January 1929, Pan Am acquired control of Compania Mexicana de Aviacion, the Mexican airline that had been in operation since 1924, and that gave Trippe a route from Brownsville, at the tip of Texas, along the Gulf of Mexico through Guatemala to Nicaragua. In September, service was extended through the Canal Zone to Barranquilla, Colombia, then continued eastward via Caracas to

Port of Spain, Trinidad, where the system turned back northward to complete its circle of the Caribbean at San Juan, Puerto Rico. That locked up for Pan Am the two primary air routes to South America from the U.S., with one approach through Texas and Central America, the other by way of Florida and the Antilles. Meanwhile, Miami replaced Key West as the Florida terminus, and America's overseas flag carrier began measuring the distances to Buenos Aires and Santiago, where some very formidable competition was firmly entrenched.

Anticipating continued expansion, Trippe sent Pan Am representatives throughout Latin America to obtain landing and operating rights. This involved State Department people, because a simple, unilateral agreement was seldom enough. Colombia, which already had a pretty good German-operated airline (and had not forgotten Teddy Roosevelt's perfidy in wrestling away Colombian territory for the Panama Canal), was particularly difficult, and bargained so stubbornly that she ended up with a bilateral agreement that gave that small nation aerial access to the entire U.S. coastline—Atlantic, Pacific, and Gulf of Mexico. That was considered meaningless by American diplomats at the time, because everyone knew that such little countries could not operate an international airline. But years later—after WWII—times had changed, and when Colombia began to eye the lucrative U.S. air travel market with its carte blanche agreement in hand, that occasioned some State Department backpedalling of truly magnificent form.

Trippe's toughest early antagonist was W.R. Grace & Company, a shipping, banking, trading monopoly that had for years been a mighty power on South America's west coast. Pan Am and Grace sparred warily for a time, then each decided that the other was too strong to risk a nose-to-nose showdown. So they formed a holding company in Peru, each taking 50 percent of the stock, and the airline that resulted was called Pan American Grace Airways (Panagra), which flew the route from Buenos Aires up the South American west coast to Panama. Not until 1965 did Panagra's name drop from the list of international air carriers as Pan Am took over the route and Pan Am subsidiaries were limited to domestic operations.

Trippe faced another determined opponent on South America's east coast, the New York, Rio & Buenos Aires Line. NYRBA (referred to as "Near Beer" by its crews), was organized in 1929 by Ralph O'Neill, formerly associated with Boeing, and was backed by James Rand of Remington-Rand (later Sperry-Rand and still later Rand Corp.), along with Lewis Pierson of the Irving Trust Company, who, as a backer of Pan American, Inc., had jousted with Trippe before. J.K. Montgomery was also back, as an NYRBA officer.

NYRBA was quite as rich as Pan Am at the time, and its fleet of 14 Consolidated Commodore flying boats was superior to Pan Am's assortment of Sikorsky S-38s, Ford and Fokker Trimotors, and Fairchild 71s. But NYRBA never really had a chance once Trippe was ready to muscle in, because its officials lacked the State Department backing that Grace's steamship lines commanded. The mail contract went to Pan Am (at the maximum rate of $2 per mile), and on 15 September 1930 Trippe acquired NYRBA and added the entire east coast of South America to his routes. That closed the big circle from Miami all the way around the South American Continent and back to Brownsville. In order to facilitate the takeover of NYRBA's Brazilian agreements, Trippe formed Panair do Brasil, and this subsidiary flew the route south of

Pan Am acquired 14 Consolidated Commodore flying boats in September 1930, when Trippe absorbed James Rand's New York, Rio, & Buenos Aires Line. (Pan Am)

The 40-passenger Sikorsky S-40, first of the famed "Clippers." Four P&W Hornet engines of 575 hp each maintained this 17-ton aerial houseboat in the air at 117 mph. (Pan Am)

Belem to Buenos Aires. It, too, disappeared as an international carrier in the mid-'60s.

In the meantime, foreseeing the need for future Pacific terminals, Trippe purchased a couple of small Alaskan lines and bought into Chiang Kai-shek's China National Aviation Corporation. He also obtained a mail contract for a Boston-Halifax route, anticipating Atlantic service.

Across the Pacific

In the end, Pan Am did not need the Alaska bases for inauguration of transpacific service, because Glenn Martin, by then building airplanes in Baltimore, provided Pan Am with new, long-range flying boats that made possible a route to the Orient from California via Hawaii, Midway, Wake, Guam, and the Philippines. That was a route that very much pleased the U.S. Navy, which lent Pan Am all possible assistance in establishing those bases, for the Navy had long been looking for an excuse to get such facilities on the stepping-stone islands of Midway, Wake, and Guam without upsetting the Department of State's delicate relations with Japan. Therefore, with help from the U.S. Navy, Post Office Department, Department of

State, and Department of Commerce (and, surely, the Good Lord Himself, all things considered), Pan Am began scheduled flights across the Pacific to Hong Kong 22 November 1935. Capt. Ed Musick was in command of the Martin M-130 *China Clipper* on her initial flight.

Across the Atlantic

Regularly scheduled Atlantic flights were delayed for several years when the British stalled negotiations on a reciprocal agreement until they possessed transport airplanes capable of flying the route. Finally, on 8 July 1939, Capt. Arthur LaPorte lifted the Boeing-built *Yankee Clipper* from the channel at Port Washington, Long Island, and headed northeast on a Great Circle course for Southhampton, England.

By that time, Pan Am faced trouble from another quarter as Hitler's aggressions in Europe at last prodded America into looking with concern at her deficient air defenses, and it became evident that the U.S. would be well-advised to build up its aerial lifeline to Britain in case of war and an attendant submarine menace in the Atlantic.

Of course, the last thing on Earth (or above it)

Sikorsky S-42 entered service with Pan Am in August 1934; it carried 42 passengers in unparalleled luxury at 140 mph. (Pan Am)

Pan Am began regular service across the Pacific—via Hawaii, Midway, Wake, Guam, and the Phillippines—on 22 November 1935, with a trio of Martin M-130 flying boats. The M-130, capable of carrying 48 passengers, was powered with four P&W R-1830 Twin Wasps of 800 hp each. (Pan Am)

that Juan Trippe wanted was to share one of his oceans with a competitor. He offered to schedule extra flights at little extra cost to the Post Office Department (Pan Am was already being paid nearly six times as much per mile for carrying the mail as any domestic airline). There was no point in wasting taxpayers' money by giving a mail contract to a competitor.

American Export Lines

But a potential competitor had quietly been preparing to challenge Pan Am's Atlantic monopoly for more than two years. This was American Export Airlines, Inc. (AMEX), which was headed by John E. Slater and James M. Eaton. Slater had earlier rescued the steamship company, American Export Lines, and put it on a paying basis through good management practices; Eaton was a former official of Ludington Lines and Pan AM. Amex was conceived as a subsidiary of the steamship company, but separated itself from its parent during the ensuing battle with Trippe after filing for a route certificate in May 1939.

Trippe bitterly fought the AMEX application

with the help of Senator Pat McCarran, who won an advantage for Pan Am even after the AMEX route certificate was approved. McCarran convinced his friends in the House that no money should be included in the Post Office appropriation for an AMEX air mail contract. Normally, that would have meant the end for AMEX, but at the beginning of WWII, AMEX found so much business waiting that it didn't need an air mail contract to survive. Then, when the Army and Navy took over all U.S. airlines upon America's entry into that conflict, the Pan Am-AMEX battle ended.

The precedent was established, however, and Juan Trippe knew that when peace returned he would be confronted with many AMEXs. But neither Trippe nor his future competition intended to wait for peace to do their planning. The State Department, too, was anticipating the problems of postwar global air travel.

Postwar Overseas Routes

Assuming Allied victory, it was clear as early as 1942 that the U.S. alone would be in position to fly international civil air routes at war's end. The

The Boeing B 314 was the last and largest of the commercial flying boats. Boeing built 12 for Pan Am, with deliveries beginning in January 1939. (Boeing)

The Douglas DC-6 was a beefed-up, speeded-up, pressurized version of the DC-4. It began airline service in November 1946 with American and United. Engines were P&W R-2800s giving a total of 8400 hp and a speed of 300 mph. Engine improvements raised the speed of the DC-6B to 370 mph. (Pan Am)

British had been forced to abandon transport airplane development in the late '30s in favor of desperately needed military aircraft. The U.S., with its own desperate hour two years delayed, meanwhile produced such excellent transport craft as the Lockheed Constellation and Douglas DC-4.

The British had no intention of allowing U.S. airlines to take over postwar international air transportation, and they were not without effective bargaining power in the matter, because Britain controlled within her (then) far-flung empire many of the overseas bases and terminals essential to such operations. Therefore, a conference was called in Chicago, during November 1944, to divvy up the postwar international air routes.

That conference wasn't as presumptuous as it may sound. No other country, except Australia and Canada, could hope to have overseas airlines soon after the war. Germany, Japan, and Italy would be out of the running. Liberated France, its economy and industry ruined, would not be an immediate factor. The Soviets could be dealt with later.

Agreement between the U.S. and British did not come easily because, under Roosevelt, the U.S.

Government had decided to discontinue the "chosen instrument" policy and encourage the operation of as many U.S. overseas airlines as the traffic would support. The English looked with horror upon that wasteful Yankee concept because their flag carrier, British Overseas Airways Corporation (BOAC), which had temporarily disappeared into war service, was a state-owned enterprise that Parliament regarded as a prestigious symbol of Britain's global influence. Really, old boy, one could hardly expect such an instrument of the government to make money, now could one?

However, after much haggling, British-American differences were settled when the airlines themselves organized the International Air Transport Association (IATA), offered membership to all nations possessing or expecting to possess an overseas airline, and proclaimed that IATA would establish international air fares.

That allayed British fear of rate-slashing by the Americans and promoted an optimistic setting for a new conference, at Bermuda, in January and February of 1946, from which delegates from most of the Free World emerged in happy agreement.

The single dissenter was Pan American. From the time of the Chicago conference, Trippe, aided by his old ally Senator McCarran and new recruit Senator Owen Brewster, had been fighting in Congress to re-establish the "chosen instrument" principle. Senator McCarran repeatedly introduced bills (S 1790, S 326, and S 1814) that would, in effect, return America to its air policies of the early '30s. When the McCarran bills failed to win much support, they were slicked up with fresh goodies to attract other interests and tried again. It was an interesting battle (McCarran never explained why a Senator from Nevada should take such an interest in transatlantic air routes), but all it engendered in the end was a lot of resentment for Pan Am, especially in the executive branch of the government. And since Harry S. Truman had become President in April 1945, resentment in the executive branch was certain to find an outlet.

There is evidence that President Truman was ready to substantially penalize Pan Am. He ignored the recommendations of his own CAB and arbitrar-ily awarded to Braniff Air Lines a route from the U.S. via Mexico City and Rio to Buenos Aires—right through the heart of Pan Am's hitherto private preserve. The President also announced that Eastern Air Lines would be granted a route from Miami to San Juan, Puerto Rico—although Eastern had not applied for it. It was another raid on exclusive Trippe territory. But then CAB Chairman L. Welch Pogue managed to calm the President, and the CAB was allowed to proceed with its task of parceling out America's portion of the world's air routes to the 18 U.S. airlines that wanted to share Mr. Trippe's air.

On 1 June 1945 the CAB ruled that three U.S. air carriers should fly the Atlantic to European terminals: TWA, Pan Am, and American Air Lines. United, alone among major U.S. domestic carriers, sought no international routes at the time. United's president, William Patterson, believed that not more than two dozen airplanes would be needed to serve the postwar Atlantic traffic.

Late in 1945, American Air Lines bought 60

Lockheed Constellation Model L49 also served Pan Am in the immediate postwar years, with a total of 28 registered to the airline. Later versions of the Connie, which began as a 48-passenger airliner, had more powerful turbo-compound engines (Wright R-3350s), and a fuselage 20 feet 11 inches longer to accommodate up to 95 passengers. (Pan Am)

The Douglas DC-7C had a total of 13,700 hp and a cruise speed of 355 mph with 104 passengers. Pan Am operated 26, the last prop-driven planes in the Pan Am fleet. (Pan Am)

Pan Am began jet operations over the Atlantic with the Boeing 707-121 in October, 1958. The 720B (pictured) went into service on Pan Am's Latin American routes in 1963. (Pan Am)

Boeing 727-21, added to Pan Am's fleet in December 1965, cruises at 35,000 ft with 128 passengers, averaging 575 mph. (Pan Am)

percent of AMEX and renamed that company American Overseas Airlines. Five years later, the President overruled the CAB and approved the sale of AOA to Pan Am.

The CAB's route decisions on Latin America were handed down in May 1946. In addition to the routes given to Braniff and Eastern by the President, National Air Lines, American Air Lines, and Chicago & Southern were awarded certificates to operate south of the border. Then, 15 months later, the CAB decided that Pan Am's competitor in the Pacific would be Northwest Air Lines (later, Northwest Orient), which would fly the Great Circle route to the Orient where it would connect with TWA to effect round-the-world service. Pan Am, retaining its prewar Pacific run, would be the other round-the-world U.S. airline. And United was at last edged into commercial ocean flying with a San Francisco-Hawaii route, duplicating Pan Am service to the islands.

These decisions, all carefully watched over by President Truman, resulted in the basic structure from which present-day international air routes evolved. There have been many additions, including foreign flag carriers that have the right to serve the U.S. in return for U.S. airline service to and across their countries, and there have been many route extensions and duplications as traffic in-

creased. Introduction of the jets brought most of this increase, and Pan Am was first with jet service, when its new Boeing 707 began flying from New York to Paris in October 1958.

Juan Trippe stepped down as Pan Am's board chairman and chief executive officer early in 1968, and Pan Am clearly lost much of its elegant arrogance. Under Trippe, Pan Am was the haughty *grand dame* of the international airways. She set the standards.

The Second World War greatly influenced the public's perception of air travel. At war's end, far more passengers awaited scheduled air service across the oceans that United's boss had suspected. The domestic airlines also enjoyed large increases in boardings.

During the war, the average citizen was all but excluded from air travel. The military requisitioned a large part of the airline fleet, beginning with the takeover of 11 Pan Am Boeing and Martin Clippers, along with five Boeing Stratoliners belonging to TWA. A priority system gave what seats there were to people flying on defense-related business. But literally millions of young Americans were introduced to air travel by the military air transports that whisked them to and from the far-flung theaters of war, and although that was air travel of the most uncomfortable and otherwise undesir-

The Lockheed L-1011-500 began service with Pan Am in 1980. This version of the TriStar is 13 1/2 feet shorter than other L-1011s, but carries 230 passengers 6200 miles, a truly long-range wide-body. (Lockheed California Company)

able kind, it was, nevertheless, a firsthand demonstration of the transport airplane's ability to compress time and distance—the basic justification for air travel in the first place.

The airlines needed those first dozen years after WWII to find their proper places in the overall system, because another quantum advance waited at the end of the '50s.

As we have seen, three major factors came together in the late '20s to touch off a transportation revolution. First, the U.S. Post Office Department, historically an important force in the development of the nation's transportation systems, offered the promise of profits to scheduled air carriers. At almost the same time, the first truly reliable and reasonably efficient aircraft engines appeared. The third factor, a significant influx of risk capital, immediately followed as a result of the first two, and it was accelerated by Lindbergh's dramatic solo flight to Paris, certainly the greatest public relations *coup* in aviation history, whether or not it was so intended.

The next great advance, the appearance of the jet airliner, would come as a result of the same factors: plenty of *risk capital* to reap the *profits* promised by more *efficient machines*.

REVIEW QUESTIONS:

1. What were the political implications of Senator Black's Committee? How did Walter Folger Brown respond to the charges against him? How was the Ludington-Eastern Air Transport bidding affair explained?

2. Why did President Roosevelt order the Army to fly the mail? What was the Army's experience from February to May 1934? How did the airlines get around the decree that no airline which had been represented at the spoils conference would be given a mail contract?

3. What were some of the provisions of the Air Mail Act of 1934 (Black-McKellar Bill)? What was the purpose of the Civil Aeronautics Authority Act of 1938? Describe the consolidation which took place.

What were the "Certificates of Convenience and Necessity"?

4. Who was Juan Trippe? How was he able to secure the Key West to Havana route? What was the "chosen instrument" policy of the Post Office and State Departments? What were some of the problems encountered by Pan Am in its expansion into Central and South America? How were these overcome? How was Pan Am able to launch service across the Pacific and Atlantic in little over 10 years from the founding of the company?

5. Describe the competition faced by Pan Am in the post WWII period. Why did the U.S. Government choose to discontinue the "chosen instrument" policy? Why didn't postwar transoceanic air travel revert back to the use of large flying boats?

Chapter 10

The New Deal and U.S. Airpower

OBJECTIVES: At the end of this chapter you should be able to:

- ☐ Give your reasons for the prevailing attitude of neutrality during the 1920s and early 1930s.

- ☐ Explain why the Army had such poor experience in flying the mail during the winter and spring months of 1934.

- ☐ Discuss the significance of the development of the Pratt & Whitney 400-hp air-cooled Wasp engine.

- ☐ Give your reasons why the U.S. Naval Air Service placed so much emphasis on rigid airships during the 1930s.

- ☐ Recognize the position of Congress and the top military leaders regarding airpower in the 1920s, and 1930s.

- ☐ Describe some of the new generation aircraft which appeared during the late 1930s.

The fact that President Franklin D. Roosevelt never admitted a mistake is insufficient evidence that he never made one. Of course, any President elected to four terms in that office, and whose supreme self-confidence leaves him unencumbered by doubt and provides him with the courage to make tough decisions without equivocation, is going to make mistakes. Nobody's perfect. And whether or not Roosevelt's "New Deal," which pointed the nation down the road to socialism, was a great mistake depends upon the politics of those who judge him, and is beyond the scope of this modest book. We are concerned here only with the effects of the New Deal on U.S. military aviation and the physical defense of our freedoms.

Still, in order to attain this limited objective we must take note of the atmosphere that gave birth to the New Deal and certain events that preceded it.

First, however, let us plainly state a couple of simple facts that our nation's leaders must heed in the planning of U.S. security: The American people will unite in support of war *only* when they believe that our very survival is at stake and that God is clearly on our side. It's just that simple. And a great many Americans view the maintenance of superior military forces as an invitation to trouble, rather than a deterrent to foreign aggressors.

These attitudes are not new; they date back to

McCook Field, located on the outskirts of Dayton, Ohio, was the most significant place in American aviation during the early '20s. Almost all new aerial hardware was either developed or tested there prior to 1927. (Merle Olmsted collection)

the Revolutionary War, and they were at least as pronounced during the '20s and '30s as they are today.

Nevertheless, the function of a leader is to lead, and a leader with a mandate from the people as great as that enjoyed by Franklin Roosevelt has little defense for his failures. The threat to the United States was clearly delineated long before he made any move to counter it, and America's tardiness in preparing to defend herself not only cost countless American lives, but encouraged military conquests that bore heavily on U.S. vital interests and, eventually, tempted attack on America herself. History offers no examples of a peace dictated from weakness.

America's reaction to the aggressions of Japan, Germany, and Italy during the mid-'30s was funding for an Army of 165,000 and the Neutrality Acts passed between 1935 and 1937. As late as 1938, the Army Air Corps' appropriation was $58.8 million (compared to $35.1 million in 1921), and total Air Corps personnel numbered 21,089. At that time, our best fighter airplanes were some 70 Curtiss P-36s in service (plus 139 more on order), and our best heavy bombers were 14 service test YB-17s (plus 39 B-17Bs on order). Just one year later, Hitler would march into Poland to start the Second World War.

There is evidence that Roosevelt shared the anti-Air Corps sentiments held by the Navy Department's battleship admirals right up to the time of Pearl Harbor. Roosevelt, born to wealth and position, a Harvard graduate and amateur yachtsman (always expected of such young men), served as assistant secretary of the Navy 1913-1921, and was obviously much perturbed at Billy Mitchell's claim that the airplane had made the battleship obsolete. "It is highly unlikely that an airplane, or a fleet of them, could ever sink a fleet of Navy vessels under battle conditions," he told the press in 1921.

Later, following Mitchell's demonstrations, Roosevelt was asked by a reporter if he'd changed his mind, to which he replied, "I once saw a man kill a lion with a .30/30 rifle . . . but that does not mean that a .30/30 is a lion gun."

Thirteen years later, the Air Corps would provide him an even greater embarrassment.

"Neither Rain, Nor Snow, Nor Politics . . ."

Early in February 1934, Roosevelt cancelled all air mail contracts with the airlines and directed that the Army fly the mail. The Air Corps took over the mail routes on 19 February, and although the 27,000-mile airway system was reduced to a basic 9,000 miles and no passengers were to be carried, it was an impossible assignment. With only ten days preparation, obsolete aircraft, and non-instrument pilots, the Air Corps tried to fly unfamiliar routes—often without so much as a compass—during the worst weather of the year. At the end of a week, five pilots were dead and six critically injured. The newspapers made the most of it.

Now, we should digress to explain that the airline system in the United States was originally made possible by the 1925 Kelly Bill which provided for payment to private contractors to fly the mail. In 1931, the McNary-Watres Act changed the rate of payment for as much as $3.10 per pound to a much larger amount based upon the cubic feet of capacity in the contractor's aircraft available for mail. This legislation, amounting to an outright subsidy, was intended to encourage the airmail contractors to place in service large, multi-engine aircraft (most had been flying the mail in open cockpit biplanes), which in turn would lead to scheduled passenger flights since it would cost the operators very little more to fill all that empty space with people.

The Post Office Department felt that this subsidy would not long be needed as the public began paying for that space, and the Post Office (in the person of President Hoover's Postmaster General, Walter Folger Brown) was right. By the time FDR took office early in 1933, postal payments to the

The Curtiss Hawk series of biplane fighters, 247 in all, were procured 1925 through 1931 inclusive. Above is a P-1F at Kelly Field. (USAF)

Lt. Otto Wienecke, one of 12 Army fliers to be killed flying the mail during the 1934 airmail moratorium, died in this Curtiss O-39 observation plane when he crashed near Cleveland in a snowstorm. (UPI)

airlines was rapidly decreasing as the public began to accept scheduled airline service in the Ford and Fokker Tri-Motor airliners.

The only trouble was that these early airliners simply were not efficient. With passenger capacities of 12 to 15, some mail pay was still necessary—was, in fact, the difference between profit and loss. However, this policy was about to bear other fruit, because it fostered development of the Douglas DC-2/DC-3 series, the first of which appeared a few days before Roosevelt ordered the Air Corps to fly the mail, and these airplanes were capable of returning profits to their operators with passenger revenues alone.

Meanwhile, the New Dealers had discovered, soon after they took possession of the White House, that ex-Postmaster General Walter Folger Brown had built America's airline system with the employment of some rather undemocratic methods. Brown had not bothered with such things as competitive bidding for the routes or a fair shake for the small, poorly financed operator. He had forced mergers and favored the well-financed bidders, and his high-handed methods had left a trail of enemies in his wake. About all that could be said in Brown's favor was that he had, using his mail pay whip, given the United States the best domestic airline system in the world.

The Democrats gleefully smelled collusion and

thievery and appointed a Senate committee to investigate the "Air Mail Scandals" of the previous Republican administration. This committee was headed by a senator from Alabama, Hugo L. Black (whose law degree, he later admitted, came from a correspondence school), and it is difficult to understand why, today, reading transcripts of the testimony given before the Black Committee, that the New Dealers should have pursued the matter, because the only provable fact was that Brown had been a dictator—a charge that Brown himself cheerfully agreed to, pointing out that his power had been bestowed upon him by the Congress of the United States.

Nevertheless, citing the Black Committee report, President Roosevelt cancelled all air mail contracts, charging that the airways system had been mapped out in a series of "spoils conferences" by W.G. Brown and a handful of his favored airline cronies. The Army Air Corps would fly the mail, the President said, until such time as the New Dealers should present their own plan for the awarding of airline routes.

But the Air Corps, though it made a valiant effort, lacked both the equipment and the trained pilots to perform the task, and by the second week in March the mounting death toll among the Army fliers appalled the nation. The President had to find a way out. On 10 March he announced that the air

This crash, 2 February 1934, claimed the life of Lt. Ed Lowry about 50 miles southwest of Toledo. Mail bags were scattered far from the scene. (USAF)

The P&W R-1340 Wasp was introduced in May 1926, rated at 400 hp; by 1938 it had evolved into a 600-hp engine. A smaller version, the R-985 Wasp Jr, similarly grew from 300 to 450 hp.

mail would be returned to the airlines as soon as possible.

A total of 12 Army fliers died before the mail could be returned to its former contractors. (*Author's Note:* Now, lest I be accused of party bias in recording this episode, I am willing to concede that had the situation been reversed—that is, had the Republicans rather than the Democrats taken over the White House in 1933 after 12 long years of the other party's rule—they, too, would have been looking for signs of maladministration to discredit their political enemies. The point is that the Democrats acted too hastily in starting a vendetta against the airlines and the Republicans because no thievery could be proved. There was probably plenty of it to be proved had they looked in the right places, but once the "Air Mail Scandals" became a media event, the New Dealers had to follow through as best they could.)

In an attempt to save face, Roosevelt decreed that no airline company represented at the 1929 meetings ("spoils conferences") with W.F. Brown,

when the air routes were parceled out, should be allowed to carry the mail in the future. That, too, became a farce, because that edict was easily handled by the airlines which, at that point, had the President over the proverbial barrel: American Airways suddenly became American Air Lines; Eastern Air Transport repainted its signs to read "Eastern Air Lines." TWA, a bit bolder, merely added "Inc." to its name, and United Air Lines remained unchanged because its original contract had been awarded to a United subsidiary.

The New Dealers gained no political mileage from the tragic witch hunt, and nothing was changed for the small, poorly financed operators in whose name all the fuss had been made in the first place. Roosevelt's Postmaster General, James Farley, continued to award air mail contracts only to those companies which had the capital to buy the best equipment and the organization to operate the most responsibly, while the small operators continued to be squeezed out and gobbled up by the growing major airlines.

The Allison V-1710 powered the P-40s, P-39s, P-63s, P-38s, A-36s and F-82s. Pictured is the V-1710-39, which was fitted to the P-40D and P-40E as well as the early Kittyhawks. (Allison Division, GM)

The whole episode was an embarrassment to Roosevelt, and he was not the kind of man to forget an embarrassment. During the ensuing four or five years he appears to have ignored the Army Air Corps as much as possible, while the Navy received authority to build no less than 34 new battleships and battle cruisers (a program that was modified after WWII began and the importance of the aircraft carrier became evident).

Engine Development Paces the Industry

You will recall from Chapter 4 that Fred Rentschler and his top enginemen at Wright Aeronautical Corporation had brought the Wright Whirlwind J-4 to the threshold of success by 1924. Although Rentschler never admitted it, it appears most likely that he recognized the opportunity of a lifetime at that point. Rather than enrich Wright Aeronautical with his foresight, he decided to start his own company. It was a decision worth millions.

Rentschler correctly judged that the 200-hp Whirlwind, when fully developed, would have a great impact on aviation and make a great deal of money for Wright. However, he also knew about the work of Sam Heron and Edward T. Jones at the Air Corps' McCook Field experimental center, which had resulted in development of the first truly reliable air-cooled cylinders in several sizes, and which featured Heron's sodium-filled exhaust valves. Further realizing that here was the key to much bigger aircraft engines that would match the Whirlwind's reliability, Rentschler resigned from Wright in September, 1924, taking his best enginemen (Mead, Willgoos, and Brown) with him.

Then, with a truly first-class dream to sell, he was able to secure the backing of the owners of the idle Pratt and Whitney Tool Company factory for production of his new 400-hp Wasp engine, Model R-1340. This engine (and others of the same basic construction that followed) were so successful that by 1933, the 1375 shares of Pratt & Whitney stock

A Sparrowhawk returns to the trapeze beneath the *Macon*. The *Macon's* engines were inside her hull. Normal crew was 10 officers and 50 enlisted men, plus four Sparrowhawk pilots. (USN)

that Rentschler had purchased for $275 in 1925 had grown to more than $21,000,000—that's correct, *twenty-one million*.

It also appears that Rentschler's principal advisor—that is, the man who encouraged him to build the Wasp engine—was none other than Adm. William Moffett, chief of the Navy's Bureau of Aeronautics. Moffett wasn't concerned with the money to be made from the production of such an engine. The Navy badly needed an aircraft power-plant of that size, and Moffett had decided that the Navy would use air-cooled radials exclusively for the foreseeable future, principally because they were much easier to service than the big liquid-cooled powerplants.

But Rentschler did not need to be told that the Air Corps and the airlines would also come knocking at his door if he had a reliable high-horsepower air-cooled radial to sell; by 1938—just 13 years after P&W was formed—the R-1340 Wasp had long since become a 600-hp engine; the R-985 Wasp Junior filled the 450-hp needs, and the R-1690 Hornet was in production at 850-hp, while the new R-1830 Twin Wasp and the R-2800 Double Wasp, at 1200- and 2000-hp respectively, had completed their tests and were just entering production.

Meanwhile, at Wright Aeronautical, the two men who had contributed the most to air-cooled aircraft engine development—Sam Heron and Ed T. Jones—had been lured from the Air Corps' experimental and development center at McCook Field (later, Wright Field, and today Wright-Patterson AFB, Ohio) by Charles Lawrance at Wright Aeronautical where they gave the J-4 Whirlwind their new cylinder and valve system to bring forth the famed J-5 Whirlwind. The J-6 series quickly followed, ranging in power from 165- to 300-hp, along with the 750-hp R-1820 Cyclone.

Wright Aeronautical was merged with the Curtiss Aeroplane and Motor Company in 1929 by wheeler-dealer financier Clement M. Keys (who had controlled Curtiss since the early '20s) to form the Curtiss-Wright Aircraft Corporation. In 1931, when Curtiss-Wright decided to abandon liquid-cooled aircraft engine development (despite the success of its D-12 and Conqueror engines during the

'20s) to concentrate on the Wright air-cooled radials, the Air Corps was forced to look elsewhere for the 1000-hp V-12 it was sure it would need within a decade.

The Air Corps favored the in-line V-12s because they presented a much smaller frontal area (and therefore less drag) than the big radials, and because cooling problems were yet to be solved with the high-horsepower radials above 15,000 ft. So the Air Corps went to General Motors miniscule (less than 30 employees) Allison Division where a new V-12 of 1710 cubic inch displacement and a planned rating of 750-hp was in its early stages of development under a Navy contract to supply engines for the Navy's huge airships *Akron* and *Macon*.

The Air Corps was mostly jawboning, because it had almost no money to spend. It bought a dozen Allison V-1710s between 1932 and mid-1934 which were shipped to Wright Field where Air Corps enginemen under the direction of Opie Chenoweth tried to uprate them to 1000 hp with no success. Not until March 1937, after Allison's Ron Hazen, Charles McDowall and Robert Atkinson had almost completely redesigned the V-1710, did it at last pass a type test at 1000-hp. This was, by the way, just a few months after the Rolls Royce Merlin passed its type test at 990-hp. Both engines were rated for 87 octane fuel. The V-1710 required pure Prestone as a coolant and weighed 1,280 pounds. The 1335 pound Merlin was cooled with a water-Prestone mix.

During WWII, Allison would produce almost 70,000 V-1710s, the last ones rated at 1600-hp. Production would continue into 1947, after a final order to equip the P-82 Twin Mustang, but none ever propelled a Navy dirigible. Both the *Akron* and *Macon* were destroyed in crashes before the Allisons meant for them could be delivered.

Navy Airships *Akron* and *Macon*

Adm. William Moffett (he wasn't the kind of man one called "Billy") never lost faith in the great rigid airships as patrol and reconnaissance vehicles for the fleet. The Germans had used Zeppelins as strategic bombers in WWI with limited success, but

Trio of Curtiss F9C-2 Sparrowhawks. Engine cowlings were red, white and blue. Engines were Wright R-975s of 420 hp which gave the Sparrowhawks a top speed of 176 mph. (USN)

the record of the huge airships subsequent to that time was not very good. The Italian-built *Roma* had crashed during test flights in the United States in 1922; the Navy's ZR-2, built in Britain as the R.38, also crashed on a test flight, and the Goodyear-built ZR-1 *Shenandoah* was lost in a storm in 1925. Only the German-built ZR-3 *Los Angeles*, in U.S. Navy service since 1924, appeared to be headed for a long and useful life (it was finally decommissioned in 1932 as an economy measure), but was inadequate for the sea duty Moffett envisioned since it was actually a WWI design. The Hoover Administration

had, in 1928, approved purchase of two airships, the ZRS-4 and ZRS-5, which were much larger than the *Los Angeles* and which were specifically designed for extended service at sea.

The two new airships, to be christened *Akron* and *Macon*, were nearly identical. The first to be completed was the *Akron*, which was 785 feet in length, 133 feet in diameter, 146 feet in height. It contained 6.5 million cu/ft of helium. Her eight engines furnished a total of 4480-hp, and she could carry a useful load of 160,000 pounds at speeds up to 84 mph. Her engines were placed inside the great

Army's Keystone LB-7 bomber of the late '20s was powered with two P&W Hornet engines of 525 hp each. A total of 210 Keystones (crews called them "Keystone Comedies") with different engine installations were procured following the Mitchell trial. (USAF)

Great Lakes G-1 torpedo bomber of 1929 was typical of the heavy biplanes procured by the Navy during the '20s for that mission. (Charles W. Meyers collection)

hull; her propellers—which could be turned in different directions for forward, reverse, or even upward thrust—were mounted outside at the end of extended driveshafts. Also inside the hull was hangar and maintenance space for five small scout-fighter planes which could be launched and returned to the airship in flight by means of a retractable trapeze. Six Curtiss F9C-2 Sparrowhawks (plus two prototypes) were built for the *Akron* and *Macon*, with more planes to be ordered as needed.

The *Akron* was placed in service in October, 1931, with Lt. Cmdr. C.E. Rosendahl as her captain, and for a year and a half she seemed well on her way to the vindication of Moffett's support, her 10,000-mile range allowing her to roam the seas for many days without refueling. But then the *Akron* was lost (unnecessarily, most believed) on 4 April 1933, just two months after the *Macon* was christened.

The *Akron* crashed in a storm off the New Jer-

Maj. Joe R. Reed and his crew chief inspect damage to Douglas O-2H observation plane after the Liberty engine failed at low altitude. (Joe R. Reed collection)

The U.S. Marine Corps' Curtiss OC-2 Falcon of 1930 was Wasp-powered, had a top speed of 155 mph. (USN)

sey Coast while flying at a very low altitude when her helmsman apparently raised her nose too abruptly and allowed the rear of the airship to strike the water. The great aerial machine broke up, and 73 of the 76 men aboard her lost their lives, including Adm. Moffett.

The *Macon* entered service in June 1933, two months after the *Akron's* loss, and received the *Akron's* Sparrowhawks, since none of the planes were aboard the *Akron* when it went down. At sea, the planes' landing gears were removed and belly tanks added to give the small scout-fighters greater range. The lack of a landing gear didn't matter, since the only place the planes could "land" was on the extended trapeze of their mother airship.

This combination—an airship of great range, plus four (usually) scouting planes fanning out to patrol all points of the compass—provided the Navy with eyes over many thousands of square miles of ocean. If the *Macon* had survived it is quite possible that other, similar airships would have been built, because they easily offered the most effective and economical means of guarding the sea approaches to America's coasts. No nation was in a better position to exploit these aerial behemoths because the United States possessed the world's only known deposits of non-flammable helium prior to WWII. Germany, the master builder of these machines, was forced to use highly-flammable hydrogen in her airships.

The *Macon* was lost to a fatal flaw in her struc-

ture. Her vertical tail atop the rear of the airship was improperly attached to the hull, and this critical component failed in flight during marginal weather off the California Coast near Big Sur on 12 February 1935. Miraculously, all but two of the 81 aboard survived the ensuing crash.

Many in the Navy believed then (and still do) that the airship program should have continued; but without Adm. Moffett's leadership, the U.S. Navy's lighter-than-air vehicles were henceforth limited to the relatively small, non-rigid "blimps," primarily used during WWII to hunt enemy submarines in U.S. coastal waters.

Transition: The Biplane Era Passes

Despite the impoverished status of the U.S. Army Air Corps during the '20s and much of the '30s, and despite the lack of promotion and the low pay, the Air Corps attracted—and often held—some very able men. It seems remarkable today that any of them should have remained in the service. Following Billy Mitchell's court martial, those officers with any rank who were known to share Mitchell's views were shown by the Army's General Staff how foolish that could be. All were exiled to lesser commands: Majors H.H. "Hap" Arnold, Carl Spaatz, Lewis Brereton and Gerald Brandt; Cols. Hugh Knerr and Frank Andrews; Lt. Cols. George Kenney and Joe McNarney all suffered career setbacks. Maj. Arnold, for example, was relieved of his post in Washington D.C. and sent to Marshall Field

Curtiss F6C-4 Hawk of VF-9M. This craft was plane number two of Fighting Nine. (USN)

where his command consisted of four tired DH-4s and 13 men. Perhaps these blatant punishments merely strengthened the resolve of such men. In any case, they all hung tough—if temporarily silenced—perhaps aware that the time would come when the nation would sorely need their counsel.

During the late '20s and early '30s, significant progress was made in aircraft and aircraft engine development, mostly due to the new and expanding markets in civil aviation. The demand for more efficient airliners and a booming market for private airplanes, along with the appearance of truly reliable engines in all power ranges, encouraged by airframe builders to push ahead with fresh ideas. By 1931, John K. "Jack" Northrop was building the first of his all-metal stressed-skin airplanes in which the metal skin carried much of the load, resulting in a lighter internal structure, and the small but talent-ridden National Advisory Committee for Aeronautics (NACA, forerunner of NASA) developed a wide array of new airfoils and provided much other useful aerodynamic data to industry with its

wind tunnel work at Langley Field, VA, including engine cowling shapes for the air-cooled radials that not only greatly reduced drag but also improved engine cooling.

These advances produced the first "modern" airliner in 1933, the Boeing 247 for United Air Lines—an all-metal, low-wing, twin-engine craft with retractable landing gear. It was limited only by its small size (10 passengers). Donald Douglas rectified that with the first of his famed DC series airliners, built for TWA, the following year. It was the DC-1, which quickly (1936) evolved into the DC-3, known as the C-47 in the Air Corps and the R4D in Navy service.

Prior to 1936, the military services normally purchased airplanes in batches of 25 or 30 at a time. The Army took delivery of only 247 Curtiss Hawk biplane fighters ("pursuits") between October 1925 when the first was delivered, and April 1932, when it accepted the last one. During the biplane era, the Army favored Curtiss fighters, Douglas observation planes, and Martin or Keystone bombers. The

Boeing P-12C Army fighter was powered with P&W R-1340-9 Wasp of 525 hp and had a top speed of 178 mph. Army took delivery of 366 of the P-12 series, 1929-1932 inclusive. Navy version was the F4B series. (USAF)

Curtiss F11C-2 Goshawk was fitted with the Wright R-1820 Cyclone of 715 hp; had a top speed of 205 mph. The Navy bought 27 of this model during the early '30s and later redesignated it the BFC-2 (bomber-fighter). (USN)

The Curtiss P-6E Hawk was the last biplane fighter purchased by the Air Corps. Its Curtiss V-1570 Conqueror V-12 engine produced 600 hp and gave the P-6E a top speed of 193 mph. The Air Corps took delivery of 45 P-6Es in early 1932, paying $12,362 each for them, plus an additional $10,000 each for engines, propellers and guns.

The *USS Lexington* as it appeared during the early '30s. The "Lady Lex" and its sister carrier *Saratoga* were commissioned in the late fall of 1927. Both were converted cruisers of 36,000 tons, and both carried 72 aircraft. (Joe R. Reed collection)

Navy favored Boeing fighters and Douglas torpedo planes. The U.S. Marines usually received castoff Navy airplanes.

The Marines were fortunate to have any airplanes at all, and probably wouldn't have had it not been for a series of incidents in Haiti and Nicaragua where the Marines were sent to restore order and protect what was then seen as America's best interests when rebel guerillas threatened those governments.

Marine Fighting Squadron Nine was also instrumental in saving Marine aviation during this period. Aware that a move was afoot to eliminate Marine aviation, Fighting Nine organized an aerial exhibition team of seven pilots who flew precision aerobatics in close formation just as today's Blue Angels do. They called themselves the *Rojas Diablos* ("Red Devils") and, performing at county fairs and other civil celebrations, gained a great deal of favorable publicity and goodwill for the Corps in general and Marine Air in particular.

Fighting Nine did it all on a shoestring, and with dedicated mechanics who kept their aging biplane fighters in service often by fabricating their own spare parts. On one occasion these crews built an airplane from the salvaged remains of several others and gave it a fictious serial number. That later caused a great flap in Marine Headquarters where there was no record of the plane's acquisition. Headquarters finally decided that the airplane did not exist and that settled the matter.

A New Generation of Aircraft

After the Navy received its first aircraft carrier, the *Langley*, in 1922, only two more were added to the Fleet during the next dozen years, the *Saratoga* and *Lexington*, converted battle cruisers that entered service in the fall of 1927. But then four more were commissioned prior to WWII: *Ranger* in 1934, *Yorktown* in 1937, *Enterprise* in 1938, and *Wasp* in 1940. President Roosevelt, always attentive to Navy needs, originally funded *Yorktown* and *Enterprise* through a provision of his National Recovery Act (NRA: "recovery" from the Great Depression), and although the Supreme Court later held the NRA to be unconstitutional, Roosevelt had no trouble getting the money from Congress to pay for them, as well as the *Wasp*. The Congress seldom argued with FDR because of his immense popular support.

The United States should have possessed at least twice that number of aircraft carriers, enough to support a two-ocean Navy, but this is a judgment made in hindsight. No one in the Navy Department

A BF2C-1 Hawk flown by Lt. Cmdr. J.D. Barnwar of VB-5B operating from the *USS Ranger* in 1935. The BF2C-1 had a top speed of 225 mph; power was the 770-hp Wright R-1820-04. Navy bought 27 of this type in 1934. (USN)

The carriers *Yorktown* and *Enterprise* were christened during 1936 and each received a squadron of Curtiss SBC-3 Helldivers. The SBC series remained in production until 1941. (Merle C. Olmsted collection)

at that time fully realized the role the aircraft carrier would play in the future defense of the country. The carrier was still a theoretical weapon, actually untried in battle.

Our point is, however, that the Navy was relatively better funded during the '30s than was the Army, and especially the Army Air Corps. Roosevelt did not overtly oppose the Air Corps, he simply ignored it as long as possible.

Unfortunately, the Army General Staff, headed by the temperamental Gen. Malin Craig during the critical late '30s, *was* overtly opposed to a modern air force and made certain that the Air Corps remained totally subservient to the presumed needs of ground commanders, while admitting no offensive role for Army aviation—a position shared by

Douglas O-46A observation plane, 90 of which were delivered to the Air Corps in 1935-1936, was a pretty airplane but already obsolescent when it appeared. (USAF)

most congressmen. The idea of a strategic bombing force was heresy, and any air officer who presumed to disagree with this doctrine was summarily transferred to the boondocks and reduced to his permanent rank. When Gen. George C. Marshall replaced Craig as Chief of Staff in 1939, Marshall rescued the "Billy Mitchell Crowd" and returned all of them to positions of high responsibility. Hap Arnold was, after a lengthy penance, promoted to Brig. Gen. and appointed Chief of the Air Corps in 1938, although that post had been diluted in 1935 with formation of the "General Headquarters Air Force" at Langley Field, which was supposed to be on an equal level with that of the Air Corps Chief. The GHQ Air Force controlled the Air Corps combat arm, while the AC Chief was responsible for training and supply. This confusing arrangement split whatever authority the top air officers possessed under Malin Craig.

Meanwhile, able Army air officers did as well as they could under the hostile Malin Craig and, in 1936, as the Congress became mildly alarmed at Hitler's occupation of the Rhineland, Italy's invasion of Ethiopia, civil war in Spain, and Japan's continuing aggressions in China, money was appropriated for 77 new Seversky P-35 fighter planes for the Air Corps.

A year later, Germany, Italy and Japan signed an anti-Comintern pact, Hitler formally renounced the Versailles Treaty, the Japanese sank a U.S. gunboat on the Yangtze River, and money was found for 210 new Curtiss P-36 fighters for the Air Corps. It was the largest single order for Army airplanes since WWI. At the same time, Wright Field issued a specification to the nation's struggling airplane industry asking for proposals for a 2000-hp fighter airplane.

That specification was a bit far out and Wright Field knew it. No 2000-hp aircraft engine existed in 1937, and the Air Corps had no money either in hand or promised to buy such planes. But all concerned knew that the gestation periods for new military aircraft was growing much longer as the planes became more complicated and that engines, especially, required several years to develop. It wasn't simply a matter of increasing the size of existing engines to obtain more power. Better fuels were needed for higher compression ratios, and improved metals had to be formulated to withstand the greater pressures and higher operating temperatures. As aircraft speeds increased, a host of new aerodynamic questions arose. Next to nothing was known about compressibility, a phenomenon that some engineers believed—and others did not—

A new era in U.S. fighter airplane design began in 1934 when Don Berlin designed the Curtiss P-36. Pictured is the wooden mock-up.

Prototype P-36 first flew in April 1935, and was penalized by use of the Wright R-1670 engine, a decided failure. Berlin had no choice but to try this engine since he worked for Curtiss-Wright. (Donovan R. Berlin)

would be encountered as planes approached the speed of sound. (Lockheed was to soon face the problem, which was indeed real).

Barely solvent Lockheed, a small company which had produced only 277 airplanes since its organization 11 years before, responded to the Air Corps' specification with exciting plans for a fighter plane fitted with a pair of 1000-hp Allison V-1710 engines (then still in development). Lockheed's proposed airplane would, if built, demand answers to questions which had not yet been asked. On paper it was a 400-mph airplane, at least 100 mph faster than the Curtiss P-36s which would begin entering service a year later, and it would certainly force the

The Air Corps asked Curtiss to install the new P&W R-1830 Twin Wasp in the P-36 and the happy result was an order for 210 such machines in June 1937, the largest U.S. fighter plane order since WWI. (Donovan R. Berlin)

In March 1938, P-36 designer Don Berlin suggested to the Air Corps Material Division at Wright Field that the P-36 be fitted with the new Allison V-1710 engine. That resulted in the P-40, and a contract for 524 of those machines in April 1939. Deliveries to the Air Corps began in June 1940, and eventually totalled 13,763, including Tomahawks and Kittyhawks to Britain and the Commonwealth countries. (USAF)

state-of-the-art beyond present limits.

But Wright Field (apparently Opie Chenoweth, head of the Air Corps Technical Service Command) liked the Lockheed proposal, which was actually the work of young Clarence "Kelly" Johnson, a recent University of Michigan graduate. Gen. Oscar Westover, who endured for three years under Malin Craig as Chief of Air Corps, approved a contract for one experimental model of the new fighter which was designed the XP-38. It was officially described as a "defensive interceptor" in order to get it past Craig and the Congress.

The Navy, too, was looking to the need for faster and better airplanes and let contracts as early as November 1935 for experimental fighters, the Grumman XF4F-1 and the Brewster XF2A-1. At that time, the Navy had 867 pilots, the Marines 110. Those figures were up to 1068 and 180 respectively when WWII began in Europe.

The Navy took delivery of 503 Brewster F2A Buffalo fighters beginning in December 1937, but those were interium craft with a number of weaknesses, and were replaced by the Grumman F4F Wildcat for fleet duty. A total of 1978 Wildcats were built for the Navy (plus 431 for Britain) beginning in 1938. The famed Chance Vought F4U Corsair was contracted that same year, designed for the P&W R-2800 2000-hp radial engine which was in its early stages of development at the time. The first Corsair would fly in 1940, and 7829 would

Lt. Col. Benjamin S. Kelsey (later, General) was the test pilot and Air Corps project officer for the P-38 program. When this photo was taken he was recovering from a broken ankle received when he parachuted from a YP-38 after pulling its tail off in a dive. (USAF)

eventually be built for the Navy and Marines.

Actually, all of the American-designed 400 mph fighters appeared as test models at about the same time, with the XP-38 leading the pack in 1939. All the rest followed in 1940, except the XP-51, which was originally built for the British and first flew in 1941. None of these craft was developed and available for combat when Pearl Harbor was attacked. It's true that the P-38 Lightning was thrown into combat in mid-1942, but it was not combat-ready until the P-38J-25 version came off the production lines in 1944. During the early, desperate months of the war for the United States, the Navy's F4F Wildcat and the Army's P-40 carried the burden.

The P-40 was simply a re-engined P-36. Originally powered with the P&W R-1830 of 1050-hp, the P-36 had a speed of 310 mph and outstanding maneuverability. It was as good as any fighter in the world when it entered squadron service in 1938. By then, however, its designer, Donovan Berlin, Chief Engineer at Curtiss-Wright, was recommending that it be fitted with the 1090-hp Allison V-1710-19, and that resulted in the 365 mph P-40, which first flew in October 1938. P-40 deliveries

The Boeing Model 299, a daring project by the Boeing Company, first flew in 1935 and evolved into the famed B-17 series of WWII. A total of 12,726 was built, although only 134 were built or on order early in 1941. (USAF)

When the U.S. was plunged into WWII all sorts of civil aircraft were drafted. The famed Beech Staggerwing (Model 17) became the UC-43 in Army dress, and was used as a "command transport." (Beech Aircraft Corp.)

to the Army began in mid-1940, and 13,737 were eventually built, many for America's allies during WWII.

The Republic P-47 Thunderbolt, more often referred to as the "Jug" by those who flew and serviced her, was a brute of a fighter plane—rugged, powerful and fast. Its prototype also appeared in 1940, and it would be the principal U.S. fighter over Europe when the Luftwaffe offered the most resistance. Therefore, America's top aces in the European Theater of Operations (ETO) were Jug jockeys. The several versions of the P-47 had top speeds ranging from 425 to above 450 mph. Power came from the 2000-hp P&W R-2800 which, with water injection, could produce 2300-hp for short periods.

On the face of it, the P-38 Lightning should have been at least as fast as the P-47, and it probably would have been had it possessed the Thunderbolt's wing. The P-38, however, was a load-carrier—it would deliver a bomb load equal to that of a medium bomber—and it could outclimb just about anything. With a top speed of 405 to 420 mph, depending upon model, it was probably fast enough, and its firepower was truly awesome. Once it received a redesigned intercooler system and automatic controls for its turbosuperchargers, maneuvering flaps, and dive brakes, all of which finally

came together in mid-1944 (but not until more than half of the 10,036 Lightnings had been built), did the P-38 come into its own. The late models were fearsome machines indeed, arguably the best all-around fighter-bomber of the war. Its long range and two engines made it the hands-down favorite of fighter pilots in the Southwest Pacific, that "extra fan" providing a large margin of security for long overwater missions.

The P-38's wing, while a great asset in one

General of the Army George C. Marshall (L) and Army Air Forces Chief, Gen. Henry H. Arnold. Insignia on Arnold's jacket pocket is Pre-WWI aviators wings. (USAF)

way, proved a liability in another, and that was quickly discovered when Maj. Signa Gilkie took one of the first service test YP-38s above 30,000 feet and entered a dive. As the airspeed built above 500mph the airplane's tail began to buffet severely. As the dive continued the machine became progressively nose-heavy, increasing its dive angle to near vertical, while the control yoke oscillated stiffly and defied Gilkie's utmost efforts to move it. He managed to recover by use of his elevator trim tab after the aircraft entered denser air below 18,000 feet.

Wind tunnel tests at Cal Tech established that the tail flutter was the result of turbulent airflow created by the sharp juncture at wing and fuselage, and that was eliminated by a wing fillet that smoothed out the airflow over the tail.

But not until October 1942, 16 months later, when a scale model of the P-38 was tested in the Ames Laboratory high-speed wind tunnel, was the loss of control in 500 mph dives explained. The P-38's wing was entering compressibility. The airflow around the wing was travelling more than 40 percent faster than the airplane itself, and was reaching Mach One (the speed of sound) and creating a shock wave when the aircraft reached an airspeed of slightly over two-thirds Mach, or Mach .67 to be exact. (Most other WWII advanced fighters could be pushed into aerodynamic compressibility, but not as early. The British Spitfire, for example, encountered compressibility at .82 Mach.)

A new wing was out of the question for the P-38; American fighter planes were desperately needed in every theater of war and production was all-important. There was no time to design and test a thinner wing. Therefore, Lockheed engineers devised a "bolt-on" dive brake that tended to limit the P-38's speed in a dive to just short of compressibility in dives of 60 degrees or less.

Col. Ben Kelsey, the Army's fighter airplane project officer, personally tested this modification and approved it in February 1943—but Lockheed was never able to satisfactorily explain why it was not incorporated into the P-38 production lines until mid-1944.

As mentioned, the other high-speed fighters also experienced this phenomenon. At least two P-47s lost their tails to it in test flights, and both Col. (later general) Kelsey and Lockheed test pilot Ralph Virden pulled the tails off P-38s recovering from high-altitude dives. Virden was killed; Kelsey successfully parachuted. The problem was not solved until after WWII when true transonic airplanes were developed.

Had President Roosevelt and his congressional leaders been properly responsive to the nation's security needs during the '30s, American pilots would not have fought for a year and a half in obsolescent and undeveloped airplanes. (Indeed, they may not have had to fight at all.) Of equal significance is the fact that if the aircraft and other key industries in the United States not had sizable arms orders from France and Britain as early as 1937, we would have been plunged into war with far less.

A $25 million order from the British for medium bombers allowed Lockheed to begin plant expansion in mid-1938 (Lockheed was building a handful of small airliners for Japan at the time) and that in turn would make P-38 production possible. In March 1940, the British ordered 667 P-38s, and that got the P-38 production line moving months before the USAAF ordered that airplane in quantity. French orders for 730 Curtiss P-36s in 1939 and 1940 similarly aided Curtiss-Wright. Martin and Douglas also sold airplanes to America's future allies prior to 1940, and all this, including a British order for 1000 P-40s, prompted the U.S. aircraft engine builders along with the airframe makers to expand their production facilities.

True, in 1938 President Roosevelt dramatically called upon the U.S. aircraft industry to produce 10,000 planes per year—and develop a capacity for twice that number—while Britain's Prime Minister Chamberlin was in Munich to sell out Czechoslovakia to Hitler's insatiable appetite in a bid for time. And less than two years later, in the summer of 1940, Roosevelt would up his appeal to 50,000 planes per year as his Secretary of War, Henry L. Stimson, was noting that "Airpower had decided the fate of nations . . ." By that time Poland was gone; Norway, Denmark, Belgium and the Netherlands had fallen to the Nazi conqueror; France was defeated, and the British stood alone, somehow both pathetic and magnificent in their awful peril.

But while Roosevelt was making these ringing pronouncements, he and his Congress were doing little to actually build U.S. airpower or the aircraft industry in the United States. Whatever expansion the aircraft factories accomplished during this period was done with private capital, which in turn was based upon their orders in hand. Not until the myopic U.S. Congress at last enacted the Lend-Lease Bill (HR 1776) on 11 March 1941—just nine months before the attack on Pearl Harbor—did the U.S. aircraft industry receive federal funds for plant expansion.

Meanwhile, after General Marshall took charge of the Army in 1939 (the first non-West Pointer to be Chief of Staff since 1914), the weak and poorly-equipped Air Corps was steadily strengthened with as much speed as could be mustered against congressional opposition. The congressional majority, obviously with Roosevelt's tacit approval, remained adamantly opposed to a U.S. strategic bombing force right up to the minute that they stared disaster in the face, and Chief of Air Corps, Gen. Arnold, had employed a deception or two in order to keep Boeing's B-17 program alive and to procure less than 100 B-17s by 7 December 1941.

Under Gen. Arnold, the divided authority of Air Corps command came to an end, and on 20 June 1941, with Gen. Marshall's strong support, the Army Air Corps became the United States Army Air Forces (USAAF), Lt. Gen. Henry H. Arnold commanding. On 9 March 1942 Gen. Marshall completely reorganized the War Department, and the Army Air Forces received virtually complete control of the development of its special weapon—the airplane. Administering its own affairs, it also came to exercise considerable influence over the Army's conduct of the war in general.

The hour was late and the enemy was upon us, but somehow, our society has always seemed to produce the kind of people we need the most and, with our survival as a free nation at stake, President Roosevelt seemed to possess the ability to recognize them when they were most needed. He passed over 34 higher ranking officers to select George Marshall as the Army's top commander. As events would prove, he never made a better decision.

REVIEW QUESTIONS:

1. Why was there such a strong feeling of neutrality during the 1920s and early 1930s? Why wasn't Congress or the top military leadership of the time impressed with Billy Mitchell's demonstrations?

2. Why did the Army have such poor experience when they flew the mail in 1934? Who was Fred Rentschler? How did Pratt & Whitney get started? What was the significance of the Wasp engine?

3. Why did the U.S. Naval Air Service place so much emphasis on rigid airships? What were the Curtiss F9C-2 Sparrowhawks used for? What happened to the Akron and Macon?

4. What was the significance of the development of the Boeing 247 and the Douglas DC-3? Name some of the U.S. Navy aircraft carriers that were commissioned during the late 1920s and 1930s. Why was the U.S. Navy better funded during the 1930s? Who was General Malin Craig? What was his attitude toward Army air power?

5. Describe some of the aircraft received by the military during the late 1930s. When did the Republic P-47 Thunderbolt first appear? What was the problem with the Lockheed P-38's wing? Why was Congress so slow in responding to the German and Japanese military threat?

Chapter 11

WWII: The Desperate Months

OBJECTIVES: At the end of this chapter you should be able to:

☐ Describe the damage and discuss the political significance of the Japanese attack on Pearl Harbor.

☐ Describe the U.S. losses in the Philippines during the months that followed the attack on Pearl Harbor.

☐ Explain why the battle of Coral Sea was a major strategic victory for the U.S.

☐ Give the reasons for and the implications of the U.S. victory in the battle of Midway.

☐ Discuss the importance of taking Guadalcanal in the southern Solomon Islands.

Sunday, 7 December 1941, dawned clear and beautiful over Hawaii with the mists, as always, scudding low among the peaks of Oahu's Koolau Range. On a lonely hill overlooking Oahu's north coast, Sgt. Joe Lockhard and Pvt. George Elliott were manning a primitive radar set, scanning the empty Pacific. They were bored and anxious for their relief crew to arrive.

It was exactly two minutes past seven A.M. when Lockhard called to his companion, "Hey, George. Come look at this." He made a note with his pencil. "I make it 136 miles."

"What is it?"

"I don't know. But it's our job to report it."

Lockhard cranked the field phone and, after some delay, reached the watch officer at Fort Shafter, a young lieutenant. He made his report, adding that the scope seemed to indicate a large

fleet of airplanes, some 130 miles away, approaching Oahu from slightly east of north.

The lieutenant acknowledged the message and hung up. Nothing to get excited about. Twelve B-17s were due about 8:00 or 8:30 from San Francisco.

The lieutenant was right; two flights of AAF B-17s were due from the mainland. He was also wrong; what Lockhard and Elliott had observed on their scope was indeed something to get excited about. It represented the radio echos from 352 Japanese airplanes from six aircraft carriers: 171 Val dive bombers, 102 Kate attack bombers, and 79 Zero fighters. At 7:55 A.M., approximately 45 minutes after Lockhard's alert was logged at Fort Shafter, that deadly aerial armada began raining destruction on Pearl Harbor.

No warning was ever sounded. The attacking

force achieved complete surprise, partly because the Japanese ambassador and a special envoy continued to negotiate settlement of U.S.-Japanese differences until, literally, the last minute. This pair of Japanese officials was actually in Secretary of State Cordell Hull's office with a note from their government when Hull was informed of the attack.

The military's primary failure at Pearl Harbor was the failure of reconnaissance, which should have been the Navy's responsibility. With a large part of the Navy's ships at anchor in Pearl Harbor, the sea approaches to the great base were essentially unguarded. Although the PBY series of long-distance patrol planes had been available since the mid-'30s, the Navy had not seen fit to procure them in sufficient number to provide a viable early warning system for vital installations vulnerable to attack by enemy fleets. And prior to WWII the U.S. was completely without another form of reconnaissance which might be classified as a "super long-range warning system," a worldwide intelligence gathering organization which could have given the President and his advisors critical data concerning the military and political composition of Japan as well as her probable intentions.

It was, of course, the question of Japan's inten-

tions that figured most prominently in America's vulnerability. Britain's Prime Minister, Winston Churchill said (*The Second World War,* Houghton Mifflin Co., 1948), "All the great Americans around the President and in his confidence felt as acutely as I did the awful danger that Japan would attack British or Dutch possessions in the Far East and would carefully avoid the United States . . ." And Gen. Hap Arnold said in his memoirs, "Like most officers in the War Department, I was under the impression that, if a Japanese attack occurred, it would be made first against the Philippines and then would be carried down the east coast of Asia to Singapore, to the Islands of Borneo, Java and Sumatra." Obviously, it never occurred to Roosevelt, Churchill, or any of their advisors, that the Japanese could misjudge us as badly as we misjudged them.

With this erroneous position permeating the thinking at the top, there should be small wonder that the Army and Navy commanders in Hawaii were lulled into similar attitudes. Both were sacked after the debacle at Pearl, however.

The Japanese Kate bombers, most of them armed with torpedos, concentrated on the Navy ships at anchor around Ford Island, while the Vals

Army fighters in Hawaii at the time of the Japanese attack included 99 P-40Bs and Cs, along with 36 P-36As, in the 15th and 18th Pursuit Groups. (USAF)

A P-36 may well have scored the first air victory for the U.S. in WWII. Six managed to get airborne and engage the enemy during the Pearl Harbor attack. Two P-40s also joined the fight. All but 27 P-40s were destroyed on the ground.

struck at Navy, Marine, and Army airfields and other key installations. The Zeros were free to strafe targets of opportunity since they encountered virtually no U.S. fighter opposition. Eight Army fighters (six P-36As and two P-40s) managed to take off during the attack, and accounted for 10 enemy bombers between them. Lt. George Welch, in a P-40, shot down four. Army and Navy antiaircraft gunners shot down another 18 of the enemy—plus one P-36.

The attack ended at approximately 0945 hours.

The departing Japanese left behind 2400 American dead, 1500 wounded, four battleships sunk, 14 ships heavily damaged, and 233 U.S. warplanes destroyed—plus the certainty that they had aroused the sleeping giant.

The surprise attack on Pearl Harbor united the American people in an outraged determination to fight more effectively than anything the President could have said or done. An hour earlier, the U.S. Congress would have rejected war. But after the news reached Washington (about 1325 hours, or

A Japanese Navy Zero fighter leaves the deck of its carrier early on the morning of 7 December 1941 for the surprise attack on Pearl Harbor and other targets on Oahu. (USN)

1:25 P.M. due to the time difference), and was flashed to a stunned public, even the isolationists were breaking out their flags and calling for vengeance against this enemy who had so greviously wounded us "without provocation."

President Roosevelt called Sunday, the 7th of December 1941, ". . . a date which will live in infamy," and the U.S. Congress responded with roars of anger. A formal declaration of war against Japan came on 8 December 1941, and when Japan's Axis partners, Germany and Italy, followed with declarations of war against the United States, the nation was embarked upon an all-out, two-front war.

The Philippines Lost

Nine and a half hours after word of the Pearl Harbor attack reached the Philippines, the Japanese treated confused U.S. forces there to a repeat performance. Again, despite those hours of warning, all U.S. aircraft were caught on the ground at Clark Field, near Manila. The Navy's Asiatic Fleet under Rear Adm. Thomas C. Hart—if three cruisers, 13 old destroyers, six motor torpedo boats and 29 submarines could be regarded as a "fleet"—was at sea. (Official Air Force records do not agree as to the time of the attack in the Philippines. Maj. (ret) Al Fernandez, who was on the flight line at Clark when the first bombs fell, told this author the time was 1220 hours and, of course, 8 December since the Philippines are east of the International Date Line, though six hours earlier on the clock. Lt. Gen. (ret) Joseph Moore, who flew one of the three P-40s which got into the air to engage the enemy, told us it was "about 1130

Japanese Kate torpedo bomber takes off for the strike against U.S. ships anchored in Pearl Harbor. (USN)

189

This captured photo, taken from a Japanese Kate, was snapped at the exact instant the first torpedo struck the battleship *Oklahoma*. The *Oklahoma* is the third from left, with the *West Virginia* anchored alongside. (USN)

hours." Official Japanese records give it as 1330 hours Tokyo time, which would have been 1230 hours Manila time.)

In overall command in the Far East was Lt. Gen. Douglas MacArthur, and just what he did with the hours of warning he was given is not easily explained. Adm. Hart's radio man picked up the Navy signal from Pearl Harbor 34 minutes after the attack there began, the same signal that was received in Washington D.C., and Hart ordered that it immediately be repeated to MacArthur's headquarters in Manila, as well as to all British and Dutch forces in the area.

It is clear that MacArthur and his staff were fully functioning no later than 0400 hours, and Air Force records show that he "alerted" all his air units at 0430 hours. But there is no record of further orders prior to the noontime attacks on Clark and Iba Airfields. There is also no explanation as

to why Navy Patrol Wing 10 at Cavite and the 17 B-17s at Clark Field were not dispatched at dawn to reconnoiter, particularly in the direction of Formosa, from which a Japanese air attack must (and did) come. MacArthur certainly knew that the President and the Chiefs of Staff all expected that the Philippines would be an early target if war came.

Air Force Gen. Lewis Brereton, who had assumed command of the Far East Air Force (FEAF) only the day before, was at MacArthur's headquarters at 0500 hours seeking permission to send his 17 B-17s against the Japanese airfields on Formosa, but MacArthur was too busy to see his air commander, and MacArthur's Chief of Staff, Gen. Southerland, told Brereton that "Americans must not fire the first shot in this part of the world." That remarkable order may or may not have been changed before noon. Later statements from those

The *Arizona* explodes, partly hiding the *Oklahoma,* as the *California* burns in background. (USN)

Curtiss P-40s, destroyed on the ground by strafing enemy planes, were bulldozed into pile of scrap during cleanup at Wheeler Field in the days following the attack. (USN)

The Douglas B-18 Bolo, a DC-2 with bomber fuselage, was the "economy bomber" on hand in Hawaii and the Phillippines when war came; it was essentially useless. (USAF)

involved do not agree on that question. It should be noted that, although MacArthur had been in Manila since the previous summer, he had no reliable telephone network between his headquarters and his units in the field. The air raid warning system consisted of a radar set at Iba Field, which was out of commission, and a number of designated ground observers along the Luzon coasts. Not one report from a ground observer reached the air units before the enemy arrived. Meanwhile, MacArthur's radioed dispatch to the President late that morning read: "Every possible defense measure is being undertaken. My message is one of serenity and confidence." MacArthur, too, was ready to fight WWI again.

On 8 December 1941, the FEAF consisted of the USAAF 19th Bomb Group, equipped with 34 B-17s (half of which were on the big island of Mindanao, 500 miles to the south of Manila); the 6th Philippine Pursuit Squadron, with 11 obsolete Boeing P-26s, and the four-squadron 24th Pursuit Group (PG), which had 72 Flyable Curtiss P-40s and 35 flyable Seversky P-35s, plus 35 P-40s and 11 P-35s in maintenance or grounded for lack of parts. Some other obsolete aircraft were at Clark Field,

Lt. Boyd D. Wagner, flying a P-40E, became America's first WWII ace when he shot down six enemy aircraft over the Phillippines on 12 and 13 December 1941. (USAF)

but they were of no practical use. The 24th PG's four squadrons, the 3rd, 17th, 29th and 21st, were scattered at Iba, Nichols, Clark, and Del Carmen Fields respectively.

The pilots of the 29th Pursuit Squadron (PS) sat in their P-40 fighters all morning awaiting orders that never came. Then, high in the western sky, someone saw a line of specks, which rapidly resolved into a large number of planes, flying line-abreast, and slanting down toward Clark Field.

Capt. (later, general) Joe Moore and Lts. Randy Keator and Eddie Gilmore were the only ones to get off the ground to meet the attacking force. Four P-40s immediately behind them were destroyed while on their takeoff runs, while fourteen others were destroyed or crippled by strafing Zeros before ever reaching the runway. Moore, Keator, and Gilmore shot down five of the enemy before faulty ammunition silenced their guns.

A few minutes after Clark Field was hit, Iba Field, across the mountains, was struck by other enemy raiders, losing 13 of its 15 P-40s. Moore's squadron lost 18 of its 23 P-40s.

After the attack, the fighter squadrons dispersed to small dirt airstrips and pooled their remaining aircraft, and at the end of a week there was but 24 P-40s left. All but one of the B-17 bombers had been destroyed on the ground at Clark. A few P-35s remained, but they were no match for the Zeros and were not flown in combat. All air combat over the Philippines during the ensuing 90 days was ridiculously one-sided. The invader never appeared with less than 30 Zeros, and the Americans never met them with more than six P-40s. Often, the pilots of the 24th PG attacked with two, sometimes four-plane elements.

Spare parts were cannibalized from wrecks, oil was strained through makeshift filters and reused, tailwheel tires were stuffed with rags, and some P-40s seemed to have more bullethole patches than original skin. The ammo problem was never solved; fully a third of it was defective, and aircraft gun oil congealed into a molasses-like varnish in cold air at high altitudes. No mail, no supplies, no help ever reached the Philippines after the war started there. Food, medicine, and eventually ammunition

was in extremely short supply, but the American and Filipino forces held out.

The main Japanese invasion, following preliminary landings, began on 22 December 1941. The attack centered on Luzon, the northern most and largest island of the archipelago, where all but a small fraction of the defending forces were concentrated. The main landings were made on the beaches of Lingayen Gulf in the northwest and Lamon Bay in the southeast, and on 23 December, MacArthur ordered a general withdrawal into the mountainous Bataan Peninsula, across Manila Bay from the capitol city. Manila itself was occupied by the Japanese without resistance. The 15,000 American troops and 45,000 sketchily-trained Filipinos had their food rations cut in half by mid-January, and their air cover had swindled to nine P-40s, while airmen without planes to fly or service took up rifles and joined the infantrymen in foxholes.

This gallant contingent of American men and women (a number of Army nurses were with the troops), without hope of relief or rescue, called themselves the "Battling Bastards of Bataan" ("no momma, no poppa, no Uncle Sam"). With Filipino patriots, they pinned down two divisions of the enemy's best assault troops and greatly upset the Japanese timetable of conquest.

By April, the defenders were subsisting on about 15 ounces of food daily, mostly rice supplemented by lizard meat, and thousands succumbed to dysentery, dengue, malaria and scurvy. The P-40s flew as long as it was possible to get one into the air, and one can guess at the mood of those airmen as revealed in a grimly humorous message relayed by an American submarine: "Dear President Roosevelt. Please send us another P-40. The one we have is full of holes."

Actually, they had two P-40s when the end came. On 8 April, Gen. Jonathan Wainwright, left in command after MacArthur's escape (by order of the President) to Australia a month earlier, retreated to the caves of Corregidor Island in Manila Bay with most of the surviving Americans, and sadly ordered the remaining defenders of Bataan to surrender. Incredibly, the Americans on Corregidor held out another month before they, too, were forced to surrender, their food and ammunition exhausted. More than most Americans, they paid the price for 20 years of what Billy Mitchell described as " . . . incompetency . . . almost treasonable administration . . . and the delusion of the American Public."

Coral Sea and Midway

The chief goal of American deployment to the Pacific during most of 1942, following the initial reinforcement of Hawaii and the Panama Canal, was to build up a base in Australia and secure the chain of islands leading to it. As early as January, a task force of division size was hastily sent to New Caledonia, and for a few weeks an effort, doomed to failure, was made to stem the enemy's invasion of Java. Thereafter, the buildup had as its first object the defense of Australia itself because, at the end of January, the Japanese had occupied Rabaul on New Britain Island, thus posing an immediate threat to Port Moresby, the weakly-held Australian base in southeastern New Guinea at Australia's doorstep. Two U.S. divisions went to Australia in March and April as construction of air bases was rushed to completion on the steppingstone islands

along the ocean routes to Australia and New Zealand. After the western anchor of this chain, New Caledonia, was secured, Army and Marine garrisons and reinforcements were sent to various other islands along the line, culminating with the arrival of American troops in the Fiji Islands in June 1942.

These moves came none too soon because during the spring, the Japanese, after occupying Rabul, pushed into the southern Solomons, within easy striking distance of the American bases on Espiritu Santo and New Caledonia. They also occupied the northeastern coast of New Guinea, just across the narrow (but mountainous) Papuan peninsula from Port Moresby, where the Americans and Australians were preparing bases and airfields.

The stage was thus set for a major test of strength in the Pacific: American forces thinly spread along an immense arc from Hawaii to Australia; the Japanese securely in possession of the vast areas north and west of that arc, prepared to strike in force at any point.

Nevertheless, as tenuous as this deployment may have appeared, the security of Australia and New Zealand was essential. Later, as American arms grew stronger, this southern semi-circle could be matched with a string of steppingstone bases

The P-40E was deployed in the Phillippines when the Japanese struck, along with some P-40Bs and Seversky P-35s. The P-40E (pictured) had a slightly narrower fuselage than earlier models, shorter landing gear legs, larger radiator scoop, and six wing guns. (USAF)

The *Lexington* was lost in the Battle of the Coral Sea. Crew abandons ship as escorts stand by. (USN)

across the Central Pacific and, with MacArthur proceeding up the east coast of New Guinea to retake the Philippines, the giant jaws of the pincer would be closed and all enemy forces within cut off from supply, reinforcement, or retreat.

All that would take time, American lives, and a great deal of America's treasure, but it did, during those early, desperate days, provide the blueprint for victory. There can be little doubt that the Joint Chiefs planned well in the Pacific war with Japan. Adm. Ernest J. King, Commander-in-Chief of the U.S. Fleet (appointed immediately after Pearl Harbor; another excellent choice made by President Roosevelt), clearly dominated most of those decisions. Adm. King was 62 in 1942, a 1901 Naval Academy graduate—fourth in his class—who spent most of his career at sea until 1927 when he qualified as a naval aviator. He became chief of the Navy's Bureau of Aeronautics in 1933, and was regarded as an "airplane admiral" thereafter.

The first test of the American military posture in the Pacific came in May, when the Japanese made an attempt from the sea to take Port Moresby. That precipitated the great aircraft carrier battle of the Coral Sea. The battle itself was indecisive, but it constituted a strategic victory for the Americans because the enemy was forced to abandon his planned invasion of Port Moresby. Thereupon the Japanese struck eastward, hoping to complete the destruction of the U.S. Pacific Fleet and to seize Midway—a bid for clear naval supremacy in the Pacific.

We should mark the boldness of the U.S. Navy as it ventured forth to fight in the Southwest Pacific when it was the inferior force and in hostile waters. Early in May 1942, two small task forces that had earlier made surprise raids against the enemy's troop buildup on New Guinea's northeast coast joined forces south of the Louisiades and moved northward to intercept the Japanese invasion fleet bound for Port Moresby.

The American units were Task Force 17 under Rear Adm. F.J. Fletcher, who had the carrier *Yorktown* and her escorts, and Task Force 11, consisting of the carrier *Lexington* and her support vessels, commanded by Rear Adm. A.W. Fitch. On 7 May, this combined force, strengthened by the addition of Australian cruisers and destroyers, sent its aircraft against the enemy force and sank the Japanese light carrier *Shoho* during a furious air battle, although some enemy planes were able to sink a U.S. destroyer and tanker. Darkness brought a lull in which both sides lost track of one another, but on the following day Japanese aircraft set fires aboard the *Lexington* which destroyed her, and severely damaged *Yorktown,* while U.S. Navy pilots seriously damaged the enemy's fleet carrier *Shokaku* and shot down most of her planes. The Japanese invasion force, with its air cover gone, had no choice but to flee.

The "Lady Lex" was a poor trade for the *Shoho,* but Moresby—and Australia—had been

Navy F4F Wildcat fighters prepare to take off from the carrier *Enterprise,* 12 May 1942. (USN)

Rare photo, dated 4 June 1942, one of the *Yorktown's* SBDs just prior to takeoff during the Battle of Midway. A handful of these aircraft were about to become the most significant planes in U.S. Naval history. (USN)

saved from invasion and all that portended.

The Battle of the Coral Sea was unique in another way: For the first time in history, a great sea battle had been fought *solely* in the air, the opposing ships never within sight or gunrange of one another. There would be many more such battles.

Less than a month later, the enemy, still confident, was ready to take Midway and deliver a knockout blow to the U.S. Pacific Fleet. It would, in the bargain, occupy Attu and Kiska in the Aleutians, and bomb the U.S. Navy base at Dutch Harbor, Alaska. All this *should* have worked out as planned. It did not because the commander of the U.S. Pacific Fleet, Adm. Chester W. Nimitz, was aware of the enemy's intentions.

Details are unavailable even today, because U.S. intelligence people are loath to talk much about codes, but we do know that U.S. Navy cryptographers in the Office of Naval Intelligence had broken the Japanese diplomatic code prior to Pearl Harbor, and since that code belonged to the same family of codes employed by the Imperial Japanese Navy, Adm. Nimitz was reading portions of the Japanese Navy's radioed messages. That is what allowed Nimitz to plan the ambush of an overwhelmingly powerful enemy force at Midway. Nimitz knew a little of Yamamoto's plan, and correctly guessed the rest of it.

Adm. Yamamoto had reason to feel confident. With the *Lexington* gone, the *Saratoga* and *Yorktown* under repair, and the *Ranger* and *Wasp* in the Atlantic, the Americans should have no more than two carriers, *Enterprise* and *Hornet,* in the Pacific (the ancient *Langley* had long since been downgraded to tender status), while Yamamoto would have an armada of truly awesome proportions. He would send two aircraft carriers and their phalanx of supporting ships northward to attack the U.S.

U.S. Navy aces in their F4F-4 Wildcats just after Midway are Lt. Cmdr. John Thatch in No. 1 and Lt. Edward ''Butch'' O'Hare in No. 13.

Naval base at Dutch Harbor, Alaska, and to occupy the Aleutian Islands of Attu and Kiska. Concurrently, far to the south, would be his Midway Invasion Force, containing one carrier, troop transports, and escorting vessels. Between these two would be his Midway Strike Force One under Adm. Chuichi Nagumo, consisting of four aircraft carriers (*Akagi, Kaga, Hiryu and Soryu*), two battleships, three battle cruisers, and 12 destroyers. Finally, Yamamoto himself would loiter about 300 miles behind Nagumo with one carrier, three battleships and a host of escorts, serving as a reserve or mop-up force. Meticulous planner Yamamoto also dispatched submarines to act as pickets in Hawaiian waters; their job was to attack the U.S. fleet as it (presumably) charged out of Pearl Harbor in response to the attack on Alaskan territory.

Meanwhile, Adm. Nimitz was doing some planning of his own. He inspired repair crews at Pearl to complete a two-month repair job on the *Yorktown* in a matter of days, sent three heavy and three light battle cruisers, with ten destroyers, to harass the enemy's Aleutian Invasion Force, and assembled two task forces with which he hoped to dry-gulch Nagumo. All were gone from Pearl Harbor by 28 May—*before* the enemy subs arrived to attempt interception.

Task Force 16, commanded by Rear Adm. Raymond A. Spruance, was made up of the carriers *Enterprise* and *Hornet,* six cruisers and nine destroyers; Task Force 17 consisted of the carrier *Yorktown,* two cruisers and five destroyers, commanded by R./Adm. Frank J. Fletcher (the senior commander over both forces). These two forces sailed to a point—Adm. Nimitz called it "Point Luck"—350 miles northeast of Midway, where they were to figuratively "lie in the bushes" and wait for Nagumo's powerful strike force.

Fletcher and Spruance reached Point Luck on 2 June and settled down to wait, Nimitz having deduced that the enemy intended to strike sometime between the 4th and 6th of June. In the meantime, Navy PBY Catalina long-range patrol planes from Midway were searching for the Japanese fleet, although they were limited by a large storm front which was advancing from the northwest. The U.S. commanders knew that Yamamoto would very likely take advantage of the rain and low clouds to make his approach undetected. (Radar was a new invention at the time and of limited value.)

Early on the morning of 3 June Yamamoto's Aleutian Invasion Force made a successful attack on Dutch Harbor, and later landed unopposed on Kiska and Attu in the Aleutians. Weather conditions were so poor that a number of Japanese pilots were lost when they failed to find their carriers after the strike—a problem shared by the U.S. task force in the area.

Also on 3 June, at about 0900 hours, Yamamoto's Midway Invasion Force, approaching Mid-

This F4F-4 on Henderson Field, Guadalcanal, 9 February 1943, has 19 aerial victory symbols on its fuselage, although several pilots had flown this craft to achieve that total for lucky No. 2. (USN)

AP-40F of the 44th FS, 18th FG, on the fighter strip at Henderson Field, Guadalcanal, June 1943. The F model P-40 was powered with a Packard-built Rolls-Royce Merlin. (USMC)

way from slightly south of west, was discovered by a Catalina patrol plane some 700 miles from its destination. Army and Marine aircraft based on Midway unsuccessfully attacked this force during the late afternoon and evening hours while, out at Point Luck, Adm. Fletcher listened to their radio chatter and decided that was not the prize he sought. He could ask no questions because his command was maintaining strict radio silence. As night fell, he and Spruance moved to a point about 200 miles north and slightly east of Midway, with about ten miles separating the two task forces. With the enemy invasion force nearing its objective, his heavy guns were certain to come charging out of the fog and rain by daylight.

Fletcher was right. Under scattered clouds ahead of the weather front, Nagumo began launching bombers and fighters from his four carriers for the attack on Midway at 0430 hours on 4 June. And just an hour later, at 0536 hours, a pair of Catalinas found Nagumo's force and immediately radioed its position, course, and speed.

At that moment, the advantage passed to Fletcher and Spruance, because Nagumo was totally unaware of their presence.

Between 0700 and 1000 hours, Midway-based planes struck at Nagumo's force but were driven back with serious losses. Then, 41 TBD Devastator torpedo planes from *Enterprise, Yorktown* and *Hornet* went in at wavetop level, but the enemy ships' massed defensive firepower, plus that of their Zero combat air patrols, was impenetrable. The Devastators achieved no meaningful hits and only four returned to the *Enterprise,* two to *Yorktown,* and none to *Hornet, Hornet's* Torpedo Squadron Eight being completely wiped out.

But those crews had not been sacrificed in vain, because their determined attacks had drawn Nagumo's Zeros down to the surface and left the defending fighters low on fuel and ammunition. As the few surviving torpedo planes left the scene, high above—unmolested at 20,000 feet—*Yorktown's* 17 SBD Dauntless dive bombers, led by Lt. Cmdr. Maxwell F. Leslie, were peeling off and taking dead aim on the Japanese carrier *Kaga.* It was 1022 hours and time had run out for Nagumo.

A minute and a half after Leslie's 17 planes began their dives, Lt. Cmdr. Clarence W. McClusky, leading 37 Dauntlesses from the *Enterprise,* arrived to select two more fat targets: Nagumo's own flagship, the carrier *Akagi,* and the smaller carrier *Soryu.*

Thus it was that, within the space of a few hundred heartbeats, the Imperial Japanese Navy suffered a blow from which it never recovered. By 1029 hours, the 51 Dauntlesses from *Yorktown* and *Enterprise* were reforming in a ragged, exuberant formation for the flight back to Point Luck, leaving behind three enemy aircraft carriers aflame and sinking.

Nagumo's fourth carrier, the *Hiryu,* had a short reprieve because the *Hornet's* air group failed to immediately locate it after the enemy fleet changed course following the initial attacks. They would sink the *Hiryu* later in the day, but not before its planes severely damaged the *Yorktown.*

By the time the Japanese realized that they were fighting three U.S. carriers, their strike force had none. Yamamoto ordered a full-speed withdrawal (including, of course, the Midway Invasion Force far to the south).

The *Yorktown* was listing at too great an angle for her flight deck to be used, so her planes returned to *Enterprise* and *Hornet.* Adm. Fletcher transferred his flag to an escorting cruiser, the *Astoria,* and the *Yorktown's* crew was ordered to abandon ship after it appeared that she would capsize. Fletcher then signaled to Spruance, ordering him to proceed as he saw fit, and that the remaining ships of Task Force 17 would follow.

Spruance pursued the fleeing Japanese for two days, and on the 6th launched two final air strikes against them, sinking the heavy cruiser *Mikuma* and heavily damaging the cruiser *Mogami.* Then, with some of his escort vessels running low on fuel, Spruance reluctantly turned back.

But the enemy managed to strike a final blow. Early the next morning, 7 June 1942, Japanese submarine I-168, commanded by Lt. Cmdr. Yahachi Tanabe, put two torpedos into the crewless *York-*

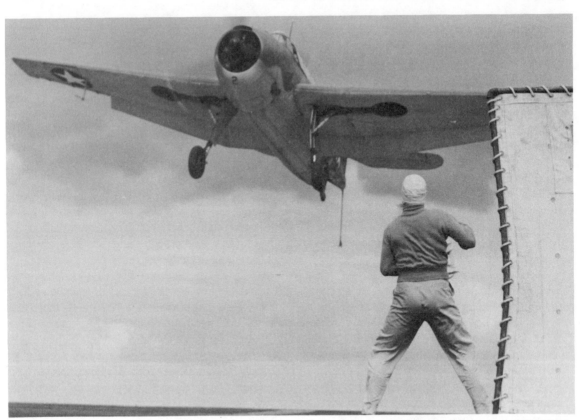

Grumman TBF Avenger comes aboard the escort carrier *Santee* during operations off Guadalcanal, January 1943. (USN)

Lockheed F-5A reconnaissance version of the P-38, with cameras rather than guns in its nose. Bars were added to the star insignia in July 1943. (USAF)

town and sent her to the bottom as she was being towed toward Pearl Harbor by the minesweeper *Vireo*. Tanabe also sank the escorting destroyer *Hammann*. Thus, alone among Yamamoto's entire sea armada, submarine I-168 could return to Japan claiming victory over an American ship at Midway.

After the Battle of Midway, strategic initiative in the Pacific belonged to the U.S. Navy. In addition to his carriers and battle cruisers, the enemy lost 258 airplanes and many of his best pilots. U.S. losses were 40 planes from Midway, and 92 aircraft from three carriers, plus the *Yorktown* and *Hammann*. Few if any Japanese airmen were rescued, although a number of U.S. Navy pilots were plucked from the sea by roving destroyers. After Midway, both the U.S. and Japan had six aircraft carriers remaining, but America would increasingly add carriers to the U.S. fleet, while Japan (actually fighting a defensive war following the defeat at Midway) was unable to replace her lost aircraft carriers and highly trained carrier pilots. Japan's far-flung oceanic empire could be maintained only as long as the Imperial Japanese Navy dominated the Pacific. That dominance was lost at the moment when U.S. Naval Aviator Maxwell Leslie peeled off in his Dauntless and centered his gunsight on the broad deck of the Japanese carrier *Kaga*.

New Guinea and the Solomons

Neither America's leaders nor the American people knew it at the time—and if they had it would not have mattered after the surprise attack on Pearl Harbor—but Japan entered WWII with limited aims and with the intention of fighting a limited war. Its objective was to secure the natural resources Japan lacked (oil, tin, rubber, etc.) in Southeast Asia and much of China, and to establish what Japan's Premier Tojo described as the "Greater East Asia Co-Prosperity Sphere." In other words, Japan would swiftly grab what she wanted, then stand firm behind a solid defensive position and negotiate a peace that would leave her in possession of most of her conquests.

Had she followed the course that President Roosevelt and his advisors expected, she might well have gotten away with it. On the eve of Pearl Harbor, there was a lot of sentiment in the United States against involvement in the war in Europe or a war with Japan. But Japan's decision to "neutralize" the U.S. Navy by a surprise attack unified a divided people, aroused America to wage a total war, and denied the Japanese any chance of conducting the war on their own terms.

After Midway, Japan's war planners had to modify their master plan considerably, and with the

Fifth Air Force's field-modified medium bombers were so successful skip-bombing and strafing in the Battle of the Bismark Sea that North American was inspired to build the B-25G and H Mitchells armed with 75mm field cannon. Beside cannon, B-25H (shown) could also bring ten forward-firing .50-caliber machine guns to bear on strafing target.

mobility of their carrier striking forces curtailed, concentrated on strengthening their existing defensive perimeter. They were far from defeat, and in fact were not ready to negotiate. According to statements made by Japan's military leaders at war's end, they expected the United States to grow weary of attempting to breach those defenses, after which Japan would consider the terms of a negotiated peace.

Meanwhile, the U.S. Joint Chiefs naturally turned to the elimination of the threat to their tenuously held bases in the Southwest Pacific, the lifeline to Australia. On 2 July 1942, they decided to begin a series of operations that would destroy the Japanese stronghold at Rabaul and establish Allied control of the Bismarck Archipelago.

The campaign would have three tasks: (1) Forces of the South Pacific Area (under V./Adm. Robert Ghormley, later commanded by Adm. William "Bull" Halsey) would seize base sites in the southern Solomons; (2) South Pacific forces would advance up the ladder of the Solomons while Southwest Pacific forces (under Gen. Douglas MacAr-

thur) would move up the north coast of New Guinea; (3) The forces of the two theaters would converge on Rabaul and clear the rest of the Bismarck Archipelago. Adm. Nimitz, overall commander of the Pacific Ocean Areas—including the North, Central, and South Pacific—would run the Solomons operations, while Gen. MacArthur would be responsible for the Southwest Pacific. Gen. Marshall and Adm. King would referee the anticipated differences between the hard-bitten Nimitz and the flamboyant MacArthur (although they did not state it quite that way).

MacArthur's air support would be provided by the USAAF Fifth Air Force, born from the ashes of the Far East Air Force in the Philippines, and commanded by Gen. George Kenney. (The former FEAF commander, the fiesty Gen. Lewis Brereton, was in India forming the USAAF 10th AF.)

Air support in the Solomons would be provided by Navy and Marine fliers, plus a handful of Army P-39s and P-40s, until formation of the USAAF 13th AF early in 1943.

The offensive began on 7 August 1942 when

The Eastern Aircraft Division of General Motors built Wildcats under the designations FM-1 and FM-2. The FM-2 was easy to recognize with its tall rudder. The British received more than a thousand Wildcats. (USN)

the 1st Marine Division landed on Guadalcanal and nearby islands in the southern Solomons. The enemy reacted vigorously, and six times during the next four months challenged the U.S. Navy in a series of sharp battles, while air fighting was almost a daily occurrence.

During the first days of bitter fighting on Guadalcanal, the Navy, Marine, and USAAF aircraft, commanded by Rear Adm. J.S. McCain, operated from bases on New Caledonia and in the New Hebrides, with some initial assistance from the air groups of *Saratoga, Enterprise,* and *Wasp.* The carriers, operating in confined waters, withdrew from direct support on 9 August. By 20 August, the Marines had pushed a stubborn enemy, a few feet at

a time, beyond the airstrip and Marine Fighting Squadron 233 and Scout Bombing Squadron 232 moved in. There were plenty of enemy soldiers in the surrounding rain forest, and would be for months, but the fliers took care of their missions and depended upon the "Gyrenes" to protect the airstrip. This was Henderson Field, known to the airmen there by its code name, "Cactus One." A week later, the *Enterprise* brought a deckload of P-40s, and in the weeks to follow other Air Force and Marine air units arrived.

During Christmas Week, Marines, strengthened by Army troops, took over the area known as "Lunga Beach" on Guadalcanal and it became Fighter One Base, with Marine Fighting Squadron

Japanese Mitsubishi G4MI Betty Bomber. P-38s of 347th FG bushwhacked Betty carrying Admiral Yamamoto, costing Japan her best military mind. (USAF)

214 (VME-214, Pappy Boyington's "Black Sheep") at one end of the strip, and the P-40-equipped 44th FS of the 18th FG* at the other. Contrary to Hollywood's portrayal of the Black Sheep, there were no Army nurses on Fighter Base One and no liquor. There were Spam, dehydrated potatoes, mosquitos, and dysentery in abundance.

Guadacanal was not declared secured until 9 February 1943. In the meantime, in addition to the fierce fighting on the island, six major sea battles were fought in the area. *Saratoga's* air groups sank the Japanese light carrier *Ryujo* during the Battle of the Eastern Solomons, 23-25 August; *Enterprise* was damaged by enemy carrier-based bombers during that battle and forced to retire. Then the *Saratoga* took a submarine torpedo on 31 August and went to Australia for repairs, and the *Wasp* was sunk by a submarine on 15 September while escorting a troop convoy to Guadalcanal. During October, the *Hornet,* in Task Force 17, repeatedly sent her planes against enemy targets on Guadalcanal and, with *Enterprise,* fought in the Battle of Santa Cruz (26-27 October) in which she was sunk by Japanese dive bombers. In the final carrier actions of the campaign, *Enterprise,* severely damaged during the Battle of Santa Cruz (the enemy threw four carriers into that battle, two of which were put out of action but not sunk), went to Noumea, New Caledonia for repairs, and was back in action by 15 November.

In the long, proud history of the U.S. Marine Corps, no pages stand out more vividly than those containing the record of the prolonged Battle for Guadalcanal. That campaign alone should provide a shining beacon of inspiration for every man and woman who has worn that uniform since. On the ground and in the air, the Marines spearheaded the bloodiest fighting, and the Marine air groups alone accounted for 427 enemy planes destroyed in combat.

The advance from Guadalcanal began 21 February 1943, in the Russells, sixty miles to the northeast. Although there were no noteworthy naval engagements for a time, aerial fighting continued unabated. Enemy air attacks on Guadalcanal, particularly on Henderson Field, did not let up until June, and on the 16th April the island was subjected to one of the most devastating air strikes of the campaign. The Japanese sent 160 bombers and fighters which were intercepted by more than 100 American fighters from the Army, Navy and Marine Corps. The enemy lost 107 planes; the Americans, six.

By the end of 1943, Adm. Nimitz was ready to begin his final assault on Rabaul, and the drive up the Solomons ended with occupation of the Green

*In May, 1942, all USAAF Pursuit Groups became "Fighter Groups," and Pursuit Squadrons became "Fighter Squadrons." Normally, a Fighter Group consisted of three squadrons of 35 aircraft per squadron—on paper, at least. In combat areas, groups were often under-strength.

Islands—just 120 miles from Rabaul—on 15 February 1944. As Adm. Arleigh Burke put it, "Behind lay bloody Guadalcanal—an epitaph, and enduring symbol of American bravery and sacrifice."

In January 1943, the USAAF 13th Air Force was formed around the 347th FG, which had been operating over Guadalcanal and adjacent waters since the previous October. The 347th contained one squadron each of P-40s, P-39s, and P-38s. The 13th AF gradually accumulated a hodgepodge of B-17s, B-25s, and other aircraft, including the 8th and 18th FGs equipped with P-38 Lightnings, and the 5th, 42nd, and 307th Bomb Groups (BG) flying B-24 Liberators and B-25 Mitchells. While the bombers went to Rabaul and attacked enemy shipping in the area, the fighters of the 13th AF opposed enemy raids over the Solomons and the advancing ground forces. Australian P-40s (Kittyhawks) joined in this effort and guarded the "back door" in the southern Solomons and New Caledonia.

Meanwhile, Gen. Kenney's 5th AF on New Guinea was being built up around the 49th, 24th, and 35th FGs, which were equipped with whatever fighter planes Kenney could lay hands on. Early in 1943, Kenney had a total of 330 fighters, of which 80 were P-38s and 72 were the decidedly inferior P-39s. The rest were P-40s, including seven Royal New Zealand Air Force squadrons and eight Royal Australian Air Force squadrons, plus one Dutch squadron. (British and Commonwealth squadrons contained 9-12 aircraft.) Kenny's bomber force would grow from the relative handful of B-17s, A-20s and B-25s of the 7th, 19th, 3rd and 22nd BGs possessed early in 1943 to a total of 11 bomb groups a year later; an eventual total of five USAAF fighter groups after the 475th and 58th FGs were added. Gen. Paul "Squeeze" Wurtsmith was the 5th AF's fighter commander.

The 5th AF, flying from airstrips in the Port Moresby area, made all the difference in the Battle of the Bismark Sea. In fact, that battle was fought primarily between enemy warships and Kenney's airplanes. On 1 March 1943 the Japanese sent a 16-ship convoy from Rabaul toward Lae on New Guinea's north coast to beef up their base there with an additional 6000 troops and thereby keep MacAr-thur contained in southern New Guinea. But F-5 Lightnings (the recce version of the P-38, fitted with cameras in place of guns) of the 17th Photo Squadron (PhS) discovered the convoy en route. On 2 March, in poor weather, 28 B-17s, escorted by 16 P-38s, sank one of the troop transports in Huon Gulf and shot down two enemy fighters. On the following day, skip-bombing and strafing, 28 Lightnings, with a mixed formation of 5th AF A-20s, B-25s, and some Australian Beaufighters, sent two destroyers and three transports to the bottom. U.S. Navy PT Boats accounted for the rest of the transports. Of the 16-ship convoy, only four destroyers survived, rescuing perhaps half of the enemy soldiers and beating a retreat to Rabaul in deteriorating weather.

It was not a large battle by WWII standards, but taken together with victory in the Solomons and devastating air strikes against the Japanese airfields on New Guinea's north coast which destroyed 200 enemy planes on the ground (made possible by use of a secret jungle airstrip built by U.S. Army engineers only a few miles from the enemy strongholds), the 5th AF over New Guinea, and the 13th AF over the Solomons, gained control of the air—with the help, of course, of the Marine Corsair units moving up through the Solomons. That greatly faciliated American strategy in the Pacific.

That strategy was predicated upon three lines of advance: Across the Central Pacific, the USAAF 7th AF in support of Naval units via the Gilberts, Marshalls, Marianas, Carolines and Palaus toward the Philippines; in the Southwest Pacific the 5th AF covering (and often leading) MacArthur's march up the north coast of New Guinea toward the Philippines; and the South Pacific line of advance up through the Solomons with the 13th AF, plus Navy, Marine and RAAF squadrons, to encircle and neutralize Raaul, which was as important to Japan as was Pearl Harbor to the U.S. as a Pacific base.

During the first two weeks of April 1943, Adm. Yamamoto moved most of his carrier air groups onto Rabaul for Operation *I-go,* and all-out attempt to regain control of the air over New Guinea and the Solomons, and in mid-month struck at Port Moresby and Milne Bay with 150-plane raids. But

Yamamoto's great aerial offensive was abruptly terminated by a flight of 14 P-38s from 347th FG on Guadalcanal. On 18 April these Lightnings were dispatched by Adm. Bull Halsey (Nimitz' deputy in the South Pacific area) to shoot down a certain Japanese Betty bomber due to arrive at an enemy airfield on Bougainville at a given time.

Halsey's information came from the Japanese themselves, by way of the Navy's decoding experts, and the prize was a big one: Adm. Isoruku Yamamoto would be aboard that bomber.

The P-38s flew a long, roundabout route, staying well out to sea to avoid detection. Counting on Adm. Yamamoto's reputation for punctuality, they carefully timed their arrival over Bougainville to coincide with that of their quarry.

Yamamoto was on time. So were the P-38s. The admiral's plane went down aflame under the guns of Capt. Thomas Lanphier, while the remaining Lightnings shot down a second Betty and engaged the escorting six Zeros. One P-38, flown by Lt. Ray Hine, was lost in the fight.

But the enemy's Operation *I-go* was called off. Japan had lost her greatest military strategist.

REVIEW QUESTIONS:

1. How many Japanese aircraft took part in the attack on Pearl Harbor? Why were we caught so unaware? Describe our losses in manpower and shipping. How was the attack on our bases in the Philippines a repeat performance? What were some of the unexplained occurrences regarding messages to General MacArthur's headquarters? What was the fate of General Wainwright's forces?

2. What was the significance of the battle of Coral Sea? How was it a unique naval engagement? Why was the battle of Midway such an incredible victory? How come the Douglas SBD Dauntless dive bombers had a clear shot at the Japanese carriers?

3. What was the strategy of the U.S. Joint Chiefs of Staff for the Southwest Pacific? Why was the battle for Guadalcanal such a long and bitterly fought campaign? Describe the battle of the Bismark Sea. What was the significance of this victory?

4. What was operation I-go? How was Admiral Yamamoto killed?

Chapter 12

The War in Europe

OBJECTIVES: At the end of this chapter you should be able to:

☐ Summarize the U.S. position on the War in Europe at the time of the fall of France in June 1940.

☐ Highlight the purpose of Operation Torch.

☐ Discuss some of the problems faced by General Eisenhower during the early part of the North African Campaign.

☐ Discuss the importance of the Italian campaign to the allied victory in Europe.

☐ Describe the combined British and American bomber offensive against Germany starting in January 1943.

☐ Describe the preparation of manpower and equipment for the Normandy invasion.

☐ Discuss the importance of tactical and strategic air power during the last year of the War in Europe.

Four days after the surprise Japanese attack on Pearl Harbor, Germany and Italy declared war on the United States, effectively settling any question there may have been in the public mind as to whether or not America would also have to fight in Europe.

President Roosevelt, his military leaders, and perhaps many Americans had accepted that fact long before. As early as 1939 the President had looked the other way as American-built warplanes were pushed by hand across the border into Canada for delivery to England, a practice that supposedly got around U.S. neutrality laws. On the eve of France's defeat in June 1940, the President directed the transfer of large stocks of Army WWI weapons, and ammunition and aircraft to both France and Great Britain; after France fell these munitions helped to replace Britain's losses in the evacuation of its forces from the Continent at Dunkerque. More aid to Britain was forthcoming in September when the United States traded 50 over-age destroyers for offshore Atlantic bases. The American position was clear by March 1941, when the Congress passed the Lend-Lease Act, sweeping away the pretense of neutrality and by openly avowing that America would become an "arsenal of democracy" against aggression.

Actually, these acts constituted a measure of self-defense, the fundamental purpose being to help contain the military might of the Axis powers—Germany, Italy and Japan—until the U.S. could build its own shaky defenses.

American military preparations and actions during the remaining months of 1941 prior to the Japanese attack were steadily toward U.S. participation in the war against Germany. In April, the President authorized an active naval patrol of the western half of the Atlantic Ocean. In May, the United States assumed responsibility for the operation of military air routes across the North Atlan-tic via Greenland, and across the South Atlantic via Brazil. In May, Roosevelt also proclaimed an unlimited national emergency and ordered the Army and Navy to prepare an expeditionary force to be sent to the Azores to block any German advance into the South Atlantic.

A few days before the Germans invaded the Soviet Union (22 June 1941), the President sent U.S. Marines and the 33rd FS to guard Iceland. The 33rd, which belonged to the 8th FG, flew its P-40s off the deck of the aircraft carrier *Wasp* to Reykjavik with orders to attack any Axis aircraft or ship found within 50 miles of shore. By October the U.S. Navy was fully engaged in ship convoy duties in the western part of the Atlantic, and Navy ships, with some assistance from Army aircraft, were join-

The P-40s of the 33rd FS, 8th FG, were sent by President Roosevelt to Iceland in August 1941 to forestall the possibility of German seizure of that strategically located island. (USAF)

Carrier *Ranger* bound for North Africa with replacement P-40Ls (Merlin-powered) as escorting destroyer drops depth charges over suspected enemy submarine. (NASM)

ing with British and Canadian forces in warring against German submarines. During the third week in October, the new U.S. Navy destroyer *Kearny* was torpedoed in the South Atlantic and President Roosevelt declared in indignation. "We have wished to avoid shooting, but the shooting has started, and history has recorded who fired the first shot . . . All that will matter is who fired the last shot!" Actually, the *Kearny* was joining British warships in an attack on a German U-boat when she was hit.

In November Congress voted to repeal prohibition against the arming of American merchant ships and their entry into combat zones, and the stage was set (as Prime Minister Churchill noted on 9 November) for "constant fighting in the Atlantic between American and German ships."

Apparently, all of the overt American moves in 1941 toward involvement in the war against Germany were acceptable to the majority of the American people, with only a small though vociferous minority criticizing the President for the nation's

departures from neutrality. America, along with the British and Dutch, had also embargoed oil shipments to Japan and imposed other trade sanctions on the Nipponese for their international misbehavior, and no one questioned the propriety of that. (Those embargos forced Japan to do *something*, even if it was wrong, because she had no oil or certain other strategic materials of her own, and the American/British/Dutch position left her with no face-saving way out, because resumption of normal trade was tied to the condition that Japan get out of China and Indochina and, in effect, renounce her treaties with Germany and Italy. Premier Tojo and his warlords never considered that alternative.)

North Africa and Italy

Once the nation was committed to war, every American, from the President to the humblest citizen, seemed to possess the same attitude toward it: a strong resolve for quick, direct, and total action. The trouble was that during 1942 the strength of our arms did not match the strength of our will.

Nevertheless, after the Battle of Midway the U.S. Navy, weak and exhausted though it was, completely confident that it would soon own the Pacific Ocean, and (although the Joint Chiefs were against it) President Roosevelt confidently placed his finger on a map of the North African coast and told them that, since the Allies were not yet ready to invade Hitler's Europe, we would invade North Africa instead, and then move up through Italy to attack Europe's "soft underbelly."

The invasion of North Africa, Operation *Torch*, was Churchill's idea, prompted by the fact that Germany's brilliant Field Marshal Erwin Rommel, the "Desert Fox," was then chasing the British 8th Army across Libya and threatening Britain's supply of Middle East oil. Also, with the Germans and their Italian allies in possession of that narrow but strategic strip of the North African littoral between Tunisia and Egypt—the Mediterranean on the north and impassable desert to the south—they denied use of the Mediterranean to Allied shipping and largely diluted the value of the Suez Canal.

Torch was scheduled for 8 November, and just five days before that Gen. Bernard Montgomery's British 8th Army broke out of its defensive position at El Alamein in Egypt (Rommel's Afrika Korps had been stopped just 70 miles short of Alexandria), and was pursuing Rommel westward into Libya. By that time, most of the 400-ship invasion force was at sea, including the U.S. Navy Task Group 34.2 under Rear Adm. E.D. McWhorter with the fleet carrier *Ranger* and the escort carriers *Sangamon, Suwannee,* and *Santee* to provide air cover for the landings. The escort carrier *Chenango* was also along, her deck containing the 33rd FG's 78 P-40s. the 1st and 14th FG's P-38s were waiting at Land's End, England, and would stage through Gibralter after the invasion was underway.

The invasion came off as scheduled, before daylight on the morning of 8 November 1942, with American troops put ashore near Casablanca in French Morocco and in Algeria near the ports of Oran and Algiers. The French fought for their German masters for three days before throwing down their arms; during that time Allied air support for the invasion came from McWhorter's carriers, bolstered by Royal Air Force (RAF) Spitfires from Malta.

On the 10th, airfields near Oran were taken and the 33rd's Warhawks immediately moved in, while P-38s of the 1st and 14th FGs began operation the following day from Tafaraoui, Algiers. These USAAF groups were part of Gen. James Doolittle's newly created 12th AF, which also included the 301st, 310th, 97th, 47th, 98th, 319th, 320th, and 17th BGs flying B-17s, B-24s, B-25s, A-20s, and

This Bf.109G of JG 27 was shot down during the Tunisian Campaign. Powered with the Daimler-Benz DB 605 of 1475 hp, it had a speed of 403 mph at 21,325 feet. Armament was two 7.9 mm machine guns and a 20mm cannon, the latter firing through the prop spinner. (USAF)

A P-40F Warhawk of the 64th FS, 57th FG, 9th AF, which fought through Egypt, Libya and Tunisia attached to the Desert Air Force. The 57th later fought in Italy. (NASM)

B-26s. The 31st FG, equipped with British Spitfires, also went into action over North Africa within a week.

The only trouble with Doolittle's 12th AF was that *Torch* commander Gen. Dwight D. Eisenhower soon had its 800 airplanes (300 fighters, 300 bombers, and support aircraft such as C-47s) spread over 600 miles of desert to serve the presumed needs of the ground commanders, which in both deployment and mission denied the American fighter pilots the opportunity to do their job as it should be done, i.e., *first* gain control of the air.

The 12th AF—and the troops on the ground depending upon it—paid heavily for Eisenhower's on-the-job training until "Ike," aware that he was doing something wrong, sent to England for Gen. Carl "Tooey" Spaatz (probably America's most able air commander) to tell him what it was. Jimmy Doolittle probably had the answer, but lacked Eisenhower's trust.

Doolittle had been a lieutenant colonel just six months before, and eighteen months before that, a civilian. He had left the Air Corps in 1930, after 12 years' service, and returned in 1940. Then, in April, 1942, he led 12 B-25 Mitchells off the deck of the carrier *Hornet* for the celebrated raid on Tokyo. Twelve medium bombers loaded with fuel—they were launched more than 800 miles at sea—could not deliver sufficient bomb tonnage to greatly damage the enemy, but the Tokyo raid did provide Americans, civilians and servicemen alike, with a tremendous morale boost at a time when all war news was bad. All of the B-25s, and some of their crews, were lost after running out of fuel over China in bad weather, but Doolittle and his surviving crews returned to the United States as heroes, and Doolittle was promoted to the rank of brigadier general by a grateful President. As commander of the 12th AF, Doolittle wore two stars. Later, as boss of the 15th and 8th AFs in turn, he was a lieutenant general—a *lot* of rank and responsibility for a reserve officer.

Gen. Eisenhower faced several unanticipated

The Junkers Ju.87 Stuka, German dive bomber, was designed for close air support of the mechanized German Army in Europe, but was easy prey for Allied fighters in North Africa. (NASM)

problems in Northwest Africa in addition to strong Luftwaffe action. The Germans reacted to the invasion with unexpected speed and began an airlift of troops into Tunisia from across the Mediterranean just one day after the American troops were landed ashore. Initially slowed by the confused French resistance, and then confronted by seasoned German forces, while depending upon a supply line that reached all the way back to the United States, Eisenhower found his drive toward Tunis slowed until it became bogged in the mud of seasonal rains. He had expected to be in Tunis by Christmas, but Rommel was retreating from the opposite direction across Libya in good order and would, in late January 1943, halt his westward retreat at the Mareth Line, a series of old French fortifications near the southern border of Tunisia, which the British 8th Army would find difficult to penetrate. Meanwhile, 100,000 German and Italian troops commanded by Gen. Juergen von Arnim blocked Eisenhower's forces in northwest Tunisia. The Allied plan to defeat both von Arnim and Rommel by squeezing them between the American and British armies east of Tunis having failed, Eisenhower had no option

but to assume defensive positions in the harsh Tunisian mountains until he could accumulate enough strength to attack in conjunction with a renewed strike by Gen. Montgomery against the Mareth Line.

In the meantime, the 12th AF was being frittered away in a seemingly endless series of scattered, uncoordinated actions. Gen. Spaatz changed that. He told Ike that all his air units must be commanded by *air* officers; that the chain of command for all air operations must be through air officers all the way to the top; that the U.S. fighter groups must concentrate on defeating the Luftwaffe and taking control of the air. Then, and only then, could the Army move with its communications and supply lines intact and with effective, dependable direct air support, with the Air Force free to destroy the enemy's vital communications and transport, whether it be by ship or by air across the Mediterranean.

Eisenhower gave Spaatz a free hand to reorganize U.S. airpower in northwest Africa. Spaatz, coordinating with Britain's Air Chief Marshall Tedder (Montgomery's air boss), formed the Northwest

The P-38J model (foreground) with intercooler radiators beneath the engines was a greatly improved machine, but did not enter combat until the war in the MTO had moved into Italy. Photo-recon F-5B in background. (USAF)

The Focke-Wulf 190 was a formidable enemy, probably the best German fighter of the war. Its 1760-hp BMW twin-row radial gave it a speed of 395 mph at 17,000 feet. Shown here is an FW 190A-8 carrying aft fuselage "defense of the Reich" bands seen in last days of the war.

African Air Forces (NAAF) around the U.S. 12th AF, with himself in command, and then placed it in the new Mediterranean Air Command with Tedder's Desert Air Force, and with Tedder in overall command.

Air Chief Marshall Tedder's commonwealth Desert Air Force, with complete control of the air, had lead Montgomery's 8th Army all the way from El Alamein in Egypt, because Montgomery as well

as Montgomery's superior, Gen. Sir Harold Alexander, Commander-in-Chief, Middle East, understood the proper use of airpower and utilized it wisely, i.e., they listened to Tedder.

Tedder's Desert Air Force mostly consisted of RAF sand SAAF (South African Air Force) squadrons flying Hurricanes, Spitfires, and Kittyhawks, along with some Beaufighters and Wellington bombers, plus the small U.S. 9th AF which had been

The Martin B-26 Marauder medium bomber had a reputation as a "widow maker," but crews swore by it. The 9th AF contained eight Marauder groups. (USAF)

Chancellor of Germany Adolf Hitler, and Reichsmarschall Herman Goering, boss of the Luftwaffe. (USIA)

formed in Egypt the previous August by Gen. Lewis Brereton.

Brereton had four Warhawk groups, the 57the, 79th, 324th and 325th FGs; two medium bomb groups, the 12th and 322nd; and two B-24 heavy bomb groups, the 98th and 376th. None possessed its normal complement of aircraft, and Brereton had equipped his understrength bomber groups partly by shanghaiing some B-24s and their crews when they stopped in Egypt for fuel en route to India.

By early March 1943, all Allied airpower in the theater was operating under a single command and run by air officers and the situation in North Africa quickly improved for the Allies. Rommel, badly in need of fuel for his panzers, made an unexpected thrust in the Tunisian mountains against Eisenhower's forces in an attempt to capture NAAF airfield gasoline supplies. The Desert Fox gained Kasserine Pass and took 2,000 American prisoners, but failed to reach the fuel he needed. He would undoubtedly have preferred not to have the prisoners because his only supplies came by airlift across the Mediterranean from Italy and Sicily and he was having trouble enough feeding his own troops.

On 7 April, the British 8th Army linked up with Eisenhower's forces in north-central Tunisia after skirting the Mareth Line. The two armies, which had started out nearly 1700 miles apart six months earlier, at last closed the pincer to surround Rommel and back him against the sea in northern Tunisia.

The German commander would hold out there until 13 May 1943 by which time, lacking the means to further resist, Rommel escaped to Italy and surrendered his 270,000 German and Italian troops. Allied airpower had swept the Luftwaffe from the air and severed Rommel's aerial supply lines across the Mediterranean.

The main blow was struck by 46 American Warhawks and 12 RAF Spitfires in a single action on 18 April, Palm Sunday, and that battle has been known ever since as the "Palm Sunday Massacre." Throughout that day, NAAF and Desert Air Force fighters had patrolled the Mediterranean off the Tunisian coast watching for the German transport planes but found nothing. Then, at 1650 hours it was the turn of the 57th FG's three squadrons, the 64th, 65th, and 66th, who could put up only 34 P-40s, so they were joined by 12 more P-40s from the 324th FG's 314th Squadron.

The Warhawks stayed low, flying abreast in four-plane formations, stair-stepped from 4000 feet to 12,000 feet. The dozen Spits were at 15,000 feet, just below an overcast watching for enemy fighters.

For an hour, they saw nothing but an empty sea. Then suddenly someone saw the enemy's aerial convoy. The three-engined Junkers Ju. 52s were painted in green and blue camouflage that blended with the water below and were flying just a few feet above the surface. There were 30 of them, then, 60, then nearly a hundred. The Warhawks attacked in pairs.

It truly was a massacre. Some of the 30 or so Bf. 109 Messerschmitt and Macchi C.202 Italian fighters escorting the transports got past the covering Spits above, but the exultant P-40 pilots turned into them and dominated that confrontation as well.

At low altitudes, the P-40 gave up nothing to the Messerschmitts or Macchis.

It was all over within ten minutes, and the P-40s, low on fuel and ammunition, turned for home. Six of their number and one Spitfire had gone down, but the enemy's very lifeline in North Africa had been cut. The official score was 58 Ju.52 transports, 14 Mc202 and four Bf.109 fighters destroyed, although there was little doubt that other Ju.52s, badly damaged, had gone down into the sea unnoticed during the confusion of battle. Three pilots of the 57th FG became "instant" aces that evening: Lts. Richard E. Duffey and Arthur B. Cleveland each got five Ju.52s, and Lt. McArthur Powers shot down four Ju.52s and one Messerschmitt.

The enemy made several more desperate at-tempts to run the Allied aerial blockade during the following week, with about 20 transport planes each time, and each time suffered disaster. A final attempt, at night, was met by night Beaufighters of the Desert Air Force.

The enemy was allowed no respite. The combined Mediterranean Air Command, ever more fat and sassy with battle experience and receiving new U.S. air groups (including the Lightning-equipped 82nd FG and the P-40-equipped all-black 99th FS), mounted a three-week air offensive against the heavily-fortified Italian island of Pantelleria which lay about 50 miles off the Tunisian coast. Pantelleria surrendered on 11 June—the first bit of enemy territory in history to be taken with airpower alone.

Later that summer, when the Warhawk pilots

Crew members inspect battle damage to the tail of their B-25 Mitchell medium bomber of the 12th AF in Italy. Mission was to Yugoslavia. (USAF)

Flight of 9th AF P-38s, returning from a mission against German targets, make the approach to their base at low altitude. Northrop P-61 Black Widows are just visible at lower left. (USAF)

of the 325th FG (the "Checkertails") felt that they had sufficiently discouraged the Italian defenders on the island of Sardinia, they dropped a note, addressed to the commanding general, suggesting that he surrender the island to the 325th FG. That undoubtedly amused Tedder and Spaatz when they heard about it, but they were forced to pass the word that any such negotiations would be handled at a higher level.

After Pantelleria fell, Sicily was next, a campaign that lasted less than a month after the NAAF destroyed nearly 1000 Axis aircraft, most of them on the ground. During the invasion by 160,000 troops of the U.S. 7th Army and British 8th Army, the Allied air cover extended well into Italy; by 13 July 1943, elements of Tedder's Mediterranean Air Command were making themselves at home on

Sicilian airfields. Three weeks later, the Germans retreated across the Strait of Messina into Italy, and the Allies could look across those scant three and a half miles of water to the tip of Italy, toward what President Roosevelt had called "Europe's soft underbelly."

The Italian Campaign

It did not prove to be very soft. Although, with invasion imminent, the Italians disposed of their dictator, Benito Mussolini, and signed a separate peace with the Allies, they remained virtual prisoners in their own country which was occupied by 26 German divisions. And the Germans intended to fight for every inch of Italy.

On 3 September 1943 British forces under Montgomery landed in extreme southern Italy, and

North American's Mustang, designed around the Allison V-1710, became a true thoroughbred when re-engined with the Rolls-Royce Merlin, built under license in the U.S. by Packard. This early P-51B shows unusual markings: RAF camouflage, serial, and fin flash with red-bordered (mid-1943) U.S. "star and bar." (USAF)

the U.S. 5th Army under Lt. Gen. Mark Clark followed with an assault on the beaches near Salerno, a point selected because it represented the northern limit of effective Allied air support operating from airfields in Sicily. The ground-based aircraft of the Mediterranean Air Command—mostly the 9th and 12th U.S. Air Forces—provided all air support because all U.S. Navy carriers were in the Pacific.

The Italian Campaign would drag out for 19 months, the Germans (under Field Marshal Albert Kesselring) at last surrendering on 2 May 1945, just

five days before the war ended in Europe with the German surrender at Eisenhower's headquarters in Reims, France.

Less generally acclaimed than other phases of WWII, the campaign in Italy nevertheless had a vital part in the overall conduct of the war. At the crucial time of the Normandy landings, 25 Allied divisions in Italy were tying down 26 German divisions that might well have upset the balance in France. As a result of this campaign, the Allies obtained airfields useful for the strategic bombing of Germany and the Balkans. Conquest of the Italian

Definitive version of the Mustang was the bubble-canopied P-51D, seen here in service with the 8th AF's 20th FG. This early "D" lacks the later-standard dorsal fin. Note the 108-gallon drop tanks, which allowed the Mustangs to escort the 8th's "heavies" to even the most distant targets. (Merle Olmstead collection)

Enemy flak severed the oil line of this Republic P-47 Thunderbolt of the 12th AF, so Lt. Edwin King returned to base thoroughly bathed in oil. He was strafing gun positions near Brascia, Italy. (USAF)

peninsula further guaranteed the safety of Allied shipping in the Mediterranean.

Gen. John Cannon's, 12th AF, operating from captured airfields around Naples and Salerno, was a tactical air force, its air groups primarily consisting of fighters and medium bombers. The newly-formed 15th AF contained B-17 and B-24 heavy bombers, along with P-47 fighters and three P-38 groups transferred from the 12th AF, and filled a strategic role under Gen. Nathan Twining. The 9th AF, which had fought from Egypt to Tunisia with Tedder, joined the 8th AF in England for the air offensive against Germany. Also to England went Gens. Eisenhower, Spaatz and Doolittle, with Air Marshal Tedder, to prepare for the cross-channel invasion, and Gen. Ira Eaker replaced Tedder as

The Messerschmitt Bf.109F had a top speed of 382 mph at 17,000 ft, and was considered by many Luftwaffe fighter pilots to be the best of the 109 series. The more powerful 109Gs and Ks which followed gained weight and lost maneuverability.

the top air commander in the Mediterranean Theater of Operations (MTO).

Gen. Eaker had approximately 1200 fighter airplanes in Italy: seven fighter groups in the 12th AF and five fighter groups in the 15th AF, plus 16 squadrons of RAF, RAAF, and SAAF fighters. The RAF squadrons were mostly equipped with Spitfires, while the Australians and South Africans went to Italy from North Africa with Kittyhawks. About half of the 12th AF fighters were Warhawks at first, but all were re-equipped with Thunderbolts (and, eventually, Mustangs). The 15th AF had three Lightning groups (plus one photo-recce F-5 group), two Thunderbolt and one

A B-24 Liberator of the 15th AF is hit by flak while attacking the marshalling yards at Munich, Germany. (USAF)

Spitfire group (31st FG). While the Thunderbolt and Spit groups switched to Mustangs late in the war, the Lightning groups in the MTO kept their P-38s.

Eaker also had 10 medium bomber and light bomber groups in the 12th AF, two flying A-36s (Allison-powered dive bomber Mustangs), four equipped with B-25 Mitchells, and three with B-26 Marauders. The 15th AF, by mid-1944, contained no less than 21 heavy bomber groups (the 15th was bombing Germany from its bases in Italy by then). Six of these groups flew B-17 Flying Fortresses, and 15 groups had B-24 Liberators.

The 325th FG, which fought with the 12th AF in North Africa and was transferred to the 15th AF in Italy, flew P-40s, P-47s and P-51s in turn, and provides us with an interesting statistic: They destroyed 3.6 enemy aircraft for each P-40 lost in combat, 3.9 for each P-47, and 3.2 for each P-51. If *that* doesn't start some arguments, nothing will.

Throughout the winter of 1943-44 the Germans occupied strong defensive positions anchored on the towering peaks around the town of Cassino, about 90 miles south of Rome. On 22 January 1944, American and British troops landed at Anzio, 60 miles behind the enemy's "Winter Line," but the Germans kept this force pinned down on its beachhead, and but for constant Allied air strikes this force could not have survived. The Winter Line was not breached until May 1944, after the 12th AF had methodically destroyed all rail and highway routes of supply to the Germans.

The enemy withdrew to the Apennines in northern Italy and stubbornly remained there until, again, with his lines of supply severed by Allied airpower, half-starved, the bereft of the means to further resist, he surrendered just a few days before the war ended in Europe.

Throughout the final year of the war in Europe, the 15th AF in Italy coordinated its mass attacks on Germany with those of the U.S. 8th AF in England, and the 15th's P-38s, because of their long range, always escorted their "Big Friends."

A typical mission was that of 2 April 1944 when 450 B-17s and B-24s of the 15th AF went to Steyr, Austria, to bomb a ball bearing plant and aircraft

" . . . into the valley of the shadow . . . " B-17s of the 91st BG, 8th AF, leave the coast of England 27,500 ft below headed for Germany, 4 January 1944. (USAF)

factory. The 82nd FG furnished initial escort; while still miles from the target, the bombers were attacked by 50 Bf.109s, FW.190s, and Macchi C.202s. The Lightnings fought them off, downing three of the Messerschmitts, and although there was another formation of enemy fighters circling above, the P-38s refused to take the bait and stayed with the bombers.

Fifteen minutes later, at 1045 hours and right on time, the 325th FG's Thunderbolts arrived to relieve the P-38s and to take the Big Friends on to the target area. During the next 45 minutes, the 325th Checkertails warded off an attack on the bombers by 21 Messerschmitts. Then, at 1130 hours, 46 P-38s from the 1st FG arrived, their assignment being to protect the bombers in the target area. But the P-47s, with fuel running low, were scarcely out of sight before the bomber formation was attacked by 70 enemy fighters. That could have resulted in a sticky situation, because there were not enough P-38s on the scene to handle the Messerschmitts and Focke-Wulfs. At that point, any western movie fan could have almost heard the sound of a U.S. Cavalry bugle in the distance, because the 14the FG charged into the melee with 37 more P-38s. With more than 80 Lightnings fighting together, only six enemy fighters were able to get through to the bomber stream, two of which went down under the guns of the bomber crews.

The Luftwaffe tried again shortly after 2100 hours as the bombers began coming off their targets and turning for home. Forty twin-engine Messerschmitt *Zerstorers* (110s and 210s), armed with rockets, struck at the bombers in head-on attacks flying four abreast. The P-38s quickly broke up these formations and, in a 20-minute running battle, destroyed 18 of them.

The 14th FG stayed with the bombers until relieved by a P-47 group just south of Klagenfurt. Later, back at base with no losses of their own to count, the 14th's pilots had a good laugh to drain away the tension when one of them, Lt. Robert Siedman, observed: "I'll bet Hitler would be real mad if he knew that a little Jewish boy had shot down three of his pilots today."

During the early summer of 1944, nine Allied divisions and many 12th and 15th AF units were withdrawn to prepare for the invasion of Southern France which would follow on 15 August against thinly held German positions and almost no Luftwaffe opposition. German airpower had been swept from the skies over Italy, and the decimated Luftwaffe, fighting a desperate, defensive battle against the great Allied bomber offensive that was methodically destroying Germany's ability to make war (and as Eisenhower's armies swept across France following the cross channel invasion the previous June), had lost control of the air over Europe.

This 8th AF B-17, returning damaged from a mission over Germany, reached its base in England only to crash on landing with its brakes shot away; the crew escaped. (USAF)

A 9th AF Douglas A-26 Invader hurtles earthward following a direct hit by German 88mm flak which blasted away one wing. (USAF)

Assault on Fortress Europe

To the American ground forces gathered in England, the shooting war against Germany began with the cross-channel invasion of the Normandy Coast on 6 June 1944. To the U.S. air forces in the European Theater of Operations (ETO), it began long before that.

The buildup of the U.S. 8th AF in England was markedly slowed at the beginning when most of its handful of air groups were taken away by the 12th AF for the North African Campaign. During the summer of 1942, P-38s, B-17s and C-47s were flown across the North Atlantic with refueling stops in southern Greenland and Iceland. Another transatlantic air route was established across the South Atlantic to Africa's Gold Coast with a mid-ocean refuelling stop at tiny Ascencion Island. Many of these aircraft went to the 12th and 15th AFs. By early 1943, however, warplanes ferried across the North Atlantic remained with the 8th and 9th AFs in England, while the South Atlantic ferry route was used to deliver aircraft to the 10th and 14th AFs

in the China-Burma-India (CBI) Theater of Operations.

President Roosevelt and Prime Minister Churchill agreed, at the Casablanca Conference in January 1943, that a combined bomber offensive against Germany was a necessary prelude to the cross-channel invasion. The primary aims were the destruction of the Luftwaffe (both in combat and by bombing the enemy's aircraft factories) and Germany's sources of oil. The RAF would bomb by night and the USAAF would bomb by day—around the clock, when the two bomber commands possessed the machines to make that possible.

The biggest problem facing the 8th AF was uncertainty. Airpower had never been used in a massive, coordinated effort to destroy the industrial base—or key parts of that base—of a modern nation. Initially, Arnold and most of his commanders believed that the U.S. heavy bombers were armed sufficiently (nine .50-cal guns) that, in large formations at least, they could protect themselves against concentrated attacks by enemy fighters. However, premature raids by two to three hundred B-24s and

Scratch one Messerschmitt. This is how it looked to the gun camera of "Jug" pilot Capt. Floyd Brandt of the 19th Tactical Air Command as he participated in the protection of Patton's exposed southern flank. (USAF)

221

Little Warrior takes a direct hit from flak over Quakenbruk, Germany 29 June 1944. Craft fell out of control a few seconds later. More Liberators were built during WWII than any other American airplane. (USAF)

B-17s, in August 1943, against the Rumanian oil fields at Ploesti and the German ball bearing and aircraft factories at Regensburg and Schweinfurt, without fighter escort, proved the fallacy of that when the bomber forces sustained losses of near 20 percent.

At that time, fighter escort deep into Germany was not possible. The P-47s of the 8th and 9th AFs lacked the range to stay with the bombers beyond the German border.

By October 1943, the 8th AF possessed two groups of P-38s and while the Lightning had the potential of becoming a very effective long-range fighter, the P-38G and H versions that equipped the 55th and 20th FGs were not truly combat-ready aircraft—certainly not for the ETO. Their super-charger system demanded more attention from the pilot than he could reasonably be expected to give it during the heat of battle, resulting in a lot of blown engines; cockpit heating and windshield defrosting were completely inadequate for the altitudes and temperatures at which the air war over Europe was fought. These craft had no dive brakes, no maneuvering flaps or aileron boost. Not until August 1944 would the P-38J-25 be available in significant numbers, the first fully developed Lightning. It and subsequent versions would be the sweethearts of the AAF fighter pilots in the Southwest Pacific, but by that time most fighter groups in the ETO were being re-equipped with the P-51

Mustang, and all but one P-38 group disappeared over Europe.

Nevertheless, throughout the late winter and early spring of 1944, the period during which the Luftwaffe was defeated, the P-38s did the job as

The concentrated fire of a P-47's eight .50-caliber guns spells doom for an enemy fighter. (USAF)

America has possessed no greater air leader than Gen. Carl "Tooey" Spaatz, whose career began in 1916 and ended with his retirement in 1948. Today's independent United States Air Force was born under his command. (USAF)

assigned to them. Air superiority in the ETO was largely won by the P-47 groups in aerial combat. There were 22 Thunderbolt groups in the 8th and 9th AFs, and seven P-38 groups by May 1944, and many of the P-47 groups were in action months before the P-38s arrived.

By late March 1944, Allied airpower was dominant over Europe (the Luftwaffe lost more than 800 fighters during February and March), and although the P-51 Mustang was probably the best air superiority fighter airplane of the war, it was not in action in large numbers until after the showdown battles with the Luftwaffe in February and March, 1944.

Throughout the winter and spring the P-38s took the bombers into Germany—Bremen, Frankfurt, Munster, Soligen, Berlin—after the P-47s had escorted the bombers across France. The intelli-

gence summaries of these raids reveal that, more often than not, the German fighters did not attack the bombers while the P-38s were with them, attacking instead while the P-47s were in escort. There is no explanation for this, because the P-47 was certainly a more deadly adversary than the early P-38. Perhaps the Germans at that time didn't think so; one captured Luftwaffe pilot referred to the P-38s as "those forked-tail devils." In any case, the German fighter pilots were ordered to avoid combat with Allied fighters if possible and to concentrate on the bombers.

Overlord: The Cross-Channel Invasion

At 0145 hours on 6 June 1944, 9000 paratroopers of the U.S. 101st and 82nd Airborne Divisions began jumping from more than 800 9th AF C-47 transports over France's Cherbourg Penin-

Flames envelop this 9th AF B-26 Marauder after a direct hit on its left engine by German antiaircraft gunners.

sula inland from the Normandy beaches. At the same time, some 200 RAF transports dropped 5000 British paratroopers, while 200 gliders followed with heavy weapons, guided to open fields by flare paths set up by the paratroopers. Concurrently, 8th and 9th AF bombers joined the U.S. Navy bombardment of the enemy's coastal defenses. At daybreak the first of the five divisions of U.S. and British troops began pouring ashore on the Normandy beaches. Behind them, the mightiest sea armada of all time—4000 ships, stretching back to the coasts of England—was bringing more men and guns. Overhead, 11,000 Allied airplanes, hastily painted the night before with special black and white "invasion stripes" (hopefully, to prevent friendly troops below from firing on them), provided an air umbrella against enemy air attack and fanned out across Normandy at treetop level to interdict enemy movement for miles behind the beachheads. Some 50,000 Allied soldiers were ashore in France before the day—"D-Day"—was over.

After D-Day, most U.S. tactical aircraft and many strategic bombers were diverted from the pure air offensive against Germany to give close air support to the advancing ground forces. The 8th and 9th AFs together possessed 2900 heavy bombers, 3000 fighters, and 400 medium bombers. If some U.S. infantrymen slogging through the mud sometimes wondered where the Air Force was, they should have been told that (1) it had been there *long* before, which was why they were advancing without fear of enemy air attack, and (2) it was presently miles ahead, systematically destroying enemy transportation, communications, troop concentrations, tank farms, and supply lines—in short, going for the enemy's vitals while the ground forces engaged his extremities. Thus, the Allied armies swept across France in almost direct proportion to the effectiveness of their airpower. They were stopped or slowed, usually, for one of two reasons: (1) when their advance was so rapid that it outstripped their lines of supply, and (2) when weather screened off a sector from their eyes in the sky and allowed the Germans to concentrate sufficient strength for a counterattack.

Although the American tactical aircraft were being efficiently employed, one U.S. General George ("Blood and Guts") Patton, Jr., a tough, bold old rooster, found a way to substitute it for a division or two of mobile ground troops. On 25 July, he sent his U.S. 3rd Army racing through a five-mile breach blasted in enemy defenses along the St. Lo-Periers Road by 8th and 9th AF planes, and dashed toward Germany depending entirely upon American fighters and medium bombers to protect his exposed southern flank. To most veteran ground commanders, such a move bordered upon madness, but the pilots—mostly from Gen. O.P. Weyland's 19th Tactical Air Command—bombed and strafed like demons (at altitudes that should

have qualified them for Combat Infantryman Badges) and proved so effective that 20,000 German soldiers, attempting to turn Patton's flank, surrendered *directly* to the Air Force—without ever engaging the 3rd Army. Later, speaking of tactical air support for his armored divisions, Gen. Patton characterized the relationship as "love at first sight."

A week after D-Day, Hitler began sending his *Vergeltungswaffe* (vengeance weapons) against London. The first of these was the V-1, a small, unmanned and gyro-stabilized aircraft powered with a pulse-jet engine and carrying a ton of explosives. About 8000 of these flying bombs were sent against London and Antwerp, about half of which were shot down by Allied fighters and antiaircraft artillery before Allied bombers snuffed out V-1 production and destroyed their launching sites. By September

The Casablanca Conference, January 1943: President Roosevelt and Prime Minister Churchill (seated). Standing, left to right: Gen. Hap Arnold, Adm. Ernest J. King, Gen. George Marshall, Adm. Sir Dudley Pound, Gen. Sir Alan Brooke, and Air Chief Marshal Sir Charles Portal. (USAF)

This B-17 somehow moved directly beneath another as the upper aircraft released its bombs over Berlin. Bomb at lower left struck the stabilizer of the Fortress with this result and the plane fell away out of control. (USAF)

1944, the V-1 was no longer a threat. Hitler, however, had another and more terrible vengeance weapon, the V-2.

The V-2 was first fired against London and Paris on 8 September 1944. It was a short-range ballistic missile carrying slightly less than a ton of explosive, and it could have—like the German jet fighter—altered the course of the war in Europe had Hitler possessed enough of them soon enough, and employed them correctly. As it was, the 2500 V-1s, and perhaps 100 V-2s, that struck England killed almost 10,000 civilians and leveled more than 200,000 buildings.

Meanwhile, Allied strategic bombers systematically eliminated the enemy's oil industry. By the spring of 1945, gasoline production in Germany and German-occupied territory had dropped to seven percent of the normal capacity and the Nazi war machine became almost immobile. The mechanized German Army was afoot; panzer units had to hoard fuel for weeks in order to make a single move. New fighter airplanes for the Luftwaffe, produced with supreme effort but in surprisingly large numbers in underground plants, were grounded with empty tanks—and there destroyed by low-flying Allied fighters.

Allied ground forces, moving swiftly beneath skies totally controlled by their own aircraft, swept over the Reich to meet Russian forces at the Elbe River on 25 April 1945. Five days later, Adolph Hitler committed suicide amid the rubble of Berlin. A few days after that, on 7 May 1945, a prostrate Germany, her cities in ruin, surrendered to the Allies' Supreme Commander, ETO, Gen. Dwight D. Eisenhower.

When the end came in the ETO. America had

This shot-up 358th FG P-47, painted with "invasion stripes," nosed up during landing. Crew chief rushes to aid pilot as others control blaze from the ruptured drop tank and medics stand by. (USAF)

Consolidated (today, General Dynamics) B-24 Liberator releases bombs over Bielefeld, Germany, 24 February 1945. (USAF)

A formation of B-24s bound for Ingolstadt, Germany, 1 March 1945. (USAF)

about 13,000 combat airplanes in that theater. The Western Allies had dropped 2,770,540 tons of bombs on the continent, of which 1,500,000 tons fell from U.S. bombers, largely during the final ten months of that conflict.

Many air commanders today believe that the Allies forfeited a chance at a relatively cheap victory in the ETO during the spring and early summer of 1944, and that invasion of Europe was not necessary. Allied airpower, they point out, was free to destroy all German industry, including Germany's ability to feed her people, after defeat of the Luftwaffe.

They are probably right; Gen. Von Rundstedt,

Troop-laden gliders, two towed behind each C-47 of the 439th Troop Carrier Group, carry reinforcements to the U.S. 9th Army for the historic crossing of the Rhine River, 24 March 1945. (USAF)

Commander-in-Chief of German Armed Forces in Western Europe, said after the war, "Three factors defeated us in the West where I was in command. First, the unheard-of superiority of your air force, which made all movement in daytime impossible. Second, the lack of motor fuel—oil and gas—so that the panzers and even the remaining Luftwaffe were unable to move. Third, the systematic destruction of all railway communications so that it was impossible to bring one single railroad train across the Rhine. This made impossible the reshuffling of troops and robbed us of all mobility."

A negotiated peace with Germany in the summer of 1944 would undoubtedly have left Germany intact, and the Soviets no farther west than the Polish border, a not unattractive thought today. It would have required the Germans to punish their own war criminals, another attractive thought. But could we, at that time, have accepted that? Probably not. The Nazi excesses were simply too horrible, and in a sense all Germany shared their guilt.

REVIEW QUESTIONS:

1. What was the significance of the Lend-Lease Act? How did the U.S. position on the War in Europe begin to change after the fall of France? Why was North Africa selected for the first invasion by Allied forces? What were some of the early problems faced by General Eisenhower? Describe how Allied air forces were organized for the North African campaign. Why couldn't the German and Italian troops escape from Northern Tunisia in May of 1943?

2. How important was the Italian campaign to the victory in Europe? Discuss why this campaign was so difficult. What was the role of the 15th Air Force?

3. What was the role of the 8th Air Force based in England? How was the P-51 Mustang used? How effective were the P-47s and P-38s against German fighter aircraft?

4. Describe the extent of manpower and equipment assembled for the D-Day invasion. How effective was the use of airpower in the allied advance across France and into Germany?

5. What were Hitler's "vengeance weapons?" Describe the situation in Germany by the Spring of 1945.

Chapter 13

Victory and the Unreal Wars

OBJECTIVES: At the end of this chapter you should be able to:

☐ Identify some of the problems encountered during the Aleutian Campaign.

☐ Describe the role and success of the American Volunteer Group (AVG) known as the Flying Tigers.

☐ Discuss the importance of the Air Transport Command (ATC) in supplying Chinese and American forces fighting the Japanese in China.

☐ Highlight the significance of the retaking of the Philippines and the Battle of Leyte Gulf.

☐ Identify several of the bloody island campaigns leading to the fire bombing and atomic bombing of the Japanese mainland.

The Second World War demanded that Americans fight in some strange and unlikely places. U.S. troops understood England, France, Italy, and even the German enemy—they are people much like ourselves, with cities and trains and homes and dogs. Even North Africa had towns. But the Aleutians were a different story. So, too, were the airstrips of northern Assam, the awesome Himalayas, China. There, as in the rain forests of the Solomons and New Guinea, the young American in uniform was prone to demand: "What am I doing in this stinking hole? Tojo can *have* it as far as I'm concerned!"

The Aleutian Campaign

Nowhere did the American serviceman have a better right to gripe than in the bleak Aleutians. Of all the unreal, "lesser" wars contained in WWII,

it was, perhaps the "unrealest." Americans had to be there to prevent the Japanese from grabbing bases from which the enemy could strike at the North American Continent. But the Japanese were not the primary enemy in that cold, mist-shrouded and desolate land—the weather was the most dangerous foe to the pilots of the 11th AF who had to fly in it. Navigating through the icy mists was likened to "flying inside a bottle of milk," and violent winds could sweep the lifeless tundra with unsuspected suddeness. Distances were great—the Aleutian chain arcs across the extreme North Pacific from the Alaskan Peninsula to within a few miles of Soviet territory. Japan is closer than Seattle.

At the time of the attack on Pearl Harbor, the U.S. had a dozen old Douglas B-18 Bolo bombers

Warhawks of the 11th AF prepare for a patrol on a typical mist-shrouded day in the Aleutians. (USAF)

and 20 even older P-26 fighters in Alaska. Not until a month before the Battle of Midway (and the Japanese occupation of Kiska and Attu in the western tip of the Aleutians) did the first P-39s and P-40s arrive at Otter Point and Cold Bay on Umnak Island to protect the U.S. Navy base at Dutch Harbor. Later that summer, a squadron of P-38s would arrive and the 343rd FG would be organized, each of its three squadrons flying a different aircraft. The 407th BG, equipped with B-24s, made up the balance of the 11th AF's combat units.

When the Japanese attacked Dutch Harbor in a diversionary thrust immediately preceding the Battle of Midway, the P-40s shot down six of the enemy's carrier-based planes, but thereafter aerial combat over the Aleutians was extremely rare. The Japanese never had more than two or three squadrons of Rufes (a floatplane version of the Zero) and some Kawasaki Ki-97 flying boats in the Aleutians, and they were anything but aggressive. But airstrips were difficult to build on the spongy tundra, and since the enemy seemed content to merely remain where he was—a thousand miles from Umnak—new airstrips had to be built, because only the P-38 fighters could reach him, barely.

A new strip at Adak, 375 miles closer to Kiska, allowed the fighters to accompany the 407th's Liberators on raids against the enemy bases. Due to the lack of enemy air opposition, the P-38s carried bombs, and due to the Aleutian weather, tucked in close to the bombers and followed their lead. (The Army's WWII fighter pilots, being hastily trained, were not particularly noted for their navigational and instrument flying skills.)

Throughout the winter and early spring of 1943 (though it's hard to tell the difference in the Aleutians) the 11th AF flew bombing and strafing missions to Kiska and Attu. Then, on 11 May, a small U.S. Navy task force operating with the Escort Carrier *Nassau* put the U.S. Army 7th Division ashore at Attu and the 2300 enemy troops on the island were soon overwhelmed. Navy and Marine aircraft from the *Nassau* added their muscle to that of the 11th AF in providing close air support for the men of the 7th Division fighting in the snowcovered mountains of Attu.

Two months later, American troops invaded Kiska, only to find that the Japanese had already slipped away in the fog.

The 343rd FG, completely equipped with P-38s, moved westward to the island of Shemya, where its hapless pilots and support people were

Lightning pilots of the 343rd FG at Adak are briefed during the battle for Attu. (USAF)

The P-40 of AVG pilot Charles Older, a Marine reserve officer who achieved 10 1/2 kills with the Flying Tigers. Older later ran his score to 22 1/2 as a Lt. Col with the 14th AF, and today is a Los Angeles Superior Court Judge. (Tom Haywood)

doomed to stand guard for the rest of the war, fighting the weather and boredom in a "stinking hole" that each would gladly give to the Japanese if only he could be sent somewhere else to fight. The U.S. Navy also set up an air station on Attu, from which planes of Fleet Air Wing 4 henceforth patrolled the North Pacific.

Over the Hump with the AVG and the 14th AF

The American Volunteer Group (AVG), more popularly known as the "Flying Tigers," is not easy to accurately describe. It was organized under the direction of Claire Lee Chennault, a retired U.S. Air Corps captain who had been in China since 1937 attempting to train and lead Chinese pilots against the Japanese invader. The AVG's personnel was recruited and its aircraft purchased through the Central Aircraft Manufacturing Company in Burma—actually, an assembly plant for Curtiss-Wright fighters (fixed-gear versions of the P-36 up to that time) sold to China by wheeler-dealer William D. Pawley. (Pawley did not actually work for Curtiss-Wright. He may be more accurately described as an international promoter who collected highly-placed friends, thought big, and had the guts

to back his schemes with action.)

The AVG flew under the flag of China, and their airplanes carried Chinese insignias. The pilots and most of the supporting personnel were American civilians. That made them, by definition, *mercenaries*. But that is an oversimplification. Almost all were reservists in the USAAF, the U.S. Navy or Marines. Most of them believed that war

Robert "Duke" Hedman's airplane. Chinese insignia is painted over the original RAF roundel on wing. The AVG P-40s actually were Curtiss H81-A2 Tomahawks ordered by Britain. (Tom Haywood)

On the China side of the Himalayas there was always plenty of hand labor to fill bomb craters and keep the airstrips open. (Don Downie)

The CBI Fighters

The 10th AF in India was made up of just seven combat groups: the 7th BG with B-24s, the 12th and 341st BGs with B-25s, and the 33rd, 51st, 80th and 311th FGs, the first three of which were equipped with P-40s, while the 311th flew P-51s.

The veteran 33rd FG, (having fought in North Africa and Italy before going to India) finally ended up in China, flying P-47s with Chennault's 14th AF while the 51st FG, after a stint in India, also joined the 14th AF in China where it eventually received P-51s, though it had a fourth squadron attached to it (the 459th FS) flying P-38s. The 80th FG, based in Upper Assam, also had one squadron of P-38s.

While based in India, these fighter groups saw little aerial combat, but were kept busy bombing and strafing in an attempt to stop the Japanese advances in Burma. Not until Col. Phil Cochran (who

Warhawks and Marauders share this base in New Guinea of the 5th AF. (USAF)

White-tailed Warhawks of the 44th FS on Munda Airstrip, late summer 1943. (USAF)

had come to India with the 33rd FG) led a daring glider assault deep into Burma behind enemy lines to cut the enemy's supply lines, did the Allies break Japan's grip on Burma.

In China, Chennault, who had assumed the rank of colonel in the Chinese Air Force as leader of the AVG, became a Brig. Gen. in the USAAF when the AVG was disbanded, and was given command of the China Air Task Force (CATF), originally consisting of the 23rd FG and a group of B-25s commanded by Col. Caleb Haynes. Early in 1943, the CATF became the U.S. 14th AF, which steadily grew in strength during the following two years as it received air units from the 10th AF, and as the ATC was increasingly able to supply it.

The 14th AF fought a makeshift war at the end of an incredibly long supply line. Until the final year of the war, the P-40 was its main fighter airplane, and the 23rd FG alone accounted for 941 enemy aircraft destroyed, although most of its missions were against ground targets.

Perhaps the best assessment of the 14th AF was offered at war's end by Gen. Takahashi, Chief of Staff of the Japanese Armies in North China: "But for the 14th Air Force, we could have gone anywhere we wished in China."

The Final Thrust

MacArthur's return to the Philippines was something the people back home could at last iden-

tify with impending victory. For almost three years Americans had died taking a series of Pacific islands that most had never heard of before, and the papers reported great sea battles in which only the enemy ever seemed to lose any ships. (Censorship was something else the American people endured during WWII, but it was counterproductive in the sense that the people quickly lost confidence in official military bulletins and most felt that they never really knew how the war was going.) But here, finally, was the kind of evidence of success that everyone understood.

Militarily, the retaking of the Philippines held

Bell P-39s and P-400s (the latter a P-39 fitted with a 20mm cannon, the former with a 37mm gun) served in all theaters but were decidedly inferior to all enemy opposition in the air. Bell's follow-on design, the P-63 shown here, used a laminar-flow wing. Most P-63s built went to Russia under Lend-Lease. (USAF)

Gen. Arnold meets with military leaders in the CBI; from left: Arnold, Gen. Chennault, Gen. Joseph "Vinegar Joe" Stilwell, Gen. Sir John Dill, Gen. Clayton Bissell. Chennault was normally at odds with all but Arnold. (USAF)

far more than psychological significance. It provided a major base of operations both for ships and land-based aircraft. Adm. Nimitz' Central Pacific forces, which included the 7th AF and the recently-created 20th AF, had moved 4000 miles across the Pacific, taking bases from Tarawa through the Gilberts and Marshalls to the Marianas, while MacArthur (whose command contained a high percentage of Australians and New Zealanders) had fought 1300 tough miles from Port Moresby to Hollandia on New Guinea's north coast and beyond to the island bases of Wakde and Biak. Adm. Halsey had moved northward through the Solomons to neutralize the great enemy base at Rabaul. With Rabaul encircled and cut off from supply, it was left to "wither on the vine" after its air

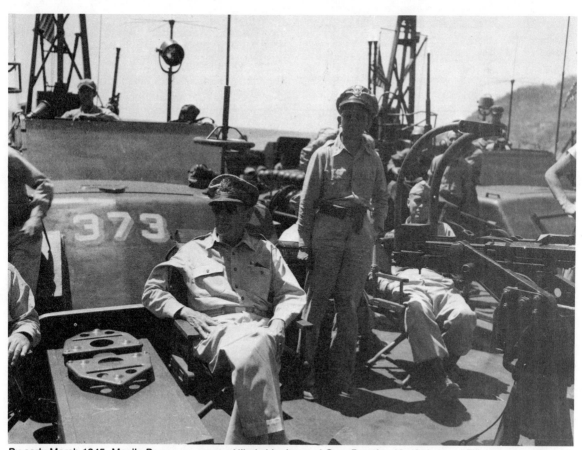

By early March 1945, Manila Bay was open to Allied shipping and Gen. Douglas MacArthur and Filipino statesman/soldier Carlos Romulo (standing) made a symbolic return aboard a U.S. Navy PT boat. (USAF)

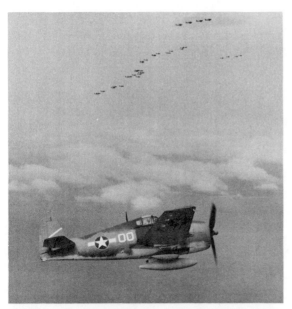

Grumman F6F Hellcat escorts TBFs and SBDs from the new *Yorktown* in the Phillipine Campaign, October 1944. (USN)

units were destroyed, invasion by Allied troops being unnecessary.

As the two forces under MacArthur and Nimitz came together southeast of Mindanao, with MacArthur on the island of Morotai and four strong U.S. Navy task groups operating from the Palaus, Yap, and Ulithi, their power was merged for the invasion of the Philippines at Leyte on 20 October 1944.

The 13th and 5th AFs were combined into the reborn Far East Air Forces (FEAF), and these

fliers, together with land-based Marine air and carrier-based Navy air units, soon took possession of the air over the Philippines and led the allied invasion of Luzon at Lingayen Gulf on 9 January 1945. Manila was liberated a month later.

Meanwhile, the Imperial Japanese Navy was decisively defeated attempting to turn back the Leyte landings. The Battle of Leyte Gulf, actually a series of actions from 10 through 29 October 1944, cost the enemy 1046 aircraft destroyed by carrier-based U.S. Navy planes alone, along with 26 major combatant ships, including three battleships, three heavy cruisers, and four aircraft carriers, the *Zuikaku*, *Chiyoda*, *Zuiho* and *Chitose*. The U.S. Navy lost the escort carriers *Gambier Bay* and *St. Lo*, the latter to Kamikaze attack. Kamikazes also damaged the carriers *Intrepid*, *Franklin*, and *Belleau Wood*.

The Kamikaze attacks would continue as the U.S. Navy operated close to the Japanese home islands, and although the censored press reports at the time minimized their effect, the truth is that this desperation tactic accounted for at least half of all U.S. Navy ships damaged and a fifth of those sunk throughout the war, most of the attacks coming during the final 10 months of the Pacific War. The Kamikazes also struck at important shore installations. Had the war not ended as it did, another 7-9,000 Kamikazes were waiting for the expected invasion of Japan.

While Allied troops were mopping up in the

Warhawks of the 80th FG at Nagahuli Airstrip in Upper Assam, India, 1944. (USAF)

PBY-5A Catalina patrol plane drops depth charge over enemy submarine in Phillippine waters. (USN)

Philippines, U.S. Navy Task Group 52, with 12 carriers, under Rear Adm. C.T. Durgin, and TG 58, containing 17 carriers and commanded by Vice Adm. Marc Mitschner, accompanied by two Marine divisions to landings on Iwo Jima 19 February 1945, where the Marines faced 23,000 Japanese in exceptionally strong defensive positions. Iwo Jima was not secured until 16 March and at the cost of 4590 Marine dead, plus the loss of the escort carrier *Bismark Sea*, sunk by Kamikazes, along with serious damage to the *Saratoga*.

The price paid for Iwo Jima was said to be justified by its location, since it gave the U.S. airfields halfway between Japan and the 20th AF's B-29 bases in the Marianas, and was later claimed to have saved no less than 2400 B-29s and their crews which would not have made it to the Marianas after missions to Japan. But that would seem to be

an overstatement since fewer than 1200 B-29s went to the Pacific before the war ended.

The B-29 air offensive against Japan began in mid-1944 when the 58th Bomb Wing of the 20th Bomber Command (the 20th and 21st Bomber Commands were part of the new 20th AF which operated directly under the Joint Chiefs as a Global Air Force) began operations from Chengtu in west central China. But that was a premature effort which served mostly to prove that meaningful numbers of Superfortresses could not be supported by the ATC airlift over the Hump. By October, however, bases taken from the enemy in the Marianas were ready to handle the B-29s and the Superforts were concentrated there on five big airfields, two each on Guam and Tinian and one on Saipan.

The air assault against Japan was resumed in November 1944, but too many B-29s were lost to

The 51st FG in India had a different idea for painting their P-40 air scoops. (USAF)

Fire rages on the forward deck of the *Saratoga* after hit by Kamikaze off Iwo Jima 21 February 1945. (USN)

Marine F4U-1 Corsair takes off from the carrier *Essex* for a strike against Formosa. (USN)

enemy defensive fighters and to fuel starvation on return to base, while results of the raids were disappointing. High level precision bombing was not markedly affecting the production of the thousands of small shops that made parts and subassemblies for the Japanese war machine.

In January 1945, Gen. Curtis E. LeMay was sent to take command of the B-29 wings in the Marianas and was informed by Arnold that the Joint Chiefs expected the same kind of job that LeMay had done over Europe as a bomber commander where he had earned the sobriquet "Iron Pants."

By early March, LeMay had all his problems sorted out. He ordered his planes loaded with incendiary bombs, stripped of guns and ammunition,

The TBM torpedo bomber was the Grumman design (TBF) built by the Eastern Aircraft Division of General Motors. TBM above is aboard the carrier *Bunker Hill* during the Battle of the Phillippine Sea. (USN)

The U.S. Navy's leading ace in WWII was Cmdr. David McCampbell, shown here in his F6F Hellcat aboard the *Essex*. (USN)

and told his crews that they would raid Tokyo at night from an altitude of 7000 feet.

Most of the crews were incredulous. The pressurized B-29 with remote controlled guns was a high-altitude strategic bomber; ol' Iron Pants was asking them to take it over the enemy's capital unarmed at low altitude and at night! Still, if one thought about it, it just might work. The enemy certainly would not expect them at low altitude and their heavy anti-aircraft guns would be set up to fire high above them. Intelligence reports indicated that the enemy had relatively few night fighters, and if the B-29s carried no guns, that would eliminate the danger of firing upon one another in the darkness, additionally, the weight saved would lower fuel consumption for the trip home. The bold plan just might work.

It did. Almost 16 square miles of Tokyo were destroyed by fire that night by 323 Superforts. During the next ten days Nagoya, Osaka, and Kobe were struck with similar raids to add another 15 square miles of fire-blackened ruins to those cities. The cost was 21 B-29s lost in 1489 sorties (a sortie being one mission one airplane).

Late in March 1945, LeMay was ordered to temporarily halt the aerial destruction of Japan's major cities and to aid in the invasion of Ryukyu Islands and Okinawa, in which the B-29s were used as tactical aircraft, attacking enemy airfields and sewing mines in the Shimonoseki Straits.

The Ryukyus were but 400 miles from Japan and the enemy resisted with everything he had. The American force of four Army and two Marine divisions, accompanied by Adm. Durgin's TG 52 and Adm. Mitschner's TG 58, along with AAF air units, were met by mass Kamikaze attacks—up to 400 at a time—despite American air superiority. During the 83 days of the Okinawan Campaign, Kamikazes sank 35 U.S. ships and damaged 288.

Okinawa was finally secured on 21 June 1945 at the price of 12,500 American lives and 763 aircraft. The enemy, fighting from a maze of tunnels and caves that were largely immune to air attack, lost 110,000 soldiers who refused to surrender.

The Okinawan Campaign was the last and most violent for the U.S. Navy. Mitschner's and Durgin's task groups, fighting with a smaller British task force containing four carriers, were constantly on station in the battle area, and most of their ships

Landing signal officer brings a Hellcat aboard the *Essex*. (USN)

243

The Northrop P-61 Black Widow night fighter appeared late in the war but saw extensive action with Air Force units over the Phillippines and subsequent battles; 9th AF also used the type late in the European war. (USAF)

The Chance Vought F4U-4 Corsair, powered with the P&W R-2800-18W Double Wasp of 2325-hp, had a maximum speed of 424 mph at 23,000 feet. The reason the Marines got such a fine fighter first was because the Navy didn't clear the Corsair for carrier operations until April 1944. The Marines, however, regularly flew Corsairs from land bases throughout the war. (USN)

This kamikaze, although burning from hits by Navy gunners, held determinedly to its final attack, smashing onto the deck of the *Essex* during the Phillippine campaign. (USN)

logged more than 60 days of consecutive combat duty. Nine U.S. aircraft carriers were damaged, some seriously, although none were sunk.

After Okinawa was taken, the Superforts of the 20th AF resumed their assault on Japan, and by the end of July had devastated more than 100 square miles of the enemy's six largest cities. With both USAAF and Navy/Marine fighters ranging at will over the enemy's homeland, B-29 losses dropped to near zero, and Gen. LeMay began announcing in advance where he would strike next in order to cut civilian casualties.

The enemy was defeated. His navy was gone, along with most of his merchant shipping. Allied airpower was free to destroy whatever it chose to attack in his island nation. True, he had thousands

The flight deck of the *Randolph* after a night kamikaze attack 12 March 1945. (USN)

Sixty-one squadrons of B-29s Superfortresses were activated in the 20th AF by war's end. Superfort engines were Wright R-3350s of 2430 war emergency hp; cabin pressurization and remote control of the ten .50-caliber and one 20mm guns were innovations. (USAF)

of Kamikazes (planes of all types, including trainers) held in reserve, and a well-equipped army prepared to resist invasion. But an army that cannot maneuver, that cannot be supplied or fed, cannot long exist. Gen. LeMay, who was unaware that

Gen. Curtis E. LeMay. (USAF)

the U.S. possessed an atomic device, recommended against the presumed invasion of Japan, telling his superiors that the enemy's unconditional surrender was only a matter of time—he judged it at "several weeks."

Iron Pants may have been right, but President Truman (who had assumed office on 12 April upon President Roosevelt's sudden death) was not willing to wait several weeks, because he said Americans were dying every day, and therefore, if he could shorten the war by *one hour*, it was his duty to do so.

At 0245 hours on 6 August 1945, the *Enola*

Corsairs of the 2nd Marine Air Wing over Okinawa. (USN)

Near the end, defeated Japan could no longer challenge the B-29s, seen here passing Mt. Fujiyama, and LeMay announced in advance where they would strike in order to spare civilian lives. (USAF)

Symbolic of peace in the Pacific and the end of countless tragic days, these Curtiss SB2C Helldivers return to their carrier, cruising serenely in the South China Sea.

Gay, a B-29 from the 509th Composite Group, 20th AF, took off from Tinian in the Marianas and headed for Hiroshima with an atomic bomb in its bays. The *Enola Gay* (named for the mother of the aircraft commander, Col. Paul Tibbets) loosed her terrible weapon above the Japanese city at 0816 hours, and four square miles of Hiroshima were obliterated. The number of human casualties was unknown at the time, but are given today as 78,150 dead, 13,083 missing, and 37,425 injured.

Three days later, the B-29 *Bock's Car* dropped the second A-bomb on Nagasaki, killing 73,884 people, and Japan sued for peace.

On 2 September 1945, in Tokyo Bay, formal surrender documents were signed aboard the battleship *Missouri.* The U.S. Navy has yet to explain why the ceremony did not take place on an aircraft carrier, the *true* symbol of victory in the Pacific.

REVIEW QUESTIONS:

1. What was the purpose of the Aleutian Campaign? What were some of the geographical and environmental problems encountered?

2. Who was Claire Chennault? Why was he in China? What was the role of the Flying Tigers? Were they successful? What happened to this group?

3. What was the function of the Air Transport Command (ATC) under Colonel Haynes? How successful was the "Assam Trucking Company" in carrying out their mission?

4. Describe the psychological and strategic importance of retaking the Philippines. Why did the Battle of Leyte Gulf virtually put an end to the Imperial Japanese Navy as a fighting force? Were the Kamikaze attacks effective? What was the importance of taking Iwo Jima?

5. Describe the fire bombing campaign ordered by General LeMay in the spring of 1945. Why did the Kamikaze attacks increase during the Okinawan Campaign? Why was General LeMay against the invasion of Japan?

Chapter 14

Uneasy, Peace, and Another War

OBJECTIVES: At the end of this chapter you should be able to:

☐ Give the reasons for and results of the Berlin airlift.

☐ Explain why the B-52 was developed and how it became such a good investment.

☐ Describe our response to the invasion of South Korea by North Korean and subsequently Chinese troops.

☐ Give President Eisenhower's ultimatum to the Communists in 1953 regarding the continued fighting in Korea.

☐ Describe the type of aircraft and source of manpower for the Korean War.

☐ Give the reason for President Truman recalling General MacArthur in 1951.

☐ Describe some of the results of the Korean War regarding military preparedness.

World War II changed the world and the peace that followed was an uneasy one. For a brief period, America felt secure. The U.S. was the sole possessor of the atomic bomb and had the means to deliver it anywhere in the world. Surely, the threat of such massive retaliation would deter the most ambitious aggressor.

The potential aggressor was, of course, the Soviet Union. Few Americans ever doubted that. At the end of WWII, while the United States and its Allies demobilized (the U.S. Army went from 8,000,000 in 1945 to 684,000 by 1950), the Russians kept much of their military intact, and repeatedly demonstrated their allegiance to the communist canon which holds that "political power comes from the barrel of a gun."

Their national character was bared to the world by their acts immediately following Germany's surrender. In Poland, and in that part of Germany occupied by the Soviets, the only women who were not raped were those few who successfully hid for months. Everything of value was stolen. Millions of German "prisoners" disappeared into Soviet Siberia. Even the railway tracks were ripped up and shipped back to the Soviet Union. The terror and pillage that came in the wake of the Soviet army

The USAF's first operational jet fighter was the 550-mph Lockheed F-80 Shooting Star which appeared in 1945. The F-80C, which entered service in 1948, had a thinner wing, allowing a higher critical Mach number. Two-seat versions became the T-33 jet trainer. (USAF)

was little different than that practiced by the Mongol hordes of Genghis Khan 700 years earlier.

So the Free World knew its Godless enemy and watched in apprehension as the Soviet Union hammered its Iron Curtain around Eastern Europe. Poor President Roosevelt—sick and debilitated, just a month before his death, he had believed that he could deal with the Soviet dictator Stalin at the Yalta Conference. But the agreements made in good faith by FDR were to be regarded by the Soviets merely as positions of advantage from which to expand their communist dominion.

Berlin Big Lift

Among those agreements—which greatly affect us all to this day—was the supposedly *temporary* occupation of Germany by the Allies. The Soviets were allowed to occupy East Germany and a portion of East Berlin (Berlin itself is 110 miles inside the Soviet sector). Britain, France and the United States occupied the remainder of Berlin and West Germany, and were guaranteed access to Berlin by rail, the *autobahn* (German express freeway), and three 20-mile wide air corridors.

By 1948, however, the Soviets possessed the secret of nuclear fission (by espionage), and were ready to test the will of the United States in Germany. It should have come as no surprise. From the start, the Soviets had refused to cooperate in Allied efforts to establish a new government that the Germans could run themselves and to begin rebuilding the German economy.

On 24 June 1948, the Russians stopped all surface transportation into the western sectors of Ber-

The Bell X-1A was a rocket-powered research aircraft; X-1 was the first airplane to exceed the speed of sound, 14 October 1947. (USAF)

lin, suspended parcel post service, and cut off electric power. They stopped barge traffic on the rivers, destroyed bridges, and tore up the tracks of the remaining railroad into the city from the west. Berlin was isolated.

Almost. The Soviets faced one problem with their blockade: Iron Pants LeMay happened to be the commander of the U.S. Air Force in Europe (USAFE). The Joint Chiefs under Truman also made some pretty good choices.

Within 48 hours, Gen. LeMay had all his C-47 transports for duty with *Operation Vittles*. Within airliner) flying milk, flour, medicines and coal into the beleagured city from Frankfurt, carefully staying within the prescribed air corridors. There was nothing the Russians could do about an airlift short of shooting down the unarmed transports, and that, of course, would have been a clear act of war.

The C-47s carried 80 tons of cargo to Berlin that first day. Meanwhile, orders went out around the world calling in Air Force C-54 four-engine transports for duty with Operation *Vittles*. Within a month a steady stream of U.S. and British transports were delivering 1500 tons of life-giving supplies to West Berlin daily. Then, after the new Military Air Transport Service (MATS)—successor to the wartime Air Transport Command and Naval Air Transport Service—took over the job with old "Hump" commander Gen. William Tunner running the show, the tonnage exceeded 5000 per

day—including candy for Berlin's children.

During the 13 months the Berlin Airlift was in operation, MATS delivered 2,231,600 tons of essential cargo into that city, average 700 flights daily, to thwart the Soviet attempt to force the Western Allies out of Berlin. In so doing, MATS also administered a sound—and responsible—diplomatic/strategic defeat to the communist aggressor. The Soviets could find no face-saving way out. They simply lifted the blockade, and contented themselves with an ultimatum to Czechoslovakia which forced the Czechs into the Russian orbit, and announcement of the detonation of the first Soviet A-bomb.

Lawrence Bell (L), who began his career as designer of the 1919 Martin GMB bomber and saw a Bell aircraft break the sound barrier only 28 years later, congratulates X-1A pilot Capt. (later General) Charles Yeager. (Bell Aerosystems)

MATS C-54s (R5D in Navy dress) were the backbone of the Berlin Airlift which averaged 700 flights daily to keep the city alive—and from total Soviet control—for 13 months. (USAF)

Birth of the B-52

The fallout from the Berlin blockade was far more significant than the Russians could have foreseen when they recklessly imposed it. Among other things, it was indirectly responsible for America's B-52 global bomber program, plus a lot of rethinking of the U.S. defensive posture *vis a vis* Russia's newly-obvious expansionist policies.

Actually, Air Force brass had sent a new strategic bomber specification to the aircraft industry seeking proposals in mid-1946; they were looking down the 'pike 10 years, by which time it was reasonable to assume that the U.S. would need a fast, high-flying nuclear carrier of extra-long range. There was, however, significant opposition to the concept within the Air Force itself.

The Strategic Air Command (SAC) had been organized on 21 March 1946 with Gen. George

Convair B-36 (in background) had a span of 230 ft, six 3500-hp engines driving pusher props, and four turbojets of 5200 lbs thrust each. SAC had 33 squadrons of B-36s to enforce the peace until the B-52 began entering service in 1955. (USAF)

This unlikely critter was the McDonnell XF-85 parasite fighter which was to be carried by the B-36 for protection against enemy fighters—one of those good ideas that didn't work out. (McDonnell-Douglas)

Boeing XB-52 had pilot and copilot sitting in tandem in blister atop the nose. The first B-52 flight came on 15 April 1952. (The Boeing Company)

Kenney as its first commander. At that time, Kenney was given 36,000 men, 18 bases and 600 aircraft—B-17s, B-29s and B-25s. The Air Force was ready to substantially restructure in anticipation of legislation that would separate it from the Army and make it an independent and co-equal branch of the U.S. military, the dream of Billy Mitchell and all other Army airmen since the First World War. That act was passed by the Congress and signed by President Truman in mid-1947, becoming law on 18 September of that year. (The National Security Act of 1947 also created the CIA, another security measure long overdue.)

The early B-52 proposals from Boeing were for large propjets that lacked the performance envisioned by the Air Force. In any case, the B-52 concept had some strong opposition in the persons of Gen. George Kenney and Gen. Lauris Norstad, Deputy Chief of Staff for Operations. Kenney felt that the B-50 (essentially, the B-29 with bigger engines) would be a lot cheaper and that, therefore, he could have more of them. Also, the B-52, if it had the performance being asked for, would require technological advances that could take years to attain. There was no engine then available that would furnish the power such a machine would require.

Meanwhile, Convair wanted to go ahead with the mammoth B-36, a 1941 program that had been sidetracked by the war. The technology was available to build the B-36 at once, but Kenney and Norstad opposed the B-36 for the same reasons they were against the B-52. Assured of plenty of overseas bases, there was no reason the B-50 couldn't do the job.

In favor of the B-36 and the follow-on B-52 was Gen. "Tooey" Spaatz, Air Force Chief of Staff, but Spaatz knew he'd have a hard time getting money from Congress for them without the support of Kenney and Norstad. Then the Soviets blockaded Berlin and literally saved both new bomber programs.

One day after the blockade went into effect, Gen. Hoyt Vandenberg, just recently appointed Air Force Chief of Staff upon Spaatz' retirement, met with Air Force Secretary Stuart Symington and, with Kenney and Norstad in agreement, determined that a fleet of B-36s would be built to ensure the capability of a U.S. nuclear deterrent strike force until the B-52 could be brought along in the mid-'50s.

The Pratt & Whitney jet engine (the J-57) that made the B-52 possible was under development by late 1948, and the first B-52 prototype made its maiden flight on 15 April 1952. Deliveries of the B-52 Stratofortress to SAC began three years later.

Drag chute deployed upon landing greatly aids in braking the 200,000-lb (488,000-lb fully loaded) Stratofortress to a safe stop. (The Boeing Company)

Wings flex upward as B-52D takes off and outrigger wheels retract. Approximately 75 B-52Ds remained in service during the early '80s, along with the G and H models. (The Boeing Company)

The Air Force should be very proud of the B-52 program. It reflected high competence upon the several commands that planned and administered it. Boeing engineers, led by Edward Wells and Art Carlsen, produced an airplane that logically should not have appeared for another ten years. The Air Force knew exactly what it needed, and the senior officers stuck to their guns through many frustrations and the long gestation period required to get it.

A total of 744 B-52s was built during the plane's nine-year production run, the last being delivered to SAC in 1962. Throughout its service life, the B-52 Stratofortress has represented one critical leg

The B-52G and H versions are the prime nuclear carriers through the 1980s, the Gs and Hs having a cut-down vertical tail. The G models are easy to differentiate from the Hs because the H model is equipped with turbofan engines and fatter engine pods than the G (above). (The Boeing Company)

of America's nuclear deterrent triad, along with the ICBMs and nuclear-armed submarines. In 1980, after 25 years as a first-line defender of the U.S. and the Free World, 300 B-52s continued in that role. In the absence of a new nuclear carrier to replace them, they were expected by the Air Force to serve until the year 2000. The B-52s originally cost slightly less than $6 million each, and perhaps an equal amount has been spent on each of those still flying for updated electronics and weapons systems. Considering that this fleet of global bombers will contribute at least 30 years of service to the security of this nation, it is safe to say that seldom has the overburdened American taxpayer received so much for his hard-earned money.

The Korean War

If the Berlin blockade pushed the B-52 program off dead center, other threats to the Free World during the early '50s provided the impetus to keep it moving. By early 1949 it was obvious that a Chinese communist army, supported by the Soviets, would defeat Chiang Kai-shek's Nationalist forces and take possession of that vast land, while the Soviets had installed a former Russian army officer as premier in North Korea and supplied the North Koreans with arms and the belief that they should rule all of Korea.

At 0400 hours on 25 June 1950, 60,000 North Korean troops, spearheaded by 100 Russian-built tanks, swept across the 38th parallel (the border between North and South Korea) and drove rapidly southward, overrunning the South Korean capitol of Seoul four days later.

The South Koreans were, of course, unprepared for the invasion. U.S. occupation troops, who had supervised the withdrawal of the Japanese at the close of WWII, had stayed in South Korea only long enough to allow those gentle people to establish a government of their own under Korean statesman Syngman Rhee.

On the afternoon of the surprise invasion (it was 24 June in the U.S.), the United Nations Security Council met in emergency session to condemn the act, and President Truman ordered the 5th AF, which had planes in Japan and Okinawa, to evacuate U.S. citizens. Two days later, as the invaders approached Seoul, Truman directed that U.S. Air Force and Navy planes give assistance to the South Koreans, and ordered Gen. MacArthur to take command of the troops being sent from 15 Free World nations (mostly the U.S.) to fight under the flag of the United Nations. President Truman termed the UN response a "police action."

F-51 Mustangs were taken from mothballs and Air Guard units for service in Korea. Shown is an F-51 supplied to the Republic of Korea Air Force (ROKAF). (USAF)

F-82 Twin Mustangs were basically stretched F-51H fuselages joined at a common wing center section and fitted witn V-1710 Allison engines. F-82s pictured were radar-carrying night fighters. (USAF)

Actually, that was an accurate description of UN's intent, because the U.S. (and other countries which sent troops), had no objective except to push the communists back across the 38th parallel and restore peace. Most also undoubtedly saw it as a test of the effectiveness of this new (1945) world organization in dealing with "brushfire" wars that could escalate into big wars.

U.S. airpower played a major role in the Ko-

rean War. American warplanes dominated the air and provided close air support that was the decisive factor in UN successes on the ground. There were four major offensives and counteroffensives in the Korean War: (1) The initial North Korean thrust which carried all the way to the southern end of the country by 15 September 1950, with the South Korean and UN troops backed into a pocket around Pusan; (2) A UN counteroffensive with an

Another retread: The T-6 Texans, armed with rockets, served as forward air control craft, spotting targets for the heavy ordnance carriers. The T-6 was an advanced trainer in WWII. (USAF)

Lockheed F-94 Starfire saw service in Korea, primarily as a night fighter. The F-94 was a member of the F-80/T-33 family with thinner wing, afterburner, and nose-mounted search radar. (USAF)

amphibious landing by the U.S. Marines at Inchon, just south of Seoul, which trapped half of the invader's army between the UN forces in the south and the Marines closing from Inchon. This done, the UN troops drove north across the 38th parallel, entered the North Korean capital of Pyongyang, and totally defeated the North Koreans as the drive reached the Yalu River, which separated North Korea from Manchuria. Then, the next day, on 3 November 1950, (3) Communist China entered the war by sending 300,000 troops across the Yalu and pushed the UN forces back below Seoul again by late January 1951. (4) The UN forces counterattacked and once again advanced into North Korea, halting along a line that stabilized by November, averaging about 20 miles north of the 38th paral-

The 670-mph North American F-86A Sabre appeared in 1949, and in December 1950 the USAF 4th Fighter Interceptor Wing went to Korea equipped with Sabres. Normal armament was six .50-caliber machine guns; later (H) versions sometimes replaced the machine guns with four 20mm cannons. (USAF)

The Douglas A-26 Invader of WWII was redesignated B-26 in 1948 after the Martin B-26 Marauder was no longer in inventory. The Invader served in Europe and the Pacific in WWII, in Korea, and (shown here) in Vietnam. (USAF)

The Black Sheep were back in Korea, operating off the escort carrier *Sicily,* and still flying Corsairs. Shown is a cannon-armed F4U-4. (USN)

lel. That would be the positions of the opposing forces when a truce was at last agreed upon on 27 July 1953.

Negotiations to end the fighting had been going on for two years when the agreement was finally reached. The unrepentant aggressors had stalled and seized upon any excuse to delay a settlement, apparently hoping to gain something from the war. But Dwight Eisenhower became President of the United States in January 1953; immediately after taking office, Ike sent a message to Moscow, Peiping, and Pyongyang saying that if satisfactory progress toward an armistice was not forthcoming, " . . . we intend to move decisively without inhibi-

tion in our use of weapons, and will no longer be responsible for confining hostilities to the Korean peninsula."

That was the kind of "negotiation" the communists understood, and it achieved the desired results.

At the outbreak of hostilities in Korea, the FEAF, made up of the 5th and 13th AFs, greatly reduced from WWII levels, had 535 operational aircraft, including 365 F-82 Twin Mustangs. The Lockheed F-80 was America's first operational jet fighter, appearing in 1945, and was obsolescent by 1950 due to the pace of jet engine development and new lessons learned in the field of aerodynamics

This frosted Mustang crash-landed after being hit by enemy ground fire. Foamite controlled fire and the pilot was not injured. (USAF)

259

Soviet MiG-15 was the standard fighter for the Soviet-bloc air forces during the '50s. In Korea, despite the fact that American pilots were not allowed to pursue the MiGs beyond the Yalu River, the F-86 pilots shot down 10 MiGs for every F-86 lost in combat. (Hudeck collection)

as jet and rocket-powered U.S. research aircraft attained ever-higher speeds. (USAF Capt. Charles Yeager had exceeded the speed of sound on 14 October 1947.) The North American F-82 was, literally, a "Twin Mustang," two stretched P-51H fuselages (F-51s after the USAF changed the Army's "P" for "pursuit" to "F" for "fighter" in 1948) joined together on a common wing center-section to make a single twin-engine aircraft. It was, however fitted with Allison rather than Rolls-Royce engines.

A month after the war started, 764 National Guard F-51s were called to active duty, and 145 of them rushed to Korea aboard the carrier *Boxer*. World War II's illustrious 4th FG, now designated the 4th Fighter Interceptor Wing and equipped with F-86A Saberjets followed in December 1950 to take on the Chinese MiG-15s.

Actually, the United States was in the process of rebuilding the Air Force into a new all-jet air force to meet America's defense needs of the '50s. At the end of WWII, the USAAF contained a whopping 218 air groups with nearly two and one quarter million men. Demobilization was so rapid and

S./Sgt. Jerry Webb, B-29 tailgunner, points to a cannon hole close to his head after attack by MiGs. Sgt. Webb shot down one MiG, another gunner on this Superfort downed a second. The B-29's rudder controls were shot out, but it landed safely at its base on Okinawa. (USAF)

ROKAF Mustangs operated under command of the 5th AF. Mustang #18 at left is flown by Major Dean Hess, ROKAF pilot training program commander. (USAF)

so thorough that the Army Air Forces were down to 52 groups on paper, with only two groups fully operational, by mid-1947. Many thousands of WWII combat aircraft—not a few of them brand new—were sold for scrap (movie flier Paul Mantz bought 500 war surplus airplanes for $50,000, sold the fuel in their tanks for $55,000, and still possessed the world's seventh largest "air force"), while a small percentage of the latest models were "mothballed" at Davis-Monthan Air Base near Tucson, Arizona, where the dry desert air contributed to their preservation.

However, the U.S. had trained more than a quarter of a million pilots during WWII and many remained in the National Guard or Air Force Reserve. These were the pilots called back to active

A North Korean YAK fighter shot down by an F-80 14 miles north of Suwon, 15 August 1950. (USAF)

duty to augment the relatively small FEAF in Korea; since most of the regulars were also WWII vets, the Air Force, Navy and Marine fliers over Korea were often called "retread tigers."

Retreads they may have been, but there is no substitute for experience, and the Americans' ten-to-one kill ratio over the North Koreans and Chinese pilots established that the old hands were quite as effective as the new breed. WWII aces became double aces in the skies over Korea, and the old saw which held that fighter pilots should be under 25 years of age was confounded by many a 30-plus retread at the controls of an F-86, F9F or F4U.

During the first enemy offensive, the F-80s and F-82s of the 5th AF shot down seven of 13 Russian-built YAK fighters and IL-10 attack planes attempting to shoot up Seoul's Kimpo Airfield, Lts. William Hudson and Charles Moran and Maj. James Little being officially credited with the first U.S. air victories over Korea.

The North Koreans apparently had but 70 of the propeller-driven YAKs and 62 IL-10s. The 5th AF quickly destroyed them all, mostly on the ground. In November 1950, when the Chinese entered the war, they had approximately 500 Russian-built MiG-15 jet fighters, some apparently manned by Russian pilots.

On 3 July the U.S. Navy attack carrier *Valley Forge*, operating with the British carrier *Triumph* in the Yellow Sea, joined the FEAF aircraft in attacks on airfields and the enemy's lines of supply around Pyongyang. Navy Panther jets (F9Fs) of

A Vultee (Stinson) L-5 liaison plane delivers mail to G.I.s at a forward gun position. The unarmed L-5s and Cessna L-19s performed many such unglamorous but essential duties in Korea. (USAF)

VF-51 shot down two YAK-9s. The two carriers worked with the Air Force to slow the communist advance. Late in the month, the attack carriers *Philippine Sea* and *Boxer* arrived, along with the escort carriers *Badoeng Strait* and *Sicily*. Eventually, the air groups from eleven U.S. aircraft carriers would operate in Korean waters, coordinating their air strikes with those of the FEAF aircraft in a ground support role, attacking enemy airfields, railroads, factories, oil refineries, and enemy troop concentrations. Marine Fighting Squadron 214, flying Corsairs from the deck of the *Sicily*, and VMF-323 aboard the *Badoeng Strait* began operations over Korea on 3 August.

Although the Navy and Marines were unhappy over the fact that MacArthur and his air commander, Gen. George Stratemeyer, were bosses of all UN air units (what did the Army know about the logistics of maintaining a Navy task force in constant touch with hostile forces for three years?), Navy and Marine air nevertheless performed as usual. After the highly successful Inchon landing (MacArthur's idea, opposed by most of the Joint Chiefs), and the resulting defeat of the North

Marine helicopters of HMR-161 carried 60,046 passengers, including almost 10,000 wounded. This front line evacuation of wounded by Marines and Army choppers proved not only lifesaving, but morale-building. (USMC)

Koreans, the U.S. Army commander, Gen. Walton Walker, declared that except for U.S. airpower, the UN troops could not have stayed in Korea—a selfevident fact, of course, but the kind of fact that ground commanders are often slow to ac-knowledge.

After the line of battle stabilized, just inside the North Korean Border in the fall of 1951, and the primary enemy was the Chinese Communists ("Chi-Coms"), the ground war became a series of small battles for advantageous outpost positions, artillery duels and reconnaissance patrols—while Navy and Air Force planes continuously struck at the enemy's supply lines and prevented a buildup of enemy forces—and the negotiators at Panmunjon argued fruitlessly over side issues such as the repatriation of one another's prisoners.

Meanwhile, Gen. MacArthur had been fired by President Truman on 11 April 1951. Gen. Matthew Ridgeway was sent to replace him after MacArthur made statements considered by the President to be at cross-purposes with the UN (and U.S.) policy in Korea. MacArthur wanted a naval blockade of the China coast, air attacks on China's war industries, and an invasion of China by Chiang Kai-shek's Na-tionalist Chinese forces from Taiwan. MacArthur said that he believed in meeting force with maxi-mum counterforce, and that " . . . if we lose this war to communism in Asia the fall of Europe is in-evitable; win it and Europe most probably could avoid war . . . there is no substitute for victory . . ."

President Truman had no intention of going to war with Red China—all-out war, that is. He kept U.S. Navy and Air Force pilots on a tight leash, giv-ing strict orders that they could not fly across the Yalu River even if in "hot pursuit" of enemy MiGs—a circumstance the ChiCom pilots soon learned to exploit—and no targets could be bombed north of the Yalu. The "police action" was not to be carried into Chinese territory. Truman was un-doubtedly right; it's better to talk than fight, even if it takes years for the talks to get anywhere. In any case, the American people would not have united behind such an action. They were, in fact, already showing signs of discontent with a war that was, for most, difficult to identify with America's

Lt/Col. Glen Eagleston, 4th Fighter Interceptor Wing's group commander, inspects damage to his Sabre after an air bat-tle with MiGs. (USAF)

best interest. Strangely, most Americans seemed to sympathize with MacArthur—there was a lot of controversy over his dismissal in the press and in Congress—although no one questioned the Com-mander-in-Chief's right to fire any general or ad-miral for cause. Civilian control of the military is essential in a free society, and is spelled out in the Constitution.

MacArthur's removal from command probably had no effect on subsequent events in Korea. UN field commanders had little latitude of action, par-ticularly after the battle lines stabilized in Novem-ber 1951.

When the final casualty report for the 37 months of fighting was prepared, total UN casual-ties reached over 550,000, including almost 95,000 dead. U.S. losses numbered 142,091, of whom 33,639 were killed, 103,284 wounded, and 5178 missing or captured. The bulk of these casualties occurred during the first year of fighting. The es-timate of enemy casualties, including prisoners, ex-

The Grumman F7F Tigercat was a 435-mph all-purpose fighter delivered to the Marines in 1945 and 1946. Most of the 364 produced were night fighter versions armed with four cannons and with a radar in the nose as shown. Engines were P&W R-2800s of 2100-hp each. (USN)

ceeded 1,500,000, of which 900,000 were Chinese.

The war's impact reached far beyond Korea. The primary result for the western bloc was a decided strengthening of the NATO alliance. Virtually without military power in June 1950, NATO would call on 50 divisions and strong air and naval contingents by 1953, a buildup directly attributable to the increased threat of general war seen in the outbreak of hostilities in Korea. The relative positions of West and East also had been affected during the war by the development of thermonuclear devices. The U.S. exploded its first such device in 1952, the USSR (Union of the Soviet Socialist Republics) in August 1953. The exact consequences of all these changes were incalculable; but it was certain that the cold war would continue and that both power blocs would face new challenges and new responses.

REVIEW QUESTIONS:

1. What was the primary reason for the Berlin Airlift? How was Berlin supplied? Why was the blockade lifted?

2. What is the function of the Strategic Air Command (SAC)? Why were the B-52 and B-36 concepts opposed by Generals George Kenney and Lauris Norstad? How many B-52s were eventually built? Why have they been a good investment?

3. What was President Truman's reaction to the North Korean attack on South Korea? What were the four major offensives and counter offensives in the Korean War? How did U.S. airpower play a major role in the War? What role did the helicopter play? What was President Eisenhower's message to Moscow in January 1953? What role did World War II aircraft and pilots play in the War?

4. Why did President Truman recall General MacArthur? Describe President Truman's position. Discuss the impact of the War on military preparedness.

Chapter 15

Johnson's War—And After

OBJECTIVES: At the end of this chapter you should be able to:

- [ ] Define the theory of flexible response as it pertained to the military during the 1960s.

- [ ] Explain why the U.S. became involved in Vietnam.

- [ ] Describe the Geneva Accords.

- [ ] Describe the powers given President Johnson under the Gulf of Tonkin resolution.

- [ ] Compare and contrast the Vietnam War with WWII and the Korean War.

- [ ] Describe the important role played by the helicopter in the Vietnam War.

- [ ] Discuss Secretary McNamara's policy of cost effectiveness regarding military procurement.

- [ ] Describe some of the aircraft that entered service with the U.S. in the 1980s.

If it is true that those who fail to learn the lessons of history are doomed to relive it, Americans should demand that every congressman and every Presidential candidate be required to pass a comprehensive examination to establish that each possesses detailed knowledge of all the contributing factors that led to America's involvement in the Vietnam War.

Although U.S. involvement in Southeast Asian affairs actually began during the Truman Administration, the tragic bungling of America's role in the war that evolved there must be laid at the doorstep of the Johnson Administration. The indictment is especially severe because never before in history were U.S. military forces so totally misdirected on so grand a scale or the President's responsibility to the American people so incompetently performed.

The decisions faced by Lyndon B. Johnson regarding the American presence in South Vietnam when he was thrust into the Presidency by President Kennedy's assassination were basic and entirely manageable. Kennedy had increased the number of U.S. military advisors in South Vietnam from 700 to approximately 16,000. They were non-combatants, ordered not to participate in the fighting, their mission being to train the South Vietnamese Army. Therefore, the questions that President Johnson had to address were: (1) Assuming that the American assistance program to the South Vietnamese was both morally defensible and in the best interest of the United States, what should be the maximum limit of that assistance? And, (2) assuming that maximum assistance led to American involvement in hostilities, what should be U.S. policy in bringing the fighting to a quick end?

Airpower and the Flexible Response

Johnson's decision was to continue with the open-ended and heretofore untried theory of "flexible response" bequeathed by the Kennedy Administration.

The theory of flexible response sounded logical. It was a term coined by President Kennedy's Secretary of Defense Robert McNamara, a former professor of economics at Harvard University and Ford Motor Company president, and it was born of the proposition that America needed a balanced combination of conventional forces available that would provide alternatives to deal with aggression other than the unhappy choice between massive nuclear retaliation or no retaliation at all.

Few would argue with that. However, the Kennedy/McNamara corollary was that, possessing a varied mix of forces, the amount of force used by the United States should always be commensurate with the threat. That was flexible response; that is what led President Johnson into a war in which the enemy could choose the kind of conflict best suited to his resources, could pick the areas of confrontation, and decide the level of the fighting. Vietnam was a war fought on the enemy's terms and at his convenience.

It was, of course, impossible to win such a war militarily, and since this enemy possessed a quasi-political organization trained in the arts of propaganda and terror, and effectively infiltrated it throughout the defended area, no stable political settlement was possible except in his favor.

President Johnson was well aware of the alternatives to flexible response. Gen. MacArthur had already stated the most obvious a decade earlier in Korea: Meet force with *maximum* counterforce. If America must fight, do so to win and get it over with as quickly as possible.

Johnson had the means at his disposal to do just that *without* the use of nuclear weapons. The USAF and the Navy's air strike forces could have, in a matter of weeks, destroyed the enemy's ability to make war or feed his people, while few, if any, U.S. ground troops need be risked. North Vietnam was especially vulnerable to a massive strategic air offensive. The destruction of its Red River Dam complex alone would have denied to that country 90 percent of its domestic food supply. A sea blockade of the enemy's coasts, the aerial mining of his harbors, and aerial interdiction of his supply line from China would have severed his source of military and other war-essential materials. Meanwhile, his industries, transportation routes, electric generating plants and troop concentrations could have been pounded into the earth by SAC's B-52s. Johnson could have told the enemy exactly the same thing that President Eisenhower told the North Koreans, China and Russia in 1953.

Instead, Johnson decided to commit " . . . our American boys to a land war in Asia," an act he had promised, during the 1964 Presidential campaign, that he would never consider. He was unwilling to unleash American airpower, with no target restrictions, for fear that it would lead to nuclear war with the Soviets. He chose instead to fight a war that would not offend the enemy too much— an incredible stance for the world's most powerful nation (or the world's weakest, for that matter).

The U.S. possessed a clear five-to-one nuclear advantage over the Soviets when President Eisenhower left office. Although that superiority had eroded some as a result of the Kennedy/McNamara adventure into "cost effectiveness" in the acquisition and maintenance of American arms, the Soviets did not have a numerically superior ICBM force in place until 1969 (1,054 American; 1,100 Russian).

To understand the U.S. presence in Vietnam,

Republic F-105 Thunderchiefs refuel from a KC-135 tanker on their way to tactical targets in North Vietnam, December 1965. Note that only two of the "Thuds" have received the new camouflage. (USAF)

we must go back a bit. Prior to WWII, the French had ruled Vietnam, then called Indochina, which included Laos and Cambodia, for nearly 100 years. Even before that the country had been divided, the people of the north ruled from Hanoi, while the people in the south were ruled by emperors in Hue. The Japanese occupied Indochina during WWII. When the French returned after the war, President Truman felt that he had to aid the French in their "recolonization" partly because Truman saw the French presence there as a barrier to Soviet moves in that direction, and also because French cooperation in the formation of the North Atlantic Treaty Organization (NATO) was needed.

Meanwhile, a typical communist organization, originally formed in 1930 by Ho Chi Minh, and which had no success opposing French rule in

northern Indochina before WWII, grew in strength during that war by playing down its communist ideology while recruiting young people for the avowed purpose of ousting the Japanese. They called themselves the Viet Minh and, during the early '50s, with Soviet and Red Chinese money and arms, fought a guerilla war to expel the French, a task they accomplished in 1954 after the famed seige of the French garrison at Dienbienphu.

Following the French defeat in North Vietnam, a multination conference in Geneva produced the Geneva Accords that established conditions for a cease-fire in Indochina, provided for the independence of Laos, Cambodia, and Vietnam, while a political dividing line was drawn at the 17th parallel across Vietnam in recognition of the centuries-old differences between the people of the north and

267

The attack carrier *Forrestal* in the Gulf of Tonkin, 29 July 1967, (USN)

and Red China, embarrassed the U.S. because it resulted in President Eisenhower's refusal to sign the accords. The CIA had informed Secretary of State John Foster Dulles that the Viet Minh had terrorist agents in almost every South Vietnamese hamlet, and that the "free election" bit would be a farce until a stable government in the south could root out the northern infiltrators.

Aware that the Geneva Accords would do nothing to ensure the independence of Southeast Asian nations, the Free World nations had already met in Manila to form the Southeast Asia Treaty Organization (SEATO), and signed an agreement on 8 September 1954 pledging aid to any Southeast Asian country which asked for it if attacked. It was under terms of the SEATO pack that President Eisenhower sent some 400 U.S. military advisors and military equipment to South Vietnam when the French pulled out the last of their troops in 1956 in compliance with the Geneva Accords.

Ho Chi Minh counted upon the 1956 elections to give him all Vietnam, but a general of the South Vietnamese Army (ARVN), Duong Van Minh ("Big Minh") led a *doup d' etat* against the tottering Bao Dai government and repudiated the Geneva Accords.

those of the south. Although the Geneva Accords called for free elections throughout Vietnam by July 1956, that provision, cleverly backed by the Soviets

CH-21 Shawnee ("Flying Banana"). These craft served in Korea and saw limited service in South Vietnam in that conflict. (U.S. Army)

An Air Force F-4C Phantom, a Mach 2-plus fighter originally procured by the U.S. Navy in 1960 and added to Air Force inventory because of its outstanding performance. It was used extensively in Vietnam. (USAF)

Due to a revolt within his own ranks, Ho was not able to increase the terror campaign by his agents in the south until 1961. At that time, he announced the formation of the "National Liberation Front" (Viet Cong), and began escalating his war below the 17th parallel. The Viet Cong, organized around hardcore Red guerillas of the old Viet Minh, murdered 1719 and kidnapped 9688 South Vietnamese that year. About 6200 Viet Cong slipped into South Vietnam during 1961, and in much of the south the Viet Cong were sufficiently in control to levy taxes in rural regions. Even though

With tail hook engaged, a Douglas A-4 Skyhawk of VA-12 returns to the attack carrier *Franklin Roosevelt* operating in the Gulf of Tonkin, 10 August 1966. (USN)

An ordnanceman wheels Sparrow missiles to F-4 Phantoms aboard the U.S. 7th Fleet attack carrier *Midway* as the aircraft are prepared for a strike against Viet Cong positions in South Vietnam. (USN)

ARVN troops might control many areas in daylight, it was generally accepted in much of the countryside that "the night belongs to the VC."

President Kennedy responded with more U.S. military advisors to help train and direct the ARVN's 200,000 men, and appeared less-than-surprised when the third corrupt and ineffective South Vietnamese government fell to still another *coup*, which some believed was CIA-inspired.

That, then, was the Southeast Asian bucket of eels inherited by Lyndon Johnson when he assumed the Presidency in November 1963. By that time, the VC were boldly launching daylight attacks against ARVN forces, and U.S. advisors began to die: 42 in 1963, 118 in 1964.

Then on 2 August 1964 North Vietnamese torpedo boats attacked the U.S. Navy destroyer *Maddox* cruising in international waters in the Gulf of Tonkin. They were damaged and driven off by aircraft from the carrier *Ticonderoga*.

Two days later, Johnson told a nationwide TV audience that a second attack had occurred and

Heavily-laden Grumman A-6 Intruder just prior to catapult launch from the attack carrier *Independence*. The A-6's electronics allow crew to "see" at night and through clouds for accurate bombing. (USN)

An F-4B Phantom of VF-102 stretches out the arresting cable as it lands on the attack carrier *America*. (USN)

that, as a result, retaliatory air strikes were underway.

There is no evidence that a second attack took place, but on 5 August, on orders from the President, 64 aircraft from the 7th Fleet carriers *Constellation* and *Ticonderoga* struck at motor torpedo boats and their supporting facilities at five points along the North Vietnamese coast and sank 25 boats along with their petroleum stores.

On that same day, Johnson used the "two" attacks on U.S. ships as his reason for asking Congressional support for " . . . all necessary action to protect our armed forces and to assist nations covered by the SEATO treaty." Congress gave him a signed, blank check. The exact wording of the Congressional resolution was: " . . . take all necessary steps, including the use of armed force, to assist any member or protocol state of the Southeast Asia Collective Defense Treaty requesting assistance in defense of its freedom." It was adopted by a vote of 416 to 0 in the House, 88 to 2 in the Senate. Johnson's War was to have a lot of sponsors.

When President Johnson obtained the Tonkin Gulf resolution, endorsing in advance whatever he decided to do in Vietnam, the Viet Cong had ap-

North American F-100 *Super Sabre* was designed as an 800-mph superiority fighter. It appeared in 1954 and saw extensive use in Vietnam as a fighter-bomber. A total of 2294 were delivered to the Air Force. (USAF)

proximately 115,000 guerillas in the south; they had murdered an estimated 5587 and a kidnapped an estimated 26,504 South Vietnamese civilians.

With North Vietnam escalating the war (whether or not it was a "civil war" is an arguable point, because the people of Indochina had never been united), and the sketchily-trained and often poorly motivated ARVN forces clearly unable to effectively oppose the enemy, it was obvious by 1965 that the U.S. would determine whether or not South Vietnam, Laos, Cambodia—and after that, perhaps, all Southeast Asia and peripheral nations—would fall to communism or mark the time and place where red aggression was contained in that part of the world.

Actually, an air offensive of sorts against North Vietnam was begun in March 1965, although it was limited to indecisive targets selected by the Joint Chiefs, who in turn were fettered by the Johnson/McNamara policy of placing important strategic targets off limits. On 26 March, F-4 Phantoms from the 7th Fleet's carriers *Hancock* and *Coral Sea*

struck at radar sites in the vicinity of Vinh Son, while Air Force F-100 Super Sabres and F-105 Thunderchiefs began a series of sustained attacks on bridges and the "Ho Chi Minh Trail," the collective name for several routes of supply through eastern Laos used by the invader to funnel men and supplies into the south. The Air Force fighters were based in Thailand.

Air action was all the U.S. was capable of for a time, as the buildup of American combat ground forces did not begin until September 1965, with the arrival of the 1st Cavalry.

On 18 June, 27 B-52F Stratofortresses from Anderson Air Force Base on Guam, each carrying 27 750-pound "iron" bombs internally and 24 on external wing pylons, began a 10-month operation against Viet Cong troop concentrations in jungle hideouts in South Vietnam. The B-52 operations were code-named *Arc Light* while the overall air offensive was known as *Rolling Thunder*.

Two weeks earlier, the U.S. Marines had an airbase in operation at Chu Lai, 52 miles south of

Douglas AD Skyraider series went into production in 1945. Its Wright R-3350 engine of 2700 hp gave it exceptional load-carrying ability. A total of 3180 were built in 28 different versions with production ending in 1957. U.S. Navy used the Skyraider until 1968. (USN)

An A-4 Skyhawk approaches for landing on the attack carrier *Hancock* in the South China Sea. (USN)

the major U.S. base an Danang, and the attack carrier *Independence* arrived in Subic Bay for duty with the 7th Fleet, making a total of five U.S. aircraft carriers operating off Vietnam. The nuclear-powered attack carrier *Enterprise* joined the action in December.

Within three years, U.S. military strength gradually built up in South Vietnam from less than 25,000 to over 500,000, including two Marine divisions. Regular ARVN forces meanwhile grew to over 340,000. South Korea sent 48,000 men; Australia, Thailand, New Zealand and the Philippines committed token forces. And despite nearly 180,000 communists killed and 70,000 captured during this period, the invader still managed to build his strength to nearly 240,000 men in the south, a feat accomplished by recruitment through terror and intimidation, and by sharply increasing the number of North Vietnamese regular army troops sent to VC units.

It was an unusual war by any standard. There were no front lines. The enemy could be anywhere and everywhere, and was often indistinguishable from the native population. The U.S. ground forces were spread around in fortified base camps from which they would strike out in search-and-destroy missions. On many such missions, particularly in

the thick jungles of the highlands, companies and battalions would be far from any road and wholly dependent upon helicopters for resupply and evacuation. Most battles were fought at the platoon or company level. Ambush and counterambush were familiar tactics on both sides. The helicopter and good radio communications were the two essential

Death of a MiG. An F-105's camera gun records this air victory over a Soviet-built MiG-17 near Hanoi. (USAF)

Army CH-37 helicopter delivers a field piece to a new firing position. (Sikorsky Aircraft)

ingredients that made it possible for the U.S. Army and Marines to engage in that kind of combat successfully, while the B-52s, Air Force and Navy fighters, despite the frustrating limitations placed upon them, limited the enemy's ability to fight and denied him the opportunity to concentrate his resources for attacks in strength. Enemy air opposition was rare except over especially sensitive targets in the north.

The first helicopter to fly in large numbers in South Vietnam was the CH-21 Flying Banana, followed in 1963 by the faster and more versatile UH-1 Huey. The helicopter became the symbol of this new kind of war, a checkboard campaign in which units might be picked up and set down swiftly almost anywhere from the forested highlands to the fertile, densely-populated river bottoms along the coast and the largely inundated rice paddies of the Mekong Delta region in the extreme south. As the enemy reacted by increasing his antiaircraft capability, the Huey Cobra appeared, a heavily armed gunship version of the UH-1.

The Huey Cobras were mostly employed in an attack role and were especially effective in close air support situations. Ground troops in radio contact with the Cobras could direct them with extreme accuracy to nearby targets. During street fighting in Hue, a U.S. Army platoon leader marvelled that "Those chopper guys would come in just a couple of feet over our heads and we could tell'em, not which building we wanted hit, but which *doorway.* Man, *that's* close air support!"

A pair of F-105 Thunderchiefs with an F-100 Super Sabre en route to strike at Viet Cong positions. (USAF)

Directing the war from Washington, the Johnson/McNamara planners, believing that the limited air strikes on North Vietnam had seriously hurt the enemy, decided that a major cutback in the air offensive could encourage the North Vietnamese to sit down in good faith at a meeting in Paris to negotiate a cease-fire.

It was true that Ho had been seriously hurt by the air attacks. By early 1968 all major railroad bridges in the north were down, petroleum storage facilities were destroyed, war material could move southward only at night, and even then the trucks were in constant danger from U.S. night fighters. All consumer goods, including food, were strictly rationed, and 300,000 people (including many Chinese "volunteers") were fully employed repairing bomb damage to roads and rail tracks.

Therefore, President Johnson announced on 31 March 1968 that 80 percent of the area north of the 17th parallel (containing 90 percent of all North Vietnamese people) would be spared further attack by U.S. aircraft. Johnson had tried short bombing moratoriums during the previous two years, but this one was tied to the Paris negotiations.

But Ho Chi Minh had no reason to seriously negotiate with Johnson offering such a major concession, and all the Paris talks accomplished at that time was to provide Ho with a breathing spell while he rebuilt his shattered supply lines to the south.

Nevertheless, on 1 November 1968 (on the eve of the elections), Johnson halted all bombing of North Vietnam. He said at the time that Ho had agreed to some reciprocal measures of deescalation. If Ho did so, there was never any evidence of it.

That was the situation when Richard M. Nixon took office in January 1969. The U.S. had half a million men in South Vietnam and American combat deaths were approaching the 33,000 mark, and

A fearsome foursome of F-105s over Vietnam. The *Thunderchief's* radar system allowed it to attack enemy ground positions through clouds from any altitude. (USAF)

The Army's Bell Huey helicopter became the symbol of the hit-and-run war in Vietnam, serving as ambulance, troop transport, gunship—name it, the *Huey* could do it. (Bob Dean)

although the Viet Cong and North Vietnamese People's Army had lost 500,000 men, they seemed prepared to lose that many more. Indeed, Ho declared that he was willing to fight for another 20 years if necessary.

Nixon, of course, was not. Nor were the American people. The average American found it difficult to understand a war with such confused beginnings fought—seemingly endlessly—for no clearly defined purpose affecting America's vital interests, and offering no chance of victory.

A month after taking office, President Nixon, acting on the advice of his new Army commander in Vietnam, Gen. Creighton Abrams, secretly authorized B-52 strikes against enemy sanctuaries in Cambodia. He later extended that authorization to include Laos as well, since those "neutral" countries had from the beginning not only been used by the North Vietnamese as bases from which to conduct the war in South Vietnam, but eventually became victims of communist "wars of liberation" themselves.

But Nixon, too, had to learn that impressive "enemy body counts" reported by U.S. Army com-

manders was not a measure of progress in this strangest of wars. The enemy knew that time was on his side, and to him life was cheap.

By May 1972, a total of 200 B-52s were committed to the war in Southeast Asia, along with their KC-135 tankers (the "tanks" also served as aerial filling stations for the fighters), but Nixon ordered that no air strikes be made north of the 20th parallel. However, after the North Vietnamese walked out of another fruitless round of cease-fire talks in Paris on 13 December 1972, Nixon lifted that ban and authorized an air offensive against selected military targets in the Hanoi/Haiphong area. Navy A-6 Intruders, operating from carriers in the Gulf of Tonkin, and Air Force F-111s from Takhli Air Base in Thailand joined the B-52s in the round-the-clock all-weather offensive (*Linebacker II*) that came to be known as the "Eleven-Day War."

At 1451 hours on 18 December 1972, the first of 87 B-52s lifted off the runway on Guam bound for Hanoi. They would be joined by 42 more flying from U-Tapao Air Base in Thailand, along with some 400 fighters, including Marine F-4s escorting the KC-135 tankers.

Over their targets at 35,000 ft., the bombers were met by hundreds of surface-to-air SAM missiles and a few MiG-21 fighters; the F-111s and A-6s going in low faced the greatest concentration of antiaircraft artillery ever assembled. But losses were remarkably light, altogether: 15 B-52s and six F-111s, and with only a 36-hour pause for Christmas (during which time the North Vietnamese stridently charged that the Americans were bombing schools and hospitals and spoiling all chance for a negotiated cease-fire), the air offensive continued, loosing over 20,000 tons of destruction on the enemy's transportation and oil facilities. On 30 December Hanoi wanted to talk again.

While the Eleven-Day War represented but a fraction of what an all-out strategic air offensive could have been, it was more than enough to force an agreement on cease-fire, effective 27 January 1973. Violations of the agreement by communist guerillas in Laos and Cambodia caused President Nixon to send the B-52s back into limited action until 15 August 1973, when the war in Southeast Asia ended—for the United States.

During the eight years the B-52 strategic bombers were in action over Southeast Asia, just six percent of their total missions were directed at decisive strategic targets.

Almost anyone who had read the *U.S. Strategic Bombing Survey,* commissioned by President Truman at the end of WWII, could have successfully planned a quick end to the Vietnam conflict in 1965. U.S. military leaders offered such a plan to President Johnson early that year, and fully explained it to the Senate Preparedness Investigating Subcommittee in mid-1967, but Johnson opted for the McNamara doctrine of flexible response, a policy not of action, but of *re*action (the "knee-jerk syndrome"). The total cost of that to America and the Free World has not yet been paid.

McNamara's Brand

Robert McNamara ran the U.S. Department of Defense just as he had the Ford Motor Company. His watchword was "cost effective," bureaucratic code for "get your money's worth," and in pursuit of his cost-effective programs, McNamara success-

Many Hueys were fitted with the 7.62 mm Gatling gun mounted above a 2.75-in rocket launcher. Such aircraft were designated UH-1Bs and UH-1Cs. (U.S. Army)

The AS-7A Corsair II light attack bomber was built by Vought and developed from the earlier F8U Crusader. The A-7 series entered squadron service in October 1966. (The Vought Corporation)

fully wrested control of weapons selection and the U.S. defense posture from the generals and admirals.

There was just one critical factor in the defense equation that McNamara's textbook efficiencies did *not* include: A dollars and cents appraisal of freedom itself.

In the name of fiscal responsibility, McNamara

The USAF also used Skyraiders over Vietnam and provided some to the South Vietnamese Air Force (VNAF). (USAF)

A Kaman HH-43F Huskie rescue helicopter with fire bottle is first on the scene as an A-1E Skyraider crash-lands at Da Nang. (USAF)

closed a number of airbases, cancelled the Skybolt air-to-air-missile program (which weakened NATO because it forced retirement of Britain's Vulcan bomber force), cancelled the B-70 supersonic strategic bomber program and the Nike-Zeus antiballistic missile which was planned to intercept Soviet ICBMs approaching targets in the United States. He expected to retire the B-52s, and planned to equip the Air Force and Navy with a single fighter airplane—one that would also serve as a *strategic bomber*. ("There's no use trying," Alice said, "One can't believe impossible things." "I dare say you haven't had much practice," said the Queen).

That airplane was then called the "TFX" for "Tactical Fighter, Experimental." It had been in the works for about 18 months when Mr. McNamara took charge of the Pentagon with John F. Kennedy's inauguration as President in January 1961. The TFX was originally conceived as the Air Force's new 1,700-mph long-range tactical fighter,

An A-4 Skyhawk approaches the flight deck of the *Ranger* in the South China Sea. (USN)

and the idea went through the usual channels: Once Tactical Air Command (TAC) settled upon the performance parameters required of the new fighter it would need during the late '60s and '70s permission to proceed with the project was obtained from Air Force Headquarters. Then, Air Force Systems Command took over to decide whether or not such a plane was feasible. Next, detailed specifications were drawn up to be sent to the aircraft manufacturers which, in turn, would produce plans showing just how they would design and build such an airplane. Finally, with input from the several commands concerned, Air Force brass would get together to select the design they liked the best and, through the Secretary of the Air Force and Secretary of Defense, ask Congress to fund it. (Since 1974 the Air Force Test and Evaluation Center at Kirtland, AFB, N.M. evaluates the prototypes, and the Defense Systems Acquisition Review Council makes the decision as to whether or not the new hardware is recommended for acquisition to the Secretary of the Air Force.)

Meanwhile, the Navy, too, had a new fighter proposal in the mill, and therefore, when these proposals appeared on the desk of Defense Secretary McNamara, scarcely before he had time to warm his chair, McNamara made his incredible de-

USAF C-130 Hercules drops South Vietnamese paratroopers into Viet Cong stronghold southwest of Saigon. (USAF)

cision: The TFX would be redesigned, in *two* versions, employing at least 90 percent "commonality of parts," to serve both the Air Force and the Navy!

An A-4 is launched from canted deck as F-4Bs prepare to follow from the main deck. (USN)

Convair F-111, originally planned as a superior tactical fighter, was downgraded by McNamara's naive theory and the resulting airplane met none of the original design specifications. (General Dynamics)

Five hundred million dollars could be saved, he said, by developing one airplane rather than two.

Now, at that time, the Air Force Chief of Staff happened to be Gen. Curtis LeMay, but LeMay held his fire and waited for the Navy's reaction, which wasn't long in coming.

The Navy pointed out that it needed an *entirely* different kind of aircraft than that required by the Air Force because their missions were different. The Air Force tactical fighter would have to be a large, heavy, offensive machine (90 ft. in length and weighing 90,000 lbs.), while the Navy needed a much smaller, lighter defensive fighter to ride shotgun for the fleet.

But McNamara was adamant. The TFX—by then designated the F-111—would proceed as decreed.

Boeing and Convair (the latter with Grumman as a sort of junior partner) responded to McNamara's specifications, and in November 1962 the

The F-111's terrain-following radar and other sophisticated systems are praised by its pilots, but the airplane itself, compromised by a multi-mission requirement, performs marginally in each role. As Gen. (ret) Eaker pointed out, it's not possible to mate a sports car and a four-ton truck. (General Dynamics)

The Navy managed to prove that the F-111 was unsuited to navy needs and did without a new fighter until the political climate changed in Washington. Then it got the fighter it wanted, the F-14 Tomcat, seen here during initial tests early in 1974. (USN)

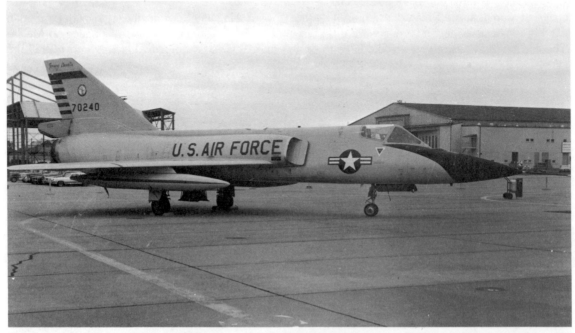

The Convair F-106A is a 1500-mph USAF fighter with a service ceiling of 60,000 feet. It has been in operation since 1959 as a home defense weapon in the U.S. It is automatically directed to its targets by advanced ground radars. (F.H. Dean)

282

The Lockheed F-104 Starfighter was introduced in 1958 and seemed slightly unbelievable with a razor-thin wing of only 22-ft span and a gross weight of 20,000 pounds. Top speed was 1600 mph, but it was an unforgiving machine and generally unpopular with pilots. (USAF)

the services chose the Boeing proposal. Eight Air Force generals and three admirals, plus the Chief of Naval Operations, Adm. Anderson, and Air Force Chief of Staff Gen. LeMay, picked the Boeing designs.

However, McNamara overruled them all because, he said, the Boeing designs contained only 34 percent commonality of parts (by weight), while the Convair designs used 92 percent identical parts. Backing the McNamara decision were Secretary of the Air Force Eugene Zuckert and Secretary of the Navy Fred Korth, who were also Kennedy appointees.

In the end, the Navy decided to stonewall it, saying that the F-4 Phantom, which it already had, was better suited to the Navy's needs than the Convair F-111B.*

The Air Force, however, ended up with 270 F-111 tactical fighters (which fell short of all original performance specifications, and was grounded a number of times until the wing carry-through structure and other weaknesses were modified), and 70 FB-111 "strategic bombers," acquisitions that were considerably eased by the retirement of Gen. LeMay in February 1965, a few days after the F-111 prototype began its flight tests. LeMay had characterized the F-111 as a "jury-rigged . . . in-

ferior stop-gap weapon system." But LeMay could not have remained as Air Force Chief of Staff in any case, because he was bitterly opposed to the policy of flexible response.

The Mitchells, MacArthurs and LeMays must always risk the foreshortening or termination of their military careers—however right they may be—because they cannot be allowed to publicly challenge the decisions of the Commander-in-Chief—however wrong he may be.

Faith, Hope, and Parity

Throughout the '60s and '70s, U.S. defense forces, including the nuclear deterrent forces, steadily eroded in comparison to those of the Soviets; and four different Presidents—Johnson, Nixon, Ford and Carter—sought solace in a series of code words when forced to defend the decline of American arms. *Equivalency, sufficiency* and *parity* were imprecise terms used to imply that, even if the Soviets had more intercontinental ballistic missiles (ICBMs), there was no need for alarm because, all things considered, the two powers actually were about even in nuclear might. The Congresses of these two decades endorsed this position.

But the assumption that nuclear confrontation

---

*Ironically, the Air Force also began buying F-4s in 1963. McDonnell's versatile Phantom proved to be one of the star performers of the Vietnam war in the air superiority, fighter-bomber, interceptor, ground support, tactical strike, and reconnaissance roles.

The Lockheed TR-1 is a larger and improved version of the famed U-2 "Spy Plane." It has a wingspan of 103 feet and cruises over 430 mph above 70,000 feet with a range of 3,000 miles. The USAF had 35 of them in mid-1986. (Lockheed-California Co.)

is thwarted by this presumed balance of terror is meaningless if the balance exists only in Presidential rhetoric. As valuable as the U.S. spy satellites may be, they cannot probe the contents of roofed structures, and therefore U.S. defense planners cannot know how many ICBMs the Soviets have in standby storage to give them a multiple reload capacity for the ICBMs that are detectable.

At the beginning of the '80s, the U.S. possessed 1,053 ICBMs: 53 Titan IIs in silos at three locations in Arkansas, Arizona and Kansas; 450 Minuteman II Solid-propellant missiles; and 550 Minuteman IIs fitted with multiple independently targetable re-entry vehicle (MIRV) warheads. The ICBMs, with a range in excess of 6,000 miles, are pre-programmed to strike strategic targets in the Soviet Union.

The second leg of America's nuclear deterrent triad is the nuclear-powered submarine fleet armed with some 640 nuclear-tipped missiles of medium range.

SAC's manned bombers represent the third leg of the U.S. strategic retaliatory force—290 B-52G and H nuclear missile carriers, 70 FB-111s and 600 supporting KC-135 tankers.

The manned bomber has one very important advantage over the ICBM: it can be launched at the first suspicion of attack and then recalled for several hours thereafter if no attack materializes. The ICBM cannot be called back once launched—indeed, it will reach a target in the Soviet Union in slightly over 20 minutes—or it may be destroyed in its silo if for any reason (including a delayed order from the Commander-in-Chief as he agonizes over the decision) it is not launched within the 15-minute warning period provided by satellite and radar surveillance.

The manned bomber is more vulnerable to

enemy defenses, which is why the B-52s would penetrate Soviet airspace at 400 mph and only 400 ft. above the surface to launch their stand-off nuclear missiles hundreds of miles from their targets.

In 1980, the stand-off nuclear missile carried by the most B-52s was the SRAM (Short Range Attack Missile), as many as 20 per plane (or, more often, depending upon each B-52s pre-selected targets, a mix of SRAMs and nuclear gravity bombs). The SRAMs may be launched with the aircraft on any heading, even 180 degrees away from the targets. It flies at 2,000 mph and its 18-inch diameter gives it a very poor signature on enemy radar. In tests, the SRAM has repeatedly impacted within 100 ft. of its programmed targets. Its only weakness is its short range—about 100 miles. It has been operational since 1972.

The Air Launched Cruise Missile (ALCM) is subsonic, but has a much greater range and therefore significantly increases the B-52 survivability

factor. The Cruise Missile program was delayed by the Carter Administration, and as a result full deployment of the ALCM could not be accomplished before 1986. Carter also delayed development of the improved Trident II nuke missile for U.S. submarine strike force, cancelled the B-52's replacement, the B-1, and delayed the MX (mobile ICBM) for three critical years. At last faced with the consequences of these acts—along with those of previous administrations—and a re-election campaign, President Carter endorsed an enormously expensive, environmentally destructive and embarrassingly ridiculous MX railway system in which the missiles were to be shuffled about in a massive shell game that, hopefully, would leave the Soviets guessing as to which shelters contained missiles at any given time. Meanwhile, Mr. Carter voiced the belief that an eventual nuclear arms limitation agreement with the Soviets was possible. The Soviets, no more concerned with adherence to their future promises than to their past ones, claimed

The Strategic Air Command's SR-71 Blackbird can cruise at 2000 mph at 80,000 feet, and is a product of Kelly Johnson's "Skunk Works" at Lockheed. (USAF)

The Convair B-58 Hustler was intended as a replacement for the medium-range Boeing B-47 bomber and entered service in 1960. With a speed in the 1600-mph range it was impressive for its time. But changing requirements, and the fact that SAC was stuck with the FB-111s, caused a phase-out of the 80 Hustlers by the end of the '70s. (General Dynamics)

The Military Airlift Command delivers whatever needs to be delivered by air, anywhere in the world, at any time, for the military services. Pictured is one of MAC's emergency hospital aircraft, a Douglas C-9 Nightingale. (USAF)

Lockheed C-130 Hercules is the Air Force combat transport, designed to operate from unimproved airstrips. It does everything from iceberg patrol (for the Coast Guard) to paratrooper drops. (Lockheed Georgia Company)

support for such an agreement while going forward with a mobile ICBM program of their own, and concurrently installing new SS-20 medium-range semi-mobile missiles in Western Russia aimed at targets in Free Europe.

Each SS-20 is fitted with three independently-targeted warheads, and a total of 300 SS-20 boosters (900 warheads) were in place by early 1982, giving the communists a clear six-to-one advantage in nuclear weaponry deployed for any kind of a so-called "limited" nuclear confrontation in Europe.

That advantage was, of course, measured against the combined nuclear strength of the NATO partners. This situation so alarmed President Reagan when he took office that it prompted him to seek deployment of ground-launchable cruise missiles in Western Europe to counter this threat. The cruise missile program, along with that of the B-1 bomber, went forward in the Reagan administration.

Earlier, on the eve of the 1980 elections, in an apparent attempt to gloss over the weaknesses in America's defenses, Carter's secretary of defense, a man by the name of Brown, decided it was time to reveal the Air Force's "Stealth" bomber program, which had been in the works since late in the Nixon administration. The Stealth bomber, Brown said, would be virtually "invisible" to current Soviet radars.

The Lockheed C-5A Galaxy of MAC is shown with a typical load. It can carry this 256,000 pounds, 2,900 miles nonstop at a speed of 530 mph and land in a distance of 5000 feet. Improved C-5B version was ordered in 1982.

A Navy Tomcat fighter of the "High Hat" squadron, a unit that dates back to the mid-20s; nowadays part of the air group on the attack carrier *John F. Kennedy*. (Francis H. Dean)

Brown's revelation impressed the news media and surely sounded reassuring to the taxpayers. But what Brown did not say was that the Soviets already had some of the key engineering data on the Stealth's radar-eating systems. It had been sold to a Polish intelligence agent for $100,000 by an engineer working for Hughes Aircraft.

As the USAF Tactical Air Command entered the '80s, it possessed some excellent new aircraft.

The F-15 Eagle had been entering squadron service since the mid-'70s. The first of a planned buy of 733 A-10 ground support planes had come along in the late '70s, and the F-16 lightweight fighter, 650 of which were replacements for the 675 F-4s acquired during the '60s, was entering service. The F-15 has a top speed in excess of Mach 2, a combat thrust-to-weight ratio of 1.4 to 1, and is superior to anything the Soviets may put into the air during

U.S. Navy P-3 Orion anti-submarine warfare (ASW) aircraft makes a mock run on an American sub during exercises held in the Sea of Japan. A perimeter of P-3 bases extending from Sigonella and Souda Bay in the Mediterranean to Norway, Iceland, United States, Japan, Okinawa, the Phillippines, Thailand, Australia, New Zealand, Guam and Hawaii make any area in the world accessible to the Orion within 30 minutes' flying time. More than 400 are in service. (USN)

The newest Air Force fighter is the McDonnell F-15 Eagle believed by the Air Force to be superior to anything the Soviets may put in the air during the '80s. (McDonnell-Douglas St. Louis)

the '80s. It carries four medium-range missiles and two short-range missiles, along with 900 rounds of ammunition for its 20mm cannon. The F-16 is not as fast or as well armed as the F-15, but is much lighter and more maneuverable.

The F-16 was originally justified as an "economy" fighter, one almost as good as the F-15 for a lot less money. But the initial cost turned out to be $14 million each, while the F-15 is $17 million.

The necessary spares and maintenance equipment add significantly to these figures, not to mention the fact that some highly trained technicians are required to keep them flying.

While such aircraft are capable of some truly amazing performances in the delivery of their ordnance against an enemy, the complexity of these high-technology combat machines is in itself a limiting factor. No matter how miraculous their systems,

The General Dynamics F-16 USAF fighter is a lightweight air combat fighter which performs so well that the gadgeteers and Pentagon Pilots added air-to-surface and all-weather radar and navigation capabilities to broaden its mission. Predictably, the new goodies have forced a quantum leap in cost. (General Dynamics)

Fairchild's A-10 ground support aircraft was literally designed around its tank-killing General Electric GAU-8 seven-barrelled cannon. (Fairchild Industries)

those out of service for high-tech maintenance have an effectiveness factor of *zero.* And if no more than half of these machines in squadron service can be put into the air at any given time, due to the amount of expert care demanded by their magical black boxes, then our air commanders must plan accordingly.

One lesson learned about airpower in WWII was that the "best" and most effective combat airplanes were simply those that were airborne and ready to fight when needed—a principle clearly established by the pilots flying the unremarkable Douglas Dauntless at Midway, the obsolescent P-40 over North Africa, and the inadequate F4F Wildcat at Guadalcanal and the Coral Sea.

This is a relevant consideration because, currently, the AF and Navy are short of the technical people needed to maintain the sophisticated systems in our first-line combat aircraft.

Anytime, Gaddafi Baby

On 19 August 1981, two Soviet-made Su-22 "Fitter" fighter-bombers of the Libyan Air Force were shot down by a pair of U.S. Navy F-14 Tomcats above the Gulf of Sidra in international waters. The fight started when the Libyan aircraft fired a missile (presumably, a Soviet Atoll) at the Americans, who were flying combat air patrol protecting the carrier *Nimitz,* participating in maneuvers with the U.S. 6th Fleet. The Tomcats, armed with Sidewinder missiles, made short work of the Fitters.

The Tomcats were flown by Cmdr. Henry Kleeman and Lt. Larry Muscyznski, and their Radar Intercept Officers (called GIBs in the Air Force, for "Guys in Back") were Lt. Davis Venlet and Lt.

James Anderson. Later, one of the F-14s seen aboard the carrier had an appropriate victory symbol painted on its fuselage above the legend: "Anytime, Gaddafi Baby."

The "Gaddafi" referred to was, of course, the Libyan dictator Muammar Gaddafi, who gained power in 1969 (at age 27) by way of a *coup d'etat,* deposing the aged King Idris. A strutting, desert dandy, Gaddafi was a supporter of Uganda's mad Idi Amin, provoked the destruction of the U.S. Embassy in Tripoli in 1979, and was to contribute more to world terrorism during the 1980s than the Soviets, Iranians, and Syrians combined. He claimed the entire Gulf of Sidra to be Libyan waters (150 miles off the Libyan Coast), declaring that any unauthorized entry into the Gulf was to cross his "Line of Death."

President Reagan, aware of the 20 terrorist training camps in Libya, and frustrated by the fact that a great many Americans, and citizens of America's Allies, had been victimized by hijackings and terrorist bombs, nevertheless would take no direct action against Libya until he possessed incontrovertible evidence of Gaddafi's involvement in a specific terrorist act. He would eventually have it.

Meanwhile, on 23 March 1986, the U.S. 6th Fleet, containing the attack carriers *Saratoga, Coral Sea,* and *America,* began exercises in the Mediterranean and when, on the following day, three U.S. ships crossed Gaddafi's so-called "Line of Death," the Libyans launched at least five SA-2 and SA-5 surface-to-air missiles at U.S. aircraft. Grumman EA-6 Prowlers diverted the SAMs with their electronic countermeasures devices, and the Libyan missiles fell harmlessly into the sea. But having been fired upon over international waters, the Americans reacted as they had five years earlier. A pair of A-7 Corsairs took out the SAM site's ra-

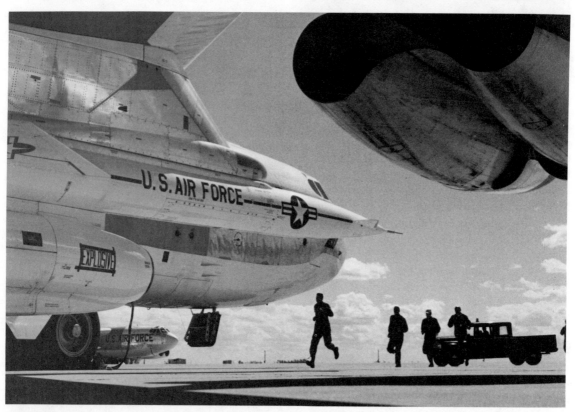

Approximately 90 B-52 nuclear carriers are on alert at all times. Quick-start ability allows simultaneous starting of all engines and a five-minute elapsed time from the scramble order to liftoff. (USAF)

The Titan II ICBM is liquid-fueled and requires extensive maintenance. America's ICBM force consisted of 53 Titans and 1000 Minutemen in 1980, a figure that had remained static throughout the '70s. By 1986 the count was 1008 Minutemen IIs and the Titans were being deactivated. (USAF)

12 A-6 Intruders from the *America* and *Coral Sea,* which struck at targets in the Benghazi area, and by 13 F-111s from bases in England, which attacked Gaddafi's headquarters/residence and the international airport in the Tripoli area. The F-111s destroyed five Libyan transport planes and damaged Gaddafi's compound. The A-6s shot up four enemy airplanes on the ground at Benghazi and inflicted an undetermined amount of damage on a military barracks. One F-111 was lost shortly after leaving the target area. Five additional F-111s were unable to bomb due to mechanical malfunctions.

The attack unquestionably shook Gaddafi—he maintained a low profile for weeks afterward—but actual damage was relatively slight. However, there were some useful truths to be gleaned from the action:

The U.S. Navy's nuclear submarine fleet contained 41 vessels in 1980, each armed with 16 nuclear missiles with a 2500-mile range. Test firing shown is of a Polaris A3, launched while the submarine was submerged. The Carter Administration refused to update with the more advanced Tridents. New Trident subs entering service late in the 80s each carry 24 Trident missiles. (Lockheed)

dar with HARM missiles (the HARM homes on the enemy radar signal), while A-6 Intruders destroyed two enemy gunboats, and the cruiser *Yorktown* blasted a third Libyan attack boat. Two Libyan MiG-25s charged toward the fray, but suddenly decided that they had something more important to do back inside Libya.

Less than two weeks later, on 5 April 1986, a terrorist bomb exploded in a West Berlin nightclub frequented by U.S. servicemen. One American soldier died (along with a 28-year-old Turkish woman), and 79 Americans were among the 230 injured. This time, U.S. intelligence people could provide the President with the hard evidence of Libyan planning and execution that Mr. Reagan had demanded. He immediately approved a retaliatory air strike against Gaddafi.

The attack was carried out at 2 A.M. on the morning of 15 April (7 P.M. on the 14th EDT) by

1. Underscored once again was the uncomfortable fact that America has no dependable allies. True, Britain's "Iron Lady," Prime Minister Margaret Thatcher, backed the U.S. play all the way, but she faced substantial criticism in Parliament for allowing the Americans to operate from British bases, while West Germany, France, Italy, and Spain opposed the attack, France and Spain going so far as to deny the American planes right of transit through their airspace.

2. The Paveway 2,000-lb. laser-guided bombs carried by the F-111s were less accurate than expected. Sixteen were delivered and, had they been squarely on target, would have left a grease spot where Gaddafi's headquarters had been. No direct hits were made.

3. The F-111s probably required more support than they were worth. A total of 17 F-111s, plus five EF-111s (countermeasures aircraft with radar jamming equipment and infrared decoys), required 28 tankers for their six airborne fuel stops during the 5,600-nm round trip. The F-111s were selected because they were equipped to deliver the laser-guided bombs, and because the Air Force insisted upon grabbing a piece of the action. The Navy could have done it all, flying 400-nm round trips from their carriers.

4. The politics of defense did not serve this mission well. It was clearly not an Air Force caper, but a job for the 6th Fleet. This mission suffered from overplanning, with input from the National Security Council, the Joint Chiefs, and others close to the President.

No one believed that the U.S. air strike against Gaddafi would mark the the end of world terrorism. The Soviet Union's surrogates—Bulgaria, Cuba, Nicaragua—would continue to aid and abet violence in the West, while Syria's ambitious King Assad, along with Iran's fanatical Ayatolla Khomeini were intent upon savaging any prospect of a mid-East peace with their own hired guns. Nevertheless, the U.S. had put the world on notice that it would make terrorism as costly as possible for its sponsors, with or without the support of America's allies.

Carrier Power

By 1982, the U.S. Navy had 14 aircraft carriers, ranging in size from the 40 year-old 45,000-ton *Midway* to the 91,000-ton nuclear-powered *Carl Vinson*. Three new *Nimitz*-class carriers were expected to join the fleet by the early 1990s. Aircraft complements are typically 50 to 80 aircraft, with up to 24 Tomcat fighters, 36 Intruder and Corsair attack craft, plus a handful of Prowlers and Hawkeyes, four to six SH-3 helos and, on the larger attack carriers, up to 10 S-3 Viking anti-submarine aircraft.

There has long been substantial opposition to operation of the supercarriers. They are expensive—$2.5 billion for the *Nimitz*-class *Carl Vinson*—and critics charge that, in all-out war with the Soviets, the big flattops would be vaporized in a matter of days, or even hours. Presumably, the Russians keep track of all U.S. carriers at all times. However, in an all-out nuclear war, the fate of our carriers wouldn't much matter. In a non-nuclear war, the big carriers would be vulnerable to the Soviets' 300 attack submarines (the U.S. has 100 submarines). Still, the Navy's ability to send these self-contained mobile airfields throughout the world

The Pershing is a short range tactical missile with a low trajectory. Based in Western Europe during the mid-1960s, and supplemented with the surface launched cruise missile in the mid-1980s, these were the weapons most likely to be affected by arms reduction talks between the superpowers. (Martin-Marietta)

The Lockheed S-3B Viking, fitted with Harpoon missiles, is a sub-hunter, and its electronic support measures and countermeasures systems make it a valuable escort for carrier-based strike aircraft. (Lockheed-California photo by Bob Ferguson)

to show the flag and serve U.S. policy is probably worth the cost. An enemy must assume that each American aircraft carrier possesses a stock of nuclear weapons, while the flattops' ever-present escorts—which can include a modernized battleship—is a formidable force in itself.

Meanwhile, we should mark the fact that U.S. spy satellites have been observing the construction of at least one, and possibly two, Soviet aircraft carriers at the Black Sea port of Nikolayev. This will be the first Russian flattop designed for the operation of fixed-wing jet aircraft.

ATF and ATA

The USAF expected to replace its F-15 Eagle fighters in the late 1980s and early '90s with a machine that, in development, was referred to as the Advanced Tactical Fighter (ATF). This may or may not have been the F-19 out of Lockheed's famed "Skunk Works," a number of which were reportedly flying (only at night) from a super-secret airstrip near Tonopah, Nevada, in mid-1986. The Air Force asked Congress to fund a secret airplane code-named "Aurora" early in 1985.

At least seven aerospace companies worked on the ATF design, which certainly incorporated stealth technology, and stealth technology appeared to consist of engines mounted atop the aircraft, a well-rounded airframe (no sharp corners), at least 40 percent composite construction, and a radar-absorbing finish, probably a ceramic.

In the meantime, the U.S. Navy also wanted a new fighter for delivery in the early '90s. Designated the Advanced Tactical Aircraft (ATA), it would also possess stealth characteristics. The new F/A-18s, meanwhile, would replace the aging A-7s.

Northrop's stealth bomber was due to appear in the same time frame. During the early fall of 1986, the first 15 B-1B bombers were delivered for service to Dyess AFB, Texas. At the time, the Air Force planned to buy 100 of the B-1Bs pending delivery of 132 Stealth bombers in the '90s.

In addition to a more extensive use of composite materials in the airframes of the ATF/ATA/Stealth machines, we can also expect to see "head up" cockpit displays, which project flight, navigation, and weapons delivery data onto transparent screens directly in front of the pilot. The most significant advance, however, will come—as it always has—in the new generation of engines. The Pratt & Whitney PW5000 and the General

294

Electric GE37 may have up to 50 percent fewer parts, 40 percent less fuel consumption at supersonic speeds, and 25 percent higher thrust-to-weight ratios than the best fighter engines of the '80s.

The Balance of Power, United States Versus USSR

Despite the fact that the U.S. enjoyed a clear 10-to-1 advantage in deliverable nukes over the Russians at the end of the Eisenhower Administration, John F. Kennedy won the Presidency claiming a dangerous "missile gap" in favor of the Soviets. The missile gap did indeed develop during the Kennedy and subsequent administrations, until President Reagan began repair of America's leaky defenses and regained, if not military superiority, at least a thoroughly credible deterrent force.

In October 1986, as President Reagan prepared to talk about nuclear arms reductions with the Soviets' General Secretary, Mikhail Gorbachev, in Reykjavik, Iceland, the Soviet Union possessed a total of 15,206 known nuclear warheads vs. 12,564 U.S. nuclear warheads. Having recorded that bit of insanity, we should now crank-in the "howevers":

However, the U.S. had 1,008 land-based intercontinental ballistic missiles (ICBMs), fitted with a total of 2,108 independently-targeted warheads, while the USSR had 1,398 ICBMs fitted with a total of 6,420 warheads.

The U.S. had 100 submarines set to fire 5,632 warheads from 640 missiles, and the Soviets had 300 submarines, carrying 940 missiles fitted with a total of 3,100 warheads.

The U.S. could deliver 4,200 nuclear devices with 260 B-52s, one B-1B, and 280 FB-111s, while

A Grumman A-6A Intruder comes aboard its carrier. The Intruder is an all-weather attack aircraft, equipped for aerial refuelling and nighttime delivery of its ordnance; in service since the mid-1960s. (Grumman Aerospace Co.)

the Soviet Union had 950 bombers (mostly short-range) carrying 3,200 nuclear bombs and missiles.

In Europe, the U.S. had 220 short-range land-based missiles, vs. 1,250 for the USSR. The Soviets also had a reported 170 SS-20 triple-warhead intermediate-range missiles aimed at China.

America's Minutemen ICBMs, scattered in underground silos in nine states in the Midwest, South, and West, each fitted with three warheads, were to be at least partially replaced by the MX Peacekeeper, each carrying 10 warheads. President Reagan asked for 100 MXs, but the Congress had agreed to only 50 late in 1986.

Midgetman

The appearance of the single-warhead Midgetman ICBM clouded the defense picture. Midgetman was mobile; it could be driven about the U.S. mounted on specially-built trucks and fired from wherever it happened to be if the President ever pushed the Doomsday button. Midgetman's mobility provided the protection against destruction by an enemy first strike that the MX originally promised but never achieved. The Pentagon big-rocket people opposed Midgetman, and when it appeared to be gaining adherents in the Congress, suggested that Midgetman be more than doubled in size (from 38,000 to 90,000 pounds) and fitted with at least three independently targeted warheads.

Meanwhile, arms reduction talks with the Russians, and President Reagan's so-called "Star Wars" research program, introduced more uncertainty into the nuclear arms standoff.

The Strategic Defense Initiative

On 23 March 1983 President Ronald Reagan proposed that the U.S. embark upon a research program that would lead to a defense system designed to intercept and destroy ICBMs before they could reach American soil or that of our allies. Reaction to this bold announcement was instantaneous and varied, at home and about the world. The Soviets and their apologizers cried "Foul," claiming that

effective protection against nuclear attack would be "destabilizing," the balance of terror would be upset, and the U.S. would have a first-strike advantage (perhaps an *only*-strike advantage) if such a system were in place. The President, anticipating that objection, said that America would share SDI technology with the Soviets, although no one could—or should have—believed *that*. If both superpowers were protected against nuclear destruction, the Soviets' massive military, equipped with conventional weapons, would have a "first-strike" capability of another kind.

In the beginning, much opposition to the SDI project in America was rooted in the belief that such a system was either impossible of attainment, or, if possible, would require decades to develop at an astronomical cost. Late in 1986, after spending more than three years and almost $5 billion on the project, SDI researchers could offer no absolute assurance of their ultimate success.

However, their efforts had sufficiently impressed the Soviets that Mikhail Gorbachev was eager to swap some Russian warheads for a curb on the American SDI program. Whether the Communist Party's General Secretary feared America's high-tech potential, or whether it was the enormous cost of attempting to circumvent an effective nuclear shield, Gorbachev appeared to be, prior to the October "Mini-Summit" in Iceland, anxious to talk about nuclear arms reductions, beginning with the European-based missiles.

Lasers

At this writing, SDI research appears to be focusing on a system that will employ submarine-launched X-ray lasers. The X-ray laser is generated by the detonation of a small nuclear device—small enough that it can be lofted into space by a submarine-launched missile. It has to be submarine-launched because it must be close enough to the Soviet Union to zap their ICBMs during their five-minute launch phase—that is, before each missile's multiple warheads, and 100 or so decoys, have separated from the missile's "bus" and greatly multiplied the problems of interception. Clearly, the big rockets are easier to track while in their boost phases, and it is more effective to kill 10 warheads at a time than to search them out in space among their decoys.

The alternative to submarine launch of the defensive lasers would be nuclear devices in Earth orbit, but there would seem to be no advantage to that from a purely technical standpoint, and world opinion would surely argue against it.

Why the X-ray laser? Because it seems to be the only weapon, not based in space, that may be effectively hidden and capable of intercepting Soviet ICBMs during their boost phase. Plus, an X-ray laser beam, nuclear-generated, will destroy its target with a mere one-second dwell. Other forms of lasers, and particle beams—which are greatly weakened passing through the Earth's atmosphere—must remain exactly focused on their targets for as long as seven seconds to cause significant damage, are much too unwieldy to be placed in Earth orbit, and require complex mirror systems to relay their beams against Soviet ICBMs during boost phase.

When President Reagan proposed SDI, he recognized that it was a ". . . formidable task, one that may not be accomplished before the end of this century." Whatever the outcome, the fallout from such an effort, in terms of jobs, technological advances and, perhaps, a substantial shove toward nuclear disarmament, may alone justify the great cost.

REVIEW QUESTIONS:

1. What was the theory of flexible response? Did President Johnson have any other choice but to commit U.S. troops to a land war in Asia? How did the Viet Minh get started? What were the Geneva Accords? What was the purpose of the Southeast Asia Treaty Organization (SEATO)? Who were the Viet Cong? Why were the South Vietnamese governments so ineffective?

2. Describe the events leading up to the Gulf of Tonkin resolution. What powers did this resolution give to the President?

3. How was the Vietnam War different from WWII and the Korean War? Why was it difficult for the average American to understand the war? Why can it be said that time was on the side of the North Vietnamese?

4. Why was the Helicopter such an effective vehicle in this conflict?

5. What was the situation when President Nixon took office in January, 1969? Why did he authorize B-52 strikes on neutral countries?

6. Discuss the implications of Secretary McNamara's cost effectiveness policy. List some of the aircraft which entered service with the U.S. Air Force during the 1980s.

Chapter 16

Gen-Av and Fun-Av

OBJECTIVES: At the end of this chapter you should be able to:

- ☐ Describe the private flying market in the immediate postwar period.

- ☐ Summarize the history of air racing in the United States.

- ☐ Define the purpose of the Experimental Aircraft Association (EAA).

- ☐ Describe the FAA position regarding Ultralights.

- ☐ Describe how Piper Aircraft Corporation was formed and the role of the J-3 Cub in its history.

- ☐ Identify some of the successful early aircraft developed by Beech Aircraft Corporation and Cessna Aircraft Company.

- ☐ Discuss some of the uses of general aviation aircraft.

- ☐ Summarize the brief history of helicopters and describe some of their uses.

Sensibly regulated by the Civil Aeronautics Act of 1938 and the Federal Aviation Act of 1958, private and commercial flying steadily advanced after World War II. Sport and pleasure flying grew apace, embracing such activities as air racing, homebuilt aircraft, and the restoration of antiques. Meanwhile, the lightplane manufacturers increasingly prospered as the U.S. businessman discovered the several advantages of airplane ownership. The helicopter took its unique place in the workaday world. The past was prelude.

WWII Surplus

The late 1940s was a time of readjustment, for the nation as well as for aviation. As soon as the shooting stopped, America dismantled—almost overnight—the mightiest military force the world had ever seen. Our fighting men and women were brought home and mustered out of uniform as fast as transport for them could be provided; the streets at home were filled for a time with members of the "52-20 Club" ($20 per week for 52 weeks; an immediate postwar measure that put a few dollars in vets' pockets while they sought jobs and reassembled their lives), each proudly wearing the little gold-colored emblem of honorable service irreverently known as the "Ruptured Duck."

Private flying returned in boom proportions after the war—at least, for a time. It was helped along by the "G.I. Bill," legislation that offered a wide

The Aeronca Champion series appeared in 1945. The first ones, Model 7AC, had 65 hp; later versions had 85 hp. All were fabric-covered and seated two in tandem. After the cost of personal flying began escalating in the late '70s such craft were sought in the used market and refurbished for economical personal flying. (Randall Brink)

WWII primary trainer, the Fairchild PT-19, was available in the immediate postwar surplus market for very little money, but most soon disappeared because of maintenance problems with internal wooden wing structure.

The Boeing-Stearman PT-17, another WWII primary trainer. Most that were purchased as surplus were converted to use as ag-planes. Nowadays, those that remain are being refurbished and returned to their original configuration by Warbird addicts. (Peter M. Bowers)

range of educational benefits, among other things, to WWII vets, including civilian flight training.

Postwar Ag-Planes

During this period the general aviation fleet was dominated by Aeronca Champions, Piper Cubs, and Taylorcrafts, sprinkled with war surplus trainers, mostly Fairchild PT-19s and Stearman PT-17s. A lot of Vultee BT-13s were to be seen at first, but most gave their engines (450-hp R-985

Wasp Juniors) to the Stearmans, which combination became the backbone of the aerial dusting and spraying businesses that rapidly spread throughout the country's agricultural areas. Later, the same fate befell many of the surplus AT-6s, their P&W R-1340 Wasp engines of 600 hp transforming the sturdy Stearman (actually, Boeing-Stearman) biplane into an excellent duster/sprayer (the Stearman military trainers were originally fitted with 220-hp Lycoming or Continental radials, R-680s and

Stearman spray plane with 600 hp P&W Wasp engine. Both maneuverable and ruggedly built, the Stearman was well suited to ag-flying.

Popular Warbird is the F4U series Vought Corsairs which served in both WWII and the Korean War with the Navy and Marines. This one is an F4U-7, originally built for the French. (Jim Larsen)

R-670s respectively). Eventually, the commercial aircraft manufacturers offered aircraft especially designed for agricultural work, beginning with the Piper Pawnee introduced in 1959.

In the early '80s, one could still find a few Stearmans working for "aerial applicators," as the dust/spray operators prefer to be called these days. However, many of the Stearmans that survive today have been returned to their original "two hole" configuration and painted as they looked when in military colors.

Warbirds

The restoration of WWII aircraft is hardly limited to Stearmans. It is an activity that started, almost imperceptibly, in the early '60s after the surplus warbirds had become scarce. It apparently began as a nostalgia trip for former military pilots,

Restored Mustang. Many Warbirds are painted to represent a particular WWII fighter, and many present-day owners are younger than their airplanes. (Dustin Carter)

A restored North American T-6, photographed at Willow Grove, Pennsylvania, in 1974. (Bob Dean)

and was spearheaded by a group of aging tigers in South Texas who loosely banded together as the "Confederate Air Force" in order to locate, finance, and refurbish the old fighters and bombers. By 1980 the CAF colonels (everyone in the CAF is a "colonel") had been joined by others who tracked down the vintage fighters, bombers, and trainers in the smaller Latin American countries, the limited air forces of which had been so equipped near the end of WWII. With the supply of such craft virtually exhausted, prices reached $200,000 and up, and most were in the hands of affluent men, as yet unborn when these machines were built, who regarded them as investments, and who obviously enjoyed the *macho* image that attached to the operation of such airplanes.

Air Racing

A number of WWII-era fighters have constituted the Unlimited class in civilian air racing since 1945. The most successful have been highly-modified P-51 Mustangs (F-51 after the Air Force redesignated its aircraft in 1948).

Air racing in America began as soon as it was possible to gather a few flying machines together

Curtiss P-40 Warhawks at the annual EAA Fly-In, Oshkosh, Wisconsin. Airplanes in foreground has Flying Tiger (American Volunteer Group) paint scheme, although the actual Flying Tiger aircraft number 47 was an earlier model. (Don Downie)

Walter Beech's Travel Air Model R, commonly called the "Mystery Ship," returned air racing to civilians in 1929 after military domination of such events throughout the '20s. (Beech Aircraft Corporation)

that could remain airborne long enough to complete such an event—which is to say, 1910. A top speed of less than 50 mph was sufficient to win, and that was quite enough for the spectators at Compton, California, many of whom still doubted that man could fly when the event was announced.

The air races of the '20s were dominated by the military until 1929, when Walter Beech's Travel Air "Mystery Ship" appeared at the Cleveland National Air Races and ran away from the best

Matty Laird's "Super Solution" of 1931 averaged 223 mph between Burbank, California, and Cleveland, Ohio, in the transcontinental Bendix Trophy race with Jimmy Doolittle as pilot. (E.M. Laird)

The Gee Bee R-1 racer of 1932, built by the Granville brothers in Springfield, Massachusetts, established a new world's speed record for landplanes at 296.28 mph. Jimmy Doolittle was the pilot. (Thompson Products Company)

military fighters. Then, until the mid-'30s, a succession of civilian racers, most of them built on a shoestring, led the U.S. and the world into the realm of high-speed flight and returned to America (from France) the world's landplane speed record.

Beech's 220-mph racer, fitted with a 420-hp Wright R-975—souped-up from its normal 300 hp—was eclipsed the following year at Chicago's National Air Races by Matty Laird's LC-DW300 "Solution" ("solution" to Beech's mystery), which was approximately 10 mph faster.

In 1931, the first of the 300-mph Gee Bee racers appeared, and a year later, Jimmy Doolittle won the Thompson Trophy Race in the Gee Bee R-1, then took the world's landplane speed record, averaging 296.28 mph in four passes over the three-kilometer course.

From 1932 until WWII suspended air racing, James Wedell's Wedell-Williams racers shared the Unlimited class purses with similar machines, fitted with engines of up to 1000 hp, all of which would be classed as "homebuilts" today (except for a couple of new Severskys, prototypes of the P-35 Air Corps fighter. That eventually evolved into the P-47 Thunderbolt of WWII).

After the war, the 400-mph surplus fighters took over Unlimited class air racing and sustain it to this day. In 1979, Ed Browning's highly modified Mustang, flown by Steve Hinton, established a new world's speed record for piston-engine airplanes at 499.059 mph, while closed-course speeds for this class were in the 430 mph range. The engine in Browning's machine was a Rolls-Royce Griffon, normally rated at 2375 hp but certainly producing more power than that for the assault on the record.

Other racing classes included the Formula I machines, tiny homebuilt monoplanes that somehow achieved closed-course racing speeds near 230 mph with engines originally rated at 100 hp; and a confused Sport Biplane class, also homebuilts, in which three or four professionally designed machines have taken all the money in recent years with average speeds around 200 mph while the amateurs trail along for the ride at 150 mph.

Air racing is a spectator sport, and the largest annual meet is the National Air Races held at Reno, Nevada, which embraces many other aerial activities such as aerobatic competitions, parachuting, etc. Air racing itself is not economically significant to the overall general aviation industry, and some feel that it promotes a negative impression of ci-

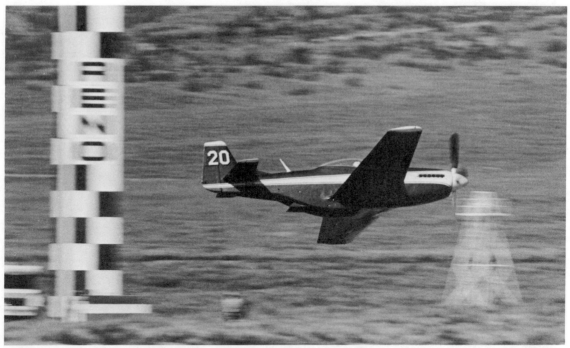

John Wright in his P-51D Mustang at Reno, 1976. (Jim Larsen)

vilian flying. It should not. Man will race whatever vehicles he may possess, and that is less a commentary on our machines than on the nature of man.

Homebuilts

That adventurous and creative nature finds other outlets in private aviation. Many free spirits build their own airplanes. That is just about the only discernible thing they have in common, because amateur plane builders are otherwise as diverse as the feathered denizens of a tropical rain forest. Homebuilt airplanes are constructed by all kinds of people, male and female, of all ages, from every economic level. Some get their creations into the air within a few months; some take years. It is possible for all because, as plane builder Peter Bowers

A typical Formula I racer at Reno, flown by Thurman Rock and built by Dick Minges. (Dustin Carter)

The Williams-Cangie sport biplane racer, Sundancer, flown by Dr. Sideny White at Reno and Mojave air races. (Dustin Carter)

Airshow performers combine skill with the spectacular, and the Cole brothers, headed by champion Duane Cole and wife Judy, are unsurpassed in this field. (Marion Cole)

once pointed out, building an airplane in one's garage is not a big job, but a collection of little jobs.

Today the cost of a ready-to-fly homebuilt airplane will range between $6,000 and $12,000 if one's labor is counted as fun. Some designs can easily cost more.

The two greatest advantages to be taken from such a project are 1) purchasing materials or kit components as needed, the airplane is paid for when completed, and 2) one has a machine tailored to his/her own personal need/preference/dream that is unavailable in the high-priced commercial market. Other benefits include the deep satisfaction that comes with the knowledge that one is transiting the skies with wings of one's own creation.

There are pitfalls. The four greatest obstacles to a successful homebuilt airplane project are 1) a spouse who is against it; 2) finding a proper engine at a reasonable price; 3) maintaining one's dedication to the task over the protracted period of time required; and 4) friends and neighbors who make the builder's garage-workshop a gathering place, drink his beer, and keep him from working.

The EAA

No special skills are required, except that some welding is usually needed, and that may be done by a professional or another amateur plane builder who possesses that skill. One should become acquainted with other builders before starting a project, because they can be very helpful, and the best way to contact such people is through membership in the Experimental Aircraft Association (EAA). This 30-year-old nonprofit organization has approximately 80,000 active members in more than 600 local chapters and is still growing. Its primary purpose is the promotion of sport aviation. While the EAA embraces all forms of recreational flying—the restoration of classic and antique airplanes, warbirds, ultralights—the hard-core membership is

In recent years, homebuilt airplane constructors have increasingly turned to foam and fiberglass, as in this advanced design by Burt Rutan of Mojave, California. Rutan's Long-EZ above flew nonstop from California to the Oshkosh Fly-In; is being built in large numbers by others. (Don Downie)

Homebuilt copy of the Travel Air Mystery Ship in flight at the Oshkosh Fly-In. At right is homebuilt replica of Lindbergh's *Spirit of St. Louis*. (Don Downie)

made up of those who build their own flying machines, and who have banded together for mutual support.

The EAA has been deftly guided by Paul Poberezny from the time that he and a handful of other homebuilt airplane enthusiasts obtained its charter in Milwaukee back in 1953. Poberezny was an Air Force pilot who had already constructed his first airplane at home. Under his leadership, the EAA soon had members nationwide and, by 1969,

The antiques go to Oshkosh, too. The antiquers have a division within the EAA, and also an Antique Aircraft Association headquartered at Ottumwa, Iowa, presided over by Bob Taylor. Pictured is Pete Ettinger of Albuquerque in his 1929 Fleet.

Paul left the Air Force to devote full time to it. Since then, aided by wife Audrey and son Tom (a champion aerobatic pilot), Poberezny has directed the EAA into a significant place in general aviation.

The EAA's annual fly-in and convention at Wittman Field, Oshkosh, Wisconsin, is far and away the single largest aviation event in the world, with an attendance of close to one million. During this week-long event each August, Wittman Field is the busiest airport in the world, with 15,000 airplanes from antiques to mini-jets, in a constant state of arrivals and departures, fly-bys, and demonstrations, all concurrent with countless activities on the ground from seminars to "fly markets."

Poberezny and his board of directors preside over a multimillion dollar budget that has allowed the purchase of 500 acres on Wittman Field for an extensive new EAA headquarters, museum, and re-search facility. The money comes from members; $25 annual dues ($1.75 million), an equal amount from the fly-in, and revenues from EAA publications, museum admissions, etc.

Ultralights

The ultralight aircraft people have their own separate division within the EAA. The ultralights have been called a phenomenon of the early '80s recession, but that was not entirely true. These minimum aircraft are not substitutes for small, private airplanes that have become too expensive for too many; they are not *substitutes* for anything. The ultralight is a distinct new class of aerial recreational vehicle, fun machines with roughly the same practical value as sailboats.

The modern ultralight aircraft was developed

A portion of the crowd at the annual EAA Fly-In at Oshkosh, Wisconsin. The EAA headquarters and museum are located there after years in Hales Corners, Wisconsin. (Don Downie)

The ultralights evolved from hang gliders, such as this Rogallo Wing type, as well as the rigid-wing designs. (Soarmaster)

from the modern hang glider. The Wright brothers began their experiments with a hang glider, and this most primitive of the heavier-than-air flying machines was reinvented in the '70s in two forms: the conventional monoplane or biplane with rigid wings, and the flexwing, or Rogallo wing, the latter being, essentially, a man-carrying kite. These were "modern" in the sense that they employed modern materials in their construction and, in the case of the rigid-wings, perhaps a more efficient air-foil shape than that worked out by the Wrights. All were/are controlled, to a degree, by the operators' shifting weight. The addition of small two-cycle engines to the rigid-wing hang gliders resulted in the first modern "ultralight aircraft"—a term adopted for the lack of a better one, since tiny airplanes weighing less than, say, 500 pounds had been called ultralight since the late '20s.

Inevitably, the powered hang gliders quickly grew in weight and power as their builder/pilots

The Mitchell P-38 illustrates the evolution from ultralight to "real airplane." (Larry Collier)

sought better performance and increased control. Movable control surfaces became necessary because the heavier the structure, the less effective the shifting weight of the operator in controlling it. And dissatisfied with chainsaw and other tiny gasoline engines, the proponents of this sport went to snowmobile and larger engines. By 1982, 30-hp ultralights were common.

The question was, at exactly what point did such a contrivance become an airplane? That was important because, as long as such machines remained "foot launchable," the FAA had a good excuse to ignore them. Their construction and operation were completely unregulated, their pilots unlicensed, and those involved in the sport regarded that as a highly desirable state of affairs.

But again, the nature of man being as it is, he will never, as the saying goes, leave well enough alone. The use of one's legs for a landing gear became next to impossible as the machines acquired weight and more power. They had to have wheels.

Still, the FAA left them alone as long as possible, although everyone knew that some sensible regulation would have to come, especially, after a couple of dimbulbs flew ultralights coast-to-coast, and began taking them to altitudes as high as 14,000 feet.

The FAA acted with remarkable restraint. It decreed, in 1982, that ultralights must not: exceed 254 pounds in weight; carry more than five gallons of fuel; operate in controlled airspace; or fly during the hours of darkness, over populated areas, or from established airports. For the time being, pilots and machines would remain unlicensed by the federal government, except for two-place ultralights. So the ultralighters got off light.

Piper

The Piper J-3 Cub did not burst upon the av-scene overnight. The concept awaited the appearance of a proper engine—and Bill Piper.

Oilman William T. Piper, Sr., at age 48 became involved with airplanes sort of by accident when, along with several other Bradford, Pennsylvania, businessmen, he invested $600 in the Taylor Brothers Aircraft Corporation a few months before the stock market crash of 1929. The Taylor Brothers company consisted of Gilbert Taylor (his brother had died in a plane crash the year before), two employees, and a parasol monoplane fitted with a 90-hp Kinner engine, which Taylor expected to produce priced at $4000.

Taylor's airplane found no buyers at the beginning of the Great Depression and, at Piper's sug-

The twin-engine Lazair ultralight is a Canadian design. (Don Downie)

The gentle, versatile Piper J-3 Cub. As an Army Air Force liaison aircraft it was known as the L-4. Pictured is a flight of L-4s in service with the South Korean Air Force. (USAF)

gestion, Taylor designed and built a smaller, much lighter airplane, powered with a 20-hp Brownbach engine. That craft, designated the Model E-2 Chummy, barely flew with such an anemic power-plant, and Taylor's backers allowed the company to slide into bankruptcy early in 1931.

But Piper retained his faith in the E-2's concept—a minimum airplane that could be sold at a minimum price. He purchased the Taylor company's assets for $1000, and cast about for a suitable engine.

Piper's timing could not have been better, for late that year Continental Motors introduced a little 4-cylinder, four-stroke, air-cooled engine of opposed configuration rated at 37 hp. It was called the A-40, and it would establish the basic lightplane engine configuration for at least the next 60 years. Mated to the Taylor E-2 Cub, the A-40 allowed Piper to sell that airplane for $1325. Piper sold 17 Cubs in 1933, 71 the following year, and 210 in 1935.

At that point, Gilbert Taylor, aware that he had

Piper's successful Cherokee series first appeared in 1960. The Cherokee 235 Pathfinder, above, was a 1974 model. Cherokees range from two-place to six-place. (Piper Aircraft Corporation)

The Piper Tomahawk is a popular two-place sport/trainer. The T-tail gives it a modern look, but offers no aerodynamic advantage to offset its disadvantage on a small, piston-powered airplane. (David Frazier)

something going, left Piper and moved to Alliance, Ohio, where he introduced a similar airplane in 1937 known as the Taylorcraft B12. The Taylorcraft would have the improved Continental A-65 (65hp) by 1941, and as the BC-12D reintroduced af-

ter WWII, about 3000 "T-Crafts" would be built before the company folded in 1947.

A lot of T-Crafts have been restored and are flying today, along with some new ones. In 1974, a new company was formed in Alliance to produce the F-19 Sportsman, a re-engineered version of the BC-12D, fitted with the Continental O-200 engine of 100 hp. It was initially priced at $9500.

In the meantime, Bill Piper had moved to Lock Haven, Pennsylvania, changed his company name to Piper Aircraft Corporation, and introduced the Piper J-3 Cub powered with a 50-hp version of the A-40. Piper sold 736 of these machines priced at $1617. His 1938 models were the first to standardize on the now famous "Cub Yellow" paint scheme, and that finish, like Henry Ford's "Model T black," stayed with the Cub until the last J-3 was built in 1947. Altogether, 14,125 Cub J-3s were produced.

In 1940, the J-3 was certified with the 65-hp Continental and Lycoming, and production jumped to more than 3000 per year as the Civilian Pilot Training Program (CPTP; later, the War Training Service) was begun in colleges across the country

The Piper Cheyenne III is a cabin-class business airplane that is representative of the big-buck market that is outpacing the once strong demand for single-engine privately owned airplanes. (Piper Aircraft Corporation)

to give primary flight training to thousands of American youngsters. When this program ended in mid-1944, 1132 educational institutions had trained 430,000 primary flight students and, according to an FAA publication (GA-20-84), "Three-quarters of those trainees had their first flights in Cubs, soloed in Cubs, and were certificated in Cubs." Just how many others earned their wings in the gentle, pokey J-3 before and since that time will never be known.

The second generation of Pipers, metal-framed and fabric-covered like the Cub, appeared immediately after WWII, and the Piper Cruisers, Clippers, Pacers, Tri-Pacers, and Colts, all in the 100 to 160-hp class, continued the Piper success story throughout the '50s. All were two to four-place, with the two-place Vagabond of 1948 being the best compromise between performance and cost at $1995.

The Cub reappeared in 1949 as the Super Cub with a red paint scheme and 90 hp. It soon went to 108 hp, 115 hp, 125 hp, and was sold in later years mostly with 150 hp, remaining in production until 1982, at which time Piper sold the manufacturing rights to an Odessa, Texas, firm.

The third generation Pipers represented a clean break with the past; they were all-metal low-wingers, beginning with the Comanche in 1958, and followed by the Cherokee series in 1961. But Piper,

with production facilities at Lock Haven and in Vero Beach, Florida, had reorganized in 1948 to acquire fresh capital—and that led to loss of control of the company by the Piper family.

Both the company's founder, and his son, William T. Piper, Jr., are gone now, and the company continues, seemingly always a little behind its competitors in its marketing practices. In 1986, Piper—by then a subsidiary of the Lear Siegler Company—offered the Malibu and the Archer single-engine craft, along with a couple of twins. The Lock Haven facility had long since been sold.

Meanwhile, both Beech and Cessna struggled in the changing market of the '80s, both counting on corporate customers for survival.

Beechcraft

Walter Beech appears to have leaned to that view from the beginning. After selling Travel Air to Curtiss-Wright in mid 1929, Walter served as president of the C-W Airplane Division until 1932. Then, at the lowest point of the Great Depression, he and wife Olive Ann (nee Olive Ann Mellor, Travel Air's office manager, whom Walter married in 1930), left Curtiss-Wright, returned to Wichita, and formed Beech Aircraft Corporation. At first working in rented space in the idle Cessna plant, Walter brought in engineers Herb Rawdon and Ted Wells, and sent them to their drafting tables with,

The first Beechcraft Model 17 Staggerwings had fixed landing gear, fully enclosed; entered the market in 1932. A total of 781 Stagger-wings was built before the last one left the factory in 1949, two years after introduction of the Model 35 Bonanza. (Beech Aircraft Corporation)

The Beechcraft Model 18 appeared in 1937. Commonly called the "Twin Beech," The Model 18 remained in production until the last Super H18 left the factory in Wichita in January, 1969. (Beech Aircraft Corporation)

reportedly, the admonition to design a reverse stagger (lower wings placed forward of the upper ones) cabin biplane that would seat four and "go like hell."

Walter got what he asked for, the classic Model 17 Staggerwing that despite its high price—$14,000 to $17,000, depending upon engine installation, which ranged from 225 hp to 420 hp—found 332 buyers prior to WWII. The military purchased an additional 427 Staggerwings, and 16, fitted with 450-hp Wasp junior engines, were produced on special order, 1946-1948, for civilian customers who preferred to pay $29,000 for a new Staggerwing rather than accept the promise of a new Beech Bonanza for less than $10,000.

The model 35 Bonanza was introduced in 1947, fitted with a 165-hp E-185 Continental engine. It was priced at $8945, weighed 1460 pounds empty, and cruised at 172 mph. Forty-six years and more than 13,000 Bonanzas later, the Bonanza cost *eighteen* times more, had gained 800 pounds in weight, possessed 125 more horsepower, and cruised about 20 mph faster. By then, it had been in continuous production longer than any other airplane.

There are, and have been, many other Beechcrafts, but the only civilian aircraft known to Walter were the Staggerwing, V-tailed Bonanza, and the Model 18 Twin Beech that entered the market in 1937. Walter died in 1950, and Olive Ann, along with Frank Hedrick and other top management

people who were there when Walter was, ran the company until after it became a subsidiary of the Raytheon Company in 1980.

Raytheon brought in its own management people, downgraded the public relations department to a two-man gofer office, and announced plans to market several new twins for the early 1990s, following certification of its composite Starship in 1987 or 1988. Insiders reported that Beech held no more than 12 orders for the highly-touted Starship late in 1986.

Cessna

When Walter rented space at Cessna in 1932, aircraft production had halted there. Three years earlier, Clyde had purchased 80 acres at Cessna's present main plant site on Pawnee Road, constructed five buildings, and had 80 employees. His products were the Cessna Model A series—clean, four-place cantilever monoplanes powered with a variety of engines—the most popular of which was the Model AW, fitted with a 125-hp Warner or 200-hp Wright Whirlwind. These Cessnas were Clyde's own designs, and were so basically sound that one can still see some Model AW in single-engine Cessnas today.

By 1932, however, Clyde was nearing retirement age, and had he not given an airplane ride to this 12-year-old nephew, Dwane L. Wallace, in Clyde's new Laird Swallow back in 1923, the

The Bonanza V-tail was priced at $126,000 in 1983. Non-Bonanza owners charge that part of that price is for the V-tail's "snob appeal." This airplane has suffered more than its share of in-flight structural failures.

Cessna story would be somewhat different.

From that time forward, young Wallace knew that his future would be in aviation. He soloed an OX-5 Travel Air in 1932, and graduated from Wichita State University in 1933 with a bachelor's degree in aeronautical engineering. Since Cessna was closed, Dwane worked briefly for Beech, then persuaded his uncle to reorganize the Cessna Aircraft Company and reopen the plant, producing a new four-place monoplane based on the Model A series. The resulting Cessna Airmaster kept the company alive for the next five years, an average of 30 per year finding buyers.

Clyde retired to his farm in 1936 (he died in 1954), and Dwane Wallace, at age 25, became president of the company—as well as the test pilot, engineer, and salesman.

Cessna's first twin-engine airplane, the T-50,

Certification of the Beechcraft Starship was delayed due to weight problems, while pre-production orders for the all-composite twin turboprop were disappointing. New management at Beech changed company character. (Beech Aircraft)

Deliveries of the Beech 1900 Airliner began in 1983. Seating 19 passengers, this pressurized turboprop cruises at 300 mph and has a range of 850 nautical miles. (Beech Aircraft Corporation)

was introduced in 1939, shortly before Hitler marched into Poland. Although intended for the civilian market (as an economy version of Beech's Model 18), the T-50 achieved a degree of success as a military trainer that Wallace had not envisioned. There was exactly $5.03 in the company's bank account when Canada bought 180 of these machines, and during WWII more than 5,400 were built as the USAAF AT-8, and UC-78. Cessna called it the Bobcat, but to the cadets who transitioned to multi-engine airplanes in it, the Bobcat was irreverently known as the "Useless 78" or the "Bamboo Bomber."

Also during the war, Cessna (along with Beech, WACO, and other general aviation plane makers who had survived the depression) produced troop-carrying gliders and subassemblies for bombers and fighters.

When the war ended, Cessna again turned to the commercial airplane business, its first postwar models being the two-place 120 and 140, 4000 of which were built in 1946.

Cessna broadened its market in 1947 with introduction of the five-place 190 and 195, essentially all-metal Airmasters with more horsepower. And the following year production was begun on the new four-place Cessna 170.

The Korean War claimed a large portion of Cessna's production capacity, turning out subassemblies for Boeing, Lockheed, and Republic, but in 1954, along with the T-37 jet trainer, the five-place twin-engine Model 310 was introduced. The

A total of 185 C-165 and C-145 Cessna Airmasters was built 1935-1941 inclusive. (Cessna Aircraft Company)

The Cessna 190 and 195 were essentially all-metal versions of the prewar Airmasters, albeit with more power. The 190/195 appeared in 1947, and a total of 1177 was produced, including 83 for the military, which were designated C-126s. (David Frazier)

Models 172 and 182 came out in 1955, and then, when the two-place Model 150 was added in 1959, the foundations of the modern Cessna company were complete.

Business Flying

Meanwhile, the American businessman had begun to recognize that the airplane could be a valuable business tool, and as such was subject to the same kind of tax writeoff as other business machines. By 1975, an estimated 40 percent of the general aviation fleet was used for business purposes, either full or part-time, and with the exodus of factories to the Sun Belt from less gentle climes, company airplanes represented an everlarger percentage of the new civil aircraft sold each year.

That, along with the rapidly rising cost of flying, changed the look of general aviation. The demand for new single-engine airplanes steadily eroded, while the market for twin-engine airplanes and corporate jets remained strong. The lowest-priced single-engine craft suffered the greatest loss in sales during the early '80s, while the costliest twins suffered the least during that recession.

The classic Cessna 120/140 series of two-place personal/trainers will each sell for more today in the used market than when new. Produced 1946-1951 inclusive with 85 or 90 hp, these craft cruised at 105 mph on five gallons of fuel per hour. (Cessna Aircraft Company)

The two-place Cessna 152 cruises at 120 mph with 108 hp. (Cessna Aircraft Company)

Cessna 152 and 172 production lines were shut down in 1982 at a time when there was a backlog of orders for the Cessna Citation business jet.

Production of the single-engine Cessnas had been completely suspended by 1986, except for the turboprop Caravan, an ungainly freight-hauler. In November 1986, Cessna offered three versions of its successful Citation bizjet, two of its twin turboprop Conquest, and two models of the Caravan.

Cessna is a subsidiary of General Dynamics, and its present boss is Russ Meyer, who moved into the top slot following Dwane Wallace's retirement.

The general aviation ("gen-av") airplane manufacturer increasingly looks to the businessman, who sees the airplane as a means of multiply-

ing the effectiveness of key management and technical personnel, especially in corporations with scattered facilities. As an efficient compressor of time and distance, the airplane places a company's decision-makers on-the-scene in several places hundreds of miles apart in a single day and will still have them home that evening. The electronic age notwithstanding, it is apparent that the most crucial determinations often demand on-the-spot analysis by management. And in competitive markets, time is often the most important single factor to correct decisions, because management decisions are not a storable commodity, but are the products of informed intellects constantly faced with changing conditions, and who are most effective when

The Cessna Skyhawk went out of production in the mid-1980s. Basic list in 1983 was $48,940 with essential avionics. Engine is the 160-hp Lycoming O-320-D2J. (Cessna Aircraft Company)

The Cessna pressurized Centurion II cruises at 200 kts at 18,000 feet, and has a 600 nautical mile range. List price in 1983 was $207,000. (Cessna Aircraft Company)

eyeball-to-eyeball with the knottiest challenges.

Company-owned airplanes are seldom identifiable as such because management often suspects that stockholders doubt the true usefulness of such machines. Therefore, most corporate airplanes do not carry the company name or logo.

Nevertheless, scheduled airlines serve only five percent of the nation's 16,000 airports, and offer multiple, daily schedules, without plane-change service, to only a fraction of those. In other words, the scheduled airlines do not—and cannot—provide the on-demand air travel that thousands of corporations often need.

The economics of the situation are not hard to grasp. A middle-level executive paid $48,000 per year is earning $25 per hour. He/she is assumed

The turbo Mooney 231 offers 210 mph cruise at 18,000 feet with 19 gph fuel economy. Engine is the Teledyne-Continental of 210-hp. (Mooney Aircraft Company)

The Cessna Ag Truck has a 280-gallon hopper capacity; is powered by the Teledyne-Continental IO-520-D engine of 285 hp. (Cessna Aircraft Company)

to be worth twice that to the company, and therefore the company cannot afford to have such a person sitting in an airport terminal waiting for an airplane during the productive hours of a business day, or on the highway somewhere at 55 mph in a rented automobile enroute to a place not served (or with limited service) by a commercial air carrier. It is the on-demand, make-your-own-schedule flexibility of the company-owned airplane (or fleet of planes in some cases) that makes economic sense to corporations.

The corporate airplane offers other, less tangible competitive advantages, including the progressive company image it projects to a company's customers. Imaginative executives may use it to gain the undivided attention of a client who has been difficult to see: "You're going to New York on Tuesday? As it happens, so am I. Why don't I stop by in our company airplane and pick you up? Our pilots will take you back to Booneyville whenever you are ready." It happens all the time, and a surprising amount of business is transacted in the posh cabins of the nation's corporate airplanes. And, yes, just as the office copier is sometimes switched on for personal use, so is the corporate airplane—and that fact won't surprise anyone, including the IRS.

The manufactuers of corporate airplanes have long since learned how to sell their products. The corporate airplane salesman is well-educated, well-dressed, and low-key. He is backed by a top accountant or two, ready to sit down with the prospect's comptroller and investigate the dollars-and-cents reality of airplane ownership/operation as it would apply to *that* company's particular situation. Usually, cost-benefits projections will be prepared

Cessna Crusader has turbocharged engines for cruising speeds above 250 mph between 10 and 20,000 feet. Single-engine service ceiling is 13,000 feet. (Cessna Aircraft Company)

The Cierva Autogiro of 1929. Principal U.S. builders of these craft, which flew with free-turning rotors, were Pitcairn and Kellett. The fixed-wing disappeared on later models before the appearance of the helicopter ended autogiro/autogyro development.

for several types of airplanes, with varying degrees of aircraft utilization rates cranked in. Since the fixed costs of airplane ownership (hangar, insurance, crew salaries, normal maintenance) are the same whether the airplane is flown or not, its cost per hour of operation goes down with increased utilization. The one thing the aircraft manufactures have learned *not* to do is oversell in this market. There is no room for hype, and not every business can profitably employ an airplane. Some are best served with a pure jet, and some with a medium-sized twin, while at the bottom of the scale a ladies' hosiery salesman may profitably extend his territory with a single-engine Cessna.

Helicopters

In recent years the corporate helicopter has begun to find buyers. A look at the top 1000 U.S. industrial firms as compiled by *Fortune* magazine reveals that, in 1981, 536 companies owned 2229 aircraft, and helicopters represented 10.6 percent of the total, or 236 corporate copters.

Actually, almost all helicopters work for a living, and they are spread throughout the business community. The central fact about the helicopter is that it is a unique machine, capable of performing tasks that no other machine possessed by man can do. It can fly backwards or sideways, straight up and straight down. It can hover motionless in the air while lifting all sorts of loads—including people—and it can operate from any reasonably level cleared space barely larger than the diameter of its rotors. Its place is secure in the modern world. Developed as a military vehicle, the helicopter is indispensable to a modern army, and in civilian dress daily transforms the impossible into the commonplace.

The concept of vertical flight, induced by rotat-

Igor Sikorsky at controls of the first successful U.S. helicopter, 14 September 1939. (Sikorsky Aircraft)

No, this is not a scene from *M*A*S*H*, but the real thing. A Bell H-13 lifts wounded in Korea, 23 July 1953. (USAF)

ing wings, was understood at the time of the Wrights, and a great many experimenters tried to build a controllable helicopter without significant success, until the Focke-Achgelis FA-61 at last flew in Germany in 1937.

The autogyro was developed in the meantime, initially by Juan de la Cierva in Spain, who first flew such a machine on 9 January 1923. The Cierva autogiro (the copyrighted spelling attendant to Cierva's patent; otherwise, "autogyro") was essentially a conventional airplane —fuselage, engine and propeller, tail, stubby low wing—to which was added freely rotating long and narrow wings mounted on a pylon above the fuselage. These wings, or rotors, were turned by the aircraft's forward motion, and were not connected to a power source. About 500 autogiros (and autogyros) were produced during the '30s, largely by Kellett and Pitcairn. (Harold Pitcairn disposed of his airline stock and the airplane manufacturing firm to concentrate on the marketing of autogiros. He later took his own life.)

In the United States, the first successful helicopter was designed by Igor Ivanovich Sikorsky, and first flew, with Sikorsky himself at the controls, on 14 September 1939.

Sikorsky was born in Kiev, Russia, 25 May 1889, and was educated at the Naval College in Petrograd (later, Leningrad). He designed and built two helicopters in 1909-1910 which did not fly.

Between 1912 and 1918, Sikorsky worked as engineering manager for the Russian Baltic Car Factory and designed four-engine bombers for the Czar. He fled Russia during the Bolshevik Revolution and reached the United States in 1919. He founded Sikorsky Engineering Corporation on Long Island in 1923 and produced a series of amphibians and flying boats. His company became a subsidiary of United Aircraft in 1929, was merged with

Twin-jet Sikorsky S-64 demonstrates its potential as a heavy lifter. (Sikorsky Aircraft)

The 30-passenger Sikorsky S-61 in service for Los Angeles Airways, a pioneer passenger helicopter operator that began operations 1 October 1947. (Sikorsky Aircraft)

Chance Vought's company, another United acquisition, and was known as Vought-Sikorsky for a time. Later, it was simply the Sikorsky Division of United.

More than 400 of the R-4 through R-6 series Sikorsky helicopters were produced for the military during WWII. But those machines were the Curtiss Jennies of rotary-winged flight, and it was the Bell H-13 (Model 47), designed by Arthur Young and Bartram Kelly, that convincingly demonstrated the helicopter's great potential during the Korean War (M*A*S*H fans will be familiar with that machine).

During the '60s, another war would greatly advance helicopter technology, and the major U.S. manufacturers would be those who started early: Sikorsky, of course; Hiller, 1942, later merged with Autolite; Huges, 1948; Bell, 1941, became a Textron company in 1960; Kaman, 1945; and the original Piasecki company, 1945, which became the Vertol Aircraft Corporation in 1956, and the Vertol Division of Boeing in 1960. There were many others, most of which disappeared, while some still limp along on short rations.

The high-water mark for commercial helicopter production in the U.S. was 1980, when 1425 units were produced. Then the early '80s recession took its toll and only 637 helicopters were delivered to the civilian market in 1982, by which time the sale of fixed-wing aircraft was markedly down.

There is almost no competition between the helicopter and the airplane; each does its own thing. Each is limited to a role that no other machine can do better or more efficiently. Our vehicles define their own spheres of service. Therefore, the helicopter will continue to earn its keep in the workaday world. Velvet seats won't alter its character.

Minority Group

There are about 850,000 licensed pilots in the U.S., although no more than 700,000 are considered active at this writing. By category, approximately 20 percent are student pilots (a slowly diminishing number during the '80s); 40 percent are private pilots; 25 percent hold a commercial rating; 15 percent are airline transport rated, and 4 percent are rated on helicopters. That will total more than 100 percent because some are rated on both fixed-wing and helicopters.

Women pilots constitute six percent of the total.

Rutan Voyager

Most of us in general aviation first heard the name Rutan in 1974, when an odd-looking homebuilt airplane, constructed of foam and fiberglass, with its propeller in back and its tail in front, won the award for the Outstanding New Design at the EAA's Oshkosh Fly-In. This improbable machine was the creation of Elbert L. "Burt" Rutan, a 31-year-old pilot and aeronautical engineer on leave from the flight test section at Edwards AFB, California.

Burt sold plans for this airplane—the *VariViggen,* named for a Swedish fighter it vaguely resembled—set up shop on the high desert airport at nearby Mojave, California, and then designed a series of outstanding homebuilt aircraft with such names as *VariEze* ("very easy") and *Long-EZ,* all of which were of composite construction (foam, fiberglass, and epoxy), pusher configuration, and fitted with a horizontal lifting surface in front in addition to the main wing in back.

These were very efficient airplanes, and they were flown to a number of speed and distance records for machines in their class, mostly piloted by Burt's elder (by five years) brother, Dick Rutan, a much-decorated former Air Force fighter pilot, and Dick's "constant companion," petite Jeana Yeager, who is Dick's junior by 14 years. Jeana had several years' experience in design drafting and management with an aerospace firm before joining Dick at Mojave in 1980 to form a partnership, Voyager Aircraft, a loose-knit organization consisting largely of EAA-type volunteers, and allied with Burt's Rutan Aircraft Factory for the purpose of designing, building, financing (lots of donations from private individuals), and—finally—flying an airplane around the world ("around the fat part") nonstop and without refueling.

Meanwhile, in 1983, Burt formed another company, SCALED Composites, with Herb Iversen, to provide aerospace companies with a complete engineering, technical, and flight test staff to develop and test scaled-down, manned prototypes of new airplanes, a concept that promised to cut development costs, while taking advantage of Burt's talent as a designer, and his experience with canard ("tail first") airplanes, as well as composite airframe construction. The Beechcraft *Starship* was spawned and tested in 85 percent scale by SCALED Composites—whereupon Beech purchased SCALED Composites, and Burt became a Beech official in his capacity as president of SCALED Composites.

Most observers felt that it would be interesting to see how long Burt's restless creativity could be contained by Raytheon's rigid corporate rituals. The management people at Beech who made the decision to go with the bold Starship program were gone before the first full-size *Starship* was built, and it was rumoured around Wichita that Beech's parent company bosses were less than enthusiastic over the Starship program. In any case, Burt's adventures with Beechcraft did not affect design and development of Dick and Jeana's *Voyager.*

The *Voyager* was completed early in 1985. It had a span of 111 feet, weighed 1800 pounds empty, and was designed to hold approximately 1800 gallons of fuel, mostly in the two 30-foot "outrigger" fuselages. The two-place craft was constructed of quarter-inch-thick panels of Hexcel honeycomb, a resin-coated paper-like polymer, covered with graphite fibers embedded in epoxy, a construction system said to be one-fifth lighter but seven times stronger than aluminum. Burt designed *Voyager's* wings with a high aspect ratio (long and narrow) and capable of flexing at the tips as much as 30 feet in each direction—a condition evident to the TV viewers who watched the historic takeoff from Edwards AFB. Fully loaded with fuel, *Voyager's* gross weight was in the neighborhood of 11,000 pounds (gasoline weighs six pounds per gallon), and that allowed the wingtips to drag on the runway during the early part of the takeoff roll, grinding away as much as a foot of each. With this type of construction, that did not weaken the structure, but did add some drag.

Voyager was built behind locked doors, and after its inspiring flight many of its specifications and construction details were not immediately released. That may have been because Dick and Jeana reportedly owed some $300,000 for expenses directly related to the project, and wanted to pay off their creditors with, among other things, book and perhaps even movie rights to their story. They complicated their financing because they refused to endorse products they did not actually use, and never considered tobacco advertisements ("There'll be no narcotics in our airplane!").

Voyager had made more than 40 test flights by mid-1986 when Dick and Jeana combined the final, most realistic test with an assault on the closed course distance record. They established a new record by remaining aloft for 111 hours and 44 minutes—2:42 P.M. 10 July, to 5:15 P.M. 15 July—flying 20 laps around a 503.73-mile course off the coast of California.

If some Rutan-watchers had expected the *Voyager's* round-the-world flight to be little noted in the press, they were surprised. By the time *Voyager* had crossed the Pacific during its second day after takeoff, much of the Free World was clearly enthralled with the brave venture, and Dick and Jeana had acquired a cheering section of millions.

They had taken off at 11:02 A.M. (EST) 14 December 1986. There were many anxious moments, including a series of storms over the South Pacific which forced a course deviation that took *Voyager* north of the Equator rather than the planned passage south of the Equator. Extreme turbulence was encountered when Dick flew blind into the edge of a nighttime thunderstorm over Africa, and a fuel shortage scare resulted from a faulty fuel transfer system. It was solved by Jeana, who rerouted some plumbing.

Voyager completed its 26,000-mile journey—nonstop and without refueling—at 11:06 A.M. (EST) 23 December at Edwards AFB, California, after nine days and four minutes in the air. A week later, Burt Rutan, Dick Rutan, and Jeana Yeager were awarded the Presidential Citizens Medal by President Regan.

REVIEW QUESTIONS:

1. Why do you think private flying boomed and then busted in the immediate postwar period? What is the Confederate Air Force? How did air racing get started in the U.S.?

2. What is the attraction for individuals to build their own aircraft? What are some of the pitfalls? Describe the purpose and role of the EAA.

3. Describe the FAA's position regarding Ultralights. Do you think it will change? Why?

4. How did William T. Piper, a successful oilman, at age 48 become involved with light aircraft? Why was the J-3 Cub so successful? List some of the successful aircraft that followed the Cub.

5. Describe some of the successful early aircraft produced by Beech Aircraft Corporation. Who took over the company upon Walter Beech's death in 1950?

6. Who was Dwane Wallace? How did he get started with Cessna Aircraft Company? What were some of the aircraft Cessna produced for the military during WWII? What were some of the postwar models?

7. Why do businesses use general aviation aircraft? What type of aircraft do they use? Describe some other uses of business aircraft. Who developed some of the early helicopters? What are civilian helicopters used for?

Chapter 17

Economic IFR

OBJECTIVES: At the end of this chapter you should be able to:

- [ ] Discuss the development of the jet engine from the 1910 Coanda jet.

- [ ] Explain why Boeing has held such a dominant position in jet aircraft development.

- [ ] Summarize the facts leading to the merger of McDonnell and Douglas.

- [ ] Highlight some of the problems and successes which Lockheed has experienced in recent years.

- [ ] Discuss some of the causes and effects of the Airline Deregulation of 1978; the Air Controllers strike; the Slot System; Flow Control.

- [ ] Highlight the extraordinary career of William P. Lear and the development of the Learjet.

As the U.S. airline industry sought to become established on-course and pick its way through economically stormy skies in the uncertain 1980s, it was buffeted from all quadrants. The old automatic pilot of federal regulation had been disengaged and the industry was being hand-flown, IFR, into rapidly changing conditions.

Meanwhile, corporate airplanes proliferated, from light twins to Learjets, the latter having been so well conceived—and marketed—that company ownership of a Learjet had become synonymous with success, affluence, and progressive business practices.

Jet Aircraft Engines

The appearance of the jet aircraft engine brought about the second great revolution in air transport. It was certain to come, although WWII hastened its arrival.

We cannot escape the fact that military spending has, from the outset, set the pace of aircraft development. The First World War advanced airframe design by as much as 20 years in the space of four years. During the early '20s, the U.S. Navy fostered development of the radial piston engine in America, which made possible the first practical airliners. Aircraft superchargers, controllable-pitch propellers, and the cylinder/valve designs featured on the Wasps and Whirlwinds were among the projects that came from the Air Service's research center at McCook Field between 1918 and 1926. The gas turbine or jet aircraft engine had a similar history.

The principle of jet propulsion had been under-

The Army Air Service research center at McCook Field (now Wright-Patterson AFB, Ohio) was experimenting with controllable and reversible-pitch propellers in 1922. This installation was on a DH-4. (USAF)

stood at least since Isaac Newton postulated his Laws of Motion, and a jet airplane was displayed at the 1910 Paris Aircraft Show. But it was the prospect of war that at last forced development of the jet aircraft engine in the late '30s.

Now, before proceeding, perhaps we should mention that there are two major methods of classifying gas turbine engines: 1) by compressor type, and 2) by the way the power produced is used.

Compressor types fit into three categories:

Aircraft supercharger development began at McCook Field in 1918. This 1931 installation was on a Curtiss P-6 fighter. Engine was a Curtiss D-12, a Prestone-cooled V-12 of 460 hp. (Robert Cavanagh)

□ Centrifugal flow.
□ Axial flow.
□ Centrifugal-axial flow.

Power usage produces four categories:

□ Turbojet.
□ Turbofan.
□ Turboprop.
□ Turboshaft.

Secondary classifications include the path the air takes through the engine, the method of power extraction, and the number of spools in the engine.

The path the air takes through the engine refers mainly to the combustion section, and leads to such variations as:

□ Straight-through flow.
□ Reverse flow.
□ Side-entry flow.

The method of power extraction refers to whether the engine has a single shaft for the compressor, turbine, and load, or a free power (independent) turbine to drive the load. An engine may have one, two, or three independently rotating spools.

The centrifugal compressor works like the modern supercharger (or the pump that drains your flooded basement). It compresses air by spinning it off its circumference. The axial flow compressor is a large spool studded with vanes, which pulls the air through in a straight line and compresses it.

How the gas turbine engine works. (General Electric)

Basic parts of a turbojet aircraft engine, the CJ-610 which powers the Learjet Model 25. (General Electric)

So, in operation, the jet engine pulls air into its compressor and packs it into a combustion section where, mixed with fuel, it is ignited. The hot gasses are then expelled out the rear, flowing across the turbine blades, which, in turn, may drive accessories and/or turn a propeller. If this energy is absorbed to turn a propeller, there isn't much left as jet thrust. Admittedly, this explanation is a tad simplified, but essentially, that is the way it works.

There are a lot of other considerations, including the desirability of controlling both the temperature and velocity of the exhausting gases in the jet pipe to gain maximum efficiency. That is why the turbofan has evolved. Its turbine turns a ducted fan at the front of the engine that not only produces a lot of thrust of its own, but directs internal airflow around the engine to cool the exhaust, thus reducing exhaust velocity for greater efficiency and less noise. Bypass air is available in some engines for this purpose which do not employ the ducted fan, but the fan provides more thrust for the energy

Pratt & Whitney turbojets. (P&W Aircraft)

329

required to turn it than that energy will provide as jet exhaust thrust. Therefore, the turbofan, or fanjet, is more fuel-efficient than the pure turbojet.

If you are still with us after all that, we will return to our story, and include that first jet airplane.

The 1910 Coanda Jet

It was designed and built by Henri Coanda, a Rumanian, and although a biplane, it was a very clean machine, both wings being full-cantilever. The powerplant consisted of a centrifugal compressor driven by a small gasoline engine. It had no propeller and depended on the velocity of its jet exhaust for propulsion. Coanda crashed this machine on takeoff, and whether or not it was capable of flight was never established. Coanda later worked on flying saucer designs in the U.S.

The Whittle Engine

In England, 21-year-old Frank Whittle wrote an exam thesis on the possibility of gas turbine engines for airplanes in 1928. He took out his first patents on such an engine two years later, at about the time Hans von Ohain began similar research in Germany.

Whittle formed a company, Power Jets, Ltd., to develop his engine in 1936, but it was not until 1939, on the eve of WWII, that the British Government went knocking on Whittle's door, probably prompted by intelligence reports on the German's activity in that field.

The von Ohain Engine

The Germans were indeed busy. They had added a gas turbine engine division to Dr. Ernst Heinkel's airplane factory, and gave von Ohain the support he needed. Therefore, on 27 August 1939, near Rostock, the Jet Age was born—in secrecy—when the Heinkel He-178 jet airplane made its maiden flight.

First U.S. Jet Engine

Almost two years later, on 25 May 1941, Britain's jet, the Gloster E-28/39, made its first flight from Cranwell, Lincolnshire, whereupon the

Pratt & Whitney fanjet, or turbofan. (P&W Aircraft)

chief of the USAAF, Gen. H.H. Arnold, managed to obtain a Whittle engine which he dispatched by air to General Electric in the U.S. with orders to study, reproduce, and improve upon it where possible. GE got the Whittle because 1) They had been producing turbines for electric generating plants for 40 years, and because 2) GE's Dr. Sanford Moss had been working on aircraft supercharger development at McCook and Wright Fields for 20 years.

GE's copy of the Whittle developed 1250 pounds of thrust, and a pair of them went into America's first jet airplane, the Bell P-59, which was first flown 1 October 1942.

Meanwhile, Secondo Campini in Italy reinvented the Coanda. His Campini-Caproni N-1 was fitted with a 900-hp piston engine driving a three-stage compressor, its single shaft turning a ducted fan in the plane's nose. The N-1 flew in August 1940, but its cruising speed of 140 mph was disappointing.

Since GE had U.S. rights to the Whittle, Pratt & Whitney made a deal with Rolls-Royce, which was producing the Nene, an engine based on the Whittle, although of greater power. Concurrently, Andy Wilgoos at P&W began development of an axial flow type engine. The Whittle, it should be noted, was of the centrifugal compressor type.

At the end of WWII, a number of German Me-262 jet fighters fell into Allied hands, and their

Jumo jet engines were available for study, bringing all U.S. enginemen abreast of the state of the art. Subsequent U.S. gas turbine engines depended upon American know-how for the direction and quality of their development.

Boeing

It would appear that Boeing developed the first U.S. jet airliner on faith alone, because the first Model 707 was rolled out of the Seattle factory on 14 May 1954, but none were sold until 13 October 1955, when Pan Am ordered six 707-120s.

If that were the whole story, then Boeing did indeed take a large gamble. However, the 707 gave its airframe to the Air Force's KC-135 tanker, ordered in August 1954, and the KC-135 was a shoo-in because it was needed to refuel the B-52 in flight, and the B-52 had entered production in April 1953—about the time the first metal was cut for the first 707.

Gamble or not, Boeing was a year ahead of the next American-designed jet airliner to appear, the Douglas DC-8. Convair was close behind with their Model 880, the first of which entered service with Delta in January 1960. Lockheed did not penetrate this big-bucks market until the early '70s with their L-1011 TriStar.

Boeing clearly dominated the jet airline market, world-wide, for 20 years after the first 707 was put in service on Pan Am's New York-London route on 26 October 1958.

Several factors contributed to Boeing's strong position. The 707 and its spinoff, the 720 (which began flying with United in July 1960), were offered in a number of sizes, configurations, and with a choice of engines that fitted those machines for a

The KC-135 Air Force tanker and the Boeing 707 were developed simultaneously around the same basic airframe. The 707 prototype was completed in May 1954; the USAF ordered the KC-135 in October 1954, and Pan Am ordered the first 707 a year later. (USAF)

The venerable Douglas DC-3, C-47, C-49, C-53, Gooney Bird, Spooky, Skytrain (officially), R4D, Dakota—she had many names, all spoken with affection. She had but one gait; she was noisy; her wingtips flapped, and her cockpit leaked, but she'd get you there. (Pan Am)

high percentage of both domestic and transoceanic routes. Well-engineered and relatively troublefree, these Boeings were built concurrently with B-52s and KC-135s and surely benefitted from the unusual amount of wind tunnel research (8,000 hours for the B-52 wing alone) and in-flight testing accorded the military machines, including that of the earlier B-47 medium-range jet bomber. And with plenty of money coming in from the military contracts to keep the Boeing Seattle and Boeing Wichita plants busy, the Boeing Commercial Airplane Division was assured of all the support it needed.

Boeing did have a serious challenge from the Douglas DC-8, DC-9, and DC-10 during those years. Douglas, after all, had dominated the airline market from the time the DC-3 went into service in 1935.

Douglas

The DC-3: There can never be another like it. No other single airplane can ever so completely represent air travel. At one time, 95 percent of all commercial air traffic was carried in DC-3s. Almost 11,000 were built (most of them as C-47s, C-49s, and C-53s for Army Air Forces during WWII), and their trial by fire generated countless reports that bordered on the unbelievable. One was dived to its

terminal velocity; it shed its wingtips, but landed safely. Designed for 21 passengers, a C-47 once carried 74 refugees out of Burma. When a strafing Japanese fighter severely damaged one wing of a CNAC DC-3, a wing from a DC-2—markedly shorter—was substituted. It flew, although it was the only DC-2 1/2 on record. As late as 1970, DC-3s (mostly refurbished C-47s) were still in service with almost 200 airlines around the globe, and one, retired by North Central Air Lines in 1968, had 52,000 hours on its airframe. In 11 million miles it had worn out 136 engines and 550 tires. It was once again refurbished and put back in service as a corporate airplane. It was registered as N21728, and it would not surprise us to learn that ol' 728 is still out there somewhere, still flying. The DC-4, DC-6, and DC-7 four-engine airliners that followed during the '40s and early '50s took much from the fabled DC-3.

These were the airplanes that built the Douglas Aircraft Company, a company started in 1920 by Donald Wills Douglas when he rented office space in the rear of a Santa Monica barbershop, possessing an order for one airplane. Douglas, the son of a Brooklyn bank cashier, had a B.S. degree in aeronautics from M.I.T., three years with Glenn Martin, and $600 in capital.

The Douglas DC-4 was ordered by American, Eastern, and United in 1939, but by the time the prototype was developed, and its triple tail redesigned into a single unit, the U.S. was at war. More than a thousand were built during the war as C-54s and R5Ds (Navy). After WWII, many entered airline service. (McDonnell-Douglas Corporation)

Douglas sold 50 torpedo planes to the Navy during the next three years, and built the Army's four World Cruisers for their 1924 round-the-world flight. By 1926, he had a payroll of 112 and an order for six M-2 mailplanes from Western Air Express.

Douglas delivered similar machines to National Air Transport and obtained a small but steady series of orders from the Army Air Corps for observation planes. Then, on 2 August 1932, Douglas decided to go for broke when he learned that TWA intended to buy "ten or more all-metal, trimotor transport airplanes." The Douglas DC-1, which flew on 1 July 1933, was the result, and Douglas

The first Douglas DC-9s went to work for Delta in November 1965. The DC-9 deserved a larger share of the market than it got, because the airlines were rushing to order larger airplanes than most of them needed.

was in the airliner business.

Douglas was financially sound through the early '50s, but the transition to jet transports was painful. Boeing had beat Douglas into the market, and Boeing outsold DC-8s two to one. The short-haul Douglas DC-9, which began service with Delta in 1969, helped some, but again, while Douglas was selling 600 DC-9s through 1970, Boeing sold almost 900 727s, and had introduced the smaller 737 to further erode the DC-9 market.

McDonnell

Douglas ended 1966 with a net loss of $27.6 million, and that attracted the attention of James S. McDonnell of the McDonnell Aircraft Corporation. McDonnell was fat with military and space contracts, could use a tax break the size of Douglas' deficit, and liked the idea of penetrating the airliner market with an old hand like Douglas.

Exactly how McDonnell and Douglas got together is not a matter of public record, but they did, and the shareholders of McDonnell and the shareholders of Douglas then voted to love, honor, and share one another's dividends, and the two companies were officially united on 28 April 1967 to become the McDonnell-Douglas Corporation.

It isn't possible to end such an account with,

Allan (R) and Malcolm Loughhead in their 1918 F-1 Twin Hydroplane. The brothers changed their name to Lockheed and, in 1926, returned to plane building with the Northrop-designed Lockheed Vega. (Lockheed California Company)

"and they lived happily ever after," because recurring cycles of boom and bust have plagued the aviation industry from the beginning.

Lockheed

Some of the bust has been traceable to management errors, some to general economic conditions, and some to the fluctuating level of military spending. Braniff's problems in the early '80s, and Lockheed's a decade earlier, are examples of the first.

The first DC-10s went to United and American in July 1971 as 206 and 222-passenger versions, but McDonnell-Douglas was too late into a dwindling market that it had to share with the Lockheed TriStar. (McDonnell-Douglas Corporation)

Pilot Bob Cantwell and an early Lockheed Vega fitted with a Wright J-5 Whirlwind engine of 200 hp.

In 1970, Lockheed enjoyed total sales in excess of $2 billion and had a backlog exceeding $5 billion, but less than two years later the federal government was forced to guarantee large cash loans to Lockheed to keep it afloat.

Lockheed's problems appear to have stemmed from the huge development costs of the L-1011 TriStar airliner, including a costly delay incurred by the bankruptcy of the L-1011's engine supplier, Rolls-Royce, compounded by the practice—not unknown to other aerospace companies—of underpricing military projects and then renegotiating payment later as the "cost overruns" became obvious. With half of its business represented by military orders, and many of them simultaneously in renegotiation (the giant C-5A transport, originally priced at $28 million, ended up costing the Air Force $55 million each), Lockheed ran out of cash. The company blamed inflation and other factors, but whatever the causes, Lockheed's predicament had to be charged to bad decisions by management. That was underscored in 1976, when Lockheed's business practices were found to be less-than-

honorable after former sales executive E.F. Hauser revealed payoffs to foreign government officials for doing business with Lockheed. That forced the resignations of several top Lockheed people, including board chairman Daniel J. Haughton, and substantially shook up the governments in Japan, Italy, and West Germany.

By 1978 Lockheed had been "regenerated" (Lockheed's term); sales exceeded $3 billion, with a backlog of more than $4 billion, and Lockheed stock was up to 16 3/4 from 7 1/4 a year earlier.

Nevertheless, the L-1011 was clearly in trouble. Only 149 had been delivered by the end of 1977. Lockheed would announce the end of TriStar production in 1982, having lost $2.5 *billion* dollars on the program since 1968. The sad part is that the L-1011 TriStar is an excellent airplane, quieter and less expensive to operate than comparable machines—until Boeing brought out its new 757 and 767 in 1982.

Lockheed takes its name from the Lockheed brothers (originally, "Loughead"), Allan and Malcolm, a pair of automobile mechanics from Niles,

Walter Varney operated Lockheed Orions between San Francisco and Los Angeles in 1931. The Orions were among the first commercial airplanes to possess retractable landing gear. Varney, then into the second of his several airlines, was also to put up half of the $40,000 needed to buy the bankrupt Lockheed company in 1932. (Lockheed California Company)

California, who were in their late twenties when they entered the airplane manufacturing business in 1916 offering, of all things, a 10-place flying boat. They struggled through WWI with a two-plane order from the Navy, then quietly went out of business in 1920 after their tiny, single-place sportplane found no buyers.

Allan sold real estate, and Malcolm worked on a hydraulic brake system for automobiles (later sold to Chrysler), while their youthful chief engineer, John K. Northrop, went to work for Donald Douglas, who was trying to build airplanes down in Santa Monica.

The success of Malcolm's invention, and the close friendship that continued between Allan and Jack Northrop, brought the three of them together again and, in December 1926, with additional financing from ceramics manufacturer Fred Keeler, and Northrop's drawings of the airplanes that would become known as the Vega and Air Express, the Lockheed Aircraft Company was formed. An early employee was Jerry Vultee.

The Lockheed airplanes of this period featured full cantilever wings and molded-shell fuselages. The unusual monocoque fuselage was made by lin-

ing the inside of a concrete mold with multiple strips of spruce plywood coated with casien glue. An inflated rubber bag forced the shell against the mold until the glue set. Then the shell, made in two halves, was mated, and a series of spruce rings added inside for extra strength. This process resulted in a very strong yet lightweight structure possessing an exceptionally smooth outer surface. It made for an efficient and aerodynamically clean airplane.

A total of 196 wooden Lockheeds—Vegas, Orions, Altairs, etc.—were produced before the brothers sold out to a Detroit group in 1929. The new owners switched to metal aircraft, but were sunk by the depression and allowed the company to slide into receivership in 1932.

At that point, investment banker Robert E. Gross, who had previously backed Lloyd Stearman in Wichita, brought together some other optimists, and together they purchased Lockheed's assets for $40,000. This group included Walter Varney, Lloyd Stearman, Thomas F. Ryan III (of Mid-Continent Air Lines), broker E.C. Walker, and Mr. & Mrs. Cyril Chappellet. Gross also brought in engineer Hall Hibbard, who had worked for Stearman after earning a degree at M.I.T. Hibbard, in turn, brought in Clarence "Kelly" Johnson, and this pair would be primarily responsible for a long line of highly successful Lockheeds, beginning with the Model 10 Electra in 1934 and the P-38 Lightening in 1937. Robert Gross was succeeded by his younger brother, Courtlandt Gross, as chief executive officer at Lockheed and held that post until Dan Haughton became board chairman in 1967. The TriStar program was initiated the following year.

Whether or not McDonnell-Douglas follows Lockheed out of the airliner market, Boeing confronted a tough market by 1983. Since the beginning of the jet age, only the 707 and 727 series had proven profitable, and the market was changing with deregulation of the air carriers. The 211-passenger 767 and the 186-passenger 757 should do well (market surveys indicated a 2500-3000 plane market for a 150-175 passenger airliner if the airlines could afford to buy them), but Boeing faced substantial competition from Airbus Industrie, a consortium organized and funded by the governments of Britain, France, and West Germany. Airbus Industrie's 200-300 passenger jets found more than 300 buyers in Europe during the

'70s, and had penetrated the U.S. market with 26 machines delivered to Eastern Air Lines by January of 1983.

Boeing's main concern, however, was the confusion and uncertainties that marked the airline scene of the early '80s. Once it had been over-regulation. Now, deregulation.

FAA Act of 1958

The CAA was restructured and renamed in 1958. The Federal Aviation Act of that year gave American aviation's governing body agency status, while the separate Civil Aeronautics Board (CAB) continued to rule the airlines. But then Lyndon Johnson reduced the Federal Aviation Agency to an "administration" and stuffed it into his new Department of Transportation (DOT) on 1 April 1967.

The effects of that were felt more in Washington than out in the real world where airplanes fly, and the CAB's five-member board continued to hold almost as much power as that which was once concentrated in the office of Postmaster General Walter F. Brown. Then, with deregulation of the

This static-test version of the TriStar, girded with 300 load frames which, when attached to hydraulic jacks, received the equivalent of 15 years' hard service in less than two years of torture testing—one of the reasons that development costs are so high for such aircraft. (Lockheed California Company)

The extended-range TriStar L-1011-100 was delivered to Saudi Arabian Airlines in June 1975. Hong Kong-based Cathay Pacific Airways also received dash-100s in 1975. (Lockheed California Company)

airlines in 1978, the CAB was expected to slowly fade away, whatever residual duties and authority it had left being transferred to the Federal Aviation Administration no later than 1 January 1985.

Wide-body jets may pack a lot of bodies in their wide cabins, but many air travellers are less enthusiastic about this dense-pack concept than are the operators. (Lockheed California Company)

After that, the Federal Trade Commission could handle such things as unfair trade practices among the airlines.

Deregulation

At the beginning of 1983, the airline situation in America bordered on the chaotic. A number of factors contributed: the lingering effects of a recession and high fuel costs, deregulation, and, in some cases, bad guesses on the part of management. Most of those would be non-problems within a year except, perhaps, that of deregulation. The unique nature of the airline business strongly suggests that the public interest (and that of the airlines) is best served with sensible regulation of routes and rates.

The free-for-all that developed following deregulation attracted hundreds of potential airline operators, all of them small, and most of which had reason for optimism because the Federal Aviation Administration (FAA) was still subsidizing local service airlines. Also, the FAA had the authority to guarantee loans to such air carriers if the FAA

LTU German Airlines had its TriStars specially fitted with a downstairs lounge (normally, cargo space) to make transatlantic flying a bit more comfortable for 16 extra-fare passengers. Upstairs, 300 others are seated nine abreast, each with 34 inches of legroom. (Lockheed California Company)

believed their organization to be sound and their proposed routes "essential."

As a result, there were more than 250 commuter airlines in operation in the United States by 1983, and well over 100 additional route applications pending.

Under the Airline Deregulation Act of 1978 the CAB was supposed to liquidate itself as soon as practicable, October 1983 being a target date, and whatever residual duties were left to it would then devolve to the FAA. When that happened there would, presumably, no longer be any restrictions on who could start an airline, or where, or the rates to be charged. Meanwhile, the CAB's only remaining function of significance was the authority to pass upon the "fitness" of a new commuter line, and that caused a lot of confusion. Airline management, big and small, found long-range planning next to impossible.

Lest the plight of the major airlines tugs too strongly at our heartstrings, we should note that they brought much of their trouble upon themselves. From the time that the big jets became available in the late '50s, they recognized that profits lay in the long haul—in getting up high and going long distances with as many seats per engine as possible. Landings and takeoffs are expensive, primarily because of the jet engine's voracious appetites for fuel at low altitudes. Domestically, the big air carriers wanted to fly only between about two dozen of the country's largest airports, which ac-

counted for as much as 80 percent of all airline boardings.

That left the smaller cities to the so-called "second level" or "regional" air carriers who flew smaller airliners—usually piston-engine craft or propjets in the 50-passenger class—and which fed as much as 30 percent of their passengers to the big trunk lines at the super terminals.

That worked reasonably well during the '60s, but the regionals were not satisfied and also looked to greater efficiency in their operations (as opposed to public service). They, too, wanted to abandon stops that cost more to service than boardings justified, particularly as the CAB pushed to lower and/or eliminate subsidies.

That led to the CAB's "Use It or Lose It" order given to smaller cities, which meant that, if those communities could not provide a minimum number of boardings, the CAB would allow the air carriers to abandon those stops. And that opened the door to the "third level" or "commuter" airline, which could place in operation 15-to-30 passenger aircraft that could, with a little subsidy, profitably serve those limited-population centers.

The commuters, however, operating aircraft tailored to their needs, not only served the smaller communities the regionals did not want on their routes, but also, on their way to hub airports,

Another reason that modern airplanes are costly in development; the wind tunnel at Lockheed's Georgia facility. (Lockheed California Company)

Lockheed engineers envision a new type of thin-bladed propeller on a wide body propjet of the future which will be quieter and more fuel-efficient. Should get about 15 seats abreast in that one. (Lockheed California Company)

A Lockheed design concept contracted by NASA resulted in the predicted machine that President Reagan called the "Orient Express," a 4000-mph 200-passenger airliner capable of flying from Los Angeles to Tokyo in two hours, 18 minutes. Turbojets would be used for landing and takeoff, while scramjets, fueled by liquid hydrogen, would boost the craft to hypersonic speeds. (Lockheed-California; drawings by Jim Speas)

The 40-seat Convair 240 entered production late in 1947 and was fitted with P&W R-2800 engines. The stretched 340 followed in 1951, then the 440 with more horsepower. Conversion of 340/440s to propjets began in the late '50s and produced the 540, 580, 600, and 640, depending upon engine installation; the 580, with an Allison, perhaps being the most numerous. Many remain in service. Metro, the nation's fifth largest regional/commuter flys them. (General Dynamics)

stopped along the way to take hefty chunks of the regional carriers' business. And as the commuters proliferated, the regionals began to disappear, for the most part either expanding or merging into major systems.

Therefore, as the airline industry entered the uncertain '80s, the domestic system consisted of the major airlines, flying between the big hub airports, and the commuters, flying from small towns and cities—from just about everywhere in the

A total of 103 Martin 404 pressurized, 40-passenger airliners were built beginning in 1949, following an in-flight structural failure in the wing of the earlier Martin 202. (TWA)

Departing from Baer Field at Fort Wayne, Indiana, Hub Airlines flies to Chicago and to Cleveland. (Beech Aircraft Corporation)

boonies—to eventually end up at the hub airports.

The future of this industry—even the immediate future—is difficult to predict as this is written, partly because of the several unusual factors (recession, controllers' strike, etc.) that have intruded into the airline picture since Teddy Kennedy pushed the Airline Deregulation Act through the Congress in 1978. Airline executives see everything from total collapse to a bright new day, although the optimists are almost exclusively commuter executives.

One factor is the outdated air traffic control system, which, like Topsy, just grew, the fact that so much air traffic is funneled through less than 30 hub air terminals, and the very inconvenient fact that most air passengers want to fly at the same time. Even the most experienced and able air controllers can safely handle no more than 50 landings and takeoffs per hour per runway in good weather. The big jets cannot be spaced any closer than that. Crank into the system any of several common weather problems in the terminal vicinity, and aircraft movements are markedly slowed. That is why private airplanes are unwelcome, or are even refused the right to land, at major airports, especially during peak traffic hours. And that was also the reason for inauguration of the "slot" system at major airports following the air traffic controllers' illegal strike and subsequent firing in September 1981.

Air Controllers Strike

The air controllers who were members of the Professional Air Traffic Controllers Organization (PATCO) decided, during the second week in August 1981, to strike. More than 12,000 walked off their jobs, demanding, among other things, $10,000 across-the-board pay increases, a shorter workweek, earlier retirement, and more respect from their superiors. They were averaging $33,000 per year (up to $50,000 after seven years on the job), about 25 hours per week, if overstressed could retire in five years at 40 percent of their pay—and were about to forfeit much of whatever respect they could claim.

The controllers struck in violation of federal law after rejecting Secretary of Transportation Drew Lewis' offer of a 34 percent pay increase over a three-year period. They were confident that the U.S. air transportation system could not function

"That was a tasty morsel. Who's next?" (*Commuter Air magazine*)

without them, and remained unmoved after President Reagan told them to return to work within 48 hours or be fired.

As unbelievable as it may sound as we review the facts, the PATCO controllers defied the President. He fired them all.

Secretary of Transportation Lewis asked FAA Administrator J. Lynn Helms to petition the Pentagon for 500 military air traffic controllers; they were added to the 2000 or so non-striking controllers and supervisory personnel, and this force, filled out with some furloughed airline pilots and recently retired controllers, manned the 23 Air Route Traffic Control Centers and the control towers at the hub airports, leaving towers in small cities unmanned or operating a limited number of hours each day.

At the end of a week, the system was function-ing at about 65 percent of its normal capacity, and it was evident that the system had been padded by at least 3000 controllers when more than 12,000 had been on the payroll. It was also clear that many of the towers at small airports were not needed except, perhaps, for the training of neophite controllers.

Meanwhile, the FAA training center in Oklahoma City began sorting through a flood of applications, and accelerated its Air Traffic Control training program to replace as many of the discharged controllers as required. The FAA expected that, while it could fully staff, with new people, the nation's control towers and air route control centers by the spring of 1983, the system would operate at a slower pace for a couple of years after that because the newly trained controllers would attain efficiency only through experience.

By the spring of 1983, the slowdown was hardly apparent. The system was operating at somewhere between 90 and 98 percent of its pre-strike level (depending upon whose figures one accepted), and there had been no accidents traceable to an air controller's error, safety having been given priority over schedules and all else from the start.

During the first days immediately following the controller walkout, air traffic was curtailed as much as 50 percent, but some of that "loss" was actually beneficial to the major air carriers because it represented their cutback of profit-draining over-scheduling and abandonment of unprofitable routes. For years, the big lines had chosen to fly half-empty airplanes on closely spaced schedules from the major terminals rather than risk the loss of a few passengers to a competing airline. That practice had been a convenience for the travelling public, but it greatly contributed to congestion at the hub airports during peak traffic hours.

It was private aviation that bore most of the post-strike restrictions, particularly, private pilots attempting to fly across country under instrument flight rules (IFR). Such a flight plan actually became an application for a reservation in the airspace, and was supposed to be submitted 12 hours in advance. Some were granted; some were not. A number of

Beechcraft 99 Airliner is 17-place propjet. P&W engines provide a top speed of 250 mph. (Beech Aircraft Corporation)

resourceful private pilots told the Flight Service Stations that they were air taxis in order to obtain clearances, but the FAA soon noticed the air taxi boom and uncovered the deceptions.

Slot System

Each scheduled airline was assigned a given number of "slots" at the major air terminals. For example, Braniff was given 12 slots per day at Oklahoma City's Will Rogers World Airport, meaning that Braniff could schedule 12 flights daily through that terminal. The slot system became unpopular due to the manner in which the CAB chose to administer it. It could have been used to protect the pioneering equities of the established carriers as deregulation tossed the entire system up for grabs, but instead, the CAB, headed by Marvin S. Cohen, took slots away from the major air carriers and gave them to new commuters. Eventually, after evidence surfaced of speculation with slots awarded to new commuters, the slots were more or less frozen, although some became available when a few of the newcomers, or an established line such as Braniff, folded. When Braniff ceased operations in May 1982, its slots were redistributed by lottery.

President Reagan's dismissal of the 12,000 PATCO controllers was applauded by a majority of the American People (according to a *Newsweek* magazine poll), certainly by most pilots, both private and commercial, and those of us accustomed to the bored, irreducible directions from air controllers were pleased to find ourselves suddenly dealing with professionals in the air route centers and towers who not only bent over backward to safely accommodate us, but were *cheerful* about it. That had its effect, because pilots are human, and just as suddenly began bending over backward in an effort to cooperate with those nice guys on the ground. The system may have been a tad slower, but it was also a lot more pleasant to use.

Flow Control

By mid-1983, the Air Traffic Control system was operating about as normally as its equipment and the terminal facilities would allow, except the FAA Administrator Helms decreed that the "flow control" of airliners be phased out at a measured pace. Flow control was first imposed back in July 1968, when a weather inversion blanketed the busy Northeast with a stagnant ocean of smog that extended from Boston to Cape Hatteras, reducing visibility to 2 1/2 miles all the way up to 10,000 feet!

All aircraft operating in that area were IFR, and that condition alone would have markedly slowed operations from the hub airports in that part of the country. But the air controllers added to the problem with a slowdown of their own. Unable to strike, they chose to space aircraft movements further apart as a "safety" measure. It was an effective tactic; airline traffic into the New York area was intolerably stacked up in holding patterns until FAA officials stepped in to hold on the ground, at their points of origin, all air traffic bound for the affected area. Those airliners waiting in Chicago, Miami, Los Angeles, etc., were then cleared for takeoff in dribbles as it became possible for them to land at their destinations.

That was flow control. And it was put in practice after the PATCO people went out on strike in August 1981, partly as a measure to save fuel, and partly because newly trained air controllers needed experience in stacking airliners temporarily when weather conditions forced delays. In February 1983, Helms said that flow control would be phased out slowly.

Fare Wars

Meanwhile, throughout the early '80s all the major airlines lost money, while most of the commuters possessed marginal balance sheets (the more successful commuters were calling themselves "regional" airlines by that time). Total airline profits plummeted from $1.3 billion in 1978, when deregulation began, to $199 million in 1979, and continued sharply downward to a loss of $550 million in 1982. The $99 coast-to-coast fare became common by late 1982, offered in desperation by major air carriers in need of instant cash. Everyone in the industry agreed that such fares were suicidal—no airline could stay in business forever flying passengers for 2 1/2¢ per seat-mile while costs went as high as 10¢ per seat-mile—but the stronger lines could very well kill off some of the weaker ones that way, and thereby expect to later fill their own empty seats.

Investors seemed to agree. Pan Am, TWA (Trans World, after WWII; formerly, Transcontinental & Western Air), and United had no trouble marketing new stock issues early in 1983, and all airline stocks were up more than 60 percent during the fall and winter of 1982-83. That, of course, coincided with the overall advances in stock prices during that period as investors in general sent the Dow-Jones industrial averages to record highs, apparently because Wall Street was convinced that the recession had bottomed out and that good times where ahead.

The worldwide oil glut that developed during that period undoubtedly had its effect. Jet fuel was down to 95¢ per gallon early in 1983 and was expected to go lower. It had cost $1.02 a year earlier. Since fuel accounts for one-third of the airlines' operating costs, a .07¢ per gallon drop in the price of fuel meant an annual savings of $500 million. Also, in 1982, the biggest airlines trimmed costs by negotiating wage freezes or cuts, and thinned out their work forces. Since labor costs represent another third of the airlines' total expenses, that, too, was significant—although it was gained at the price of poorer union relations in some cases.

No one really expected the industry to completely collapse, but the economic dogfights resulting from deregulation seemed certain to leave the survivors bidding for passengers on the basis of minimum air fares alone. The day of truly "no frills" air travel had arrived, echoing the Scrooge-like operating practices of the Ludington Lines in the 1930s.

Survival of the Richest

By mid-1986, it was not hard to predict the ultimate effects of deregulation on the U.S. airline industry. Two or three super carriers would have it all by the end of the decade. These would be United, American, and perhaps Texas Air, rudely elbowing its way to a financially shaky third position.

Far out? Not if you consider that 1) United bought Pan Am's lucrative Pacific routes—for $750 million—in April 1985 (Pan Am had previously sold its Manhattan headquarters and International Hotel chain); 2) TWA, on the edge of bankruptcy, hoped to buy its way to solvency by acquiring Ozark Air Lines for $225 million, and 3) Texas Air, which had already digested Continental and New York Air, had recently paid $600 million for Eastern Air

Lines, and offered to take Frontier Air Lines off the hands of ailing People's Express (People's Express had given $305 million for Frontier just eight months earlier).

People's Express epitomized the spirit and intent of airline deregulation—haul as many people as possible as cheaply as possible—and for a time it seemed to work very well. A 40 year-old entrepreneur by the name of Donald Burr started People's Express with three airplanes, and in five years was operating 116 jets to more than 100 cities in North America, plus an Atlantic route. PE had become America's fifth-largest air carrier, with revenues exceeding $1 billion in 1985. Non-union Peoples was operating for 5 1/4¢ per seat-mile, against an industry average of nearly 8¢ per seat-mile, which was a significant factor in People's low fares; but profits did not keep pace with revenues, the competition began meeting Burr's low fares at key terminals, and People's Express became a money-loser in 1986. True, almost all other major air carriers were also losing money due to the cut-rate fares, but airlines like United and American, with deeper pockets, were much better prepared to ride out the rough weather. Industry observers expected People's Express to merge or die.

TEFRA

In 1982, the Tax Equity and Fiscal Responsibility Act (TEFRA) struck another blow at the already beleaguered private pilot by allowing the Reagan Administration to increase the federal tax on aviation fuel used for noncommercial purposes from 4¢ per gallon to 12¢ per gallon. A tax of 14¢ per gallon was slapped on noncommercial jet fuel as well. The rationale was that those who use the public airports and the airways system should be the ones who pay for them. It sounds fair—but it is not. The big airports, the air navigation aids, and the air traffic control system were primarily designed for the benefit of the scheduled air carriers. The private pilots could get along with a lot less. The general aviation fleet does not need runways two feet thick and 8000 feet long. Most of the electronic navaids are of no use to VFR pilots, who represent four out of 10 of the nation's licensed airmen.

The ever-increasing cost of private flying resulted in a marked downturn in such activity by 1980. A steady decrease in the number of student pilot permits continued through the 1980s.

But the system and all air regulations have, historically, favored the scheduled airlines, both in the letter of the law and in practice, and the reason given for that has always been that the government must favor that kind of air travel which serves the "greater good," and that presupposes that, since the scheduled air carriers transport more people inter-city than do private and business airplanes, the airlines serve the greater good.

Bill Lear

William P. Lear, Sr. opened the bizjet market back in the mid-'60s, when he was almost the only person around who believed that such a market existed.

Bill Lear came from a tenement district on Chicago's south side. His parents had separated when Bill was six. He spent a lot of time in the streets, dropped out of school after the eighth grade, and quietly left home, such as it was, at age 16. That was in 1918. Bill went from job to job, and his lifelong affair with airplanes began when he worked as a flunky at Chicago's Grant Park Airport, where Matty Laird, the Stinsons, and other well-known pilots of that time were often seen. Bill moved on to other jobs, tinkered with wireless sets, was an apprentice automobile mechanic and, in 1922, opened a shop in Quincy, Illinois to repair the recently developed home radio sets.

Bill miniaturized coils and worked out other improvements on those primitive sets that soon had him working for Motorola at an excellent salary.

By 1931, Lear had learned to fly, bought a WACO cabin biplane, and toured the U.S. demonstrating his new aircraft radio receiver. The Lear Radioaire worked well, but few pilots of that era could see much use for it.

Broke again in 1934, Lear returned to his workbench and designed a component for home radios that he called a "Magic Brain." RCA paid him a quarter-million dollars for it.

Bill's next project was the Lear Radio Compass for airplanes (which we call an automatic direction finder—ADF—today). A 35-watt transceiver followed, and then the Learmatic Omninavigator, the latter being identical in principle to present-day OMNIs, except that it was necessarily low frequency. Lear expanded into the electromechanical field during WWII and, during the late '40s, developed a three-axis autopilot so advanced that it brought him the Collier Trophy (civil aviation's highest award), presented by President Truman in 1950.

So it was that by 1959 Bill Lear headed a company that grossed $100 million per year. He was

Bill Lear in his 1931 Monocoupe. (Gates Learjet Corporation)

a rich man and could have retired to a less stressful life. He never considered it. "I'd rather wear out than rust out," he explained. Besides, Bill had a great new idea, the Learjet airplane.

But it was an idea that frightened his board of directors, and they wanted no part of it. Bill's vision of a six-place executive jet was, at the time, a bit startling. Who in the blue-eyed world would buy such an airplane? It would have to be priced

Learjet Model 23, the first of the Learjets, which first flew in September 1964. FAA certification followed in mid-1965. (Gates Learjet Corporation)

at close to a million dollars, and U.S. corporations weren't exactly lining up to purchase the piston-engine twins then available for less than a tenth of that amount.

But Bill, who at age 57 had lost none of his boldness, sold his share of Lear, Incorporated and went into the jet airplane manufacturing business. He invested his own $10 million personal fortune, borrowed another $8 million from Wichita banks, built a factory on Wichita's Municipal Airport, and on 7 October 1963 saw his Learjet Model 23 make its first flight.

It was an elegant machine, based on Switzerland's P-16 fighter plane, so strongly built that it far exceeded the FAA's requirements for structural integrity. It was designed—with a great deal of input from Bill—by an engineering team headed by Dr. Hans Studer and Gordon Israel. Israel was an old-timer who had, during the '30s, designed airplanes for Curtiss and Stinson, as well as the famed racing planes flown by Ben O. Howard. Hans Studer, a veteran designer formerly with the German firm of Dornier, had been associated with the P-16 program. The first Learjet was delivered in October 1964, by which time Bill had firm orders for 72 more. The market was there, all right, and Lear had a two-year lead on the rash of competitors he knew would be certain to follow.

Lear had given himself that lead by taking what most would have regarded as a gamble of enormous

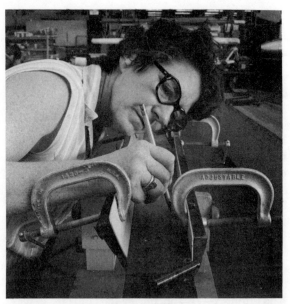

Another reason why airplanes are expensive: They are, by necessity, largely hand-built by skilled labor. (Gates Learjet Corporation)

proportions. He had ordered the production tooling *before* building and testing the prototype airplane. That meant that the Learjet would have to be near-perfect as it came off the drawing board. Otherwise, some very expensive tooling would have to be junked. This unheard-of procedure did cut Lear's "start-up" costs, and offered the competition a very short Lear coattail to grab, but as Bill himself remarked at the time, "In a situation like this, you are either very right, or very wrong."

Bill was very right. However, the $18 million had been spent, so Lear went public with 50,000 shares of Learjet common priced at $10 per share. He kept 62 percent of that issue for himself and wife Moya (whom he had married in 1942).

The Learjet's impact on the gen-av scene is well known today. Less well known is that, for all of the brilliance and pure guts that Bill Lear displayed in bringing this series of airplanes into the market, Bill did not plan his sales and product support network well, and by the end of 1967 Learjet Industries was losing money at an alarming rate. And that is when Charles C. Gates, president of the Denver-based Gates Rubber Company, appeared on the scene.

Bill and Moya Lear with what's-his-name, a presidential candidate. Lear contributed to his campaign. (Gates Learjet Corporation)

Gates Learjet

Unless Gates himself decides to tell it someday, we shall never know of the chain of events that brought Gates to Wichita with his checkbook in hand, just as the maneuvering that brought McDonnell and Douglas together must remain untold. Maybe Charles Gates merely picked up his phone, called Wichita, and asked, "Hey, Bill, you wanna sell?"

Anyway, Gates, a pilot himself since 1942, and a longtime user of corporate aircraft, paid a reported $16 million for controlling interest in Learjet Industries, restructured the company, paying particular attention to the establishment of a sound marketing and product support program, then coaxed Harry Combs to take charge of it all.

Combs has since been a key factor in Gates Learjet's success. When Combs—with some reluctance, it is said—assumed command of Gates Learjet in October 1971, he had been in aviation for more than 40 years, having soloed an open-cockpit biplane in 1928 when he was 15 years old. Combs had later built one of the largest fixed base flight operations in the world on Denver's Stapelton International Airport, and was semi-retired, a rich man, when old friend Charles Gates offered him a challenge that was irresistible to Combs' natural instincts.

Today, with well over 1000 Learjets in operation worldwide, the company has a large, new factory on Tucson's International Airport in addition to the Wichita facility.

Learjet produced less than a dozen airplanes in 1986. Harry Combs had retired, and Charles Gates negotiated the sale of his 64 percent of Gates Learjet stock late that year to the New York investment firm of M.J. Rosenthal & Associates.

Meanwhile, Bill Lear moved on to Reno, Nevada, where he spent several years and an estimated $10 million in an unsuccessful attempt to produce a practical steam-powered automobile. That didn't break Bill—at least, not for long. He next made somewhere between $13 and $15 million in Nevada real estate. Of course, that also was soon at risk. He was betting that poke on another revolutionary airplane—one made of carbon fiber plastic—when he died in 1977. Wife Moya, every bit as gutsy as Bill, attempted to carry on with the project, but encountered a succession of enervating problems (including lawsuits from her own children) that repeatedly halted development of the machine. In 1986, Moya insisted that she had not given up her lonely battle for the Learfan, while industry observers had written if off as a dying dream.

Bill Lear didn't win 'em all—and that is a most significant part of his story.

There are other Bill Lears out there, talented people with bold ideas and the courage to bet on them, and in our free society we will hear from them; we will certainly hear from them.

The Learjet Longhorn, announced in 1977 and first delivered in 1980, features winglets that turn the normal wingtip vortex into additional lift and thereby reduces induced drag as much as 20 percent in cruising flight. (Gates Learjet Corporation)

1. What is the relationship between the development of aircraft and engines for the military and civilian markets? How are gas turbine engines classified?

2. Who developed the first jet engines? How did GE develop their first jet engine?

3. Why was Boeing successful in selling their 707 to both the civilian and military markets? How did Douglas get started? What caused the company to fall on hard times? Why was McDonnell interested in the Douglas Aircraft Company?

4. Discuss some of Lockheed's problems starting in the mid-1970s. How was the Company formed? What was their first successful aircraft? Identify several other aircraft built during the 1930s and '40s.

5. What was the purpose of the FAA Act of 1958? Discuss some of the causes and effects of the Airline Deregulation Act of 1978. Why did the Professional Air Traffic Controllers Organization (PATCO) strike in 1981? Discuss some of the results of this illegal action. What is the Slot System? What is meant by "flow control?" What was the rationale for the Tax Equity and Fiscal Responsibility Act of 1982?

6. What were some of Bill Lear's earlier inventions? Why was the Learjet a big gamble? How successful has it been?

Chapter 18

America into Space

OBJECTIVES: At the end of this chapter you should be able to:

- ☐ Identify some of the early pioneers in rocketry and discuss their accomplishments.

- ☐ Describe the U.S. development of rocketry during the immediate postwar period.

- ☐ Describe the U.S. reaction to the Soviet launching of Sputnik I on October 4, 1957.

- ☐ Give the purpose of the Mercury and Gemini series of space probes.

- ☐ Discuss the development of the Apollo program leading to the landing on the moon.

- ☐ Give the purpose of the Space Shuttle program and the unmanned space probes of recent years.

Modern rocketry was fathered by an American, Robert H. Goddard. Goddard spent his life building a sound foundation for this new technology, then, like the Wright brothers, saw European experimenters take over initial development of his discoveries. Once again, the pupils surpassed the teacher, and when America at last began to recognize all that this new science portended, we appropriated the fruits of *their* labors to nourish an industry that should have grown up here in the first place.

At the end of WWII, U.S. intelligence people scrambled around Germany tracking down German rocket experts. We didn't get them all—the Soviets were looking for them, too—but we found the ones at the top of the list, particularly Gen. Walter Dorn-

berger and Werner von Braun, along with several of their best technicians, and brought them to the United States. We also sought Maj. Gen. Wolfgang von Chamier-Glisczinski, but accepted the report that he had died in an American bombing raid on Peenemunde. When the Soviets orbited Sputnik I in 1957, we had reason to doubt that report.

In the U.S., von Braun was placed in charge of the test firing of some captured German V-2 rockets (called the A-4 by the Germans) at White Sands Missile Test Center near Alamagordo, New Mexico, and when our engineers asked von Braun about his early research and basic formulas, he seemed surprised. "Why, of course," he replied. "We started with the published papers of your Dr. Goddard!"

Dr. Robert H. Goddard, Father of Modern Rocketry, began his work before WWI; he fired the world's first liquid-fueled rocket on 16 March 1926. Aided by Charles Lindbergh's intervention on his behalf, Goddard, with Guggenheim grants, made significant progress during the '30s. (USIA)

Dr. Robert Goddard was a rare person; he dedicated himself to a task that offered no tangible reward in his lifetime. Most people thought he was a nut.

Goddard was 17 years old when he decided that man would someday go to the moon. He always remembered the day—19 October 1899—and thereafter celebrated that date as the anniversary of his life's work.

After finishing high school in his hometown, Worcester, Massachusetts, Goddard attended Worcester Polytechnic Institute where he authored a paper suggesting the use of radioactive material as a fuel for deep space flight. The idea was ridiculed.

Goddard worked as a teacher while earning his Master's degree, and then a PhD, after which he moved on to Princeton as a research fellow. But a year later he was told by his doctor that he was so seriously infected with tuberculosis that he had not long to live. He went to bed as ordered, but continued his computations.

A year later, in 1912, the disease was arrested and Goddard received patents on a multi-stage rocket system designed while bedridden.

During the next four years Goddard worked as an assistant professor at Clark University and spent much of his salary on experiments with small rockets; he authored a paper describing his experiments and what he had learned to date about rocket propulsion. He sent copies to several non-profit organizations, noting that he needed more money for additional research. That resulted in a $5,000 grant from the Smithsonian Institution early in 1917, along with the suggestion that Goddard design a small battlefield rocket for the U.S. Army.

By the time Goddard's infantry rocket had been proven in Army tests, WWI was over, and then the device was forgotten until, 25 years later, he reminded Army authorities that it should prove useful against Hitler's panzers. It was. Produced as the 2.36-inch antitank weapon, it became known to American GIs as the "Bazooka."

But it was during the period between World Wars One and Two that Goddard accomplished his most significant work. On 16 March 1926 he tested the world's first liquid-propelled rocket. It was 10 feet in length, and had only a 2 1/2-second burn, which took it to an altitude of a mere 184 feet, but

America's first intercontinental ballistic missile, the Atlas, first flew in June 1957, and became operational under the direction of the Strategic Air Command in September 1959. The Atlas had a range of 9000 miles and was built by General Dynamics. (General Dynamics)

Gemini command module, built by McDonnell Aircraft Corp. America's Gemini Program of two-man Earth-orbit space missions began in March 1965; by the time Gemini 12 flew in November 1966, the Soviets' demonstrated space technology had been eclipsed in all areas of accomplishment by Americans. (McDonnell-Douglas)

it represented Goddard's proof-of-concept vehicle, and as far as he was concerned *it* represented man's "first small step" into space.

Goddard tested two improved rockets during the next three years; then, on 17 July 1929, he tested a rocket that was far more successful than it at first appeared to be. It weighed 55 pounds, was 11 1/2 feet in length, and was fueled with 14 pounds of gasoline and 11 pounds of LOX (liquid oxygen). It flew (from a converted windmill tower) a distance of 171 feet at about 90 feet of altitude. Most importantly, its gyro guidance system and on-board instrument package functioned perfectly. Unfortunately, the vehicle's thunderous and fiery flight, from the pasture of Aunt Effie Ward's farm near Auburn, Massachusetts, panicked a number of people and brought police, firemen, sheriff, and countless small boys with their dogs to investigate. As a result, newspapers jibed that the professor's "moon rocket" had missed its target by approximately 239,000 miles, and the state fire marshal forbid any more nonsense of that kind.

The ridicule paid off that time, because the news wire services picked up the story and among those who read it was a man who saw past the crude humor. He was a man who, just two years earlier, had demonstrated how one could parlay courage, vision, and good planning into unmatched success. His name was Charles A. Lindbergh.

Lindbergh went to see Goddard and was clearly impressed, because shortly afterwards he phoned to say that he had talked with Daniel Guggenheim about Goddard's work, and Guggenheim had agreed to furnish $50,000 for rocket research over a two-year period. If Goddard were able to report reasonable progress at the end of that time, more money would be waiting.

Goddard and his wife Esther (a former Clark University honor student whom he had married in 1924 after she volunteered to type his papers for him) moved to New Mexico. There, in a barren valley some 15 miles northwest of Roswell, Goddard continued his experiments, disturbing only those secretive four-footed inhabitants of the high desert.

By March 1935, a 75-pound Goddard rocket exceeded Mach 1 as it streaked beyond a mile in height and flew 9000 feet downrange. There were some failures, but Goddard learned something from each, and he maintained careful records. He fired rockets with a cluster of four engines, with gyro-controlled, gimbal-mounted tails, and with steering vanes positioned within the exhaust stream. In 1938 he made a series of demonstrations for the National Aeronautic Association, and although those representatives, as most others of the scientific world, were impressed, it is obvious that no one in America then knew quite what to do with Goddard's fire-breathing birds.

In Germany, however, there were men who *did* know—men who saw rockets as a form of extra-long-range artillery. They were members of the clandestine General Staff, and they especially liked the idea of rockets because such weapons could be made secretly, and outside conventional arms factories. The Treaty of Versailles forbid Germany to have an air force and severely limited the other military weapons she was allowed. The generals turned to Hermann Oberth, whose interest in rocketry was generally known and who, as it turned out, had been corresponding with Goddard on the subject. Gen. von Chamier-Glisczinski, a ballistics specialist, took charge of the Germans' first rocket research facility at Kummersdorf. Later, with Dornberger and the youthful von Braun aboard, a new facility was secretly opened at Peenemunde, on the Baltic Coast.

The Peenemunde complex became operational in 1937, and two years later, on the eve of WWII, a von Braun rocket attained an altitude of five miles. But Hitler then cancelled the priority for rocket research in order to concentrate Germany's resources on the buildup of his panzers and aircraft designed for close support of the highly mobile *Wehrmacht* in the conquest of Europe. It was therefore not until four years later—3 October 1943—that the 5 1/2-ton A-4 rocket (V-2) was deemed a success when it left the Earth's atmosphere and flew a distance of 124 miles.

By that time, Hitler's drive into Russia had proven disastrous, Rommel had been defeated in North Africa, the Allies were moving north through Italy, the buildup of American airpower in Britain portended a massive assault on *Festung Europa,* and Hitler turned in desperation to the German rocket program. He was too late. There was no way that a sufficient number of A-4 rockets could be produced at that late date to alter the course of the war. Von Braun later said that the A-4 could have been ready at least a year earlier had not Hitler cancelled Peenemunde's first priority, and the A-10 trans-Atlantic rocket, capable of striking New York City, would have been operational by 1946.

But wars are not decided by the "what ifs." Victory favors the side that makes the fewest mistakes.

The First U.S. Rockets

During the years immediately following WWII, the U.S. rocket program was limited to what could be learned from the firing of the captured A-4/V-2s

This is how a Lockheed-built Agena Target Vehicle appeared to Gemini astronauts as they approached for docking in Earth orbit. Space docking, extravehicular activity, and orbit manipulation were among new space skills acquired during Gemini flights. (Lockheed Missiles & Space Company)

(while Convair, as early as 1947, produced some slightly improved versions of this missile), and a low-priority effort was made at developing short-range artillery rockets such as the Corporal, along with an antiaircraft missile, the Nike-Ajax, both of which became operational in 1953. The Air Force meanwhile concentrated on flying bombs, unmanned miniature jet airplanes such as the Matador and Snark—with one notable exception.

In 1951, the Redstone Intercontinental Ballistics Missile program was born and nourished by Maj. Gen. Donald L. Putt and Brig. Gen. John W. Sessums, Jr. This pair of Air Force generals, arguing that the Soviets were already working feverishly in this field, faced a lot of high-level opposition but managed to slowly gain adherents. In 1953, Air Force Secretary Harold Talbot and Air Force Chief of Research and Development Trevor Gardner joined this minority crusade, and then others in the executive branch and in the Congress began to listen. Finally, in 1954, President Eisenhower gave America's ICBM program top priority. That sparked a crash program for development of a 6000-mile ballistics missile booster.

Born of that activity was the 100-ton, 80-foot Atlas, built by Convair, which first flew in June 1957 and became operational in September 1959. By March 1962, 119 Atlases had been fired, with the Air Force terming 80 completely successful. Four months earlier, an Atlas booster sent a chimpanzee named Enos twice around the Earth in a prelude to the Project Mercury manned orbital flights. On 20 February 1962 an Atlas-Mercury launch vehicle boosted Astronaut John H. Glenn, Jr., into America's first manned orbit of the Earth.

As Putt and Sessums had warned, the Soviets had, from the end of WWII, made an all-out effort to develop ICBMs. When they succeeded in orbiting the 184-pound Sputnik I on 4 October 1957, it became clear that they had gained a substantial lead in missile booster capability. Sputnik II, weighing 1121 pounds, was lofted into orbit on 3 November carrying a dog named Laika. The U.S. managed to put its first satellite into earth orbit on 31 January 1958 when a Jupiter C booster sent 31-pound Explorer I into space to discover the Van Allen Radiation Belt.

In October 1958, the National Aeronautics and Space Administration (NASA) was created from that venerable wellspring of aviation technology, the National Advisory Committee for Aeronautics (NACA), and NASA became the official agency for all exploratory and scientific programs in space as well as in the air. Therefore, in 1961, when newly elected President Kennedy challenged the Soviets to a race for the moon, the U.S. had a proper organization to call its space shots, three years experience with its Explorer and Discoverer series, and a bold and youthful engineering force daily designing space hardware that had to be named as it was created.

By 1968 man had ridden thunderous rockets into space 24 times—the Americans 16 times, the Soviets eight times—but none had yet left Earth orbit to venture into deep space. America's Mercury shots, with Redstone and Atlas boosters, carried a single astronaut during the early '60s. Then came the Gemini series, with two astronauts aboard, thrust into orbit by the mighty Titan. It was, however, the Apollo series that took man to the moon, and at this writing, no Soviet manned spacecraft had been farther into space than you can drive your car in half a day.

The Lunar Landing Program had been suggested by NASA back in July 1960, and feasibility studies by several aerospace companies were handed to President Kennedy in mid-May, 1961. The President presented a plan to Congress ten days later, along with his dramatic commitment to put Americans on the moon by the end of the decade. Congress promised the money and the first engineering contracts were let in 1962. More than 20,000 companies were involved in the program, and the first unmanned Apollo was tested on 26 February 1966 (Apollo was the name given the complete vehicle; its Saturn V booster had three stages). Several more unmanned test flights were made, plus a manned orbital mission with three astronauts aboard—Walter Schirra, Donn Eisele, and Walter Cunningham—before Apollos 8 and 10 flew

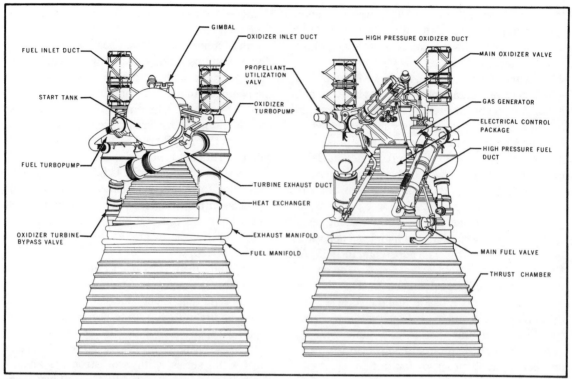

Rocketdyne J-2 rocket engine. (North American Rockwell)

to the moon and back prior to the actual moon landing by Apollo 11's lunar module 20 July 1969. Apollo 9 was the Earth orbit mission, that checked out the Lunar Excursion Module, the little space taxi that would actually land on the moon with two astronauts while the command module remained in moon orbit.

In the meantime, on 27 January 1967, three astronauts—Virgil Grissom, Edward White, and Roger Chaffee—died in an accident at Florida's Kennedy Space Center during a prelaunch test when the pure oxygen atmosphere in their Apollo command module was ignited by a short in the electrical system (three months later, Soviet Cosmonaut Komarov was killed on landing after an 18-orbit mission).

When man eventually travels into deep space to explore and perhaps colonize planets in another solar system (the closest sun besides our own is 4.5 light years away; it may or may not have a planetary system), his children will undoubtedly be re-

quired to memorize the date of 21 December 1968 as that point in time when man first shed the bonds of Earth's gravity to fly free into the cosmos. At 10:41 A.M. EST on that date, Air Force Colonel Frank Borman, Navy Captain James Lovell, and Air Force Major William Anders, in Earth orbit in the predawn darkness 118 miles above Hawaii, ignited Apollo 8's third stage booster for a 302-second burn to thrust their craft into translunar injection at a speed of 24,196 mph. Translunar injection (TLI) results when just the right amount of thrust is applied, at the proper moment during Earth orbit, to propel a spacecraft onto an intercepting course for the moon. It of course takes into account that the moon will be somewhere else by the time the spacecraft gets there (now that is "deflection shooting" on a grand scale!).

Apollo 8 then coasted for the next 53 hours, gradually slowed by the Earth's gravitational pull. Then it passed that point in space 214,000 miles from Earth where the pull of the moon's gravity be-

300

200

SATURN V

363 FT

POLARIS
31 FT LONG

100

TITAN

ATLAS

'102 FT

MINUTEMAN

82.5 FT

396 IN

192 IN.

120 IN.

59 FT

70 IN.

0

Comparison of Saturn V with ICBMs. (TRW)

came stronger than that of Earth's. By then slowed to 2217 mph, its velocity began to increase as it was drawn toward the moon.

Passing close to the moon the next morning, Christmas Eve, and turned so that the spacecraft's rocket engines faced forward, a 240-second burn slowed Apollo 8 from 5758 mph to 3643 mph to balance its speed with the moon's gravitational pull, which gave an elliptical lunar orbit 194.5 miles at apogee and 69.6 miles at perigee. (Actually, *apogee* and *perigee* are correctly applied only to the orbits of objects circling the Earth. In lunar orbit the high point is the *apocynthion,* and the low point the *pericynthion.*)

Apollo 8 circled the moon until shortly after noon on Christmas Day. Then a 198-second burn of its service module rockets accelerated the space-

ship to an escape velocity of nearly 6000 mph and the three astronauts began their journey back to the "big blue marble" in the blackness of space that was their home.

Apollo streaked through the first thinly-spread molecules of earth's atmosphere 35 hours later. Reentry, beginning at about 400,000 feet, was made at a seven-degree angle, 1600 miles from the landing zone, in order to dissipate at an acceptable rate as much of the spacecraft's 24,630-mph velocity as possible before encountering denser air at lower altitudes. Nevertheless, Apollo 8 arced Earthward like a giant meteor as air friction built up a temperature of nearly 5000 degrees F on its ablative heat shield. Inside the command module the temperature remained a comfortable 70 degrees F, although the astronauts were subjected to decel-

This photo, taken from atop the assembly building, shows Apollo-Saturn at Kennedy Space Center as the 363-foot space vehicle and its launch umbilical tower move out of the assembly building for the launch pad on the crawler-transporter. (North American Rockwell)

Four days later, on Sunday afternoon, 20 July, Armstrong and Aldrin separated from the command module in the LEM and, at 3:08 P.M. EDT Earth time, as Apollo 11 emerged from behind the moon's dark side, fired the LEM's braking rockets for half a minute to drop down into a moon orbit with a pericynthion of ten miles above the lunar surface.

Further use of the LEM's descent-stage rockets took the moon taxi out of orbit and to within 350 feet of the lunar surface by 4:15 P.M. Noting that the landing would be within a crater, Armstrong maneuvered the LEM to a more suitable spot within an area known to astronomers as *Mare Tranquillitatis* (Sea of Tranquility), and at 4:17 P.M. touched down gently.

The two astronauts rested and ate a leisurely supper. Then at 10:56 P.M. EDT 20 July 1969, Armstrong descended the LEM's ladder and set foot on the moon. "That's one small step for [a] man; one giant leap for mankind," he said to the

eration forces of near seven Gs.

Four and a half miles above the surface, Apollo's pair of 16-foot stabilizing parachutes opened, slowing the CM to 300 mph. A minute later the trio of orange-and-white main 'chutes were deployed, and at 10:51 A.M. EST on 27 December 1968, Apollo 8 splashed into the Pacific 1450 miles southwest of Hawaii and three miles from the carrier *Yorktown*, which was standing by with helicopters ready to retrieve the CM and its crew. The spacecraft had completed a 537,000-mile journey in 147 hours.

Apollo 9 flew in March 1969 to check out the lunar excursion module (LEM), or "moon taxi." Apollo 10 took the LEM for a dry run to the moon in May, and then on Wednesday, 16 July 1969, Apollo 11 left Planet Earth to carry out the first moon landing. In command was civilian Astronaut Neil Armstrong, a former Navy pilot. His crew were Air Force Lt. Col. Michael Collins, the Command Module pilot, and Air Force Col. Edwin Aldrin, Jr.

The Apollo spacecraft (L) represents the upper 82-feet of the Saturn V space vehicle (North American Rockwell)

The Apollo-Saturn vehicles weighted 6,200,000 pounds when fueled. Here an Apollo mission is transported toward its launch pad, 9 November 1967. (North American Rockwell)

latter-day astronauts may find it amusing to examine the primitive hardware left there by Apollo crews—the descent stages of their LEMs, for example, and the electric car, Moon Rover.

The Mercury series space capsules of the early '60s, each of which carried a single astronaut, put America in space as the wood-and-cloth airplanes of 1910 put us into the air. Then Project Gemini, each capsule of that series carrying two astronauts into Earth orbit, represented great advances in all areas of the U.S. space effort and in a remarkably short time. In 1965, Geminis 6 and 7 rendezvoused in orbit, flew in formation a few feet apart, and proved the concept of space-docking that followed with the Skylabs in the early '70s.

When President Nixon assumed office, he drastically cut funding for the space program, and except for a single docking mission in 1975, American astronauts did not leave Earth again until April 1981, in the first of four tests of the new Space Shuttles.

The control panel for the three-man Apollo command module had 250 switches and controllers, displayed 137 quantity measurements, and recorded 142 events. (North American Rockwell)

millions of Earthlings who watched the event via live television.

Aldrin joined Armstrong to plant the American flag, set up some experiments, and gather rock and dirt samples. Then they returned to the LEM for a few hours of sleep before blasting off to rendezvous with Mike Collins, orbiting above in the command module.

Apollo 11 returned to Earth at 12:50 P.M. EDT on 24 July. The three astronauts were held in quarantine for three weeks while doctors looked for signs of any exotic malady that may have been brought back from the moon, then they were freed to face hordes of news reporters—that part of the mission for which they were *least* prepared.

Subsequently, American astronauts would spend much more time on the lunar surface for scientific studies and exploration, and if, as has been suggested, the moon one day becomes a sort of base camp for space safaris far beyond, those

A Space Shuttle orbiter test vehicle in Lockheed-California Company's "reaction frame" which contains more than 350 hydraulic jacks that exert loads on the orbiter of up to one million pounds to prove its structural integrity. (Lockheed-California)

The Space Shuttles

The shuttles, officially known as Space Transportation Systems (STS), were conceived as space trucks—primarily to serve the Air Force, but also to serve commercial customers. The program was initially directed by Air Force Lt. Gen. James Abrahamson (who would later direct SDI), and the most interesting cargoes delivered into space by the shuttles were not announced to the public. In the early 1990s, the shuttles would be used to construct a permanent American space station operated by the Air Force.

Between April 1981 and July 1982, shuttle flights 1 through 4, with two-man crews, completed the test phase of this program; by the spring of 1984, two shuttles were operational, the *Columbia* and *Challenger*. A third, *Discovery,* made its first flight that August, and *Atlantis* followed the next

year (the test vehicle was the *Enterprise*).

In the meantime, a second launch and recovery complex was begun near Vandenberg AFB in California, which would have allowed the shuttles to place their payloads in polar orbits (those sent aloft from the Kennedy Space Center in Florida achieve equatorial orbits), but construction was halted on the Vandenberg shuttle port following the loss of the *Challenger* and its crew in January 1986, about which, more momentarily.

From the beginning, NASA took the position that for the shuttle program to be "economically viable," 24 flights per year, carrying significant commercial cargoes, were necessary.

The civilian customers were waiting, although the European Space Agency's unmanned Ariane rockets, which began flying in 1979 from a launch pad in French Guiana, were ready to accept a share of such business, primarily consisting of communications satellites.

NASA has taken the position that the manned shuttles are far more versatile than unmanned boosters, and some of that versatility was demonstrated on 8 April 1984 when George Nelson and James van Hoften, part of the five-man crew of STS 11, retrieved the satellite Solar Max from its orbit for maintenance and repair in space. The shuttles were also developed for the purpose of building a

A Lockheed technician examines some of the silica tiles that shield the Space Shuttle from fiery temperatures when it returns from space to Earth's atmosphere. No two tiles are alike, and 24,000 are required for each of the four Shuttles. (Lockheed-California)

permanent American space station.

In any event, the shuttles were deemed essential to the nation's security, and were the most cost-effective space vehicles for the several unique chores they would be called upon to perform. These huge, pressurized cargo gliders, serviced after each trip into space to fly again, actually have many emergency landing runways available when returning from a space mission, because the pilot has sufficient maneuverability to deviate as much as 1500 miles from his planned landing approach. He will always prefer to land at the launch site, because otherwise the shuttle must be (expensively) transported piggyback on a Boeing 747 to its launch facility. Edwards AFB is currently the shuttle's first alternate landing field because of its 15,000-foot runway, and because a specially-built structure is located there to facilitate mounting the shuttles on the NASA 747 for cross-country ferry.

Lockheed-built space telescopes will be able to see objects 50 times fainter and almost ten times farther away than the best Earth-bound telescopes. (Lockheed-California)

The Inevitable Tragedy

On 28 January 1986 space shuttle *Challenger* exploded into a huge fireball 73.5 seconds after lift-

View of a Space Shuttle's cargo bay with doors open. (Lockheed-California)

off. The seven astronauts aboard probably died instantly. Their remains were later recovered in the wreckage of their control cabin 100 feet beneath the surface of the Atlantic 18 miles downrange from Kennedy Space Center. The seven were: Cmdr. Francis R. Scobee, shuttle pilot Michael J. Smith, Judith Resnik, Ronald E. McNair, Ellison S. Onizuka, Sharon Christa McAuliffe, and Gregory Jarvis.*

The disaster struck on the 25th shuttle flight with the failure of a rubber O-ring employed as a seal between two sections of a solid-fuel booster. Two such boosters, manufactured by Morton Thiokol, were attached externally to the large main fuel tank to send each shuttle into orbit. A lengthy investigation revealed that NASA officials, al-

*Neither Judy Resnik nor Christa McAuliffe was the first American woman in space; that distinction belongs to Sally Kristen Ride, who flew in shuttle 7 in June, 1983. First American woman to walk in space was Kathryn Sullivan who, during her October, 1984 sojourn outside shuttle 13 to repair an antenna, remarked to helper astronaut Leetsma about the crew members inside, "I'll bet they ate our lunch." The first Soviet woman in space was Valentina Tereshkova, who flew in Vostok 6, June, 1963.

Astronauts Joseph Allen and Navy Commander Gardner stow equipment in the cargo bay of the Shuttle Discovery after snaring a communications satellite and bringing it aboard for repair. (NASA)

while the Air Force said it would require at least 45 flights by 1992 in order to meet its defense obligations. In mid-1986, the Air Force had but one (out of nine launched since 1978) Keyhole spy satellite in polar orbit to watch the Soviets. Therefore, the Air Force began turning to unmanned launch vehicles for its immediate needs. A dozen old Titan IIs were ordered refurbished, along with some of the 40 Titan ICBMs deactivated by the installation of Minutemen and MX ICBMs.

Meanwhile, the West European consortium that operated the Arianes announced construction of a second launch facility in South America which would allow an increase to 10 launchings per year, while Japan and China developed their own unmanned rockets for satellite deployment, and in the U.S. at least two private companies—one of them headed by former astronaut Deke Slayton—hoped to get their unmanned boosters ready for commercial customers before the end of the decade.

Unmanned Space Vehicles

While the manned spacecraft may be of more

though repeatedly warned about problems with the O-rings, nevertheless chose to continue shuttle launchings, in part due to pressure by a self-imposed goal of 24 launchings annually by 1988. It was evident that, following the departure of Gen. Abrahamson, a leadership vacuum had developed at NASA; schedules and public relations projects were overriding more important considerations. The O-ring design flaw had been well documented prior to *Challenger's* fatal flight, and with no fix in the works it was only a matter of time until *Challenger* or one of her sister space trucks would be lost. There is no law against incompetence. All we can do is bury our heros and press on.

The *Challenger* tragedy set back America's space program at least two years. When *Challenger* was lost, NASA had a waiting list of 26 satellites scheduled for shuttle deployment in 1986 and 1987,

Space Shuttle Columbia lifts off from Cape Canaveral. (NASA)

2001 Space colony features artificial gravity living quarters and control center, three zero-gravity modules for scientific research, and three tetrahedral beam platforms connected by "shirt sleeve" air tubes. Each platform is positioned to allow 360-degree line-of-sight communications, while leaving open flight paths for shuttles. (Lockheed Missiles & Space Co., Joe Boyer, artist)

Some of our space probes surprise us. Pioneer 10, built by TRW and launched by NASA on 3 March 1972—hopefully to make the first reconnaissance of Jupiter, if the 500-pound craft could survive passage through the asteroid belt beyond Mars—was one. If, by any chance, Pioneer 10 got that far, it might also confirm the outer limit of the heliosphere, the bubble of particles blown into space by the solar wind, and believed to be in the vicinity of Jupiter.

Pioneer 10 did indeed reach Jupiter—and then, accelerated by that great planet's gravitational field, raced beyond, passing the orbit of Uranus and, in June 1983 Earth time, crossed Neptune's orbit headed out of our solar system into the realm of the stars. It had discovered the heliosphere to be far beyond its predicted boundary, and had sent back intriguing evidence of an unseen source of gravity—perhaps another planet beyond Pluto—as it left our solar system on its journey into infinity. It was traveling at 30,550 mph, three billion miles away, and scientists at the Ames Research Center in California hoped to receive its signals through 1986. Pioneer 10 was not expected to approach another sun for 10,000 years.

Voyager II flew past Jupiter to investigate Saturn and its rings in August 1981, then tracked toward Uranus. If its radio continued to function, it was expected to send back data about Neptune when reaching there in 1989.

immediate use to us, the unmanned probes into deep space serve a longer-range and more compelling function. These little instrument packages, roaming among the planets, help satisfy our compulsive need to know more about ourselves and our place in the universe. We launch them in the name of scientific investigation, but we seek greater truths than they are designed to discover. True, we send them to sample the atmosphere of Jupiter, mark the edge of the heliosphere, and chart the carrier waves of gravitational force, along with a hundred other measurements, but ultimately we hope to learn from these clues how our solar system was formed, and then the universe. Whether it was all an accident, a "Big Bang" in which the universe somehow created itself out of nothing (the theory currently fashionable among many scientists), or whether there is a Supreme Intelligence—and therefore, purpose—behind it all, is a question each of us must decide for ourselves, Charles Darwin and Carl Sagan notwithstanding.

Space Shuttle Columbia returns to the Kennedy Space Center riding piggyback on a Boeing 747, following a landing at Edwards AFB, California. (NASA)

Earlier, in 1962, Mariner II gave us the first reports on Venus's hostile environment. Three subsequent unmanned spacecraft went to Venus. Mariner IV flew by Mars for a preliminary look in 1965, and Mariner IX went to Mars in 1971 to fill in the details. The soil of the Red Planet really is red, but there are no canals—and no visible Martians.

Our next scientific space vehicle (if Congress funds it), the Galileo Probe, originally scheduled to be launched from the Shuttle *Atlantis* in mid-1986, is intended to thoroughly investigate Jupiter and its atmosphere.

We have other means of searching the cosmos—a huge radiotelescope in New Mexico, for example, and the infrared Astronomical Satellite. The latter, launched in January 1983, is an infrared "telescope," placed in Earth orbit in order to allow it to operate above the disturbing influences of Earth's atmosphere. Within months, it found "something" orbiting the star Vega (all stars are suns). H.H. Aumann of the Jet Propulsion Laboratory, and Fred Gillett of Arizona's Kitt Peak Observatory, working at the telescope's tracking station at Chilton, England, made the discovery.

The infrared data cannot reveal the size or composition of Vega's satellites, but it does give us firm evidence that another sun out there—this one 150 trillion miles away—has a satellite system of some kind and, perhaps, planets like those of our own sun.

Extraterrestrials?

And, of course, the question that always comes up when laymen talk about space: Is there anyone else out there?

Well, consider: We live in the Milky Way Galaxy, which is an enormous pinwheel of suns (stars), perhaps as many as ten billion of them. There are millions of other galaxies similar to our own. We would have to possess a very narrow concept of life and the universe to conclude that, of all those billions of suns, only our own has a planetary system containing a habitable world.

There are many kinds of suns, ranging from the red giants to the white dwarfs. Ours is a yellow star, a very common type.

Draw your own conclusions.

REVIEW QUESTIONS:

1. How did the Germans get such a lead on us in rocket development after the pioneering efforts of Robert Goddard? Who was Wernher Von Braun? How did Charles Lindbergh assist Robert Goddard? What were some of the practical developments of Goddard's research? Where did the German rocket research take place? Why was it given secondary priority until the end of the war?

2. How was the Redstone Intercontinental Ballistics Missile program started? What was the U.S. reaction to the Soviet launching of Sputnik I on October 4, 1957? When was the National Aeronautics and Space Administration (NASA) created? What was the purpose of the Mercury and Gemini series?

3. What was the objective of the Apollo program? Discuss the successes of Apollo 8 and 11. Why are Space Shuttles now used? What relation do they have to national security?

4. What is the purpose of the unmanned space probes into outer space? How was the Universe formed? Why?

Appendix A

Objective Questions

Prelude

I. Multiple Choice: Circle the letter that corresponds to the best answer:

1. This individual holds the distinction of being the first to fly.
   - a. Etienne Montgolfier.
   - b. Pilatre de Rozier.
   - c. Ferdinand von Zeppelin.
   - d. Octave Chanute.

2. This Englishman designed the first true aircraft as we know it today with wings, fuselage, and tail section. Several of his gliders were successfully test flown.
   - a. Samuel P. Langley.
   - b. Charles Manley.
   - c. George Cayley.
   - d. Glenn H. Curtiss.

3. Between 1891 and 1896 this German glider pilot made a number of flights in his biplane, some reaching 750 feet in length. His work was studied closely by the Wrights.
   - a. Ferdinand von Zeppelin.
   - b. Otto Lilienthal.
   - c. Octave Chanute.
   - d. Alexander Mozhaisky.

4. Secretary of the Smithsonian Institute and a noted scientist, this individual developed an "Aerodrome" which crashed on takeoff after two unsuccessful launchings from a houseboat on the Potomac river.
   - a. Alexander Graham Bell.
   - b. Thomas Walker.
   - c. George Cayley.
   - d. Samuel P. Langley.

5. Wing warping was the first step in the development of:
   - a. wing camber ratio.
   - b. ailerons.
   - c. wing aspect ratio.
   - d. rudder pedals.

6. The Wright brothers completed their epic flight on:
   - a. October 7, 1903.
   - b. December 8, 1903.
   - c. December 17, 1903.
   - d. January 5, 1904.

7. The Aerial Experimental Association was formed by:
   - a. Alexander Graham Bell.
   - b. Samuel P. Langley.
   - c. Wilbur Wright.
   - d. Griffith Brewer.

II. True/False: Circle "T" if the statement is true; circle "F" if it is false.

T   F   1.   Sir George Cayley published a paper entitled *On Aerial Navigation* in 1810.

T   F   2.   Known as Germany's birdman, Otto Lilienthal completed his hang glider experiments from an artificial hill near Berlin.

T   F   3.   Stephen M. Balzer piloted professor Langley's Aerodrome on its two unsuccessful flights.

T	F	4.	The first flight of the Wright brothers' on December 17, 1903 lasted 12 seconds and covered a distance of 120 feet.
T	F	5.	The Wright brothers received considerable press coverage after their historic flight and consequently were immediately recognized as the first to achieve powered flight.
T	F	6.	The U.S. Army was quick to recognize the potential of the Wright brothers' machine and shortly after the historic flight they placed a substantial order.
T	F	7.	Professor Langley's Aerodrome was modified by Glenn Curtiss in 1914 and then successfully flown.
T	F	8.	Dr. Albert P. Zahm of the Smithsonian Institute confirmed that Glenn Curtiss had not made any major changes to Professor Langley's Aerodrome.

Chapter 1

I. Multiple Choice: Circle the letter that corresponds to the best answer:

1. In August 1909, the first great air meet was held near:
   a. Rheims, France.
   b. Los Angeles, California.
   c. Boston, Massachusetts.
   d. Martiques, France.

2. The Bennett Cup race at Belmont Park in October 1910 was won by:
   a. Glenn Curtiss.
   b. Alberto Santos-Dumont.
   c. Ralph Johnstone.
   d. Jacques de Lesseps.

3. One of the most daring of the early showmen in the pre-World War I era was:
   a. Claude Graham-White.
   b. Lincoln Beachey.
   c. Roy Knabenshue.
   d. Louis Bleriot.

4. The control system which incorporated foot-operated pedals for rudder control and a wheel that activated both elevators and ailerons was developed by:
   a. Glenn Curtiss.
   b. Orville Wright.
   c. Louis Becherau.
   d. Louis Bleriot.

5. Calbraith P. Rodgers:
   a. performed the first inside loop in a Curtiss biplane.
   b. established the speed record at the 1909 Rheims meet.
   c. was the first to fly coast-to-coast across the United States.
   d. was killed while performing at San Francisco's Panama Pacific Exposition.

II. True/False: Circle "T" if the statement is true; circle "F" if it is false.

T	F	1.	Wilbur Wright won the first Gordon Bennett cup race with a speed of 47 mph.
T	F	2.	John Moisant won the Bennett Cup race at Belmont Park but was disqualified on a technicality.
T	F	3.	An altitude record of 4,165 feet was established in January 1910 at an air meet held near Los Angeles.
T	F	4.	Louis Bleriot was the first to fly across the English Channel in a heavier-than-air aircraft on July 25, 1909.
T	F	5.	Katherine Stinson was one of the first pilots to perform a loop-the-loop in her air show appearances.
T	F	6.	Matty Laird, Buck Weaver, Clyde Cessna and others established their aircraft manufacturing facilities in Wichita, Kansas.

Chapter 2

I. Multiple Choice: Circle the letter that corresponds to the best answer:

1. In March 1916, the First Aero Squadron received orders to report to:
   a. Texas.
   b. France.
   c. New Mexico.
   d. England.

2. Naval aviation was born in November 1910 when _____ made the first takeoff from a platform on the bow of the cruiser Birmingham.
   a. Harold E. Geiger
   b. Eugene Ely
   c. Benjamin Foulois
   d. Glenn Curtiss

3. The synchronized machine gun mounted in front of the pilot was first developed by:
   a. A.V. Roe & Co.
   b. Handley Page.
   c. Rumpler.
   d. Morane-Saulnier.

4. At the beginning of the war, most military strategists looked upon the aircraft as a(n):
   a. observation post.
   b. tactical fighter.
   c. long range bomber.
   d. novelty which had little military significance.

5. Germany's ace of aces, "The Red Baron," with 80 confirmed victories was:
   a. Max Immelman.
   b. Kurt Wintgens.
   c. Manfred von Richthofen.
   d. Ritter von Tutschek.

6. Considered by many as the best allied fighter aircraft of the war, this aircraft had a distinctive humped engine cowling.
   a. Nieuport 17
   b. Curtiss JN-2
   c. Vickers Gunship
   d. Sopwith Camel

7. This British aircraft was manufactured in the United States under contract but very few reached the front lines by the war's end.
   a. de Havilland DH-4
   b. Bristol F-2B
   c. Vickers Gunbus
   d. Handley Page 0/400

8. This superior German fighter aircraft was developed toward the end of the war and presented a match for any of the allied aircraft.
   a. Fokker E-1 Eindecker
   b. Albatros D-III
   c. Pfalz D-III
   d. Fokker D-VII

9. Head of the Royal Flying Corps and one of the earliest air war strategists, this individual had a strong influence on America's Billy Mitchell.
   a. Mason Patrick
   b. Hugh Trenchard
   c. Edward Deeds
   d. Elliot White Springs

10. America's leading ace during World War I was:
    a. Major Raoul Lufberry.
    b. Captain Eddie Rickenbacker.
    c. Lt. Frank Luke.
    d. Lt. Joseph F. Wehner.

II. True/False: Circle "T" if the statement is true; circle "F" if it is false.

T F 1. The First Aero Squadron was led by Captain Benjamin Foulois.

T F 2. If World War I had continued into 1919, the Allies would have controlled the air because of numerical superiority.

T F 3. A popular aircraft used for training many U.S. pilots was the Curtiss JN-2 Jenny.

T F 4. British, French and German aircraft development during World War I was greatly advanced over our aircraft development.

T F 5. The Lafayette Escadrille was one of the most famous squadrons of French fighter pilots during World War I.

T F 6. The Germans used their Zeppelins as long-range (strategic) bombers during the early years of the war.

T F 7. Early aircraft production in the U.S. was controlled by automobile manufacturers.

T F 8. The water-cooled Liberty engine was developed by the Wright-Aeronautical Company.

T F 9. General William "Billy" Mitchell was Commander of the Army Air Services during World War I.

T F 10. The SPAD was a rugged aircraft developed by the British Sopwith Company.

T F 11. Observation balloons were used by both sides during World War I.

T F 12. Significant technical developments took place during World War I which resulted in improved aircraft performance, greater engine power output, greater speeds, stronger airframes and larger payloads.

T   F   13. Frank Luke was known as the balloon buster from Arizona because of his dogged pursuit of German *drachens* (observation balloons).

T   F   14. The U.S. Air Service was actually part of the Army Signal Corps until May 1918.

III. Matching (Individuals)

1. First pilot to use a synchronized machine gun on his Morane-Saulnier Bullet monoplane.
2. France's top scoring ace during World War I.
3. Scored 17 victories as a member of the Lafayette Escadrille before transferring to the U.S. Air Service.
4. The balloon buster from Arizona who was awarded the Medal of Honor posthumously.
5. Head of the Royal Flying Corps.
6. Commander of the Army Air Services.
7. Proposed that the Air Service be a separate and equal department of the U.S. Military.
8. Commanding officer of the U.S. First Aero Squadron.
9. Germany's leading ace.
10. America's leading ace.

a. Hugh Trenchard
b. Manfred von Richthofen
c. Eddie Rickenbacker
d. Frank Luke
e. Raoul Lufberry
f. Rene Fonck
g. Benjamin Foulois
h. Roland Garros
i. Mason Patrick
j. Billy Mitchell

IV. Matching (Aircraft)

1. Used by the British early in the war primarily as an observation plane.
2. Early German fighter which became the scourge of the skies during 1915 with its synchronized machine guns.
3. Flown by Von Richthofen's Jagdstaffel 11 during the Spring of 1917 and the aircraft in which he scored the greatest number of victories.
4. One of Great Britain's best fighter aircraft during World War I.
5. British heavy bomber designed to carry 1,000 lbs. of bombs to Berlin.
6. British aircraft manufactured in the U.S. under contract.
7. A French fighter that was flown by many American pilots.
8. Used to train U.S. pilots.

a. de Havilland DH-4
b. Albatros D-III
c. JN-4
d. SE-5
e. SPAD
f. Fokker Eindecker
g. BE2
h. Handley page V/1500

Chapter 3

I. Multiple Choice: Circle the letter that corresponds to the best answer:

1. During the 1920s, U.S. military aircraft were primarily designed for:
   a. long-range bombing missions.   c. tactical ground support.
   b. defensive purposes.   d. none of these.

2. During the 1920s, military appropriations for the Air Service:
   a. expanded significantly.
   b. increased in the immediate postwar period, then leveled off.
   c. were adequate.
   d. were not a high priority.

3. The Treaty of Versailles:
   a. stripped Germany of all overseas territories.
   b. required that Germany pay billions of dollars in reparations.
   c. forbid Germany from having any military aircraft.
   d. all of these.
   e. only b and c.

4. The first men to fly the Atlantic nonstop from Newfoundland to Ireland and claim the $50,000 prize offered by a British newspaper were:
   a. Tower and Read.
   b. Alcock and Brown.
   c. Smith and Arnold.
   d. Nelson and Harding.

5. Lt. Commander _____ and his five-man crew, aboard the NC-4, successfully flew across the Atlantic from Long Island to England in May 1919.
   a. Douglas Taylor
   b. Charles Menoher
   c. Albert C. Read
   d. Lowell H. Smith

6. The World Cruisers, specially built for the Army's epic flight around the world, were developed by:
   a. Curtiss.
   b. Martin.
   c. Douglas.
   d. Boeing.

7. Which of the following World Cruisers completed the epic flight around the world?
   a. *Seattle* and *Boston*
   b. *Boston* and *Chicago*
   c. *Chicago* and *New Orleans*
   d. *New Orleans* and *Seattle*

8. General Mitchell's secret report to the War Department in October 1924:
   a. predicted a naval air attack by the Japanese on Pearl Harbor.
   b. suggested that the U.S. Pacific Fleet stop the flow of war materials to Japan.
   c. provided the basis for a substantial buildup of military air power in the late 1920s.
   d. predicted the German attack on Poland in 1939.

9. Which of the following statements is *not* true?
   a. General Charles Menoher, an infantry commander with no aviation background, replaced General Mason Patrick as Chief of the Air Service.
   b. The R-34, commanded by Major G. H. Scott, completed the first aerial round trip across the Atlantic.
   c. Captain St. Clair Street completed a round-trip flight from New York to Nome, Alaska, in June 1920.
   d. The World Cruisers *Chicago* and *New Orleans* completed their epic flight in a total of 97 days or roughly three months.

10. An outspoken proponent of military aviation, this individual attempted to demonstrate the importance of aviation by sending his army pilots on numerous record-breaking flights:
    a. Glen L. Martin.
    b. Mason M. Patrick.
    c. William E. Mitchell.
    d. James Doolittle.

II. True/False: Circle "T" if the statement is true; circle "F" if it is false.

T   F   1. It can be said that the peace treaty signed with Germany at the close of World War I led to the Nazi takeover of Germany.

T   F   2. Adolf Hitler was elected chancellor of Germany by an overwhelming majority.

T   F   3. Commander John Tower successfully flew the NC-4 from Rockaway Beach, Long Island to Plymouth, England, in May 1919.

T   F   4. The German dirigible R-34, commanded by Hugo Eckener, was the first airship to cross the Atlantic both ways.

T   F   5. The U.S. Navy acquired one of its first dirigibles from the Germans under a post-war reparations agreement.

T   F   6. The U.S. and Germany signed a separate peace treaty in 1921.

T   F   7. The NC number originally stood for "Navy-Curtiss."

T   F   8. Many of the epic flights by General Mitchell's army pilots served to gain significant congressional support.

T   F   9. Although several World Cruisers were slightly damaged, all completed the flight around the world.

T   F   10. General Billy Mitchell's secret report to the War Department in October 1924 resulted in a significant buildup in military airpower during the late 1920s.

Chapter 4

I. Multiple Choice: Circle the letter that corresponds to the best answer:

1. A strong proponent of Navy aviation who became Director of Naval Aviation in March 1921 was:
   a. Josephus Daniels.
   b. William S. Benson.
   c. William A. Moffet.
   d. Bruce G. Leighton.

2. Bombers developed by which of the following companies were used by the Army Air Service to sink the *Ostfriesland* in July 1921.
   a. Curtiss
   b. Douglas
   c. Martin
   d. Wright

3. The Wright Whirlwind engine was first developed by:
   a. George J. Mead.
   b. Charles L. Lawrance.
   c. Bruce G. Leighton.
   d. Frederick B. Rentschler.

4. The Navy was particularly interested in Lawrance's engine because it:
   a. was water-cooled and easier to maintain.
   b. had more horsepower for less weight.
   c. was air-cooled and developed 400 hp.
   d. had a water-cooled rotary radial engine.

5. The Navy's first aircraft carrier was named the USS:
   a. *Maryland.*
   b. *Shenandoah.*
   c. *Langley.*
   d. *Los Angeles.*

6. The evolution of large multi-engine flying boats used by the Navy developed slowly for all of the following reasons, *except:*
   a. lack of reliable engines of sufficient power.
   b. smaller float planes catapulted from ships were more effective in covering greater distances.
   c. Admiral Moffet had great faith in large rigid dirigibles.
   d. none of these.

7. Which of the following statements is *not* true concerning Billy Mitchell?
   a. He was reduced in rank to colonel and transferred to Fort Sam Houston, Texas.
   b. Major General Mason Patrick quietly supported his position.
   c. He lost public support when he criticized the War Department.
   d. He demanded that the President appoint a panel of representative Americans to investigate the War and Navy Departments.

8. The Morrow Board:
   a. found Mitchell guilty of treasonable acts.
   b. investigated the best means of developing and applying aircraft in national defense.
   c. represented a cross-section of nonpartial business and military leaders.
   d. supported Mitchell's charges.

9. Which of the following statements regarding the use of airplanes by the military during the 1920s is *not* correct?
   a. The Navy feared that Congress might support an independent air force.
   b. The Navy placed more emphasis in developing dirigibles partly due to the lack of reliable engines for large aircraft.
   c. Congress strongly supported the development of military airplanes.
   d. none of these.

II. True/False: Circle "T" if the statement is true; circle "F" if it is false.

T   F   1. In his crusade for an independent air force, General Mitchell claimed that the airplane had made the Navy's surface ships obsolete.

T   F   2. Admiral William S. Benson was a strong proponent of Naval air power.

T   F   3. The sinking of the German battleship *Ostfriesland* had proved Mitchell's point to the top Navy brass.

T	F	4.	Lawrance's J-1 engine evolved into the Wright J-4 Whirlwind.
T	F	5.	The Navy first used airplane catapults mounted on the stern of battleships and cruisers.
T	F	6.	Admiral William A. Moffet discouraged the development of dirigibles but was over-riden by the CNO.
T	F	7.	The first turntable airplane catapult was fitted to the stern of the USS Jupiter in 1922.
T	F	8.	The Navy's ZR-3 Los Angeles was ordered from the Zeppelin works at Friedrich-shafen, Germany.
T	F	9.	Major General Mason Patrick was vehemently opposed to Billy Mitchell's crusade for a strong independent air force.
T	F	10.	The Navy dirigible Shenandoah had a long and productive career before it was decommissioned in 1929.
T	F	11.	The Lampert-Perkins Committee made recommendations largely favorable to Mitch-ell's position.
T	F	12.	Mitchell was charged with "conduct prejudicial to good order and military discipline" but was found not guilty.

Chapter 5

I. Multiple Choice: Circle the letter that corresponds to the best answer:
1. Air mail service was inaugurated on May 15, 1918 when _____ attempted to fly the first leg between Washington, D.C. and New York City.
   a. Reuben H. Fleet
   b. Albert Burleson
   c. James H. Knight
   d. George L. Boyle

2. Between August 12, 1918 and the end of 1925 the mail was flown by:
   a. Army pilots.
   b. Navy pilots.
   c. Post Office pilots.
   d. private contractors.

3. The Air Mail Act of 1925 (Kelly Bill):
   a. turned over the carriage of air mail to private contractors.
   b. eliminated all subsidies for air mail carriage.
   c. turned over the carriage of air mail to the Post Office Department.
   d. set limits on the amount of mail that could be transported by air.

4. One of the problems of early air mail service was:
   a. lack of support from the postmasters general and congress.
   b. no market for new civil aircraft.
   c. how to justify the unusually high profits.
   d. pilot training.

5. The primary purpose of the cross-country flight staged by the Post Office Department in February 1921 was:
   a. to influence the Army to give up air mail service.
   b. to influence the public and congress for financial assistance.
   c. to eliminate carriage of the mail by rail.
   d. to obtain better equipped aircraft.

6. This Post Office pilot flew three legs of a cross-country flight in February 1921 and became a na-tional hero:
   a. Frank Yeager.
   b. Homer Berry.
   c. Ernest Allison.
   d. Jack Knight.

7. The airway system was lighted from coast to coast by:
   a. August 12, 1918.
   b. February 22, 1921.
   c. July 1, 1924.
   d. February 2, 1925.

II. True/False: Circle "T" if the statement is true; circle "F" if it is false.
   T   F   1. The first air mail service was established between Washington, D.C., and Boston.

T	F	2.	Curtiss Jennies were first used to fly the mail.
T	F	3.	Early air mail service was very profitable for the Post Office Department.
T	F	4.	By the end of 1921 de Havilland DH-4's became the standard air mail airplane.
T	F	5.	By the summer of 1919 air mail service had been established between New York and Chicago.
T	F	6.	During the time the Post Office operated the air mail service, very few pilots were killed primarily because parachutes were used from 1919.
T	F	7.	President Warren Harding first took the position that air mail was a waste of money.
T	F	8.	Jack Knight's epic flight was between North Platt, Nebraska and Chicago.
T	F	9.	The first cross-country air mail flight took seven pilots a total of 108 flying hours.
T	F	10.	The Post Office Department primarily used war surplus aircraft for air mail service.

Chapter 6

I. Multiple Choice: Circle the letter that corresponds to the best answer:

1. Which of the following aircraft was *not* generally used by the barnstormers for their aerial shows?
   a. Standard
   b. Curtiss Jenny
   c. Thomas Morse Scout
   d. de Havilland DH-4

2. All but one of the following barnstormers started their own airplane manufacturing company. Which one did not?
   a. Buck Weaver
   b. Matty Laird
   c. Lloyd Stearman
   d. Wiley Post

3. The Air Commerce Act of 1926:
   a. transferred the carriage of air mail to private contractors.
   b. provided for the first aviation regulations and required federal licenses for all civil pilots and aircraft.
   c. gave the Postmaster General authority to consolidate air mail routes.
   d. established the Federal Aviation Administration.

4. Described in the June 1920 issue of *Aviation* as the "First commercial airplane capable of carrying a pilot and two passengers with fuel enough for 225 miles at full speed," this was the:
   a. Laird Swallow.
   b. Travel Air.
   c. Cessna Model A.
   d. Stearman C-1.

5. Wichita, Kansas, became the home of general aviation largely because of this individual:
   a. Charlie Meyers.
   b. Jake Moellendick.
   c. Clyde Pangborn.
   d. Roscoe Turner.

6. Clyde Cessna's 1912 Silver Wings was a homebuilt copy of the:
   a. Curtiss Jenny.
   b. Thomas Morse Scout.
   c. Bleriot.
   d. Standard.

7. In 1924, Beech, Cessna, and Stearman formed the:
   a. WACO Aircraft Company.
   b. Swallow Airplane Company.
   c. Travel Air Manufacturing Company.
   d. Advance Airplane Company.

8. Stearman Aircraft Company eventually became a part of:
   a. Boeing Airplane Company.
   b. Cessna Aircraft Corporation.
   c. Douglas Aircraft Corporation.
   d. Lockheed Aircraft Corporation.

9. Cessna Aircraft Corporation's first aircraft was the:
   a. Standard.
   b. Model 6.
   c. Model A.
   d. Scout.

10. This aircraft was advertised as a sister ship to Lindbergh's famous airplane:
    a. Stinson Detroiter.
    b. Ryan Brougham.
    c. Great Lakes Sport Trainer.
    d. Meyers Midget.

II. True/False: Circle "T" if the statement is true; circle "F" if it is false.

T   F   1. Many of the barnstormers in the early 1920s flew Curtiss Jennies.

T   F   2. Walter Beech, Clyde Cessna, and Charles Lindbergh got their start in aviation on the barnstorming circuit.

T   F   3. During the early 1920s, there were no aviation regulations, no federal pilot licenses, and no airworthiness certificates for airplanes.

T   F   4. The Air Commerce Act of 1926 was the result of recommendations from the Morrow Board.

T   F   5. Many of the barnstormers used wing walkers who performed gymnastics in flight as a means of attracting crowds.

T   F   6. Clyde Cessna preferred biplanes over monoplanes during his early years in aircraft manufacturing.

T   F   7. Charles Lindbergh's Ryan monoplane was called the *Dallas Spirit*.

T   F   8. Winners of the 1927 "Pineapple Derby" were Art Goebel and Lt. Bill Davis, flying a Travel Air 5000.

T   F   9. By the late 1920s, WACO had become one of the most popular civilian aircraft.

T   F   10. The first Travel Air was a monoplane powered by a 120-hp Anzani engine.

Chapter 7

I. Multiple Choice: Circle the letter that corresponds to the best answer:

1. The Postmaster General during the Hoover Administration was:
   a. Walter Varney.
   b. Elmer Partridge.
   c. Walter Folger Brown.
   d. J. Paul Riddle.

2. CAM-1 was awarded to:
   a. Colonial Air Transport.
   b. National Air Transport.
   c. Boeing Air Transport.
   d. Pacific Air Transport.

3. Under the Kelly Bill, the Post Office Department:
   a. exercised very little control over the air carriers.
   b. encouraged the air carriers to add passenger service.
   c. made adequate profits through 1929.
   d. matched the subsidies given to the railroads.

4. CAM-9 between Chicago and Minneapolis-St. Paul was started by Charles Dickinson and formed the foundation for:
   a. United Airlines.
   b. American Air Lines.
   c. Northwest Orient Air Lines.
   d. Trans World Airlines.

5. Varney Air Lines, Pacific Air Transport, Boeing Air Transport, and National Air Transport formed the foundation for today's:
   a. American Air Lines.
   b. Western Airlines.
   c. Trans World Airlines.
   d. United Airlines.

6. Boeing Air Transport, Pratt & Whitney, Hamilton Propellers, Stearman, Northrop, and Sikorsky all came under which of the following holding companies?
   a. AVCO
   b. North American Aviation
   c. United Aircraft and Transport
   d. Transcontinental Air Transport

7. The North American Aviation holding company was formed by:
   a. William B. Boeing.
   b. Frederick Rentschler.
   c. Clement Keys.
   d. Sherman Fairchild.

8. Southern Air Transport became a part of:
   a. AVCO.
   b. United Aircraft and Transport Corporation.
   c. North American Aviation.
   d. National Air Transport.

9. American Airways was organized under:
   a. AVCO.
   b. United Aircraft and Transport Corporation.
   c. North American Aviation.
   d. Universal Aviation Corporation.

10. Eastern Air Transport, the forerunners of Eastern Airlines, was acquired by:
    a. AVCO.
    b. United Aircraft and Transport Corporation.
    c. North American Aviation.
    d. Universal Aviation Corporation.

II. True/False: Circle "T" if the statement is true; circle "F" if it is false.

T F 1. Charles Lindbergh completed his epic flight in May 1927.
T F 2. Lindbergh's specially-built Ryan monoplane was powered by Pratt & Whitney 400-hp Wasp engine.
T F 3. Most of the early contract air mail carriers were not particularly interested in carrying passengers.
T F 4. Charles Lindbergh was an air mail pilot flying for the Robertson brothers on CAM-2 between St. Louis and Chicago.
T F 5. David L. Behncke, a pilot for Northwest Airways, was one of the founders of the Air Line Pilots Association.
T F 6. Henry Ford was the successful bidder on two early CAM routes.
T F 7. Harry Chandler founded and edited *Aerial Age*, one of the earliest U.S. aviation magazines.
T F 8. The Ford TriMotor was affectionately dubbed the "Tin Goose."
T F 9. Pacific Aero Products Company formed the beginning of Douglas Aircraft Corporation.
T F 10. The Boeing Model 40A biplane was used to fly the air mail route between Chicago and San Francisco.
T F 11. During 1933, General Motors actually gained control of North American Aviation.
T F 12. Transcontinental Air Transport merged with Western Air Express to form the beginnings of today's TWA.
T F 13. National Air Transport was a combination air and rail service across the United States.
T F 14. Pratt & Whitney's first engine was the air-cooled 400-hp Wasp.
T F 15. William Boeing designed the merger of Curtiss Aeroplane and Motor with Wright Aeronautical Corporation.

III. Matching:

1. Postmaster General during the Hoover Administration.
2. Formed Pacific Air Transport.
3. Formed Western Air Express.
4. Started Pacific Aero Products Company in 1915.
5. Left Wright Aeronautical to form Pratt & Whitney.
6. Formed North American Aviation.
7. Aircraft manufacturer whose company was bought by Ford Motor Company.
8. Flew a Ford TriMotor over the North Pole.
9. Developed a successful monoplane called the Detroiter.
10. Former Chief of the U.S. Air Service.

a. Harris Hanshue
b. William Stout
c. Frederick Rentschler
d. Mason Patrick
e. Edward Stinson
f. Walter Folger Brown
g. Clement M. Keys
h. Richard Byrd
i. Vern C. Gorst
j. William E. Boeing

Chapter 8

I. Multiple Choice: Circle the letter that corresponds to the best answer:

1. The Air Mail Act of 1930 (McNary-Watres) included all of the following provisions except:
   a. operators were paid for flying the mail according to space available for mail in their airplanes.
   b. the Postmaster General could extend or consolidate routes according to his judgment.
   c. it designated three transcontinental routes which would be opened for competitive bidding.
   d. routes would be awarded to the lowest bidder who had offered a daily schedule of at least 250 miles over a period of six months.

2. The Air Mail Act of 1930 (McNary-Watres):
   a. gave the operators an incentive to acquire large multi-engine aircraft.
   b. discouraged passenger service.
   c. encouraged smaller, newly established operators.
   d. eliminated subsidies.

3. Which of the following did *not* occur during the "Spoils Conferences"?
   a. The merger of TAT and Western Air Service.
   b. American Airways acquired the southern route after purchasing SAFEway and Delta Air Service.
   c. United Aircraft and Transport Corporation acquired National Air Transport.
   d. Qualified bidders must have flown at night for six months over a route of not less than 250 miles.

4. Delta Air Service:
   a. was acquired by TAT.
   b. was merged into SAFEway.
   c. shared the southern route with American Airways.
   d. was acquired by American Airways.

5. The three transcontinental routes included all but one of the following carriers. Which one?
   a. United
   b. TWA
   c. American
   d. Delta

6. This carrier actually submitted the low bid for the air mail contract between New York and Washington, DC, but the route was given to Eastern Air Transport:
   a. Reed Airline.
   b. Century Air Lines.
   c. Ludington Lines.
   d. Central Air Lines.

7. Ludington Lines operated:
   a. Douglas M-2s.
   b. Northrop Alphas.
   c. Stinson TriMotors.
   d. Ford TriMotors.

8. E. L. Cord, founder of Century Air Lines and Century Pacific Lines, claimed that the major carriers:
   a. were grossly overpaid for flying the mail.
   b. were poorly managed.
   c. were favored by the Post Office Department.
   d. all of these.

II. **True/False:** Circle "T" if the statement is true; circle "F" if it is false.

T	F	1.	Postmaster Brown was the primary author of the Air Mail Act of 1930.
T	F	2.	The McNary-Watres Act gave the postmaster almost absolute control over the airlines.
T	F	3.	Postmaster Brown favored competition and smaller operators with limited resources.
T	F	4.	The "Spoils Conferences" favored smaller independent operators.
T	F	5.	The president and directors of Western Air Express were generally in favor of the merger with Transcontinental Air Transport.
T	F	6.	Both Delta Air Service and SAFEway were excluded from bidding on the southern route because they had not flown at night for six months over a route of not less than 250 miles.
T	F	7.	Delta Air Service began as a crop-dusting business in Louisiana in the early 1920s.
T	F	8.	Small carriers such as Reed Airline and Century Air Lines were favored by the Post Office Department.
T	F	9.	Ludington Lines flew passengers profitably, which was unusual for most carriers during the early 1930s.
T	F	10.	Fulton Lewis's publisher refused to print his story regarding the scandalous air mail bidding practices.

Chapter 9

I. Multiple Choice: Circle the letter that corresponds to the best answer:

1. Walter Folger Brown testified before Senator Black's committee that he:
   a. favored small independent carriers.
   b. was determined to develop an outstanding air carrier network in the United States.
   c. discouraged carriers from developing passenger service.
   d. did not force any major carriers to accept route extensions.

2. One of the results of Senator Black's committee was:
   a. Postmaster Brown was charged with violation of proper code of conduct while in office.
   b. the cancellation of all air mail contracts.
   c. substantial fines levied on all major air carriers who were overpaid for carrying the mail.
   d. the transfer of all air mail contracts held by Eastern Air Transport to Ludington Lines.

3. Under the Air Mail Act of 1934 (Black-McKellar Bill), the Bureau of Air Commerce:
   a. approved air mail contracts, routes, and schedules.
   b. established air mail rates.
   c. provided subsidies to the air carriers.
   d. regulated the airway system and the licensing of pilots and aircraft.

4. Which of the following was *not* a provision of the Black-McKellar Act?
   a. It subjected the air carriers to control by the Post Office Department, Interstate Commerce Commission, and the Bureau of Air Commerce.
   b. All airlines were required to separate themselves from manufacturing firms.
   c. Transferred authority for establishing air mail routes and schedules from the Post Office Department to the Interstate Commerce Commission.
   d. Required that all routes were to be rebid each year.

5. Certificates of Public Convenience and Necessity were issued by the:
   a. Air Carrier Economic Regulation Division of the CAA.
   b. Post Office Department.
   c. Bureau of Air Commerce.
   d. Interstate Commerce Commission.

6. The Civil Aeronautics Board (CAB) was created in 1940 to:
   a. license pilots and aircraft.
   b. operate the airway system.
   c. regulate the airlines and investigate air accidents.
   d. only regulate the airlines.

7. Pan American Airways began scheduled service on October 28, 1927 between Key West, Florida and:
   a. Cuba.   c. Puerto Rico.
   b. Haiti.   d. Dominican Republic.

8. Which of the following was *not* a problem faced by Juan Tripp in expanding Pan Am's routes into the Caribbean, Central and South America?
   a. Columbian government
   b. Cuban government
   c. W. R. Grace & Company
   d. New York, Rio & Buenos Aires Line (NYRBA)

9. The arrival of the _____ gave Pan Am the range to cross the Atlantic nonstop.
   a. Sikorsky S-38   c. Martin M-130
   b. Sikorsky S-42   d. Boeing B-314

10. Which of the following carriers did not seek international routes in the postwar period?
    a. American   c. TWA
    b. Braniff   d. United

11. AMEX was purchased by:
   a. American.
   b. Northwest.
   c. Pan Am.
   d. United.

12. Which of the following companies was not *entirely* controlled by Pan Am?
   a. West Indian Aerial Express
   b. Compania Mexicana de Aviacion
   c. Panagra
   d. Panair do Brasil

13. Pan Am's chief competitor in the Pacific after WWII was:
   a. American.
   b. National.
   c. Northwest.
   d. TWA.

14. On June 1, 1945 the CAB ruled that three U.S. air carriers should fly the Atlantic to European terminals. Which of the following was *not* included?
   a. American
   b. Braniff
   c. Pan Am
   d. TWA

II. True/False: Circle "T" if the statement is true; circle "F" if it is false.

T   F   1. The Special Committee on Investigation of the Air Mail and Ocean Mail Contracts was chaired by Senator Pat McCarran.

T   F   2. Postmaster Brown testified that Ludington was merely "skimming cream from a short, high-density route."

T   F   3. Eastern Air Transport's costs per mile were higher than Ludington's because it served a much wider airway network with many low density routes.

T   F   4. The Black Committee established that Postmaster Brown had been a dictator.

T   F   5. The accident experience by the Army during the period in which they flew the mail was so low that the President considered leaving it with them on a permanent basis.

T   F   6. Many of the air carriers changed their names after the Black Committee hearings so that they could submit air mail bids.

T   F   7. In the first few years following passage of the Black-McKellar Act, the major air carriers enjoyed very high profits.

T   F   8. The arrival of the Douglas DC-3 enabled the carriers to earn profits on passenger traffic alone.

T   F   9. There were about 8,000 individuals employed by the air carriers in 1935.

T   F   10. The Civil Aeronautics Board (CAB) was created in 1940.

T   F   11. Pan Am's first route was between Miami, Florida and Havana, Cuba.

T   F   12. NYRBA flew Consolidated Commodore flying boats which were superior to Pan Am's Sikorsky S-38s.

T   F   13. Pan Am began scheduled service across the mid-Pacific in November 1935.

T   F   14. The U.S. State Department decided to continue the "chosen instrument" policy in the immediate postwar period.

Chapter 10

I. Multiple Choice: Circle the letter that corresponds to the best answer:

1. America's reaction to the aggressive actions by Japan, Germany and Italy during the mid-1930s was:
   a. outrage.
   b. neutrality.
   c. a massive military buildup.
   d. a declaration of war.

2. The Curtiss Sparrowhawks were used with the Navy dirigibles as:
   a. torpedo bombers.
   b. dive bombers.
   c. scout-fighter planes.
   d. long range bombers.

3. Which of the following Navy dirigibles was *not* lost in an accident?
   a. *Shenandoah*
   b. *Akron*
   c. *Macon*
   d. *Los Angeles*

4. The famous Douglas DC-3 saw service during the war as the Army:
   a. R4D.
   b. 0-46A.
   c. C-47.
   d. P-12C.

5. The first military precision flying team was the:
   a. Red Devils.
   b. Blue Angels.
   c. Fighting Hawks.
   d. Thunderbolts.

6. Built in 1922, the Navy's first aircraft carrier was the:
   a. Saratoga.
   b. Lexington.
   c. Langley.
   d. Ranger.

7. A new era in U.S. fighter airplane design began in 1934 when Don Berlin designed the:
   a. Curtiss P-36.
   b. Republic P-47.
   c. Lockheed P-38.
   d. Curtiss P-40.

8. The _____ first appeared in 1940 and became the principal U.S. fighter in Europe. America's top aces in the European Theater flew this aircraft.
   a. Curtiss P-40
   b. Republic P-47
   c. Lockheed P-38
   d. Curtiss P-36

9. The _____ first flew in 1935 and evolved into the famous B-17 series of WWII.
   a. Boeing 247
   b. Boeing 299
   c. Douglas 0-4A
   d. Boeing P-12C

10. The United States Army Air Forces (USAAF) was created on:
    a. March 11, 1941.
    b. June 20, 1941.
    c. December 7, 1941.
    d. March 9, 1942.

II. **True/False:** Circle "T" if the statement is true; circle "F" if it is false.

T F 1. As assistant secretary of the Navy from 1913 to 1921, future President Roosevelt was a strong advocate of military aviation.

T F 2. Postmaster Walter Folger Brown had built America's airline system by some rather undemocratic methods.

T F 3. The U.S. Navy had reasonably good success with their dirigibles during the 1930s and many Naval personnel felt that the airship program should have continued.

T F 4. Admiral Moffet was killed when the Akron crashed in a storm off the New Jersey coast.

T F 5. The first modern airliner, the Boeing 247, was produced in 1933 for United Air Lines—an all metal, low-wing, twin-engine aircraft with seating for 10 passengers.

T F 6. The Navy's first aircraft carrier was the *Yorktown*.

T F 7. Naval aviation was relatively better funded during the 1930s than Army aviation.

T F 8. Henry "Hap" Arnold was appointed Chief of the Army Air Corps in 1938.

T F 9. The Lockheed XP-38 was officially described as a defensive interceptor in order to get it past General Craig and Congress.

T F 10. The Curtiss P-40 was simply a P-36 with a more powerful engine.

Chapter 11

I. **Multiple Choice:** Circle the letter that corresponds to the best answer:

1. The U.S. military's primary failure at Pearl Harbor was:
   a. inadequate number of aircraft.
   b. lack of reconnaissance.
   c. poor training.
   d. the inability to supply our forces.

2. This Japanese fighter aircraft was used in the attack on Pearl Harbor and throughout the war in the Pacific:
   a. Nakajima Hayate.
   b. Kawasaki Hien.
   c. Mitsubishi Zero.
   d. Kawanishi Shiden.

3. This was the first sea battle in which neither side ever sighted the other from a surface ship; the entire battle was fought with air power.
   a. Bismark Sea
   b. Coral Sea
   c. Midway
   d. Leyte Gulf

4. The battle of _____ was an incredible victory for the U.S. Navy and a severe blow to the Japanese from which it never recovered.
   a. Bismark Sea
   b. Coral Sea
   c. Midway
   d. Santa Cruz

5. Japan entered WWII with the primary objective of:
   a. allying with Germany to obtain world domination.
   b. securing natural resources and fighting a defensive war.
   c. neutralizing the U.S. Navy in Hawaii and then attacking the U.S. mainland.
   d. controlling the Pacific Ocean.

6. One of the first amphibious assaults took place on August 7, 1942, in the southern Soloman island chain. It would take until February 1943 to secure this island:
   a. New Guinea.
   b. Okinawa.
   c. Iwo Jima.
   d. Guadalcanal.

7. The U.S. Pacific Fleet Commander during WWII was:
   a. Frank J. Fletcher.
   b. Chester W. Nimitz.
   c. Raymond A. Spruance.
   d. Ernest J. King.

8. Japanese fleet commander and military strategist in the Pacific during WWII was:
   a. Chuichi Nagumo.
   b. Yahachi Tanabe.
   c. Isoruku Yamamoto.
   d. Chiang Kai-shek.

II. True/False: Circle "T" if the statement is true; circle "F" if it is false

T	F	1.	The attack on Pearl Harbor took place on December 7, 1941.
T	F	2.	Most military analysts of the time expected that any possible Japanese attack would be made first against the Philippines.
T	F	3.	U.S. bases in the Philippines were attacked by Japanese air forces shortly after the attack on Pearl Harbor.
T	F	4.	General Jonathan Wainwright's forces repelled the Japanese invasion of the Philippines and took many prisoners, which was a severe blow to the Japanese early in the war.
T	F	5.	The battle of Coral Sea was probably a slight tactical victory for the Japanese but a major strategic victory for the U.S. because it forced the enemy to abandon their planned invasion of Port Moresby.
T	F	6.	The U.S. aircraft carriers that participated in the battle of Midway were the *Enterprise*, the *Yorktown*, and the *Hornet*.
T	F	7.	The most severe damage to the Japanese Fleet during the battle of Midway was done by Douglas SBD Dauntless dive bombers.
T	F	8.	The USAAF Fifth Air Force was commanded by General Douglas MacArthur.

Chapter 12

I. MULTIPLE Choice: Circle the letter that corresponds to the best answer:

1. The invasion of North Africa was referred to as operation:
   a. D-Day.
   b. Overlord.
   c. Torch.
   d. Tunisia.

2. The German General, known as the "Desert Fox," who faced allied forces in the North African campaign was:
   a. Carl Spaatz.
   b. Albert Kesselring.
   c. Juergen Von Arnim.
   d. Erwin Rommel.

3. Colonel Jimmy Doolittle led a flight of 12 B-25 Mitchell bombers off the deck of the carrier _____ in April 1942.
   a. *Hornet*
   b. *Wasp*
   c. *Ranger*
   d. *Yorktown*

4. This aircraft was probably the best German fighter during the war. Its 1760-hp BMW engine gave it a speed of close to 400 mph at 17,000 feet.
   a. Junkers JU-87
   b. Messerschmitt Bf-109F
   c. Focke-Wulf 190
   d. Junkers JU-52

5. Which of the following U.S. aircraft was the predominant fighter used during the North African campaign?
   a. Lockheed P-38J
   b. Curtiss P-40F
   c. Republic P-47
   d. North American P-51

6. The Italian Campaign:
   a. ended in September 1943.
   b. resulted in heavy losses of allied aircraft.
   c. was decided during the first two months of combat.
   d. lasted until shortly before the war in Europe ended.

.7. The primary aims of the combined British and American bomber offensive decided at the Casablanca Conference was the:
   a. destruction of German cities to break the morale of the people.
   b. elimination of the Luftwaffe and Germany's sources of oil.
   c. breaking down of all communications and rail lines.
   d. cut off of all supply lines and demoralization of German ground troops.

8. _____ with 108-gallon drop tanks were used to escort B-17s on bombing runs over Germany during the last year of the war.
   a. P-38 Lightnings
   b. P-47 Thunderbolts
   c. P-51 Mustangs
   d. A-26 Invaders

9. The war in Europe ended on:
   a. July 25, 1944.
   b. September 8, 1944.
   c. April 25, 1945.
   d. May 7, 1945.

10. General Von Rundstedt, Commander-in-chief of German Armed Forces in Western Europe attributed Germany's defeat to three factors. Which of the following was *not* one of those factors?
    a. Superiority of the Allied Air Force
    b. Lack of fuel
    c. Demoralization of troops due to bombing
    d. Destruction of all rail lines

II. **True/False:** Circle "T" if the statement is true; circle "F" if it is false.

T   F   1. The Lend-Lease Act swept away any pretense of neutrality on the part of America.

T   F   2. General Eisenhower put General Doolittle in command of the 12th Air Force during the North African campaign.

T   F   3. Over 270,000 German and Italian troops escaped from North Africa in Junkers JU-52 transport aircraft.

T   F   4. The Republic P-47 Thunderbolts were referred to by Luftwaffe pilots as "forked-tail devils."

T   F   5. General Ira Eaker replaced Air Chief Marshall Tedder as air commander in the Mediterranean Theater of Operations.

T   F   6. The B-17 Flying Fortress was flown by the 8th Air Force on long range bombing missions from England to Germany.

T	F	7.	By late March 1944, Allied airpower was dominant over the European skies.
T	F	8.	Over 11,000 Allied airplanes were used during the D-Day invasion.
T	F	9.	In July 1944, 20,000 German soldiers attempting to outflank General Patton's U.S. 3rd Army, surrendered directly to the Air Force.
T	F	10.	The V-2 rocket was first used against the Allies during the Normandy invasion.

III. Matching (Individuals):

1. Led the B-25 raid over Tokyo in April 1942.
2. Supreme Allied Commander.
3. Reichmarschall of the Luftwaffe.
4. The Desert Fox.
5. German commander in Italy.
6. Head of the U.S. 8th Air Force.
7. British Air Chief Marshal.
8. U.S. air commander in the Mediterranean.
9. Head of the U.S. 3rd Army.
10. Head of the USAAF.

a. Herman Goering
b. Carl Spaatz
c. Ira Eaker
d. Albert Kesselring
e. Dwight D. Eisenhower
f. Charles Portal
g. George Patton, Jr.
h. James Doolittle
i. Henry Arnold
j. Erwin Rommel

IV. Matching (Aircraft):

1. German dive bomber.
2. Flying Fortress heavy bomber.
3. U.S. fighter used in North Africa.
4. German fighter aircraft.
5. German transport aircraft.
6. Rugged U.S. fighter called the Jug.
7. U.S. fighter flown with drop tanks to escort bombers.
8. Germans referred to this U.S. fighter as a forked-tail devil.
9. Italian fighter aircraft.
10. U.S. bomber known as the Liberator.

a. Focke-Wulf 190
b. Junkers JU 52
c. Boeing B-17
d. Macchi C 202
e. Republic P-47 Thunderbolt
f. North American P-51 Mustang
g. Junkers JU 87 Stuka
h. Lockheed P-38 Lightning
i. Consolidated B-24
j. Curtiss P-40 Warhawk

Chapter 13

I. Multiple Choice: Circle the letter that corresponds to the best answer:

1. The major problem during the Aleutian campaign was the:
   a. difficulty in supplying our troops.
   b. weather conditions.
   c. large concentration of Japanese troops.
   d. Japanese Navy.

2. The Flying Tigers were organized and commanded by:
   a. Claire L. Chennault.
   b. Lewis Brereton.
   c. Albert Baumler.
   d. David Campbell.

3. The Air Transport Command (ATC) serving in the Far East and referred to as the "Assam Trucking Company":
   a. played a limited role in supplying the Flying Tigers.
   b. was under a command of Colonel David Hill.
   c. supplied Chiang Kai-shek's forces.
   d. formed the major supply line between Australia and China.

4. The retaking of the Philippines:
   a. was primarily a psychological victory.
   b. Virtually ended the war in the Pacific.
   c. had little strategic importance.
   d. provided a major base of operations for U.S. forces.

5. The Imperial Japanese Navy was decisively defeated in this battle which took place during October 1944.
   - a. Bismark Sea
   - b. Lingayen Gulf
   - c. Leyte Gulf
   - d. Tokyo Bay

6. The name of the B-29 that dropped the first atomic bomb was:
   - a. *Lady be Good.*
   - b. *My Fair Lady.*
   - c. *Miss Fortune.*
   - d. *Enola Gay.*

7. Which of the following statements is *not* true?
   - a. During the Okinawan campaign, Kamikazes sank 35 U.S. ships and damaged 288.
   - b. General Curtis Le May recommended against the invasion of Japan.
   - c. Had the war not ended as it did, another 7-9,000 Kamikazes were waiting for the expected invasion of Japan.
   - d. The price paid for Iwo Jima was probably too high considering the fact that we recently acquired bases in the Marianas for our B-29s.

8. This fighter flown by Marine squadrons throughout the Pacific theater had a speed of 424 mph at 23,000 feet.
   - a. Northrop P-61 Black Widow
   - b. Grumman F6F Hellcat
   - c. Chance Vought F4U Corsair
   - d. Curtiss P-40 Warhawk

9. On August 6, 1945 the first A-bomb was dropped from a B-29 on which of the following Japanese cities?
   - a. Hiroshima
   - b. Nagasaki
   - c. Tokyo
   - d. Toyama

II. True/False: Circle "T" if the statement is true; circle "F" if it is false.

T   F   1. The Aleutian Islands had to be controlled to prevent a possible strike by the Japanese on the North American Continent.

T   F   2. The Flying Tigers primarily flew Northrop P-61 Black Widow night fighter aircraft.

T   F   3. The American Volunteer Group (Flying Tigers) were fighting the Japanese in China six months before the attack on Pearl Harbor.

T   F   4. The China National Aviation Corporation (CNAC) was established and partly owned by Pan Am.

T   F   5. Kamikaze attacks accounted for at least half of all damage to U.S. Navy ships during the war.

T   F   6. The primary purpose of taking Iwo Jima was the fact that we needed a fueling base for our fleet.

T   F   7. In the Spring of 1945, B-29s were loaded with incendiary bombs and used on low-level fire-bombing raids over Tokyo and other Japanese cities.

T   F   8. Kamikazes came out in force during the Okinawa campaign, causing a high loss of ships and lives.

T   F   9. After Okinawa was taken, General Le May began announcing in advance where his B-29s would strike next in order to reduce civilian casualties.

T   F   10. Japan surrendered on September 2, 1945, aboard the battleship *Missouri* in Tokyo Bay.

Chapter 14

I. Multiple Choice: Circle the letter that corresponds to the best answer:

1. The USAF's first operational jet fighter was the:
   - a. Bell X-1A.
   - b. Lockheed F-94 Starfire.
   - c. North American F-86 Sabre.
   - d. Lockheed F-80 Shooting Star.

2. The wartime Air Transport Command (ATC) became the:
   - a. Air Transport Service Command (ATSC).
   - b. Military Air Transport Service (MATS).
   - c. Strategic Air Command (SAC).
   - d. Tactical Air Command (TAC).

3. The Boeing B-52 Stratofortress:
   a. preceded the Convair B-36.
   b. is still being used today by SAC.
   c. was first flown in 1941.
   d. is powered by four prop-jet engines.

4. When North Korean troops crossed the 38th parallel in June 1950:
   a. the South Korean army backed by U.S. occupation forces were prepared for the invasion.
   b. General MacArthur was put in command of troops from 15 nations.
   c. President Truman ordered the 5th Air Force to commence attacking North Korean cities.
   d. UN forces started a counter offensive with an amphibious landing at Inchon.

5. In January, 1953 President Eisenhower warned the Communists that if negotiations did not progress:
   a. hostilities may no longer be confined to the Korean peninsula.
   b. we would drop the A-bomb as we did on Japan.
   c. their next defensive position would be the outskirts of Moscow.
   d. North Korea would be asked to leave the United Nations.

6. With the combination of veteran World War II pilots and the arrival of this aircraft the kill ratio jumped to ten-to-one in the skies over Korea.
   a. North American F-51 Mustang.   c. Grumman F7F Tigercat.
   c. Douglas A-26 Invader.   d. North American F-86 Sabre.

7. In 1951, General MacArthur called for all of the following *except*:
   a. a naval blockade of the China coast.
   b. an amphibious assault at selected points along the Chinese coastline by U.S. Marines.
   c. an invasion of China by Chiang Kai-shek's Nationalist Chinese forces.
   d. air attacks on China's war industries.

8. Which of the following is a direct result of the Korean War?
   a. better relations with the USSR during the latter 1950s
   b. Strengthening of the NATO alliance
   c. U.S. withdrawal from the United Nations in 1955
   d. the Vietnam conflict during the 1960s

9. Helicopters were primarily used during the Korean War for:
   a. construction work.   c. medical evacuation.
   b. troop support.   d. low-level bombing.

II. True/False: Circle "T" if the statement is true; circle "F" if it is false.

T	F	1.	The C-47 (civilian DC-3) provided the backbone of the Berlin airlift.
T	F	2.	General George Kenney, the first commander of the Strategic Air Command (SAC), was a strong proponent of the B-52 and B-36.
T	F	3.	The B-52 has been the backbone of the Strategic Air Command (SAC) for the past 30 years.
T	F	4.	The first B-52 prototype made its maiden flight in April 1952.
T	F	5.	President Truman termed the UN response to the North Korean invasion a "total war."
T	F	6.	Helicopters were used during the Korean war primarily for evacuation of wounded troops.
T	F	7.	P-51 Mustangs were primarily used for air-to-air combat during the Korean War.
T	F	8.	UN field commanders had great latitude in developing and implementing battle plans during the Korean War because of the multiplicity of authority.
T	F	9.	The Vultee (Stinson) L-5s and Cessna L-19s were primarily used as tactical support fighters.
T	F	10.	The Soviet MiG-15 was the standard fighter for the Soviet-bloc air forces during the 1950s.

Chapter 15

I. Multiple Choice: Circle the letter that corresponds to the best answer:
1. The theory of *flexible response* postulated that:
   a. we must meet force with maximum counterforce.
   b. the amount of force used should always be commensurate with the threat.
   c. we should do nothing unless the threat jeopardized national security.
   d. the amount of force used should enable us to win and eliminate the threat as soon as possible.

2. The Geneva Accords:
   a. established conditions for a cease-fire in Indochina.
   b. provided for the independence of Laos and Cambodia as well as Vietnam.
   c. called for free elections throughout Vietnam.
   d. all of the above.

3. The Southeast Asia Treaty Organization (SEATO):
   a. tried to re-establish French rule in Indochina.
   b. was set up to ensure free elections in Vietnam.
   c. pledged aid to any Southeast Asian country which asked for help if attacked.
   d. supported the North Vietnamese.

4. The Gulf of Tonkin resolution:
   a. greatly curtailed presidential action.
   b. warned North Vietnam that shipping in the Gulf of Tonkin would be attacked by U.S. forces.
   c. committed military aid to all countries bordering the Gulf of Tonkin.
   d. virtually gave the President a blank check to do what was necessary.

5. The Army's AH-1G HueyCobras were primarily used for:
   a. medical evacuation.   c. delivering supplies.
   b. ground attack support.   d. observation purposes.

6. Which of the following statements is *not* true?
   a. In November 1968, President Johnson halted all bombing of North Vietnam.
   b. President Nixon secretly authorized B-52 strikes against enemy sanctuaries in Cambodia.
   c. Secretary McNamara planned to equip the Air Force and Navy with a single fighter airplane—
      which could also serve as a strategic bomber.
   d. General Creighton Abrams recommended that we increase troop strength to two million men.

7. The Convair F-111:
   a. was originally designed to serve both the Air Force and Navy.
   b. has experienced an outstanding performance record.
   c. was strongly favored by the Navy during its early stage of development, but not by the Air Force.
   d. was originally designed as a light defensive tactical fighter for the Air Force.

8. Which of the following statements is true?
   a. With the growth of ICBMs, manned bombers have been relegated to a minor role as a nuclear
      retaliatory strike force.
   b. Our nuclear defense forces relative to the Soviets was strengthened during the 1970s.
   c. The manned bomber is more vulnerable to enemy defenses.
   d. None of these.

II. True/False: Circle "T" if the statement is true; circle "F" if it is false.

T	F	1.	The USAF and Navy air strike forces could have eliminated North Vietnam's ability to make war or feed its people.
T	F	2.	The French attempted to recolonize Indochina after WWII.
T	F	3.	The Geneva Accords provided for the independence of Vietnam and called for free elections.
T	F	4.	The CIA warned against free elections in Vietnam because the Viet Minh had terrorist agents throughout South Vietnam.

T	F	5.	President Truman tried to defuse the deteriorating situation between North and South Vietnam by withdrawing some of our military advisors.
T	F	6.	On August 2, 1964, North Vietnamese torpedo boats attacked the U.S. Navy destroyer *Maddox* in the Gulf of Tonkin.
T	F	7.	The Vietnamese conflict was unquestionably a civil war.
T	F	8.	The first major U.S. offensive in Vietnam involved air power.
T	F	9.	The Vietnam War was unusual in that there were no front lines; the enemy could be anywhere.
T	F	10.	Helicopters were used as an attack vehicle during the Vietnam War.
T	F	11.	President Nixon was elected on a platform which committed us to winning the war.
T	F	12.	President Nixon secretly authorized B-52 strikes against enemy santuaries in neutral Cambodia.

III. Matching: Match the aircraft on the right with the description on the left.

1. A liquid-fueled ICBM.
2. An anti-submarine warfare (ASW) aircraft.
3. A lightweigth air combat fighter flown by the USAF.
4. A submarine-based missile.
5. A MAC aircraft used as an emergency hospital aircraft.
6. Largest of the transport aircraft flown by MAC.
7. A high-altitude spy plane.
8. A carrier-based fighter aircraft.
9. A SAC bomber.
10. An Army helicopter.

a. General Dynamics F-16
b. Boeing B-52
c. Douglas C-9
d. U-2
e. Polaris A3
f. McDonnell F-4
g. Titan II
h. AH-1G HueyCobra
i. Lockheed C-5A
j. P-3 Orion

Chapter 16

I. Multiple Choice: Circle the letter that corresponds to the best answer:

1. In 1931, Jimmy Doolittle won the Thompson Trophy Race in a:
   a. Travel Air Model R.
   b. Laird DW 300.
   c. Gee Bee R-1.
   d. Stearman PT-17.

2. The National Air Races are held at:
   a. Las Vegas, Nevada.
   b. Phoenix, Arizona.
   c. Roswell, New Mexico.
   d. Reno, Nevada.

3. This nonprofit organization has over 80,000 members in six hundred local chapters and promotes sport aviation. Many members build their own aircraft.
   a. AOPA
   b. EAA
   c. GAMA
   d. NBAA

4. The FAA has decreed that Ultralights must not:
   a. exceed 254 pounds in weight.
   b. operate in controlled airspace.
   c. fly over populated areas.
   d. all of these.

5. Piper's most successful aircraft has been the:
   a. J-3 Cub.
   b. Tripacer.
   c. Cherokee.
   d. Tomahawk.

6. Which of the following Beech aircraft has been in continuous production since 1947?
   a. Twin Beech Model 18
   b. King Air B-99
   c. Bonanza Model 35
   d. Baron Model 55

7. Cessna's first postwar models were the:
   a. 120/140 series.
   b. 170/172 series.
   c. 180/182 series.
   d. 190/195 series.

8. One of the most popular civilian training and business aircraft has been the:
   a. Cessna 190.
   b. Piper Cheyenne.
   c. Cessna 172.
   d. Beech Baron.

9. The general aviation manufacturers have looked upon which of the following markets as offering the greatest potential?
   a. pleasure   c. training
   b. agriculture   d. business

10. The first successful helicopter in the United States was developed by:
   a. Juan de la Cierva.   c. Dwane Wallace.
   b. Igor Sikorsky.   d. Paul Poberezny.

II. **True/False:** Circle "T" if the statement is true; circle "F" if it is false.

T	F	1.	The G.I. Bill and the exposure to military aviation expanded private flying for the first few years after the war.
T	F	2.	Prewar general aviation aircraft and ex-military aircraft were flown by private fliers after the war.
T	F	3.	Air racing during the 1920s was dominated by the military.
T	F	4.	The EAA's annual fly-in and convention is held in Reno, Nevada.
T	F	5.	Ultralights can only operate during the hours of darkness with an FAA approved lighting system.
T	F	6.	Primary flight training during WWII at many colleges and Universities was given in Piper Tri-Pacers.
T	F	7.	William T. Piper, Sr., got his start in aviation working for Walter Beech at Travel Air Manufacturing Company.
T	F	8.	Beech Aircraft Corporation's first successful aircraft was the Model 17 Staggerwing.
T	F	9.	Cessna's UC-78 multi-engine transition trainer used by the USAAF during WWII was referred to as the "Bamboo Bomber."
T	F	10.	Business aviation is declining as a result of the tremendous growth in airline service since deregulation.
T	F	11.	The Germans used helicopters quite extensively during WWII.
T	F	12.	The autogyro was developed by Juan de la Cierva in 1923.

Chapter 17

I. **Multiple Choice:** Circle the letter that corresponds to the best answer:
1. The first jet aircraft was a 1910 biplane powered by a centrifugal compressor driven by a small gasoline engine. It was developed by:
   a. Papst Von Ohain.   c. Frank Whittle.
   b. Henri Coanda   d. Ernst Heinkel.

2. The Boeing 707 has the same basic airframe as the Air Force's:
   a. A-26.   c. C-5A.
   b. B-52.   d. KC-135.

3. The wide-bodied DC-10 was designed to compete with which of the following aircraft?
   a. Boeing B-737   c. Martin 404
   b. Convair 240   d. Lockheed L-1011

4. Which of the following was *not* a problem with Lockheed during the 1970s?
   a. Developement costs of the L-1011 TriStar airliner
   b. Lack of new military contracts
   c. Bankruptcy of the L-1011's engine supplier
   d. Poor cash flow position

5. One of the earliest Lockheed aircraft was the:
   a. Electra.   c. TriStar.
   b. P-38 Lightning.   d. Vega.

6. Which of the following was *not* an effect of deregulation?
   a. phase-out of the CAB
   b. concentration of service at large hubs by the major carriers
   c. growth in the number of commuter carriers
   d. Air Traffic Controllers strike

7. Flow control means:
   a. not clearing aircraft to take-off unless they can land at their destination.
   b. assigning landing slots at selected airports.
   c. keeping the flow of landing aircraft in homogenous groupings to avoid a slowdown due to varying speeds.
   d. assigning quotas to the twenty-three Air Route Traffic Control Centers.

8. The Learjet Model 23:
   a. was conceived by Charles C Gates.
   b. was based on Switzerland's P-16 fighter plane.
   c. was not in great demand by corporate buyers for the first several years after production started.
   d. had competition from several other aircraft as soon as it became available.

II. True/False: Circle "T" if the statement is true; circle "F" if it is false.

T	F	1.	The principle of jet propulsion had been understood at least since Isaac Newton.
T	F	2.	The jet engine pulls air into its compressor and packs it into a combustion chamber where, mixed with fuel, it is ignited.
T	F	3.	The Germans developed the Me 109F jet fighter during WWII.
T	F	4.	United Airlines became the first airline to order jet aircraft when they purchased six 707-120s on October 13, 1955.
T	F	5.	Boeing 707s outsold Douglas DC-8s by two to one.
T	F	6.	Lockheed lost about $2.5 billion on the L-1011 TriStar production.
T	F	7.	One of Boeing's chief competitors, particularly in the international market, comes from Airbus Industrie.
T	F	8.	The Federal Aviation Administration was created by the Federal Aviation Act in 1958.
T	F	9.	The Air Traffic Control System was not impacted as greatly as PATCO had anticipated when they went on strike.
T	F	10.	The slot system became very popular because it was the only equitable way of assigning landing rights.
T	F	11.	Fare wars were very prevalent in the early 1980s.
T	F	12.	The Tax Equity and Fiscal Responsibility Act (TEFRA) of 1982 was welcomed by the general aviation community.

Chapter 18

I. Multiple Choice: Circle the letter that corresponds to the best answer:

1. The father of modern rocketry is:
   a. Virgil Grissom.
   b. Wernher von Braun.
   c. Richard Gordon.
   d. Robert Goddard.

2. Which of the following individuals was *not* an early German rocket scientist?
   a. Herman Oberth
   b. Walter Dornberger
   c. Wernher von Braun
   d. Paul Weitz

3. German rocket research during WWII:
   a. was very limited compared to Goddard's work.
   b. was given high priority in 1941 but curtailed greatly by Hitler in 1944.
   c. took place in Berlin, under the control of the German military command.
   d. led to the development of American ICBM.

4. America's first series of space missions was called:
   a. Mercury.
   b. Titan.
   c. Gemini.
   d. Satturn.

5. The first suborbital flight by a U.S. astronaut was made on April 12, 1961 by:
   a. Thomas Stafford.
   b. John Glenn.
   c. Alan Shepard.
   d. Virgil Grissom.

6. The purpose of Apollo 8 was to:
   a. perfect the space-docking procedure.
   b. land on the moon.
   c. circle the moon.
   d. leave supplies on the moon.

7. The first astronaut to step foot on the moon was:
   a. Frank Borman.
   b. Neil Armstrong.
   c. Michael Collins.
   d. Alan Shepard.

8. The first moon landing mission was Apollo:
   a. 8.
   b. 9.
   c. 10.
   d. 11.

II. True/False: Circle "T" if the statement is true; circle "F" if it is false.

T   F   1. The German rocket research facility during WWII was located at Warnemunde, on the Baltic Coast.

T   F   2. Robert Goddard's research led to the WWII antitank weapon called the Bazooka.

T   F   3. Robert Goddard was helped by Charles Lindbergh in getting a grant so that he could continue his rocket research in New Mexico.

T   F   4. German V-2 rockets were brought to the United States after WWII, which established the foundation for our ICBM program.

T   F   5. In 1954, President Eisenhower gave America's ICBM program top priority.

T   F   6. The Soviet Sputnik I was launched in April, 1961.

T   F   7. The National Aeronautics and Space Administration (NASA) was first established as part of the U.S. Air Force research efforts.

T   F   8. The Gemini series was primarily designed to perfect space docking.

T   F   9. The Apollo II moon landing took place on July 20, 1969.

T   F   10. Three astronauts were killed during the Gemini series.

T   F   11. The Space Shuttle was developed as a reusable vehicle.

T   F   12. The unmanned space probes are primarily for military purposes.

III. Matching: Match the individual on the right with the description on the left.

1. Commander of Apollo 8 Mission.
2. American pioneer in rocketry.
3. German rocket scientist who developed the V-1 and V-2 rockets.
4. The first astronaut to set foot on the moon.
5. Pre-WWII German rocket scientist.
6. First astronaut to orbit the earth.
7. Command Module pilot during the Apollo 11 flight.
8. First astronaut killed during a pre-launch test.
9. Air Force Chief of Research and Development who favored rocket development.
10. America's first astronaut.

  a. Neil Armstrong
  b. Trevor Gardner
  c. John Glenn
  d. Robert Goddard
  e. Hermann Oberth
  f. Virgil Grissom
  g. Frank Borman
  h. Michael Collins
  i. Alan Shepard
  j. Wernher von Braun

Appendix B

Answers to Objective Questions

Prelude

I. Multiple Choice

1. b   5. b
2. c   6. c
3. b   7. a
4. d

II. True/False

1. T   5. F
2. T   6. F
3. F   7. T
4. T   8. T

Chapter 1

I. Multiple Choice

1. a   4. c
2. d   5. c
3. b

II. True/False

1. F   4. T
2. T   5. T
3. T   6. T

Chapter 2

I. Multiple Choice

1. c   6. d
2. b   7. a
3. d   8. d
4. a   9. b
5. c   10. b

II. True/False

1. T   8. F
2. T   9. F
3. T   10. F
4. T   11. T
5. F   12. T
6. T   13. T
7. T   14. T

III. Matching (Individuals)

1. h   6. i
2. f   7. j
3. e   8. g
4. d   9. b
5. a   10. c

IV. Matching (Aircraft)

1. g   5. h
2. f   6. a
3. b   7. e
4. d   8. c

Chapter 3

I. Multiple Choice

1. b   6. c
2. d   7. c
3. d   8. a
4. b   9. d
5. c   10. c

II. True/False

1. T   6. T
2. F   7. T
3. F   8. F
4. F   9. F
5. T   10. F

Chapter 4

I. Multiple Choice

1. c   6. b
2. c   7. c
3. b   8. b
4. b   9. c
5. c

II. True/False

1. T   7. F
2. F   8. T
3. F   9. F
4. T   10. F
5. T   11. T
6. F   12. F

Chapter 5

I. Multiple Choice

1. d   5. b
2. c   6. d
3. a   7. c
4. b

II. True/False

1. F   6. F
2. T   7. T
3. F   8. T
4. T   9. F
5. F   10. T

Chapter 6

I. Multiple Choice

1. d   6. c

2. d	7. c
3. b	8. a
4. a	9. c
5. b	10. b

II. True/False

1. T	6. F
2. T	7. F
3. T	8. T
4. T	9. T
5. T	10. F

Chapter 7

I. Multiple Choice

1. c	6. c
2. a	7. c
3. b	8. a
4. c	9. a
5. d	10. c

II. True/False

1. T	6. T	11. T
2. F	7. F	12. T
3. T	8. T	13. F
4. T	9. F	14. T
5. T	10. T	15. F

III. Matching

1. f	6. g
2. i	7. b
3. a	8. h
4. j	9. e
5. c	10. d

Chapter 8

I. Multiple Choice

1. c	5. d
2. a	6. c
3. c	7. c
4. d	8. d

II. True/False

1. T	6. T
2. T	7. T
3. F	8. F
4. F	9. T
5. F	10. T

Chapter 9

I. Multiple Choice

1. b	8. b
2. b	9. d
3. d	10. d
4. c	11. a
5. a	12. c
6. c	13. c
7. a	14. b

II. True/False

1. F	8. T
2. T	9. T
3. T	10. T
4. T	11. F
5. F	12. T
6. T	13. T
7. F	14. F

Chapter 10

I. Multiple Choice

1. b	6. c
2. c	7. a
3. d	8. b
4. c	9. b
5. a	10. b

II. True/False

1. F	6. F
2. T	7. T
3. F	8. T
4. T	9. T
5. T	10. T

Chapter 11

I. Multiple Choice

1. b	5. b
2. c	6. d
3. b	7. b
4. c	8. c

II. True/False

1. T	5. T
2. T	6. T
3. T	7. T
4. F	8. F

Chapter 12

I. Multiple Choice

1. c	6. d
2. d	7. b
3. a	8. c
4. c	9. d
5. b	10. c

II. True/False

1. T	6. T
2. F	7. T
3. F	8. T
4. F	9. T
5. T	10. F

III. Matching (Individuals)

1. h	6. b
2. e	7. f
3. a	8. c
4. j	9. g
5. d	10. i

IV. Matching (Aircraft)

1. g	6. e
2. c	7. f
3. j	8. h
4. a	9. d
5. b	10. i

Chapter 13

I. Multiple Choice

1. b	6. d
2. a	7. d
3. c	8. c
4. d	9. a
5. c	

II. True/False

1. T	6. F
2. F	7. T
3. F	8. T
4. T	9. T
5. T	10. T

Chapter 14

I. Multiple Choice

1. d	6. d
2. b	7. b

3. b   8. b
4. b   9. c
5. a

II. True/False

1. T   6. T
2. F   7. F
3. T   8. F
4. T   9. F
5. F   10. T

Chapter 15

I. Multiple Choice

1. b   5. b
2. d   6. d
3. c   7. a
4. d   8. c

II. True/False

1. T   6. T   11. F
2. T   7. F   12. T
3. T   8. T
4. T   9. T
5. F   10. T

III. Matching

1. g   6. i
2. j   7. d

3. a   8. f
4. e   9. b
5. c   10. h

Chapter 16

I. Multiple Choice

1. c   6. c
2. d   7. a
3. b   8. c
4. d   9. d
5. a   10. b

II. True/False

1. T   7. F
2. T   8. T
3. T   9. T
4. F   10. F
5. F   11. F
6. F   12. T

Chapter 17

I. Multiple Choice

1. b   5. d
2. d   6. d
3. d   7. a
4. b   8. b

II. True/False

1. T   7. T
2. T   8. F
3. F   9. T
4. F   10. F
5. T   11. T
6. T   12. F

Chapter 18

I. Multiple Choice

1. d   5. c
2. d   6. c
3. d   7. b
4. a   8. d

II. True/False

1. F   7. F
2. T   8. T
3. T   9. T
4. T   10. T
5. T   11. T
6. F   12. F

III. Matching

1. g   6. c
2. d   7. h
3. j   8. f
4. a   9. b
5. e   10. i

148th Aero Squadron, 48
1910 coanda jet, 330

A

A-4 Skyhawk, 273, 279
ABF2C-1 Hawk, 177
Advanced Tactical Fighter (ATF), 294
aerobatics, 15
aeronautical industry, engine development in, 169
Aeronca Champion, 299
ag-planes, 300
Air Commerce Act of 1926, 92
air mail, 78-86
    Army flight of, 146, 166
    Kelly Bill and, 115
    Post Office regulation of, 80
    transcontinental flight of, 84-86
Air Mail Act of 1934, 148
air races, 302
air traffic control, 344
aircraft carriers
    early development of, 176, 177
    present-day power of, 293
airlines
    air controllers strike of 1981 and, 342
    deregulation and, 338
    development of major, 131
    evolution of 114-130
    fare wars in, 345
    mergers in, 345
    postwar overseas routes of, 157
    trans-Atlantic flight of, 155
    trans-Pacific flight of, 155
airships, 170
Akron airship, 170
Albatros DIII, 33, 40
Alexander Eaglerock biplane, 104
American Airlines, 141
American Airways, 129
American Export Lines, 157
American Volunteer Group, 232
Apollo Program, 357
Army and Navy racers (post WWI), 60
AS-7A Corsair II light attack bomber, 278
Assam Trucking Company, 234
Atlantic flight, first, 58
Atlas missile, 352
AVCO, 126
"aviatrices," 13

B

B-17 bombers, 220, 226
    development of, 182
B-24 Liberator bomber, 219., 227
B-25 bomber, 202, 215
B-26 Marauder bomber, 224, 258
B-29 Superfortress, 246
B-52 bomber
    development of, 251-255

nuclear arsenal aboard, 291
balloons, 1
barnstorming era, 87-113
    Air Commerce act of 1926 and, 92
    Morrow Board and, 92
BE2 observation plane, 35
Beachey, Lincoln, 20
Becherau, Louis, 18
Beech 1900 Airliner, 317
Beech Staggerwing Model 17, 183, 314
Beech, Walter, 101
Beechcraft, 314
Beechcraft Model 18, 315
Beechcraft Starship, 316
Bell H-13 helicopter, 323
Bell P-39 fighters, 238
Bell X-1A rocket plane, 250
Berlin Air Lift, 249-251
biplanes, demise of, 173
"Black Committee," 144
Black-McKellar Bill of 1934, 148
Bleriot XI, 16
Boeing 707, 160
Boeing 727, 161
Boeing P-12C Army fighter, 175
Boeing-Stearman PT-17 trainer, 300
Bonanza V-tail private plane, 316
Boyle, George, 79
Brown, D.S., 2
Brown, Walter F., 131
Buhl Air Sedan sesquiwings, 139
Burke, Billie, 93, 95
business flying, 318

C

C-165 Cessna Airmaster, 317
Campbell, Douglas, 52
Canucks, 26, 90
Casablance Conference, 225
Caudron C-3, 38
Cayley, George, 2
CBI fighters, 237
Century Airlines, 141
Cessna 120/140 series, 318
Cessna 152, 319
Cessna 190, 318
Cessna Ag Truck, 321
Cessna Aircraft, 315
    formation of, 103
Cessna Centurion II, 320
Cessna Crusader, 321
Cessna DC-6A, 104
Cessna Model A, 103
Cessna Skyhawk, 319
Cessna, Clyde, 99
CH-21 Shawnee helicopter, 268
CH-37 helicopter, 274
Chanute, Octave, 2
Cierva Autogiro, 322
Civil Aeronautics Authority (CAA)
    Act of 1938, 150
Consolidated Commodore flying boats, 154

contract air mail (CAM) routes, 116-119
Convair 240 airliner, 341
Convair B-36, 251
Convair B-58 Hustler, 286
Convair F-106A, 282
Convair F-111, 281
Cord, E.L., 139
Curtis O-39 observation plane, 147
Curtiss Aeroplane and Motor Co., 38
    Wright Aeronautical Corp. merger with, 129
Curtiss C-46 Commando, 235
Curtiss Carrier Pigeon, 116
Curtiss CR-2 racer, 62
Curtiss D-12 engine, 60-63
Curtiss F11C-2 Goshawk, 175
Curtiss F6C-4Hawk, 174
Curtiss F9C-2 Sparrowhawk, 171
Curtiss H-12L flying boat, 44
Curtiss Hawk biplane fighter, 166
Curtis JN-2, 33, 48
Curtiss June Bug, 8
Curtiss machines, 18
Curtiss Model R, 93
Curtiss N-9H Navy trainer, 46
Curtiss OC-2 Falcon, 173
Curtiss P-36, 179-182, 179
Curtiss P-6E hawk, 176
Curtiss R3C-1 racer, 63
Curtiss SBC-3 Helldivers, 178
Curtiss T-32 Condor, 146
Curtiss triplane, 32
Curtiss Wright Aeronautical Corp., 26
Curtiss, Glenn H., 8-10, 13
Curtiss-Robertson Robin, 112
Curtiss-Wright Aeronautical Corp., 10

D

d'Arlands, Marquis, 1
de Rozier, Pilatre, 1
DeHavilland DH-4 fighter, 36-39, 45, 57
Delta airline, 135
Demoiselle, 12
Deperdussion planes, 18
DH-4B airmail plane, 81
dirigibles, Navy, 74-76
Douglas A-26 Invader bomber, 221, 258
Douglas A-4 Skyhawk jet fighter, 269
Douglas AD Skyraider, 272
Douglas B-18 Bolo bomber, 192
Douglas C-1, 59
Douglas C-54 transport, 235
Douglas DC-10, 334
Douglas DC-3, 332
Douglas DC-4, 333
Douglas DC-6, 158
Douglas DC-7C, 160
Douglas DC-9, 333
Douglas O-2H observation plane, 172

Douglas O-46A observation plane, 178
Douglas, Donald, 61

E

Eastern Airlines, 113
Enola Gay, 247
Experimental Aircraft Association (EAA), 307

F

F-105 Thunderchiefs, 274, 275
F-4B Phantom, 270
F-4C Phantom jet fighter, 269
F-51 Mustangs, 255
F-82 Mustangs, 256
F.E. 2d fighter bomber, 37
F4F Wildcat Navy fighters, 196, 197, 198, 203
F4U Vought Corsairs Navy fighters, 242, 244, 258, 301
FAA Act of 1958, 337
Fairchild A-10 ground support aircraft, 290
Fairchild PT-19, 299
Farman, Henri, 6
Farman, Maurice, 37
First Aero Squadron, 29
flexible response theory, 266
flying boats, 21, 44, 60, 154
Flying Tigers, 232
Focke-Wulf 190 fighter, 213
Fokker DRI triplane, 33, 43
Fokker DVII, 34
Fokker E-1 Eindecker monoplane, 35
Fokker F-10, 123
Fokker F-32, 127
Fokker TriMotor, 122, 151
Ford TriMotor, 121, 123
Formula I racer, 305
Fort 5-AT-B airliner, 153
French aeronautical pioneers, 12

G

Garros, Roland, 33
Gates Learjet, 349
Gee Bee R-1 racer, 304
Gemini capsule, 353
general aviation
  agricultural use of, 300
  World War II surplus in, 298
General Dynamics F-16 fighter, 289
Goddard, Robert H., 352
Goering, Herman, 214
Gordon Bennet cup races, 13
Great Lakes biplane, 111
Great Lakes Corporation, 109
Great Lakes G-1 torpedo bomber, 172
Great Lakes Sport-Trainer, 109
Grumman A-6 Intruder 271, 270, 295
Grumman F6F Hellcat, 240
Grumman F7F Tigercat fighter, 264
Grumman TBF Avenger, 200

H

Hamilton Metalplanes, 118

Handley Page V1500, 42
Hanoveraner CL-II observation plane, 51
helicopters
  non-military use of, 322
  prototype of, 322
Henry Farman biplane, 13
Hiroshima and Nagasaki, 247
homebuilt aircraft, 305
Huey helicopter, 274, 276
"Hump," The, 234

I

Immelmann, Max, 43
inter-city record flights, 93
international air meets, 13

J

Japanese Kate torpedo bomber, 189
Japanese Mitsubishi G4MI Betty Bomber, 204
Japanese Zero fighter, 188
jet aircraft, 327-350
  airline deregulation and, 338
  Boeing, 331
  Douglas, 332
  engine development for, 327
  engines for, 330
  FAA Act of 1958 and, 337
  first U.S. engine for, 330
  future designs for, 340
  Lockheed, 334
  McDonnell, 334
JN-4 training plane, 38
JN-6H airmail "Jenny", 80
Junkers J-1, 119
Junkers JU.87 dive bomber, 211

K

Kaman HH-43F Huskie rescue helicopter, 279
kamikaze attacks, 240-245
KC-135 Air Force tanker, 331
Kelly Bill of 1926, 115
Keys, Clement, 26, 126
Keystone LB-7 bomber, 171
Kirkham, Charles, 8
Knight, Jack, 83
Korean War, 255-264
  helicopters used in, 262

L

Lafayette Escadrille, 41, 49
Laird Commercial, 117
Laird Speedwing, 117
Laird "Super Solution" racer, 303
Laird Swallow, 95
Laird Transport, 97
Laird, Matty, 22-24
Langley Aerodrome, 3
Langley, Samuel P., 2
laser development, 296
Lazair ultralight, 311
Lear, William, 346
Learjet Longhorn, 349
Learjet Model 23, 347
Liberty engine, 36, 37, 49
Lilienthal, Otto, 2
Lincoln Beachey Flyers, 15

Lindbergh, Charles A., 59, 114
Lockheed, 102
Lockheed C-130 Hercules combat transport, 287
Lockheed C-5A Galaxy, 287
Lockheed Constellation Model L49, 159
Lockheed F-104 Starfighter, 283
Lockheed F-5A reconnaissance plane, 201
Lockheed F-80 Shooting Star jet fighter, 249
Lockheed F-94 Starfire night fighter, 257
Lockheed L-1011 TriStar, 162
Lockheed Orion, 336
Lockheed S-3B Viking, 294
Lockheed TR-1, 284
Lockheed TriStar, 337
Long-EZ, 307
Ludington Lines, 142
Ludington-Eastern Air Transport affair, 145
Lufberry, Raoul, 49
Luke, Frank, 49-55
Lunar Landing Program, 355
Lund, Freddie, 108

L

Macon airship, 170
Manley, Charles, 2
Marr, Kenneth, 52
Martin 404 airliners, 341
Martin B-26 Marauder bomber, 213
Martin GMB bombers, 70
Martin M-130 flying boats, 156
Martin, Glenn, 25
MATS C-54, 251
McDonnell F-15 Eagle, 289
McDonnell XF-85 parasite fighter, 252
McNary-Watres Act of 1930, 131
Messerschmitt Bf.109, 210, 218,
metal planes, development of, 119
Mexican campaign, 29
Meyers Midget, 110
Meyers, Charlie, 87, 110
Midgetman missile, 296
Military Flyer, 28
Mitchell P-38 ultralight, 310
Mitchell, William, 39-42, 68-77
  courtmartial of, 74
Model 113 Monocoupe, 111
Moellendick, Jake, 95, 104
monoplanes, development of, 105
Montgolfier, E. and J., 1
Mooney 231 turbo, 320
Morane-Saulnier Bullet monoplane, 33
Morrow Board, 92
Mozhaisky, Alexander, 2

N

Naval Air force, 68-77
Naval aircraft engine development, 71
Navy P-3 Orion anti-submarine aircraft, 288
Navy Tomcat fighter, 288
NC flying boats, 60

NC "Nancy" Navy Curtiss, 58, 61
New Swallow biplane, 104
Nieuport 17 fighters, 41, 47
North American Aviation, 125
North American F-100 Super Sabre, 270
North American F-86A Sabre, 257
North American Mustang P-51, 217
North American T-6, 302
North Korean YAK fighter, 261
Northrop Alpha all-metal airplane, 134
Northrop P-61 Black Widow night fighter, 244
nuclear missiles, 292

O

observation balloons, 51
Operation Overlord, 223-229
Orenco D fighter, 34, 58
Oshkosh air show, 308

P

P-36, 188
P-38, 216
P-38J bomber, 212
P-40 Warhawk, 194, 199, 211, 232
P-47, 227
P-51 Mustang, 305
Pacific Air Transport, 133
Pan Am, formation of, 151
PATCO, 342
PBY-5A Catalina patrol plane, 241
Pearl Harbor, 186-192, 186
Pershing, John J., 29
Pfalz DIII, 33
Pilcher, Percy, 2
Piper aircraft, 311
Piper Cherokee, 312
Piper Cheyenne III, 313
Piper Cub, 312
Piper Tomahawk, 313
Pratt & Whitney Wasp (R-1340) engine, 125, 168

R

Reed Airline, 136
Republic F-105 Thunderchiefs, 267
Republic P-47 Thunderbolt, 183, 218
Rheims Racer, 13
Rickenbacker, Eddie, 52
Rodgers, Calbraith, 17, 19
ROKAF Mustang fighters, 261
Rutan, Dick, 325
Ryan B-5, 112
Ryan M-1, 133
Ryan monoplane, 115

S

SAFEway, 135
Salmson observation plane, 50
Santos-Dumont, Alberto, 12
SE-4, 28
SE-5a, 33

Shenandoah dirigibles, 73
ship board takeoff, 30
Signal Corps, 39
Sikorsky S-38 amphibious biplane, 152
Sikorsky S-40 "Clipper" airliner, 155
Sikorsky S-42 airliner, 156
Sikorsky, Igor, 322
"Silver Wings" Cessna, 99
Skikorsky S-61 helicopter, 324
Skylab, 359
Skyraiders, 278
Sopwith Camel, 33, 47
Soviet MiG-15 fighter, 260
space exploration, 351-364
    first U.S. rockets in, 354
    unmanned vehicles in, 362
space shuttle, 360
SPADs, 19, 33
"Spirit of St. Louis," 115
"spoils conferences," 132
SR-71 Blackbird, 285
Standard biplane, 104
Stealth bombers, 294
Stearman, Lloyd, 101
Stinson 6000 TriMotor airliner, 128, 141
Stinson Aircraft, 129
Stinson Model A, 149
Stinson SM-1 Detroiter, 111, 128
Stinson, Eddie, 20, 23
Stinson, Katherine, 19, 20, 24-25
Stinson, Marjorie, 24-25
Stout 2-ATs, 118
Stout Air Pullman, 121
Stout Air Sedan, 119
Stout Navy torpedo bomber, 119
Stout, Bill, 119
Strategic Defense Initiative, 296

T

T-6 Texan forward air control planes, 256
TBM torpedo bomber, 242
TEFRA, 346
Thomas Morse MB-3 fighters, 34
Thomas Morse Scout, 90
TLR Flying Circus, 91
Transcontinental Air Transport, 126
transcontinental flight, 17
TransWorld Airlines, formation of, 134
Travel Air 5000, 105
Travel Air 6000B Romancer, 138
Travel Air biplane, 101
Travel Air Manufacturing Company, 100
Travel Air Model R, 303
Trippe, Juan, 151
Twin-jet Sikorsky S-64 helicopter, 323

U

U-2 spy plane, 284
UC-43 Army biplane, 183

ultralights, 309
United Aircraft and Transport Corp., 124
United States Air Force, 39
unmanned space vehicles, 362

V

Vietnam War, 265-297
von Ohian jet engine, 330
von Zeppelin, Ferdinand, 1
Voyager airplane, 325
Voyager spacecraft, 363
Vultee L-5 liaison plane, 262

W

WACO, 88, 107
WACO 10 biplane, 104
WACO Taperwing, 108
Wagner, Boyd D., 192
Walker, Thomas, 2
"warbirds," 301
Warhawks, 231
Western Air Express, 133
Whittle jet engine, 330
Wichita Aircraft Company, 95
Williams-Cangie sport biplane, 306
Willys, John N., 26, 38
wingwalking, 94
World Cruisers, 62, 64
world flight, first attempts at, 61-67
World War I, 28-55
    combat planes of, 45
    U.S. naval air in, 42
World War II, 186-247
    Aleutian Campaign of, 230-232
    Assam "Hump" in, 234
    assault on European mainland during, 221
    battle for the Phillippines during, 189
    CBI fighters in, 237
    Coral Sea and Midway in, 194-201
    end of, 238
    European air war during, 207-229
    fighter plane development for, 181-185
    Hiroshima and Nagasaki in, 247
    Italian Campaign during, 216-221
    New Guinea and the Solomons in, 201-206
    North Africa and Italy, 209-216
    Operation Overlord during, 223-229
Wright brothers, 1, 4-7
Wright J-5 Whirlwind engine, 71, 335
Wright Model A, 28
Wright Model B, 17
Wright Whirlwind J-6 engines, 124

Y

Yeager, Jeana, 325

Z

Zeppelins, 1, 36

Edited by Steven Mesner